ILLUSTRATED WORLD ENCYCLOPEDIA

ILLUSTRATED WORLD ENCYCLOPEDIA

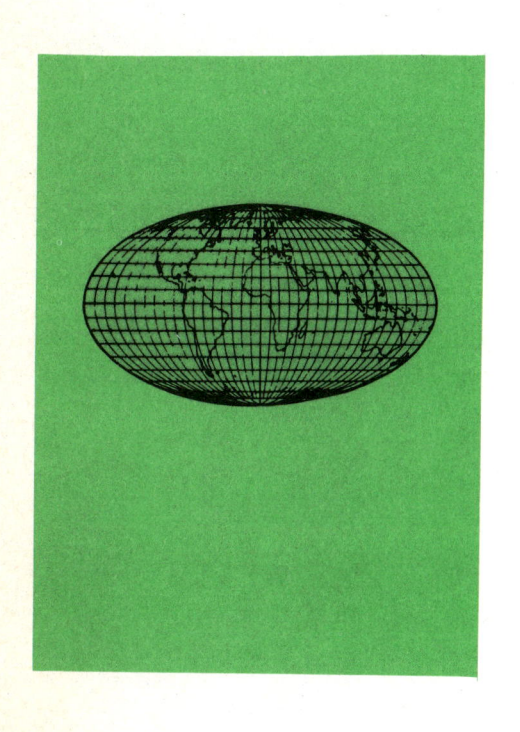

4

ILLUSTRATED WORLD ENCYCLOPEDIA, INC.
NEW YORK

Prepared and Edited by

THE NATIONAL LEXICOGRAPHIC BOARD

ALBERT H. MOREHEAD, *Chairman and General Editor*
WALDEMAR VON ZEDTWITZ, *President*
LOY C. MOREHEAD, *Vice President & Secretary;* LOYD F. GEHRES, SALVATORE RAMONDINO, *Vice Presidents;* DONALD D. WOLF, WILLIAM C. CAMPBELL, GEORGE H. COPELAND, JACK LUZZATTO.

Staff for The Illustrated World Encyclopedia

ALBERT H. MOREHEAD, *Editor* (1954-1966)
DONALD D. WOLF, *Vice-President in Charge*

HAROLD J. BLUM, *Executive Editor;* WILLIAM BIRMINGHAM, BETTY W. BRINKERHOFF, CHRISTINE PARKER, KATHRYN STOVER, *Associate Editors*

ARTHUR DIENER, EDMUND EPSTEIN, PHYLLIS FORWARD, CHARLOTTE FREED, MARTIN KEEN, SHELDON KRANZ, JACK LUZZATTO, ELIZABETH MACLEAN, MARGARET PARRAVICINI, E. MITCHELL SCHRERO, NANCY STARRELS, *Staff Editors and Writers*

MARGOT L. WOLF, *Associate Art Editor;* JANE McDOWELL, PAUL PETER PORGES, *Staff Artists*

Lionel Abel, Peter Ajello, Stockman Barner, Nat Barnett, Roberta Blaché, Letitia Bolton, Hallowell Bowser, Michael Brophy, Eileen Burns, Leonard Cohen, Dorothy Culhertson, Caleb Davis, Ormonde deKay, Susan Diener, Ruth Dym, Edwin Fadiman, Jr., John Fancher, Anne Fielding, Richard Forward, Ronald Foster, Dvora Frumhartz, Crosby George, Robert Gilkey, Louis Goldman, Nancy Gross, Nicholas Guppy, Peter Herrick, Alice Ihling, Elizabeth Kaup, Helen Keane, Dorothy Koppelman, Jean Liedloff, Benjamin Linder, Joan McDonald, Albert Meadows, Marvin Mondlin, James Morehead, Robert Mullen, Jack Peterson, Nancy A. Potter, Herbert Rabb, Philip Reichert, Arnold Romney, Jerry Schur, Irene Shapiro, Max Shufer, Ruth Silver, Alice Skodzas, William Slattery, Judy Stecher, Victor Tamerlis, Barbara Tolnai, Arthur Urrows, Eileen Walker: *Writers.*

Drawings by RAFAELLO BUSONI
Typographic Design by ANDOR BRAUN

Illustrated Encyclopedia of Knowledge
© *1954, 1955, 1956, 1957*
by Educational Book Guild, Inc.

Illustrated World Encyclopedia
© *1958, 1959, 1960, 1961*
by Educational Book Guild, Inc.

Illustrated Library of Literary Treasures
© *1958, 1959, 1960, 1961*
by Educational Book Guild, Inc.

Illustrated World Encyclopedia
© *1963, 1964, 1965, 1966*
by Bobley Publishing Corp.

Illustrated Library of Literary Treasures
© *1963, 1964, 1965, 1966*
by Bobley Publishing Corp.

Illustrated World Encyclopedia
© *1967, 1968*
by Illustrated World Encyclopedia, Inc.

This edition © 1969 by Illustrated World Encyclopedia, Inc. Copyright © under International Copyright Union 1967 by Illustrated World Encyclopedia, Inc. All rights reserved under the Inter-American Copyright Union and under the Pan-American Copyright Conventions.

PRINTED IN UNITED STATES OF AMERICA

Bolivia

Bolivia is one of the largest countries of South America. It is about five thousand miles from the United States. It has an area of about 400,000 square miles, which is about two-thirds as big as Alaska. About three and a half million people live in Bolivia. It is the biggest independent country on earth without a seacoast. It is not a rich country, but it has the biggest tin mines in the world, and this made some of the people very rich until in 1952 the government nationalized (took over ownership of) the mines.

THE PEOPLE WHO LIVE THERE

As in all the Americas, the first people in South America were Indians. More than half of the people in Bolivia now are Indians. Some of these, called the Lowland Indians, are still quite primitive and live today much as their ancestors did thousands of years ago. They speak their own languages and have their own customs.

About one in every seven of the people of Bolivia belongs to the "white" race. The white people are descendants of the Spaniards and Portuguese who went to South America hundreds of years ago. They are the most powerful and richest group in the country. The next most powerful group is called the *mestizos*. A mestizo is part white and part Indian. More than a quarter of the people of Bolivia are mestizos.

The Lowland Indians live in forests and valleys far from the cities, and get along by hunting and fishing. The other Indians, called Highland Indians, work at mining, farming, and sheep herding. Tin-mining is the most important industry. The farms produce cocoa, coffee, and grains, and there are many rubber plantations.

The biggest city in Bolivia is La Paz. More than 347,000 people live there. Most of the government offices of Bolivia are in La Paz, but it is not officially the capital of the country. The official capital is Sucre, which has only about 60,000 people. The only government building in Sucre is the Supreme Court building. Life in La Paz and Sucre is very much like life in North American cities.

WHAT KIND OF PLACE IT IS

A high mountain range, part of the Andes, runs through Bolivia. Most of the people live on the high plains between the mountain peaks. This high part is called the Altiplano. The cities of La Paz and Sucre are on the Altiplano. There is a beautiful large lake on the Altiplano, called Lake Titicaca. It is the largest lake in South America. Many steamships travel back and forth across Lake Titicaca. No other lake at such a high altitude can be used for commerce.

The climate on the Altiplano is cool

BOLIVIA

The picture at the left shows a residential section of La Paz, capital of Bolivia. There are many fine modern buildings in this beautiful sky-top mountain city. You can see how clean the streets are kept, and how neatly the decorative trees and hedges are trimmed. Traffic runs along the left side of the streets and roads in Bolivia. The name of this beautiful street is El Prado.

In the picture at the right, below, is a typical scene on Lake Titicaca, the highest navigable lake in the world. It is on the border of Peru and Bolivia. The Indians are sailing a balsa boat made of the reeds that grow on the shores of this lake. Even the sail is made of balsa reeds.

Left below: La Paz has open-air sidewalk stands where people do their shopping. Indian women wear several brightly colored petticoats. They wear them all at once, and usually add a new one each year.

Right, below: Women of Tarija are waiting with their market baskets and bowls for the meat market to open. The pretty little Indian girl is going shopping for her mother. She will pay with coins called bolivianos.

Grace Line & Unations Photos

BOLIVIA

1. Bolivian Indians push their reed boats around Lake Titicaca with long poles.
2. The little girl is making friends with a great beaked Bolivian toucan.
3. Funny masks and costumes are worn for festival dances in Warizata, Bolivia.
4. The houses of the rich old families in Bolivia are built around inner courts.
5. Llamas patiently carry their loads over the winding mountain roads of Bolivia.

and pleasant. There is a rainy season and a dry season.

Higher up in the Andes mountains it is always cold, and there is snow all year round. Shepherds live on the mountains. They tend flocks of llamas, vicuñas, and chinchillas. These animals have valuable hair and furs. In the valleys and jungles where the Lowland Indians live, it is hot and wet, very much as it is in the jungles and valleys of Africa.

Bolivia is a very beautiful place, with many different kinds of country and many different kinds of wild life. There are colorful birds flying through the tropical jungles. Fierce wild animals roam around the dense forests—jaguars, wildcats, and others.

HOW THE PEOPLE ARE GOVERNED

Bolivia is a republic. It has a president, a congress, and a supreme court, as the United States has. Both men and women are allowed to vote—men when they are 18 and women when they are 21. However, a married woman can vote at 18. Bolivia has been a republic for more than one hundred years, but it has had many stormy revolutions to decide which party will hold power.

Every man goes into the army at the age of 19 to serve two years, and until he is 49 he must serve for short periods in various army duties. Also, boys and girls between 14 and 18 are given what is called "pre-military training." The Roman Catholic religion is the official religion in Bolivia, but people who believe in other religions are allowed to worship as they please.

Every child in Bolivia must go to grammar school. After that, he can leave school and go to work. Many people in Bolivia do not know how to read and write, but the government is working very hard to teach them. One of the problems the government has is that many of the Indians who live in Bolivia do not speak Spanish, the official language, but speak their own Indian language.

BOLIVIA IN THE PAST

About a thousand years ago, the country that is Bolivia today was part of a very powerful Indian kingdom in South America, called the Inca Empire. The Incas had a wonderfully advanced civilization, but they did not know about gunpowder. When the Spaniards went to South America about four hundred years ago, they were able to defeat the Incas. Like the other countries of South America, Bolivia came under Spanish rule.

In 1825, Bolivia gained independence from Spain and became a republic. The name Bolivia was chosen in honor of the leader of the fight for independence, Simón Bolívar. There have been many stormy fights and arguments among the people of Bolivia, and one war with the neighboring country of Paraguay about which country should control a section called the Chaco. (See the article on GRAN CHACO.)

BOLIVIA. Area, 424,162 square miles. Population (UN estimate, 1964) 3,653,000. Language, Spanish. Religion, Roman Catholic. Government, republic. Monetary unit, the boliviano, worth 8½ cents (U.S.). Flag, three bars going across: red, yellow, green.

boll weevil

The boll weevil is an insect of the beetle family. It is about a quarter of an inch long, and lives on cotton plants. Every year the boll weevil causes losses of more than $100,000,000. The boll weevil has a long snout, which is a kind of beak. With this snout it bites into the blossom buds of the cotton plant and destroys the flower. It also feeds on the young bolls and lays its eggs in some of the holes it makes. The eggs hatch into little, white, wormlike things, called *grubs,* which also feed on the bolls.

The boll weevil originally came from Mexico or Central America. Until about sixty years ago there were no boll weevils in the United States. Then gradually the boll weevils invaded all the states where

The boll weevil feeds by thrusting its long snout into the bud of a cotton plant.

cotton is grown. Chemicals have been found that will kill the boll weevil but many escape and manage to do a great deal of damage.

Bologna

Bologna is a city in Italy. It lies at the foot of the Apennine Mountains, about 185 miles northwest of Rome. Bologna has been a center of culture for nearly two thousand years—since the time of the Roman Empire. It is known for its churches, which are beautiful and which contain thousands of art treasures. At one time the University of Bologna was a famous law school, and it later became famous as a medical school.

The people of Bologna manufacture many things, including soap, silk, candles, and musical instruments. A kind of sausage from Bologna has become famous as "baloney."

Bologna was the place where Allied troops broke through into the Po Valley of Italy during World War II. The city was badly damaged then, but most of its beautiful buildings may still be seen. Its population in 1960 was 431,949, which makes it about the same size as Phoenix, Arizona.

Bolshevism is a former name for the policies of the present Communist Party in Russia. See COMMUNISM and UNION OF SOVIET SOCIALIST REPUBLICS.

bomb

A bomb is a container that holds an explosive or some other substance to hurt people. Most bombs hold powerful explosives. Police sometimes use *tear bombs,* which release gases to make people cry so hard that they are blinded and can easily be captured. *Stench bombs* release a gas that smells terrible but is not harmful. Gangsters sometimes use bombs to kill their enemies. But most bombs are used in warfare, and in modern warfare they are dropped from airplanes or carried by rockets.

In World War II, Germany was so badly hurt by bombs dropped from Allied planes that she had to give up. The most powerful of these bombs held about two tons of the explosive called TNT. It was called a "blockbuster" because it would destroy a whole city block. But the atomic and hydrogen bombs that have been developed since then are more than twenty thousand times more powerful.

There are four main parts to most bombs, the outside shell, or case; the explosive or fire-producing material inside; the tail fin, which helps it move through the air or water; and the fuse, which sets the bomb off when it hits a target.

THE MAIN TYPES OF BOMBS

There are five main types of bombs; demolition, fragmentation, incendiary, armor-piercing, and atomic.

The *demolition bomb* has a thin case and a large amount of explosive inside. It was the most destructive bomb used generally in World War II. Demolition bombs often weigh as much as two tons. The fuse that sets off the bomb acts very fast. When the bomb hits the target it immediately explodes with a great blast. The "blockbuster" is a demolition bomb. These bombs are used to blow up factories, bridges, and other big targets.

The *fragmentation bomb* is a small bomb which is dropped on enemy troops by an airplane that often flies close to the ground. The fragmentation bomb has a metal case that scatters in small pieces when the bomb explodes. The pieces serve as bullets when they hit soldiers. The fuse that sets this bomb off works more slowly than the fuse of a demolition bomb. An airplane can drop these bombs while flying close to the ground and still have time to get away before the bomb explodes. This type of bomb usually weighs no more than 50 pounds.

The *incendiary bomb* is not explosive. Its purpose is to start a fire. There are two kinds of incendiary bombs. One kind weighs only a few pounds and has a case made of magnesium. This kind of incendiary bomb is used at night, because magnesium is a metal that burns very brightly and lights up the target. When the target is lit up other airplanes can see it and drop large demolition bombs to destroy it. The other kind of incendiary bomb weighs about twenty-five pounds. It has a thin case, and is filled with a gasoline jelly. When this bomb hits the target the gasoline jelly is set on fire and scattered. This bomb is used to burn down buildings.

The *armor-piercing* bomb is a large bomb with a very strong, heavy case. It weighs about half a ton. The armor-piercing bomb is used against warships. This bomb is made to go through the steel decks of a ship. It does not explode until it gets inside the ship. Ordinary TNT would explode too quickly because TNT is a very sensitive chemical. This bomb is filled with a chemical that is much less sensitive than TNT.

There are two types of atomic bombs, the ATOMIC BOMB and the HYDROGEN BOMB. There is a separate article about each. These are the most terrible weapons of war that have ever been invented. A single atomic bomb is powerful enough to destroy a whole city. The hydrogen bomb is even more powerful.

OTHER TYPES OF BOMBS

A *guided missile* is a demolition bomb that has its own engine and fuel for flying and is guided to its target by radio. No guided missiles of this kind were used during World War II.

The *depth charge* and the *torpedo* are two important types of bombs used in naval warfare. The depth charge is a bomb used against submarines. In World War I the depth charge was called an "ashcan" because it looked just like one. But the depth charge that people use today looks like a huge black teardrop. Depth charges are fired in pairs from the stern (rear end) of a ship that is chasing a submarine. This bomb does not have an ordinary fuse. It explodes when it reaches a certain depth under water. It is the pressure of the water that sets off the depth charge. When it explodes near a submarine the submarine is crushed by the blast.

A torpedo is a large and powerful bomb that submarines, torpedo boats and airplanes fire at a ship. Torpedoes are sometimes more than twenty feet long. Some of them cost twenty thousand dollars to build. Torpedoes travel as boats do, across the water or underwater to their targets. The front of the torpedo carries the explosive and is called the warhead. In the rear are the engines that drive the torpedo and a gyroscope that steers it.

A *time bomb* is usually a small bomb that is set off by an electric current. It is called a time bomb because it is attached to a clocklike instrument. When the hands of this clock reach a certain time, the electric circuit is closed, causing the bomb to explode. This bomb is much used by spies and saboteurs because it can be placed somewhere and be made to explode hours after the spy or saboteur has escaped.

A *hand grenade* is a small bomb that soldiers carry and throw at the enemy. It is nicknamed "pineapple" because it looks somewhat like one. The fuse that

BOMB

U.S. Air Force Photos

1. These bombs are being hauled to a Flying Fortress, before a World War II bombing mission.

2. A bombardier has just released his bombs over a railroad yard. The puffs of smoke on the target show where other bombs have already exploded.

3. American bombers have just destroyed this German-held bridge in Yugoslavia in World War II.

4. This torpedo will move underwater to a target.

5. Many cities were badly bombed in World War II.

British Inform. Services

sets it off is a little button that the soldier pulls out before he throws it.

PROXIMITY FUSE

The United States had one great advantage over its enemies in World War II—the proximity fuse. This is a device that will explode a bomb when it gets close to its target. A built-in radar device sets off the bomb.

BOMBSIGHT

A bomber flying at several hundred miles per hour at heights several thousand feet above the target needs very delicate aiming instruments. These instruments are called *bombsights*. They work out automatically and mathematically where the bomb will land.

The United States has had the best bombsights in the world for about twenty years, and this helped to win World War II. The best bombsights have always been military secrets. They are built with little bombs inside them. If a plane crashes, or is in danger of being captured, the bomb explodes and destroys the bombsight so that the enemy cannot take it and copy it. Before World War II, the Sperry bombsight was the best. During World War II an improved design called the Norden bombsight was used. Better bombsights have been developed since World War II.

Bombay

Bombay is a great city on the western coast of India, and a seaport on the Arabian Sea. It is the largest city in Western India and, with Calcutta, is one of the two largest cities in all of India. Each is bigger than any American city except New York and Chicago. Bombay is built on an island, with a harbor that is the finest in India and is also closer to Europe than any other. Bombay was also the name of what was formerly India's largest state, and the city of Bombay was the capital of that state. But in May, 1960, the state of Bombay was divided into two states: Maharashtra, and Gujarat, giving India 15 states. The temporary capital of Gujarat is AHMEDABAD (see separate article), and Bombay is the capital of Maharashtra.

The people of Bombay are of many different origins. Thousands of Englishmen and other Europeans live and work there. A Hindu people called Mahrattas make up the largest single group in the population. Parsees, although there are only about a hundred thousand of them, have an importance out of proportion to their number; many great businesses and much property is in their hands. Besides these groups Bombay has Arab traders from the Persian Gulf, Afghans from Afghanistan, tall Sikhs, Tibetans from the northern frontier, Senegalese, Jews, Japanese, and many other nationalities.

The two main languages of Bombay are Mahrathi and Gujarati, but almost everybody also speaks and understands a local language called "Bombay Bat," which includes words from several languages.

Most of Bombay's people follow the Hindu religion but there are many Mohammedans and Buddhists and there are some Christians. The Parsees are a separate religious group.

The name "Bombay" comes from *Mumba,* a goddess who was worshipped on Bombay and neighboring islands at about the time of Christ. King Bhima, a Hindu ruler, built the first town on Bombay Island. About five hundred years ago, Mohammedan invaders captured it, and about two hundred years after that it was ruled by Portugal. England acquired Bombay when King Charles II married a Portuguese princess. It remained under British control until India became independent in 1950.

Bombay has a big university, founded in 1857, and many fine buildings and parks.

BOMBAY, INDIA. City. Population (1960 U.N. est.) 4,941,000. Capital of state of Maharashtra.

BOMBAY

Am. President Line   *Unations*

1. The great city of Bombay is a mixture of old and new buildings. Here we see a residential section with a fine, wide beach where people can swim.
2. This little boy in Bombay is hard at work on his reading lesson. For centuries, very few people in this city could read or write, but now more and more children go to school.
3. The beautiful arch shown in this picture is known as the "Gateway to India." It is on a Bombay street named Apollo Bunder, and it was built in 1907 to remember the visit of King George V and Queen Mary of England.

Trans World Airlines, Inc.

The streets of Bombay are a fascinating and curious mixture of modern and ancient civilization. In the noisy hubbub of this busy city, modern motor cars are often held up by the old carts drawn by plodding oxen. People in stylish modern clothes rub elbows with people who still wear the traditional dress of India.

Bonaparte

Bonaparte was the family name of the French emperor, NAPOLEON, about whom there is a separate article. He made many members of his family kings or noblemen, about 150 years ago.

All of the Bonapartes are descended from Napoleon's father and mother, Carlo and Letizia Buonaparte. The Buonapartes were an old Italian family that had moved to the island of Corsica, nearly three hundred years before Napoleon was born in 1769. Corsica was taken over by France in 1768, so Napoleon and his younger brothers and sisters were all born French citizens. It was Napoleon who changed the spelling of the name to a French way, Bonaparte.

Joseph Bonaparte was the oldest son of Carlo Buonaparte. He was born in 1768, a year older than Napoleon, and the two brothers were very close. Joseph served in the French army under Napoleon in 1796. Napoleon made Joseph King of Naples, and later King of Spain, when those countries came under French control. Joseph was very active in government and politics until 1815, when Napoleon was finally beaten and sent into exile. Joseph retired from government work, came to America, and became an American citizen. He later returned to Europe, where he died in 1844.

Lucien Bonaparte was another brother of Napoleon. He was born in 1775. In 1797 he became a member of one of the groups that ruled France after the Revolution of 1789. This group was called the Council of the Five Hundred. For a while Lucien and Napoleon got along well, but Lucien believed in democracy and was disturbed because Napoleon wanted to be emperor. The two brothers had many quarrels, and Lucien was the only one of the Bonaparte brothers who was not made a king. Lucien died in 1840.

Louis Bonaparte was Napoleon's next-youngest brother, born in 1778. Napoleon was very fond of Louis, and kept Louis with him during many of his battles and campaigns. But later the relations between the two brothers became very unfriendly. Louis was made king of Holland in 1806. He was married to Napoleon's stepdaughter, Hortense Beauharnais. One of their sons, named Charles Louis Napoleon, became president and then emperor of France in 1852. He was known as NAPOLEON III, and there is a separate article about him.

Jerome Bonaparte was Napoleon's youngest brother, born in 1784. Napoleon made him King of Westphalia. Before that, Jerome was married to an American girl, Elizabeth Patterson, from Baltimore. Napoleon was very angry about this. He made Jerome divorce her, and she went back to the United States, where there have been several prominent descendants of Jerome and Elizabeth.

Napoleon also had three sisters, Maria-Anna Elisa, Pauline, and Caroline. He gave them all many honors. But at that time women were not as active in public life as they are today.

bond

A bond is a written agreement to pay a certain amount of money in the future. Bonds are used to borrow money for long periods, such as 20 or even 50 years. The best-known kind of bond is the *mortgage bond,* which is one of the documents a person signs when he borrows money to buy or build a house (see MORTGAGE). Billions of dollars are borrowed by governments, by public utilities such as gas and electric companies, and by big businesses such as railroads and manufacturers, by issuing bonds. The borrowed money is used to put up big buildings, build highways and bridges, buy heavy machinery, and for other long-term investments.

Usually the whole amount of money borrowed is split up into bonds of $1,000 each. A firm of brokers called *underwriters* may buy the entire issue of bonds, making a profit by reselling the bonds to the public at a higher price. A bondholder, or owner of a bond, may sell it at any time, but the price is not necessarily the face value (such as $1,000). A bond may rise or fall in value like any other property, depending on how sure it seems that the borrower will be able to *redeem* it (pay the promised amount) when it *matures* (becomes due), and will pay the interest in the meantime.

All bonds bear interest, ranging from 2½% to 7% (see INTEREST). On many bonds, *coupons* are printed on every bond and once or twice a year the bondholder clips off a coupon and the issuer of the bond gives him money for it, that being his interest for the period. Some bonds are *discounted*—that is, the interest is taken off the purchase price. An example is Series E Savings Bonds of the United States. The buyer pays $18.75 for the bond and receives $25 seven years later, the difference of $6.25 being his interest for seven years. (It is about 4-1/7% per year.)

A *secured* bond names some particular property as security or *collateral;* if the borrowed money is not repaid, the bondholder may take the property. Usually, as in the case of a mortgage bond, the security is real estate, but it may also be income such as the tolls from a bridge or highway, or such things as a railroad train or machinery. An unsecured bond, also called a *debenture,* is backed by the borrower's total assets, or net worth, but not by any particular property.

A *negotiable* bond, like paper money, belongs to whoever has it; a *registered* bond is payable only to the person whose name is recorded with the corporation that issued the bond. However, both kinds may be traded—bought and sold—and the buyer of a registered bond simply has his name recorded in place of the previous owner's.

Real estate bonds are like mortgage bonds except that the total amount borrowed is split up into bonds of $1,000 each so that there may be many lenders. *State* and *municipal* (city) bonds, which are issued for such purposes as building schools and other public buildings, are taxfree securities, which means that the bondholder does not have to pay income tax on the interest he receives. They pay low interest rates but are much in demand by rich people whose income taxes are high.

All national governments issue bonds of several different kinds, especially to finance wars. The United States financed World War I with Liberty Bonds and, after the war was won, Victory Bonds. To rearm for World War II it issued Defense Bonds, then War Bonds, and later Savings Bonds. After a series of expensive wars a government may have to turn its bonds into a permanent bonded fund, with no redemption date for the bonds. The British government, after its costly wars against Napoleon in the early 1800s, issued bonds called *consols* (because they consolidated, or combined, previous bonds) and these are still bought and sold. The government redeems some of them whenever it wishes. Many issues of corporate bonds (issued by private companies) are redeemed a few at a time, the company drawing lots to see which it will redeem.

OTHER FORMS OF BONDING

Another kind of bond is an agreement to pay a certain amount of money if some event does or does not occur. This kind of bond is usually issued by a *bonding company,* which is a kind of insurance company.

A *fidelity bond* is a guarantee that a trusted employee will remain honest. Bank tellers, cashiers, collectors, and others who handle money are usually bonded. If they steal, the bonding company makes good. A *bail bond* is a promise to pay an amount established by a court if a person charged with a crime runs away instead of facing trial. A *performance bond* is a promise to pay a certain amount if a person does not do what he agrees to do. For example, a con-

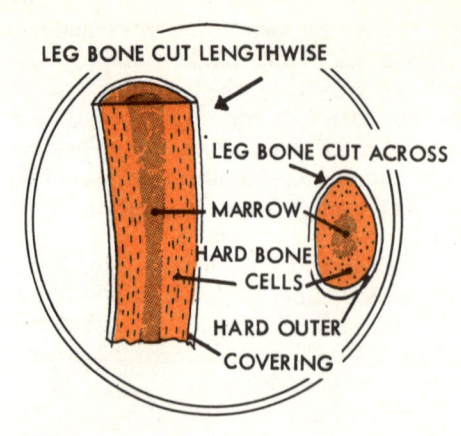

This is how the inside of a leg bone looks.

tractor agrees to finish a building by a certain date and posts (supplies) a bond that is payable if the building is not finished by that date.

A *bonded warehouse* posts a bond that it will keep goods in storage until taxes are paid on them.

bone

Bone is one of the tissues of the body. It is the hard substance of which the skeletons of animals such as fish, reptiles, birds and mammals are made. In young animals, before bone is formed, the skeleton is made of a tough elastic material called cartilage. Then the body uses various substances—salts of calcium, phosphorus, and other minerals—to make it hard.

In the human body there are about 212 bones of various shapes and sizes. The long thin bones, such as arm and leg bones, are specially important because they are hollow and filled with marrow, which makes part of the blood.

Bones are not solid. They are full of tiny holes and canals; and on the outside, bones are covered with a tissue full of blood vessels and nerves that feed them and keep them alive.

Bonheur, Marie Rosalie

This French painter is always called "Rosa," a nickname for Rosalie. She is best known for one picture called "The Horse Fair." It is a painting of big farm horses being led home after being bought at an auction. There are all kinds of different colored horses in the picture. Some of them are big, strong white ones, others are brown, black or gray. The picture is filled with movement and you can almost see the horses walking. Rosa Bonheur was born in France in 1822, and spent most of her life there. She came from an artistic family. When she was quite young, she became the head of a school for girls in Paris. Before Rosa Bonheur died in 1899, she had become world-famous as a painter of animals.

Boniface

Boniface was a missionary who set out from England to teach the Christian religion to the people of Germany, France, and Holland. All this was long, long ago, about the year 700, when the people in most of Europe were still barbarians. St. Boniface, whose name was Wynfrith before he became a saint, built

German Tourist Bureau

This church in Bonn, Germany, is more than 800 years old. It is a fine example of Romanesque architecture.

so many churches in Germany that he is called the Apostle of Germany. His special day is June 5.

Nine Popes, or heads of the Roman Catholic Church, have taken the name of Boniface. The first was Pope just about four hundred years after the time of Jesus Christ; the last Boniface was Pope almost six hundred years ago.

Bonn

Bonn is a city in Germany. It is on the Rhine River, about 16 miles southeast of Cologne. Since 1949, it has been the capital of the Federal Republic of Germany (West Germany). About 144,300 people live there. Most of them work in factories, making chemicals, machinery, and musical instruments. Bonn is a very old city, and its most famous building is a church that is more than eight hundred years old. If you visit Bonn, you can see the famous Friedrich Wilhelm University, and the house in which the great German composer, Ludwig van Beethoven, was born. You can also see the grave of another famous German composer, Robert Schumann. A beautiful bridge crosses the Rhine River at Bonn, and along the river you can see fine houses, called villas. In World War II, much of the city was destroyed or damaged.

Bonneville Dam and Lake

Bonneville Dam and Bonneville Lake were both named for Benjamin Bonneville, an American military engineer and explorer who lived in the early 1800s.

Bonneville Lake is not a lake at all. It is a desert in the state of Utah. Many, many, thousands of years ago it was a very large lake. It had an area of 20,000 square miles and was 1,000 feet deep in some places. It almost dried out once, but it refilled naturally. Then it dried out again and it has never been refilled. It turned into a desert. Its shore lines can still be seen, high on the mountainsides.

Bonneville Dam is a real dam. It is on

Bureau of Reclamation

Tons of water, pouring over the Bonneville Dam, turn turbines that supply electricity to many homes and factories.

the Columbia River, between the states of Washington and Oregon. Its main purpose is to supply electric power for the people of those two states. Bonneville Dam was built by the United States Army Engineer Corps, and is operated by the United States Army. There are many salmon in the Columbia River, and they all go upstream in the spring to lay their eggs. The Bonneville Dam has a special ladder for the salmon, to help them jump over the dam.

bonus

The word *bonus,* in the Latin language, means "good." We use it to mean extra money that is paid to a person, besides any regular wages he may have earned.

A government often gives special money to men who have served in the army or other armed forces. This is called a "soldier's" (or veteran's) bonus. Many businesses give bonuses to their workers at Christmas time. These bonuses are like Christmas presents. If a worker does a particularly good job, his company may give him a bonus.

If a company has made a very big profit, this extra money may be distributed to the owners of the company. Very often a company gives a "stock bonus." Instead of money, it gives extra shares of stock (ownership) in the company.

book

The purpose of a book is to save mens' best thoughts so that other men may make use of them. Civilization and science depend more on books than on anything else.

A book must record thousands of words and still be small enough to store and handle easily. The earliest writing was on stone slabs or clay tablets and there could be no real books, for these were too bulky. The first real "books" were long rolls of thin animal skins such as parchment or an early kind of paper called papyrus; the reader unrolled the long roll, reading as he went along. The first books of the modern kind, a sheaf of pieces of paper bound together, were made a little more than a thousand years ago. Today, about 10,000 to 15,000 new books are published each year in the United States and about the same number, more or less, in each other civilized country.

A book may be intended to entertain, as a story book or novel does; or it may be intended to instruct, as a schoolbook does; or it may be intended to make a record of things that might otherwise be forgotten. A blank book, such as a diary or a bookkeeping book, becomes a record book when things are written down in it, just as it would be if those things were printed in it to begin with.

All modern books are printed. A separate article on PRINTING tells how the type is set and how the paper is printed in a press. When a book is printed, a big sheet of paper is used. As many as 128 pages may be printed at one time.

To see how this is done, take a sheet of paper and fold it in exact halves. Then fold it again. And then again.

The place where you last folded it is where the back of the book will be. Take a pencil and number all the separate flat surfaces into which you folded the large sheet. You will find that there are sixteen of these. They will be the pages of the book.

Now unfold the sheet again. You will find that pages 1, 8, 9, 16, 12, 13, 4, and 5 are on one side of the big sheet, and pages 2, 7, 10, 15, 3, 6, 11, and 14 are on the other side. The printer makes up his type so that each page is arranged in the proper position to print in the proper

These Babylonian clay tablets are the oldest "books" in existence. The words were carved by men thousands of years ago, and they have given us information about those times. This is part of the ancient Egyptian *Book of the Dead*. It contains funeral prayers and a story of what the Egyptians believed happened to the soul after death. There are also magic words for the dead to say for a happy life after death.

Am. Museum of Natural History

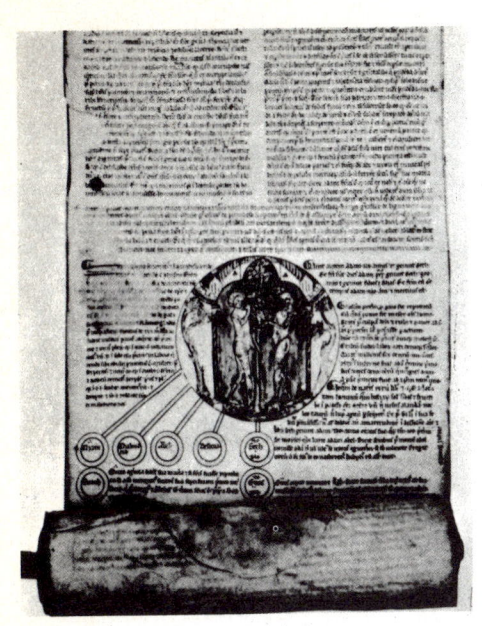

The first real books were written on long rolls of parchment more than 2,000 years ago, and some of them still exist today.

Many persons paste personal book plates in the front of their books. This book plate is from a woodcut by Albrecht Dürer.

place on the sheet; this arrangement of the type is called the *imposition*. He prints one side of the sheet, then the other. Then he folds the sheet, just as you did, and he has sixteen pages in the proper order to make one section of a book. This section is called a *signature*.

Fold your sheet again, and with scissors trim off the outside and bottom edges. You will find that you have a booklet whose pages open properly and read in order from 1 to 16. There are only eight separate leaves, but each leaf makes two pages.

What you have just done is the same thing a printer does when he prints a book, except that he does it in a more complicated way because his books must have hundreds of pages and he must make thousands of them at a time.

BOOKBINDING

Usually the printer does not do the folding of the book. He ships the big printed sheets to a bookbinder. The bookbinder takes care of all the other steps that go into the making of the book.

First, the bookbinder puts the big sheets on an automatic folding machine. This machine has arms that lift edges of the sheet, and rollers that fold them over much more smoothly than it can be done by hand. Even though 64 or 128 may be printed on one sheet, the folding machine folds them in signatures of only 16 or 32 pages.

These signatures are then *gathered*—that is, put in proper order so that page 17 will follow page 16, and page 33 will follow page 32, and so on through the book, and also arranged so that the edges are even at the ends and sides.

When all the signatures have been assembled in proper order, they are taken to a sewing machine and the backs of them are sewed together. This is very much like the sewing that a housewife does on her sewing machine at home, except that of course the bookbinder's sewing machines are specially built to handle

BOOK

N.Y. Public Library

Monks in the Middle Ages made bindings for books with great care and skill. It sometimes took years to finish the beautiful binding of a book like the one at the left. The binding on the right is decorated with semiprecious stones, and the clasps that held the book together were made of precious metal and carefully designed.

books. If the cover has come off a book of yours, you can see how it is sewed. Or if you take nearly any book and count off the first eight leaves (which make sixteen pages) and open the book wide, you can see the thread.

You now have a *sewed book*. A single folded sheet of heavy paper is now pasted to the back edges of the first page and last page of the sewed book. These are the *end papers*. They will later be used to fasten the book to its cover.

The next operations are: The book is *smashed;* that is, a heavy weight is dropped on it in a special press, to flatten it out all over. Then the book is *rounded and backed;* this means that the backbone of the book is formed into a rounder shape, which is more attractive than a flat back, and then a piece of cloth is glued to the backbone to strengthen it. On a well-made book, *headbands* are added at the same time. That is the piece of decorative woven cloth you can see at the top of this book.

The sewed book is now ready for *casing-in.*

MAKING THE CASE

The cover of the book is called a *case.* The bookbinder takes two heavy pieces of cardboard to make the front and back covers. He wraps this in bookbinder's cloth, which is specially made to be attractive, long-lasting, and resistant to soil and water. Bibles and some other books are bound in leather, or in various artificial leathers made of cloth and plastics. A case-making machine automatically wraps the cloth around the pieces of cardboard and glues down the edges, and also leaves a portion in the center that will be the back of the book. From this book you are reading, you can see the result of these operations.

The case is then *stamped.* Heavy metal

1. Today books are swiftly printed and bound by machinery. This woman is placing the sewn pages of a book on a moving belt. It will carry the book to another department.

2. A man takes each book off the belt and places it in a "smasher" to make all the pages lie flat. Then the books move on.
3. Now glue is put on the backs of the books to fasten the sections of each book together. After they are dried, they are sent to the cutting room.
4. Here the edges of the books are neatly trimmed and ready to be bound in their covers. Then they will be ready to be shipped. Now, 40,000 books can be bound in a single day by a bookbinding plant.

George McKibbin & Son

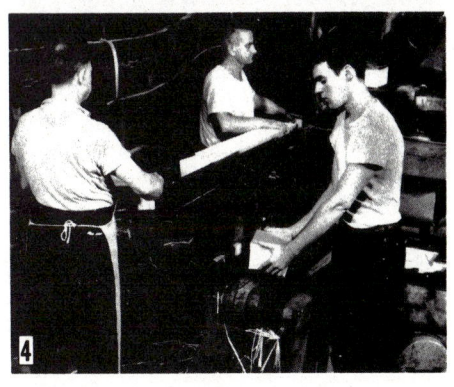

dies, which are like printing plates but much stronger, stamp colored inks, or gold, or other metals, on the book, so that its name can be read and also to give it beauty. This book requires three separate stampings to make the lettering and the design on its cover.

When the case has been made and the sewed book is complete, they meet at the casing-in machine. Both the end papers of the book are coated with a very strong glue. Then they are pressed to the inside of the case. The book is now complete. Nearly every step has been done by automatic machinery.

PAPERBOUND BOOKS

There are other methods of bookbinding that are much cheaper. The principal one is called *perfect binding*. A perfect-bound book is not sewed. The folded signatures are trimmed all the way around. Then glue and a piece of light cloth are

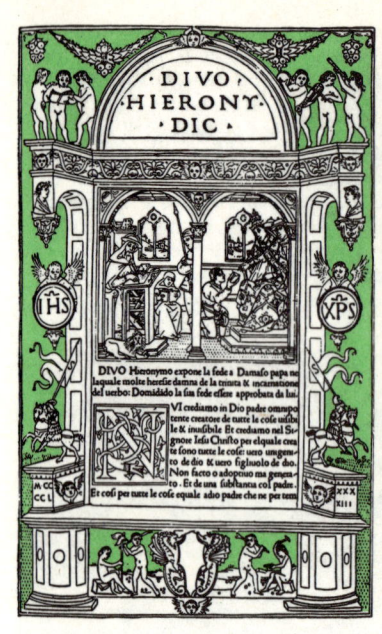

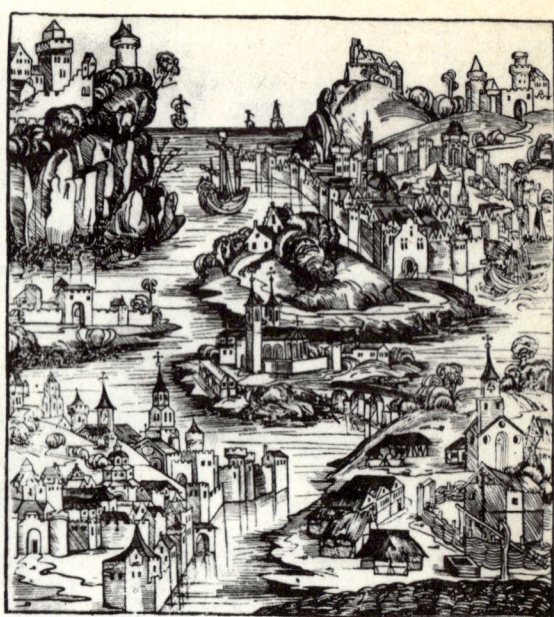

Left: A page from a book made in Italy almost 500 years ago. These early books were very beautiful and they had many fine woodcuts and pictures. *Right:* A woodcut from a 15th-century book. These early books are very rare and are kept in museums.

added to the back, to hold the pages together. This is the same way a writing tablet is made. The telephone books in all big cities are bound in this way. So are the paperbound books that sell for 25 cents or 35 cents at newsstands. It is because so much money is saved in the binding that the publishers of these books can give such great values for so little money.

Many magazines are folded just as books are, but are not sewed. Instead, heavy staples are driven through the sides. Then a paper cover is pasted over the entire magazine. Still other magazines are saddle-stitched, which means that the staple is driven through the center of the fold.

HANDMADE BOOKS

Bookbinding is a hobby with some people, and it is an art with some very fine bookbinders who make beautiful books that can cost hundreds of dollars. The finest leathers are often used, or cloths of rare weaves and patterns. The lettering and designs on the covers are put on by hand, with brass types and instruments that are heated and pressed into the covers. This is called *hand-tooling*. Of course, very few handmade books are made, because they are so expensive. In the early days of books, hundreds of years ago, many more books were made by hand, and some of them are still among the most beautiful of all books.

HOW BOOKS DEVELOPED

Thousands of years ago, when warlike nations such as Greece and Rome would capture the educated men of other countries and make slaves of them, books were written by hand, by slaves who were forced to be copyists. Of course, that was long before printing was invented.

Then came the Dark Ages. They were called dark because men forgot the advantages of education and became ignorant. Only the Christian Church kept learning alive. In the monasteries of Europe, monks worked for years making copies of the Bible and other books that were worth preserving. This went on for nearly a thousand years—from the time when the Roman Empire was conquered by barbarians, in 476, to the time when the Renaissance, or "rebirth of learning," began in the 1300s.

During this period, the monks of Europe made some of the most beautiful of all books. These are called *illuminated manuscripts.* The *manuscript* part means they were written by hand, and *illuminated* means decorated with beautiful designs and pictures in brilliant colors. These books were usually written on *vellum,* which is calfskin, or on *parchment,* which is sheepskin or goatskin, prepared in a smooth, white finish that is very beautiful, easy to write on, and very long-lasting.

The Chinese invented printing, but printed books didn't appear in Europe until about five hundred years ago. They were made from wood blocks on which an entire page was carved. Then, about the year 1455, Johannes Gutenberg, at his printing press in Mainz, Germany, made the first book ever printed from movable type. He printed the entire Bible, and it took him six years to do it. Today there are several copies of the Gutenberg Bible in existence, and they are the most valuable of all printed books. Gutenberg Bibles have been sold for prices as high as $200,000.

Movable type made it much easier to make many books, and by the end of Gutenberg's century, there were more than 150 printers in Europe making books from movable type. One of the most famous of these was Aldus Manutius, who lived about the year 1500 in Italy. He printed editions of the great Greek and Latin writers whose works had almost been forgotten. His books are called Aldine editions, and some of those are still in existence and are very valuable. William Caxton was the first

N.Y. Public Library
This copy of Chaucer's *Canterbury Tales,* printed in 1532, had hand-carved letters.

N.Y. Public Library
Beautifully designed books like this were printed in England about 100 years ago.

printer of English books. He printed books of more different kinds than any other printer. Between about 1475 and about 1490, he printed books on chess, medicine, history, religion; schoolbooks, poems, and romances. In all he printed about eighty books.

After the year 1600, books were being printed all over Europe. Booksellers' shops began to be seen on the streets, and it became worthwhile for men to make a profession of writing, for the booksellers would pay them.

In America, the first book printed was the Bay Psalm Book. It was a book of psalms, and was printed in Massachusetts in 1640. A copy of this very rare book has sold for $150,000.

Up to about a hundred years ago, only one to three thousand copies of a book were printed at one time. After the Civil War, better printing presses were invented. Books could be made cheaper. More people went to school and learned to read. As a result, books began to be sold in much greater quantities. Today, as many as 750,000 copies of a book are printed at one time. It is not unusual to print 50,000 or 100,000 copies of a book in the first edition (the first time it is printed) and a book may be reprinted many times.

HOW BOOKS ARE PUBLISHED

Until about the year 1800, the printer of a book was also the bookseller and the publisher. Then some companies began to make a business of publishing books (having them set in type, printed, and bound, but not selling them to the public). Other companies were booksellers only. They opened bookstores to sell the books of other publishers.

That is the way the publishing business works today. The author of a book takes it to a publisher. If the publisher likes the book and thinks it will sell, he pays all the expense of manufacturing the book. He pays the author a certain amount of money, called a *royalty,* on each copy that is sold. He sells the book to booksellers all over the world, and they resell the books to the public. When a book sells in a bookstore for $2.50, it means that the bookseller paid about $1.50 for it. The publisher received the $1.50. He paid the author a royalty of 25 cents to 35 cents. Out of the rest of the money, the publisher paid the cost of manufacturing the book.

Mass production and quantity sales can reduce the cost of books, just as they have reduced the cost of automobiles and other things. Sometimes a publisher makes millions of books at one time, and puts them on sale in supermarkets and such stores where nearly everyone goes. The stores accept much less profit than usual, and the authors are paid very tiny royalties or none at all, and as a result people get great bargains in books.

Many other books are offered for sale by mail, or are sold by book clubs, which pick books they think their members will want to read, and sell those books to their members. Still other books are sold by salesmen who represent the publishers and bring the books right to your house.

BEST-SELLERS

When many copies of a book are sold, it is called a *best-seller.* The biggest of all best-sellers is the Bible. So many million copies of it have been sold that no one knows how many.

There are many books of which several million copies have been sold. Some of these are "standard" books, such as dictionaries and encyclopedias and cookbooks. Every few years there may be a novel that sells a million books or more. Several American best-sellers have had sales of more than ten million copies in all editions, but most of these large sales are in paperbound copies at low prices. The best-seller among books for boys has been *Treasure Island,* by Robert Louis Stevenson, and the best-seller among books for girls has been *Little Women,* by Louisa May Alcott.

Bookkeeping

bookkeeping

Bookkeeping is writing down a record that has to do with money—how much you have received and where you got it; how much you spent and what you spent it for; how much you owe, and how much is owed to you. It is called bookkeeping because these records are written into blank books. A bookkeeper is a person who does this work for a living, and millions of Americans make their livings as bookkeepers; but every other man, woman, or child who jots down notes or reminders about money is doing a kind of bookkeeping.

The first and greatest importance of bookkeeping is to put things down so they will not be forgotten. If you lend a friend a dollar, you do not have to write it down. You will not forget it. But if you were to lend money to fifty different friends, in amounts ranging from thirty cents to a dollar and forty-two cents, you would have to write them all down or you would surely forget some of them. That is why a store or other business house, to which hundreds or thousands of persons may owe money, has to have bookkeeping. If you have five dollars in your pocket and want to buy something that costs four dollars, you know you can afford it—except that you remember something you have to do on Saturday that will cost you two dollars, so you can't afford it after all—unless you remember that on Friday you will be getting another three dollars, so you can afford it after all. Businesses that are constantly receiving money from many different places and that have dozens of bills to pay at different times in the future cannot trust to figuring out such things without written records called bookkeeping.

Bookkeeping can be very simple or very, very complicated, depending on the kind of records that have to be kept, but the job of bookkeeping is always to write the figures down. The job of telling what those figures mean—how much profit a company has made, or how much it has lost—is not bookkeeping but ACCOUNTING, about which there is a separate article.

SINGLE-ENTRY BOOKKEEPING

In the earliest and simplest form of bookkeeping, you take a blank book and use one page of it for each person you do business with. (Each page is said to represent one *account*.) Suppose you own a grocery store, and you have a customer named John Smith. At the top of one page you write "John Smith." Then your record will be something like this:

May 18	He bought groceries worth	$ 3.87
May 22	He bought groceries worth	12.66
	Now he owes	16.53
May 25	He paid	15.00
	He still owes	1.53

Of course, you wouldn't bother to write

out so fully the explanation of the figures you put down; you might simply jot down, "groceries," "1 ham," "canned goods," and so on. But that is how your bookkeeping would work, and you could always look at the book and tell how much John Smith owes.

Most people who have checking accounts at banks do their personal bookkeeping in the same way. It is just as though they had a page in the bookkeeping book with "Bank" at the top, except that actually the record is kept in the checkbook. It may read something like this:

May 18	Opened bank account by depositing	$500.00
May 22	Made out check for groceries	15.00
	Money left in bank	485.00
May 25	Made out check for taxes	212.00
	Money left in bank	273.00
May 28	Deposited in bank	200.00
	Money now in bank	473.00

If you stop to consider for a moment, you will realize that the money in the bank is money that the bank owes you and must pay you whenever you ask for it; therefore the bookkeeping record is the same kind as the one that showed how much John Smith owed for groceries.

This is called single-entry bookkeeping because each figure is written down only once. An amount of money recorded in a book is said to be *entered* in the book, and each amount written down is called an *entry*.

The method of single-entry bookkeeping shown above, in which every entry is put in the same column, is very simple but takes up a lot of space. So, hundreds of years ago, bookkeepers figured out a new way. Each account still had its own page, but the page was divided down the middle, so that there could be a column of figures on each side. The column on the left was called the *debit* column, and the column on the right was called the *credit* column. (In the Latin language, *debit* means "he owes," so a person who owes something is called a *debtor; credit* means "he entrusts," so a person to whom something is owed is called a *creditor*. The abbreviation for debit is *dr.*, and for credit is *cr.*)

In the debit column is written down anything the person owes you, or any money you pay him. In the credit column is written down anything he pays you or you owe him.

Here is the way the account with the bank would look if it were done in the two-column system instead of in the single-column system shown above:

BANK

	DR.		CR.
May 18	500.00	May 22	15.00
May 28	200.00	May 25	212.00

To find out how much money you have in the bank at any time, you add up the two figures in the debit column, which come to $700.00, and the two figures in the credit column, which come to $227.00. You subtract the smaller figure and it gives you $473.00, which is the same figure you arrived at by the other system. This figure is called a *balance*. Since it is in the debit column, it means that the bank owes you that much money. At any convenient time, such as the end of a month or the end of a year, or when the page is full and a new page must be begun, the two columns are added up and the difference between the totals begins a new account. For instance, at the end of May you might total up the columns shown above, then begin a new page and enter in its debit column, "May 31, Balance, $473.00." The $473.00 would be included when you add up the columns on the next page.

DOUBLE-ENTRY BOOKKEEPING

Single-entry bookkeeping is simple enough, but there are several ways in which it is not good enough for a business firm of any size. A simple mistake in adding up a column might not be noticed for months. The system could show a businessman how much money he had, owed, and was owed, but it could not show him how much profit he was making at any given time. To solve these and other problems, double-entry bookkeeping was invented.

Three principles are the key to understanding double-entry bookkeeping:

1. Not only people and companies, but also properties such as furniture and business ideas such as sales, or profit and loss, have their own pages, or accounts, in the bookkeeping books.

2. Every figure entered *must* be entered *twice*. once in the debit column of one account and the second time in the credit column of another account.

3. The total of all the debit entries must be exactly the same as the total of all the credit entries. This cannot fail to be the case if the same figure is entered twice, once in each. Therefore if the totals are not the same, there is a mistake somewhere and the bookkeeper must keep looking until it is found.

Suppose you open an office to carry on your business. First, you buy $1,000.00 worth of furniture for it. You do not have to pay for it in cash; the furniture store simply sends you a bill, which you must pay next month. You credit the store with $1,000.00, because that is money you owe. At the same time you debit an account called *Furniture* with the same $1,000.00. This means that the furniture owes your business $1,000.00, because that is what it cost.

Then you receive a bill for the first month's rent, which is $100.00. You credit your landlord with $100.00, because you owe it to him, and you debit an account called *Expense*, or perhaps you will choose to set up a special account called *Rent*, with the same $100.00.

All the money you owe makes an account called *Accounts Payable*, and all the money that is owed to you makes an account called *Accounts Receivable*. When the time comes to pay for the furniture, you make out a check and send it to the store. You credit your bank with $1,000.00, because it has paid back that much that it owed you. You debit Accounts Payable $1,000.00, because you owe your Accounts Payable that much less. Again there are two entries that are exactly the same in amount—they *balance* each other.

At certain times a *trial balance* is taken by a bookkeeper. All the columns on all the accounts are added up. All debit balances are added together, and all credit balances are added together. If the totals are the same, the books are in balance. If the totals are not the same, there must be a mistake and enough searching will find it.

On the trial balance, all debit balances are called *assets,* meaning values or amounts you own or that are owed to you; and all credit balances are called *liabilities,* meaning amounts that you owe.

The double-entry bookkeeping system is based on a principle called the *accrual basis.* The idea of the accrual basis is that there is no real difference between money you have in cash and money that is owed to you and will be paid to you sooner or later; and that there is no real difference between bills you received and have paid for, and bills you received and have to pay for later. In other words, if you have $10,000.00 in the bank and owe $5,000.00 you are no better off than if you have $5,000.00 in the bank and do not owe anything.

Many special accounts go on the books to show how much a business is actually worth, but these are jobs for the accountant and not for the bookkeeper. See the article on ACCOUNTING.

THE BOOKS USED

Bookkeeping is done in books that have specially ruled paper—that is, paper

BOOMERANG

with lines drawn at the proper places to make bookkeeping easier. Usually these are looseleaf books, so that pages may be changed as often as necessary.

There are two main types of books. One is called the *journal* and the other is called the *ledger*. Journal comes from the French word *jour,* meaning "day"; a journal is a day book, in which every separate item of business is entered. A journal is called a *book of original entry*. It is used to make immediate records, and show what they apply to. Many separate journals are kept, depending on the size of the business. There are the *cash receipts book,* to record all money received; the *cash disbursements book,* to record all money paid out; the *sales book,* the *purchases book,* and finally the *general journal,* in which you record anything for which you do not have a special journal.

The other type of bookkeeping book is the ledger. There are usually three ledgers. The *accounts receivable ledger* has a page for every customer who owes money to the company. The *accounts payable book* has a page for everyone from whom the company buys. The *general ledger* combines all the bookkeeping information that is in all the journals, or books of original entry. The bookkeeper first makes the entries in the journal, then transfers them—it is called *posting* them—to the proper page in the general ledger. This book has a page for every account; for example, Cash (how much money is in the bank); Sales (the total of all the goods sold); Purchases (the total of all the goods bought); and so on.

When an amount in one of the columns is to be subtracted from the total, instead of added to it, the amount is written in red ink. When a business has lost money, the amount of the loss is shown in red ink, and that is why a business is said to be "in the red" when it is losing money. Sometimes red ink is not handy and then the bookkeeper puts a circle around the figure. This gives us another phrase you often hear, "in the hole," which means the same thing as "in the red."

MACHINE BOOKKEEPING

In big companies, there is so much business that it would be a waste of time for bookkeepers to make all the entries by hand. For such companies, special machinery has been made to do much of the job of bookkeeping. The "bookkeepers" often type the names of the accounts, and the amounts of the entries, on an electric machine, and then the machine does the rest. Even for quite small companies, there are machines that save them a great deal of time and work. But these machines do not alter the fact that double-entry bookkeeping is being used. The system is exactly the same. The machines have merely been built to do the work mechanically.

boomerang

The boomerang is a weapon that was used by the savage people who lived in Australia before any white men went there. It is a curved piece of wood, rounded on one side and flat on the other. A boomerang is held at one end and thrown at an animal one is hunting, or at an enemy in warfare.

One kind of boomerang is called the *return boomerang*. It is used for hunt-

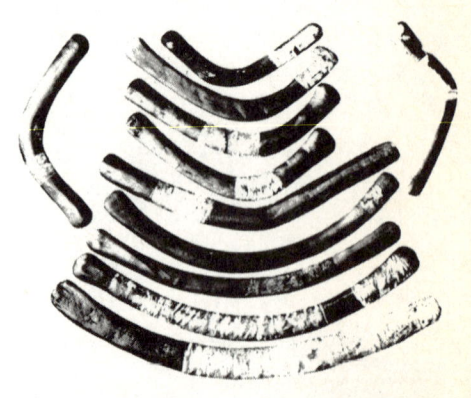

N.Y. Public Library

These boomerangs are very old. Some were used for hunting and others were used in tribal ceremonies. Sometimes the people bound them with bark or painted them.

An Australian native is about to fling his boomerang at a fleeing kangaroo.

ing. When the return boomerang is thrown, it will fly straight for about thirty yards. Then it will curve and fly back to the man who threw it. It can be used to kill birds when they are flying. The man who throws it must be careful not to be hit by the boomerang when it returns to him.

The *nonreturn boomerang* is bigger and heavier than the return boomerang. Sometimes it is as long as four feet. It is used in war. As it flies through the air, it makes a whistling sound. It travels so fast that it can kill a man if it hits him.

Some of the native people of Australia still use boomerangs. The Hopi Indians, who live in Arizona, once used the boomerang, and so did the ancient Egyptians.

Boone, Daniel

Daniel Boone went into Kentucky more than two hundred years ago, when no one lived there but savage Indians who attacked every white man that came along. The whole territory then was covered with thick forests. Only an expert woodsman could travel through them without being lost or killed. Daniel Boone led new settlers into Kentucky, helped them to fight the Indians, and opened up that part of the western United States.

There was no United States when Daniel Boone was a young man. He was born in Pennsylvania, which was then a British colony, about the year 1735. When he was just a boy he learned to hunt and to trap wild animals. All his life he was a famous hunter. He probably didn't go to school, and knew just a little about reading and writing and arithmetic. But he learned all about the wilds and the streams, about hunting and fishing and exploring. He learned how to find his way through trackless forests, and how to hunt out the wild animals. He could move as silently as an Indian, making no sound and leaving no tracks. The thing he loved best was to live alone in the woods. Nothing frightened him. No hardship seemed too great.

When Daniel Boone was still a boy, his family moved to North Carolina. There Boone worked as a farmer, grew up, married, and tried to settle down. But he liked to live away from settled places. In 1769, when he was 35 years old, he went as leader of a small group on a long trip into the frontier wilderness, the western country that had not been explored. The party crossed the Appalachian Mountains through a passage that is called the Cumberland Gap, into land that is now part of the state of Kentucky. After two years they returned, bringing with them many valuable animal skins, and telling wonderful stories about the beautiful land and their fights with the Indians.

Daniel Boone guided many groups of settlers into the Kentucky wilderness more than 150 years ago. They traveled over a famous route known as the Wilderness Trail.

After this, Daniel Boone became famous as a guide and Indian fighter. He was sometimes hired to lead people to the frontier, and to help them settle there. He lived in Kentucky for many years, hunting and exploring. He was a brave leader in battles with the Indians. Once he was captured by the Shawnee Indians, and taken far to the west. The Indians liked him. They treated him well, and they even adopted him as a member of their tribe. But Boone was always loyal to his friends. One day he heard that the Indians were planning to attack Boonesborough, the Kentucky settlement he had founded. He managed to escape from the Indians. Traveling on foot, he covered more than a hundred miles in a few days. He managed to reach Boonesborough in time to warn the people. With his help, the people beat off the Indian attack.

When he was almost 65 years old, Daniel Boone moved farther west, to land that is now part of the state of Missouri. There he continued to hunt and trap animals. There is a story about Daniel Boone's great honesty: When he left Kentucky, he owed money to many people, but could not pay them. He saved carefully for a long time. Then he went back to Kentucky to pay all his old debts. Afterward he had nothing left at all, but he was very happy.

Daniel Boone died in the Missouri country, in 1820. He was very famous in his own time, and is still remembered as a man who helped America become a great country.

Booth

Booth was the name of a famous American family of actors. Junius Brutus Booth was an English actor who came to the United States in 1821 and spent the rest of his life traveling about the country giving plays. Two of his sons were John Wilkes Booth and Edwin Booth. When they were children they appeared with their father in small parts in his plays.

John Wilkes Booth was the man who shot Abraham Lincoln. He was born in 1839. During the Civil War he believed strongly in the Southern cause. When the war ended Booth was very angry because the South had been defeated. In revenge he planned to shoot the president, the vice president and all of the cabinet. His first target was President Lincoln. On the evening of April 14, 1865, Lincoln and his wife were watching a play in Ford's Theater in Washington. Booth slipped past the guards in the theater and entered the box where Lincoln was sitting. He shot Lincoln in the head. When he jumped from the box down to the stage he broke his ankle. He escaped through the stage door, leaped on a horse and rode toward Maryland. He stopped to have a doctor fix his ankle and then rode on into Virginia. But on April 20 he was cornered in a barn at Bowling Green. He was shot trying to escape.

Edwin Booth, John Wilkes Booth's older brother, was born in 1833. He became America's first great Shakespearean actor. For many years he had to live down the fact that his brother had shot Lincoln. After Edwin had appeared in his father's troupe as a child, he formed his own company. He made a great name for himself in *Hamlet, Othello,* and other plays by Shakespeare. During his life he appeared with all the famous actors of the time, both here and in Europe. He died in New York in 1893.

Booth, William

William Booth was the founder of the Salvation Army. He was born in Nottingham, England, in 1829. From the time he was 15 years old, Booth was very religious. He liked to travel around the country reminding people to love God. After Booth married, he and his wife, Catherine Mumford Booth, did this together. One thing they did was gather together a group of men and women who had been bad but who now believed in God. These men told others what had happened to them. This group was called a "Hallelujah Band."

In 1878, Booth founded the Salvation

Salvation Army
General William and Evangeline Booth

Army. It was organized somewhat like a military army. Booth was called "General." The Salvation Army preached and sang about God on street corners and in parks. They visited prisons and hospitals, and tried to help sick and unhappy people everywhere. In the beginning it was very difficult, but General Booth believed in what he was doing and the Salvation Army grew bigger and bigger. Organizations were set up in the United States, Australia, Europe, India, Africa, South America, and many other places.

William Booth died in 1912. The Booths had eight children, and all but one of them became important leaders in the Salvation Army. **Evangeline Booth**, their daughter, born in 1865, became general of the Salvation Army in the United States in 1904 and world commander in 1934. She died in 1950.

bootlegging

Bootlegging is making or selling alcoholic liquor when that is against the law. For many years, bootleggers were simply men who made whiskey and would not pay the government tax on it. Most of these bootleggers lived in mountain and country districts. The whiskey they made was called "moonshine," or "bootleg liquor" (perhaps because they carried bottles of it in the high boots that they wore). The law was enforced by "Revenuers," detectives of the Internal Revenue (tax-collecting) branch of the United States Treasury Department.

BORAX

From 1920 to 1933, the United States had a Prohibition law that forbade all making and selling of liquor. During this period bootlegging became a national problem. Bootleggers formed big criminal gangs and became rich by selling bootleg liquor. Some of the liquor was smuggled in from foreign countries and some was made in the United States.

Since 1933, when the Prohibition law was repealed (canceled), there has again been much bootlegging of liquor on which no tax is paid. In states and districts where local laws forbid the sale of liquor, there are bootleggers who bring in liquor from other states or districts and sell it illegally.

borax

Borax is a chemical that is used as a water softener, as a cleanser, and in the making of glass, shellac, and glazes. It looks like little grayish-white transparent crystals. Borax is found in nature and also is made by man.

Man has known about borax for many hundreds of years. Most borax used to come from the salt lakes of Tibet, where it is called *tincal*. The natural borax that we use today is mined in California and Nevada in the United States, and in the South American desert of Atacama. Borax can be manufactured by combining boric acid with another chemical, sodium carbonate.

When borax is heated to a very high temperature it melts into a glasslike substance. This is why it is good for making glazes.

Melted borax has another quality that is very useful. It changes color when it touches metallic oxides. When a chemist is not sure what a particular metal is, he can find out by combining the metal with melted borax and seeing what color the borax turns. If, for instance, it turns green or blue, the chemist knows that the metal is copper. If it turns amethyst, the metal is manganese; and if it turns brown, the metal is nickel.

Bordeaux

Bordeaux is an important city in France. It is on the Garonne River, and although it is about 75 miles from the Atlantic Ocean, it is the busiest Atlantic seaport in the southern part of France. This is because the Garonne River is deep enough for ocean-going ships to sail all the way up the river to Bordeaux. The harbor is very large, and a thousand ships can get into it at one time.

Bordeaux is about the size of Richmond, Virginia. About 250,000 people live there. Many of them work in the shipbulding yards and in factories. Others make Bordeaux wines, which are famous all over the world.

The city is very old and in it there are churches that were built more than seven hundred years ago. Bordeaux University was founded before Columbus discovered America. Three times Bordeaux has been the capital of France, when the regular capital, Paris, was threatened by German armies and the French government had to move. The

French Gov't Tourist Bureau

The bell tower of this old church in Bordeaux has rung out the hour for centuries.

last time was during World War II. Bordeaux harbor was bombed many times during the war because it was a favorite hiding place for German submarines.

BORDEAUX, FRANCE. Capital of the department of the Gironde. Population, 257,946.

Borden, Gail

Gail Borden was the first man to find a good way of making evaporated milk. This is milk which is heated until most of the water goes off into steam. Evaporated milk can be kept much longer than fresh milk because it does not spoil if kept in sealed cans. Before Borden's invention, people could have no milk at all unless they lived near a farmer who had cows, or in a place where fresh milk could be bought in stores. Fresh milk does not stay sweet for very long, and Gail Borden realized how useful it would be if there were some way to preserve the food values in milk, so that people on long journeys or soldiers in battle could have milk to drink and to cook with.

Gail Borden was born in Norwich, New York, in 1801, and one of his first jobs was as a land surveyor in Mississippi. He later went to Texas with Stephen A. Austin, and laid out the plans for the city of Galveston. Later he returned to the East and worked for years trying to develop a process for evaporating and canning milk. At last he succeeded, and got a patent for his invention in 1856. This was just in time for the soldiers in the Civil War to benefit from his idea, and the invention was very important in the development of the food-packing industry. Borden died in 1874.

Borden, Sir Robert Laird

Sir Robert Laird Borden was prime minister of Canada at the time of World War I. He was born in 1854 at Grand Pré, Nova Scotia, and held many government jobs before he became prime minister in 1911. After World War I, he worked hard to help Canada become one of the world's important independent nations. He was responsible for the start of Canada's parcel-post system. He also helped a great deal in getting Canada a seat in the League of Nations as an independent country instead of just as part of the British Commonwealth's delegation. At one time he was a member of the Canadian government's embassy in Washington. He died in 1937.

border

The boundary or frontier between two countries or states is called the border. In the history of the United States, borders were important at several different times. The Border War was a bitter fight in Kansas that started in 1854 and lasted for more than six years. Kansas was about to become a state, and the question was whether it should be a slave state or a free state. Slavery was a big problem all over the country at that time. The people who were in favor of slavery and the people who were against it both sent men to live in the Kansas Territory so they could vote for their side. An open war broke out, and terrible violence followed. Many people were killed, and the territory became known as "bleeding Kansas." The Border War ended when Kansas was admitted to the United States as a free state in 1861.

In the Civil War, the "border states" were the states that were between the North and the South and had many sympathizers for each side. The states were Delaware, Kentucky, Missouri, and Maryland. President Abraham Lincoln was very anxious that these important states should not join the Confederacy, or South. He arrested the leaders of Maryland who wanted their state to secede.

In the United States today, "South of the Border" means "in Mexico."

The Border is also the frontier between England and Scotland. Many poems and stories have been written about the battles that took place there long ago. The most famous writer about the Border was Sir Walter Scott.

Borgia

Borgia was the name of a famous family in Italy about five hundred years ago. The name *Borgia* always makes people think of poison and murder, and the most famous man of this family certainly deserved such evil fame. He was Cesare Borgia, and even in a time when war and cruelty were common, he was outstanding. When he wanted something he would use the most terrible ways to get it, including murder.

Cesare Borgia was born about 1475. His father became Pope Alexander VI. Cesare used his father's power to get what he wanted, and schemed against many of the Italian rulers.

Italy was then made up of many little states, each governed by a ruler who really owned the country. These rulers were almost always fighting with one another, each trying to conquer as much as he could. Cesare Borgia set out to fight the local rulers of Romagna, which was an area in northeastern Italy. He conquered many small states and captured forts and castles, usually killing the rulers. Sometimes he did not bother with wars. He just had people murdered and then seized their property. Poison was his favorite way of murdering. Finally he was lord over a large territory and he became Duke of Romagna.

Cesare was very powerful and very lucky. But plots were always being made against him. In 1503 his father died, and Cesare himself was very ill. The new Pope was an enemy of his and Cesare had to give up all his castles and leave Rome. For a while he was a prisoner of the king of Spain, but he escaped. He commanded an army for the king of Navarre, and in 1507 he was killed in a battle.

Another famous member of this family was Lucrezia Borgia, sister of Cesare. She was very beautiful and intelligent. But she was suspected of helping her father in his crimes.

There are many stories of Lucrezia's wickedness. One story tells of a marvelous ring she wore. It was said to have a secret compartment under the stone where Lucrezia kept a little poison—just in case she should need it suddenly! It is very hard to tell whether these stories are true. Nowadays many people who have studied history say they are not true, but others still believe them.

Lucrezia was born about 1480. She was married several times. Her father arranged several of her marriages, but often he would change his mind and break the marriage off.

There is a story that one of her husbands was murdered on the order of her brother Cesare. In 1501 Lucrezia was married to the son of an Italian ruler, who later became the Duke of Ferrara. From that time on her life was peaceful. She had several children. She became noted for helping people. Many artists and writers lived and worked at her court, and she was always friendly and helpful to them.

Borglum, Gutzon

Gutzon Borglum was an American sculptor. He is most famous for making a mountain into a national monument. He carved huge heads of George Washington, Thomas Jefferson, Abraham Lincoln and Theodore Roosevelt out of the peak of Mount Rushmore in South Dakota. Congress passed a law authorizing him to do this great work, and it is now called the Mount Rushmore National Memorial. Borglum needed to be an artist and also an engineer to do this unusual task, and he was both. He made the largest sculpture ever done by any man.

Borglum was born in Idaho in 1871. He learned his art as a boy from his father who was a Danish wood-carver. Borglum also carved the statue of Lincoln which you can see in the Capitol in Washington, D.C. Many other of his statues are in museums. The work on the Mount Rushmore National Memorial was almost complete when he died in 1941, and his son, Lincoln Borglum, finished the monument.

boric acid

Boric acid (which is sometimes called *boracic acid*) is a very weak acid that can be found in nature or manufactured. It looks somewhat like powdered sugar. It is often used as an antiseptic, which means something that kills germs. Boric acid is either dissolved in water or made into an ointment or salve. The ointment is often used to relieve the sting of a burn or a scratch. The powder can be dissolved in water and used as an eyewash. Boric acid is also used in industry, chiefly for making glazes and enamels. It is chemically related to BORAX, about which you can read in another article.

Boris Godunoff

Boris Godunoff is a Russian grand opera. It was based on a historical play by the Russian poet Pushkin and was first sung in 1874, in St. Petersburg (now Leningrad), which was then the capital. The music was written by Modeste Moussorgsky, and he changed it several times. His friend Nicolai Rimsky-Korsakoff, who was also a Russian composer, helped him change it in some places.

STORY OF THE OPERA

The story is about a czar, or emperor, of Russia named Boris Godunoff, who lived about 350 years ago. He became ruler of Russia by murdering Dmitri, the real czar's brother, who would have become czar when the real czar died. Then Boris went to live in a monastery (where men live a religious life) so that the people would think that he did not really want to be czar. But Boris had many followers and when the czar did die, they knew what to do. They made a lot of people gather together and beg Boris to come back and rule over them.

Meanwhile Gregory, a young man who was just the same age as the murdered Dmitri, pretended that he was Dmitri. Many people believed him, and he was able to raise an army to fight Boris. Even Boris was afraid that Gregory really was Dmitri, and that he had come back to be the rightful ruler of Russia. Fear and a guilty conscience had made Boris so unhappy that all he could do was pray and hope that God would forgive him for his awful sin. At the end of the opera he sings a farewell to his son Feodor, telling him to be a good and kind czar, and then he kills himself.

Borneo

Borneo is a large island in the East Indies, southwest of the Philippine Islands. It is the third-largest island in the world. Although it is about the size of Texas, not half as many people live there. Most of the people of the forests are natives called *Dyaks*. There are different tribes of Dyaks, and all of them are very backward and uncivilized. They live in the jungle in low huts, and they farm, hunt, and fish. Another group in Borneo are the Malays. They are more civilized than the Dyaks. Most of them live on the coast, and are farmers and fishermen. There are also many Chinese in Borneo.

Borneo is an unusual place because parts of it are very wild and other parts are quite modern. The cities have schools and well-built houses, and there are quite a few automobiles. Many of the people who live in the cities work at mining coal, gold, and diamonds. Others work in the oil fields, and in rubber and tobacco factories. The central part of

BORNEO

782

Most of the people in Borneo live in primitive houses made of sticks. But they like nice things, and when they can, they plant little gardens around their houses.

Unations

The people of Borneo perform many ancient dances. The man above is doing a skillful sword dance, while the man behind accompanies him on a drum. At the right, a doctor is treating a Borneo boy. With the help of the United Nations, the government sends doctors and medical supplies to distant places where they are needed. People come long distances to meet the boat and get medical attention. They even carry sick people to consult the doctors of these traveling hospitals. At the lower right, elephants are being used in place of bulldozers and tractors to clear the roads. These powerful animals are not fast, but they know how to push dead logs aside.

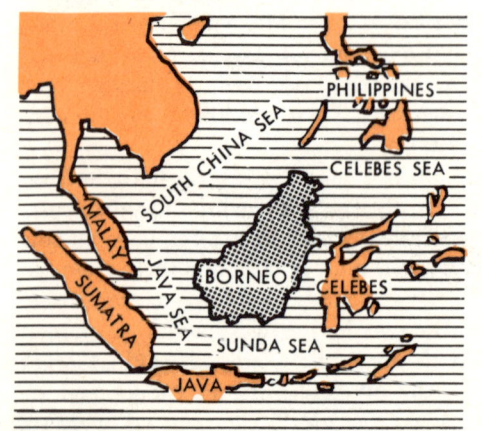

Borneo is a dense, wild jungle, with valuable forests of ebony and teak trees. Elephants, leopards, orang-utans and other wild animals roam through the jungle.

Borneo has many mountains and rivers. The rivers are important because they are one of the best ways for people to get from one place to another. The weather in Borneo is hot and sticky. Very often there are heavy rains, and sometimes there are small earthquakes.

Borneo was discovered by the Portuguese about 450 years ago. Later the Dutch moved in and drove the Portuguese out. About a hundred years later the British came and also settled. They controlled the northern part of Borneo, and the southern part (about three-quarters of the island) was owned by the Dutch. During World War II the Japanese invaded the island and stayed there for four years. When Japan surrendered to the Allies the Japanese left the island. In 1950, Dutch Borneo became part of the independent state of Indonesia, and in 1963 British Borneo, consisting of Sarawak, Brunei, and North Borneo, became part of Malaysia.

BORNEO, island in the East Indies. Area, 290,012 square miles. Population 4,958,000. These figures are divided into: Malaysian Borneo, area 81,726 square miles; population, 1,258,000. Indonesian Borneo, area, 208,286 square miles; population, 3,700,000.

Borodin, Alexander

Alexander Borodin was a great Russian composer, or writer of original music. He was born in 1833 in St. Petersburg, which is now called Leningrad. He started to study music as a very small boy. When he was only 9 he composed a polka, which is the music for a kind of dance. When he was older he studied medicine and became a doctor and scientist, but he never stopped writing music. We sometimes wonder how he was able to do so many things and do them all well, for he also wrote many books. His most famous pieces of music are three symphonies (music for a big orchestra), and a grand opera called *Prince Igor*. Borodin died in 1887.

borzoi

One of the fastest-running dogs in the world is the borzoi, or Russian wolfhound. Borzois are slender, graceful dogs. They were developed in Russia more than three hundred years ago and were used in wolf-hunting by Russian noblemen. They are still used for hunting, but in the United States they are often kept as pets because they are very beautiful, gentle, and quiet.

The borzoi is a tall, long-legged dog, with an arched back. It stands about 2½ feet high at the shoulders, and it may weigh between 75 and 110 pounds. Its head, for a large dog, is narrow and rather small, with tiny, pointed ears. The borzoi's tail is long, and curves down low under its body. Its coat is long and silky and is sometimes brown, tan, or white, or a mixture of white and any other color.

A. Brock

This beautiful borzoi has won many prizes at dog shows and at exhibitions.

Ephrom Gallery

Bosch painted this famous picture of *The Temptation of St. Anthony*.

Bosch, Hieronymus

Hieronymus Bosch was a Dutch painter who lived more than four hundred years ago. His pictures are filled with demons and monsters and all kinds of weird places. Some of the pictures are of religious subjects, like *The Temptation of St. Anthony*. Bosch tried to make everything look as real as possible in his paintings. Sometimes it seems that you can actually feel the cloth in his pictures. Bosch was born in 1470 and died in 1530. He spent part of his life in Spain. The Spanish king, Philip II, bought many of Bosch's paintings to hang in his palaces. They still hang there and every year many people go to see them.

Bosnia-Herzegovina

Bosnia-Herzegovina is the name of a part of Yugoslavia, on the Balkan Peninsula. It is more than 19,000 square miles in size, which is about twice as large as Maryland. Almost three million people live there. Most of the people are farmers, and they raise grain and cattle. Others work in the valuable copper, iron and chromium mines in the northern part of the country. In the cities people work in factories where they produce sugar, prepare chemicals of various kinds, and manufacture iron products. The capital and also the largest city of Bosnia-Herzegovina is Sarajevo. It was in this city that the Archduke Ferdinand of Austria was assassinated in 1914, and it was this event which set off World War I. For more than four-hundred years, Bosnia-Herzegovina belonged to Turkey, but in 1878, it was given to Austria-Hungary. After World War I, in 1918, it was given to Yugoslavia.

BOSNIA - HERZEGOVINA, YUGOSLAVIA. Area, 19,909 square miles. Population, 2,847,790. Capital, Sarajevo.

Bosporus

The Bosporus is a narrow *strait*, or channel, in Turkey, that connects the Black Sea and the Sea of Marmara. It also separates the continents of Europe and Asia. Although the Bosporus is very small, it is of great importance to trading ships. Together with the Dardanelles, it is the only way to sail from the Black Sea to the Mediterranean. (You can read about the DARDANELLES in a separate article.) The Bosporus is about eighteen miles long, and about one mile wide. It has swift currents and fogs that make it dangerous for ships, and lighthouses have been built to help vessels get safely through the strait. The region around the Bosporus is very beautiful. Along the high shores, you can see woods, old castles, and ancient villages. The famous city of Istanbul is at the southern end of the Bosporus.

For the past five hundred years, the Bosporus has belonged to Turkey. No warships of other nations are allowed to pass through the strait without the permission of the Turkish government. During World War II, Turkey allowed German ships to pass through the strait. Later, toward the end of the war, they also allowed Allied vessels to ship war supplies through the Bosporus to the Russians.

Boston

Boston is the capital and the largest city in Massachusetts. Its nickname is "the Hub" because for many years it was the center of American culture. Boston is an important seaport on Massachusetts Bay and a great business and manufacturing city. It has the principal wool market and the largest shoe industry in the country. There are also huge fisheries, printing plants, and business offices and shops.

Boston itself has a population of more than 697,000 crowded into an area that is hemmed in by suburbs and cannot grow. With its suburbs Boston has almost three million people and is seventh among the biggest metropolitan areas in the United States. Among the famous sections of Boston are Beacon Hill and the Back Bay (a former sea marsh that was filled in). There are many fine hotels, and shops.

COLLEGES AND UNIVERSITIES

Boston has long been a center of education. In the city of Cambridge, just across the Charles River from Boston, are some of the country's most famous schools. They include Harvard University, Radcliffe College, and the Massachusetts Institute of Technology (or M.I.T.). Important colleges in Boston include:

Boston College. Enrollment 7,854 in 1961. One of the largest Roman Catholic colleges in the United States.

Boston University. Enrollment 16,645 in 1961.

Boston Conservatory of Music. Enrollment 200 in 1961.

Northeastern University. Enrollment 18,000 in 1961.

Simmons College, for women. Enrollment 1,600 in 1961.

Tufts College. Enrollment 4,300 in 1961.

BOSTON IN THE PAST

Boston is one of the oldest cities in the United States. It was settled in 1630 by colonists who came from Salem, in the Massachusetts Bay Colony. Two years later Boston was made the capital of the colony. The people of Boston were among the leaders in the Revolutionary War, and the Battle of Bunker Hill took place in Boston in 1775. After the war the city grew rapidly, and about one hundred years ago it was the center of American learning.

Boston still has many historic buildings and monuments. Some of them are: the Old North Church, from which Paul Revere received a signal telling him that British soldiers were going to attack the American colonists; Paul Revere's house, the oldest house in Boston, built in 1676; and Faneuil Hall, called "the cradle of Liberty," where the colonists planned the Boston Tea Party. The Massachusetts State House, on Beacon Hill, is a famous old building. Boston Common is a famous park in the heart of the city.

In the late 1800s so many people from Ireland settled in Boston that it was once called "the biggest Irish city in the world." More than half a million people in Boston and its suburbs are of Irish ancestry. The largest group in Boston, however, is of New England ancestry.

BOSTON, MASSACHUSETTS. Population (1960 census) 697,197, with suburbs (estimate) 2,913,500. Capital of Massachusetts.

Boston Massacre

A massacre is the cruel killing of a number of helpless persons. The Boston Massacre was called that because it happened at a time when the people of the American Colonies were very angry with the British and were always ready to think the worst of the British soldiers, but it was more like a street fight than a massacre. It happened on March 5, 1770, before the American Revolution really began. Some of the people of Boston were constantly tormenting the Brit-

BOSTON

The picture at the right shows a corner of the Boston Common, most famous of Boston's parks. It is in the center of the business district, and Beacon Hill rises above it. The Park Street Church, shown in the picture, has a small graveyard beside it. For other pictures of Boston, see the article on Massachusetts.

N.Y. Public Library

To the left is a picture of the Boston Tea Party. In the middle of the night, fifty colonists silently crept aboard a British ship and dumped all the chests of tea into the bay. Then they crept away as silently as they had come. Below is a scene from the Boston Massacre. The old Boston Customs House is in the background.

ish soldiers who patrolled the streets. One day a British soldier became frightened when a crowd started to make fun of him and throw things. He called for help, and other British soldiers came running. They fired at the crowd of Americans and killed four people. The British soldiers were tried for murder, but John Adams and Josiah Quincy were the lawyers for the defense, and the soldiers were found not guilty.

Boston Tea Party

The Boston Tea Party was one of the first acts of rebellion by the American Colonies against the rule of England. It took place about a year before the American Revolution. The British had put a heavy tax on all the tea that was sent from England to America. The Americans thought this tax unfair and did not want to pay it. Then some British ships carrying tea came into the harbor at Boston, Massachusetts. The company selling the tea had agreed to pay the tax itself. But the Americans did not want the tax to be paid by anyone. Late on the night of December 16, 1773, a group of Americans dressed up like Indians and boarded the ships. They didn't get excited or noisy, but very quietly dumped all the tea overboard.

Boston terrier

The only breed of dog that originated in the United States is the Boston terrier, named for the city of Boston, Massachusetts, where it was first developed. It came from a cross between the English bulldog and the English white terrier, but the dog that resulted from this combination was like neither of these other two breeds. It became popular very quickly, and now there are many homes in the United States and Canada where the Boston terrier is kept as a gentle, loyal, affectionate pet.

It stands about 11 to 14 inches high at the shoulder, and weighs between 15 and 25 pounds. It has a short tail, and a straight, sturdy body. Its head is round, and its ears are small, and stand up close to the head. The Boston terrier's coat is short and smooth, with a satiny shine. In color it is a dark "brindle," which is a combination of black and brown hairs, with large white markings, usually on the head, chest, legs, and underside.

Boswell, James

James Boswell was a Scotsman who was famous for writing one of the best biographies in the English language, *The Life of Samuel Johnson*. A biography is the story of a person's life. JOHNSON himself was a very famous Englishman, and you can read about him in a separate article. Boswell was born in Edinburgh in 1740. He was the son of a judge with the title of Lord Auchinleck. When his father died, Boswell inherited the title, but he never became a judge. He did become a lawyer, but he felt that writing was more interesting than law. He was also a very fashionable young man who liked to meet beautiful ladies, writers, and other important people. Boswell was sociable and friendly, and many people called him by the nickname "Bozzy."

When "Bozzy" was 23 years old, he went to London where he became friends with Johnson. He also traveled to Holland and to France. One of Boswell's first books was about his visit to the island of Corsica. Then he returned to Edinburgh, and in 1769 he was married. He took many trips to London to see Johnson. One year Johnson came to Scotland, where he and Boswell visited the Hebrides islands, and Boswell wrote a book about this trip, too. Johnson died in 1784 and the next year Boswell published his biography of him. The book made him famous immediately, but for a long time after he died, in 1795, people thought Boswell was important only because he wrote about Johnson. Today we know more about him because other books that he wrote have just been published for the first time. From these we learn that he was truly a great writer.

botany

Botany is the study of plants and how they grow. It is a branch of BIOLOGY, which is the study of all living things, and which you can read about in another article. Plants are different from all other living things because they make their own food out of chemicals, building up living tissue out of matter that has never lived. By using *chlorophyll,* they use the energy of sunlight to make food out of air and water. This is one of the most wonderful facts in nature, even though it is happening every minute all around us. Man has never been able to do this, and all animals including human beings depend upon plants for food. Without plants, life could not exist on earth. The study of plants, therefore, is very important to us because it helps us to live better. Botany is the foundation of all agriculture, forestry, and gardening. Through botany man has been able to increase the fertility or growing power of the soil, to produce bigger crops, and to control the insects that attack them.

Men have grown some plants, such as wheat, barley, rice, flax, hemp, the date palm, olive, fig, apple, and grape, for more than four thousand years. You might say that the first botanists were these first farmers, the first men who studied the plants they used for food. The Greek scholar Aristotle and his pupil Theophrastus wrote the first scientific descriptions of plants. Then people became interested in the use of plants in medicine. Dioscorides, in the 1st century, gave a list of four hundred plants which could be used as medicine. This list was used for 1,500 years.

Many men were puzzled by the problem of how to name plants. This was settled by Linnaeus, a Swedish botanist who lived about 200 years ago. Linnaeus had the idea of giving each plant two names in the Latin language. *Pisum sativum,* for example, is the garden pea. *Pisum* means pea, and *sativum* tells how it is different from all other kinds of pea. Linnaeus named 5,950 plants. Since then more than 300,000 have been described, and nearly 5,000 new ones are named every year by men called *systematists* or *taxonomists.* These men not only name plants, but they try to find out how plants are related to one another in their various families. Since Linnaeus, other botanists have made schemes for grouping or classifying plants. The system most used today was devised by a German named Adolf Engler.

bo tree

The bo tree is a fig tree found especially in India and Ceylon. It grows to great size and age, and its leaves have long flexible stems so that they rustle in the slightest breeze. The bo tree is sacred to those whose religion is Buddhism. Its name, *bo,* or *bodhi,* means "tree of wisdom." Gotama Buddha, the founder of the Buddhist religion, is said to have gained his wisdom while sitting under the bo tree. Buddha also died under the bo tree after many years of teaching. The original bo tree was at Gaya, a city in the north of India. A slip from this tree was planted at Anuradhapura, on the island of Ceylon, just south of India. This "daughter" tree is now one of the world's oldest known trees, and crowds of people come to visit it. In Ceylon, there is a bo tree planted near every temple.

Botticelli, Sandro

Sandro Botticelli was one of the greatest painters who ever lived. He was born in 1444 in Florence, Italy. When he was a very young boy he worked for a goldsmith, or jewelry maker. He showed great artistic talent and began to study painting with a famous teacher

N.Y. Public Library

One of Botticelli's most famous paintings, *The Birth of Venus*, shows the goddess Venus rising from the ocean in a sea shell.

named Fra Filippo Lippi. He learned all he could about painting. When he was about twenty years old, Botticelli started to paint in the style for which he became famous. His paintings were full of lovely and delicate detail, and rich and beautiful colors. Botticelli often used gold to make them even more magnificent. The paintings were mostly portraits (pictures of people), or about religious subjects. The faces Botticelli painted were beautiful and angelic. A very wealthy and powerful family called Medici liked Botticelli's painting. They bought many of his masterpieces, and also gave him money to continue his painting. When the Medici family was driven out of the country, Botticelli was given help and encouragement by a famous Italian priest named Savonarola. Some of Botticelli's best-known paintings are *Spring, Birth of Venus,* and *Portrait of a Youth,* which is now at the Metropolitan Museum of Art in New York City. Botticelli died in 1510.

bottle, a container for holding liquids and other things: see the articles on BOTTLING and GLASS.

bottled gas

Bottled gas is gas that is put into steel tanks to be delivered to homes far out in the country where there are no gas pipes. Bottled gas is also used in making chemicals and other things. When all the gas is used up, the empty tank can be refilled. The gas is usually PROPANE or BUTANE, about which you can read in separate articles.

bottling

Bottling is the process of filling bottles with liquid. Bottles are used as containers for many kinds of liquid, such as soft drinks, medicine, and milk. They are also used for many foods, such as pickles and olives. Many foods and drinks are sold in enormous quantities, so bottling is very important and must be very efficient.

The first and most important thing in bottling is to make sure that the bottles are absolutely clean. After careful washing and rinsing, they are made *sterile,* or free from harmful bacteria and other germs. Then the bottles are ready to be filled. They are placed on a conveyor, or moving belt, which carries them to the large vat containing the liquid to be bottled. The belt stops for a moment as each bottle comes under the vat, and the bottle is filled through a tube attached to the vat. Then the belt moves on and another bottle is filled. The filled bottles move on to a section where they are covered with metal caps or cardboard covers.

Many liquids that used to be packaged in bottles are sold in other kinds of containers nowadays. Bottles are good for liquids that have to be shipped a long way between the place where they are made and the place where they are sold. But milk is often put in cardboard containers because it has only a short distance to travel. Soft drinks, which can be

BOULDER DAM

Right: Since ancient times, people have carried water in goatskin bottles. *Left:* In a modern plant, milk is bottled and capped very swiftly by large machines.

made and packaged at one end of the country and sold at the other end, are usually put in bottles, though some manufacturers recently have begun to use cans. Certain liquids, like shampoo, are now packed in plastic bottles. These do not break as easily as glass bottles. They are easier to use because the liquid is not poured out, but is squeezed out like toothpaste from a tube. This is a convenient kind of bottle when only small amounts of liquid are needed at one time.

Boulder Dam, one of the largest dams in the world: see **HOOVER DAM.**

Bounty, Mutiny on the

The *Bounty* was the name of an English ship on which a famous mutiny took place. When a group of soldiers or sailors decide they are not going to obey their commander, it is called a mutiny, and this is a very serious crime.

The *Bounty* was making a peaceful voyage in April, 1789. It was carrying a cargo of plants from Tahiti to the West Indies. The *Bounty* had been at sea three weeks when without warning the mutiny broke out. A sailor named Fletcher Christian was the leader, and he and most of the crew forced the captain, William Bligh, and eighteen men into a small open boat and set them adrift in the Pacific Ocean, very far from any shore. They had no map, and very little food or water. Christian and the crew never expected to hear of them again, but that is not the way things turned out. With good luck, and because Captain Bligh was a very fine seaman, these men managed to sail four thousand miles to safety. They landed at Timor about six weeks later, and not one man was lost.

Captain Bligh returned to England, and wrote all about what had happened. At first everyone admired his courage and felt very sorry for him. They began to search for the wicked crew. Some of

When the men of the *Bounty* mutinied, they took Captain Bligh prisoner.

the men had returned to Tahiti, and they were quickly caught and most of them were executed. But the *Bounty* and some of the crew had disappeared, and for ten years no one could find them. It was only by accident that the *Bounty* was discovered, when an American ship landed at Pitcairn Island, a small island in the Pacific Ocean. Only one man of all the crew was still alive. By this time people had found out that Captain Bligh was a cruel man, and they understood why there had been a mutiny on the *Bounty*. There is a famous book, *Mutiny on the Bounty,* by two American writers, Charles B. Nordhoff and James N. Hall.

Bourbon

Bourbon was the name of a French family. They took their name from the part of France they came from. This section was called the Barony of Bourbonnais about a thousand years ago. For two hundred years before the French Revolution in 1789, the kings of France were all members of the Bourbon family. For nearly a hundred years after that, the government of France was very unsettled, but there were several more Bourbon kings. From 1746 until 1931, the kings of Spain were also members of the Bourbon family.

Henry IV

All of the Bourbons were descended from King Henry IV, who became the first Bourbon king of France in 1589. His grandson was King Louis XIV of France, and one of Louis' grandsons was Philip V, who became the first Bourbon king of Spain. Louis XIV was king of France from 1643 to 1715. He was a strong king, and under his rule France became very important and powerful. Louis XVI, who was king at the time of the French Revolution, was the great-great-great-grandson of Louis XIV. He was executed during the Revolution. Later two of Louis XVI's brothers, Louis XVIII and Charles X, became kings of France. The last Bourbon king of France was Louis Philippe. He ruled until the Revolution of 1848.

The Bourbon rule in Spain was much more peaceful than the Bourbon rule in France. Until 1931 there were only two important interruptions. The first was in the early 1800s, when Napoleon took over Spain. The second was in the late 1800s, when Spain became a republic for a short time. In 1931, there was a revolution in Spain. Alfonso XIII, the king, gave up his throne, but his son or grandson retained a chance to regain it.

bourgeoisie

Bourgeoisie is a French word meaning "the people who live in towns." It comes from the word *bourg,* which means "town" in French. When the word *bourgeoisie* was invented, the people who lived in towns and cities were mostly shopkeepers, craftsmen, doctors, lawyers, and so forth. They were the people we call the middle class. Bourgeoisie has come to mean all middle-class people, no matter where they live.

The bourgeoisie were very important in the French Revolution, which took place in 1789. Before the Revolution, the nobles and the church ran the French government. The bourgeoisie wanted to run their own government. They knew all about the American Revolution, and they wanted to have the same kind of democratic government that the people in America had won.

After the French Revolution, the bourgeoisie became very powerful all over Europe and America. Many people felt that the bourgeoisie had also become much too self-satisfied and narrow-minded. They began to use the word *bourgeois* to describe anyone who had those qualities, no matter what class he came from.

bow and arrow

The bow and arrow is a weapon that men have been using for many thousands of years, in hunting, in warfare, and in the sport called ARCHERY (about which there is a separate article). The weapon shoots the arrow—a sort of slender, sharp-pointed spear—with great force, to strike and pierce its target. There are three parts—bow, bowstring, and arrow.

The *bow* is made of wood. It is a very springy stick that will bend without breaking, and is usually about as long as you are tall. It is thicker in the center than at the ends. At each end there is a notch, called a *nock,* to which the bowstring is fastened.

The *bowstring,* or *string,* is made of strong cord—now usually of linen—and is a little bit shorter than the bow. You can *string your bow* in one of two ways: 1, you tie the string to one end of the bow and tie a loop at the other end of the string. Then you bend the bow while you hold the bottom against your foot, and slip the loop into the nock at the top of the bow; or, 2, you tie a loop at each end of the string; then you put it on the bow just as you would in the first way.

When the bow is strung, there should be about five or six inches between the middle of the string and the middle of the bow, and the string should be very tight.

The *arrows* are made of wood. They are round like pencils, but thicker, and as long as several pencils—about as long as your arm. There are different kinds of arrows. To go hunting you need arrows with sharp steel points, but to shoot at a target you use arrows with plain points. Arrows are "fletched"—that is, feathers are stuck on them at the opposite end from the point. This makes them fly straight. Each arrow has a notch, or *nock,* at the end where the feathers are.

You may also have a *quiver,* or long, narrow bag, to keep your arrows in. A quiver is made of leather, or canvas, or plastic, and has a strap on it, so that you can hang it over your shoulder. It should hold ten to twenty arrows, depending upon how wide it is. As you shoot each arrow, you reach into the quiver and get out a new one.

SHOOTING A BOW AND ARROW

When you shoot a bow and arrow you hold the bow in one hand so that it is straight up and down and in front of you. The hand that you hold the bow with should be just below the middle of the bow. Then you take an arrow in the other hand and fit the nock at the end of the arrow into the string on the bow. Then you rest the front end of the arrow over the finger of the hand that holds the bow, *never over the thumb,* and pull back the arrow.

When you pull back the arrows, put three fingers on the string. Hold the the arrow between the top finger and the string just at the tips of the fingers, with next-to-the-top finger. Now you turn sideward toward where you want the arrow to go, the "mark" or target you are shooting at. Straighten the arm that holds the bow (but not too stiff!), and pull back the arrow until the hand holding the string and arrow is just below your chin. Sight along the arrow and let go. The string will snap, and the arrow will fly toward the mark.

MARKSMANSHIP

Marksmanship is the ability to make the arrow go where you want it to. This takes practice as well as knowledge of the right way to shoot.

No two bows are exactly the same. The "pull" of a bow is measured in pounds, and it means that if the bow is put on a solid place, it would take a weight that weighed that many pounds to make the string go down and bend the bow as far as you would to shoot an arrow. The proper pull is about 30 to 40 pounds for men (although bows for big-game hunting go up to 100 pounds and more, which takes a very strong man);

BOW AND ARROW

American Indians were great hunters with bows and arrows. They not only used them to hunt animals, but also to catch fish in the rivers and streams.

Dow Chemical Co.

This modern hunter is using a bow and arrow to hunt deer. You need a keen eye and a steady hand for this.

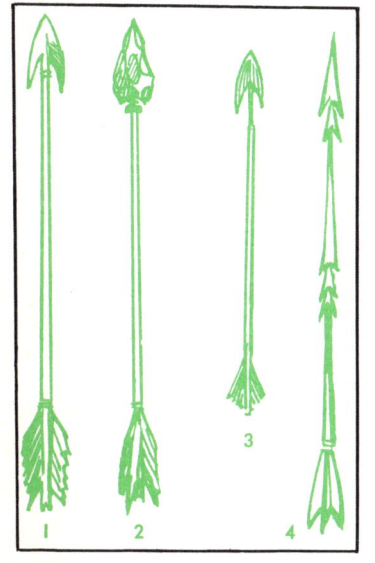

1. A steel-tipped military arrow used in Europe nine hundred years ago. 2. An American Indian arrow with a flint head. 3. An African arrow. 4. An arrow from the South Seas.

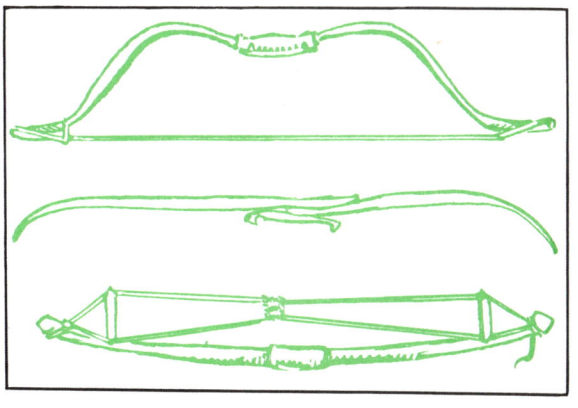

Top: The warriors under Genghis Khan used bows like this, more than seven hundred years ago. *Center:* The two parts of this American Indian bow were bound together with rawhide thongs. *Bottom:* This powerful bow is used by Indians in the forests of South America. It is used to shoot small rocks and pebbles.

30 to 40 pounds for women; 12 to 30 pounds for boys 10 to 14 years old; and 10 to 25 pounds for girls 10 to 14 years old. You have to learn by experiment where the arrows go with each bow.

If the target is far away, you aim above the place you want to hit, because the arrow *falls* as it flies through the air. The stronger the pull of the bow, the less fall there is, but you find this out by practicing. When you can picture in your head the curve that the arrow makes as it flies through the air, as soon as you are used to the bow, you can shoot at something and hit it most of the time.

Bowie, James

James Bowie was a man who lived in Texas more than a hundred years ago. He became a colonel in the Texas army and helped Texas to win independence from Mexico, but he was killed in the battle of the ALAMO, about which there is a separate article. He was born in 1796 and died in 1836. A kind of hunting knife, the Bowie knife, is named for him. It has a blade about 10 inches long, sharpened on one edge, and it is kept in a sheath. Millions of people since his time have used Bowie knives. James Bowie is said to have made the first knife of this kind in 1827, grinding it into shape from a steel file.

bowlegs

Bowlegs is a condition in which a person's legs are curved outward. It is usually caused in childhood by a disease called *rickets*. Children get this disease when their bodies lack calcium and phosphorus (the minerals that build bones), or vitamin D (the substance that enables the body to use calcium and phosphorus). The bones of young children are quite soft. A child should never be forced to walk too young, or to put too much strain on his legs. But some poor children do not get foods that contain minerals and vitamins, or enough sunlight to make vitamin D in the skin. They develop rickets. Their bones become so soft that their legs bend under the weight of their bodies. They become bowlegged or knock-kneed (so that their legs are curved inward), and even their backbones may become curved. Once the bones have hardened out of shape it is a very long and difficult process to get them right again. With modern knowledge of medicine, there is no need for anyone to have rickets, and such things as bowlegs are becoming less common every year.

bowling

Bowling is one of the oldest games in the world. It goes back to ancient times and has been played in some form ever since. The Dutch settlers brought the game with them to what is now the state of New York, more than three hundred years ago. In the story of *Rip van Winkle*, by Washington Irving, we read about the "thunder" of bowling.

The game of bowling as it is played in the United States is also known as *ten pins*. The object is to roll a ball and knock down "pins," or bottle-shaped wooden pegs. It is America's most popular indoor game, and is played by millions of people.

Until about three hundred years ago, the game was called "ninepins" because only nine pins were used. There were a great many people who thought all games were wrong, and they passed laws against playing "ninepins." So the bowlers simply added another pin and kept on playing, because there was no law against playing "tenpins."

There are two kinds of bowling, called *big-pin*, and *duck-pin* bowling. The rules and scoring are the same, and the same alleys may be used. The difference is in the size of the ball and pins, which are much smaller in duckpins. Big-pin bowling is too hard for very young people, because the ball weighs between 10 and 16 pounds and is too heavy for them to swing. Duckpins is very popular with young people in schools and YMCA bowling alleys. Grownups often play

BOWLING

The Athletic Inst., Chicago

1. Egyptians, more than five thousand years ago, played a nine-pin bowling game.
2 & 3. How a bowling ball is held. Some balls have three finger-holes, some have two.  
4. Position of the bowler from the front.
5. The front pins struck by the ball fly back and knock down other pins. In the picture, all ten pins will go down—a strike. To get a strike, the bowler must make the ball hit "in the slot"—between the 1 and 3 pins.
6. A "four-step" bowler.

duckpins too, and it used to be called "summer bowling."

Bowling is done on a long, narrow wooden *alley* with a hardwood floor. It must be highly polished and very level, so that the balls roll straight. The alley is almost 63 feet long and about 41 inches wide. Several alleys are usually built side by side, and along the sides of each alley there is a *gutter*, or trough, so that when a ball rolls off the alley it will not go into the next alley. At one end of the alley where the players stand there is a *foul line* (over which the player must not step), and behind that a runway about 15 feet long. At the other end the pins are set up in rows of 1, 2, 3, and 4, a few inches apart. They form a triangle with the "single," or No. 1, pin in front. Behind the pins there is a *pit*, and when the pins are knocked down they fall into the pit. There may be a *pin boy* in the pit to set up the pins again and roll the bowler's ball back on a chute beside the alley, or all this may be done by automatic machinery.

Here is how you keep score. A game is made up of ten *frames*, or turns at rolling the ball. You "throw" your first ball down the alley at the pins. If you knock down all ten pins with this throw, it ends the frame; you have a *strike* and you score 10 points plus the number of pins you knock down in your next two throws. If your first throw does not knock down all the pins, you get a second throw in the same frame. If your second throw knocks down the rest of the pins you have a *spare*. You score 10 points plus the number of pins you knock down in the first throw of the next frame. When you do not have a strike or spare, your score for the frame is the number of pins you knock down in two throws. A strike in the tenth frame entitles you to two more throws, so a perfect score is 300, made up of strikes in all ten regular frames and in both extra throws. A spare in the tenth frame entitles you to one extra throw.

Few bowlers can average much more than 200 per game.

There are many bowling teams in the United States. Some are made up of men, some of women. Usually they are clubs made up of persons who work for the same company or go to the same school. Rules and regulations for tournaments and matches are made by the "A.B.C.," or American Bowling Congress, by the Woman's International Bowling Congress, and by other organizations.

bowls

Bowls is the name of a game that was very popular in England hundreds of years ago. It was played in America before the Revolution and gave the name Bowling Green to many places. Now bowls is played mostly in Scotland.

Bowls is played outdoors. The field on which it is played is called a *bowling green*. The bowling green is a lawn about 120 feet square, with a ditch running around it. The game is played with big balls called *bowls* and one small white ball called a *jack*. The jack stands in one place, and the object of each player is to roll his bowl closest to the jack. The jack is like the pins in bowling, but in bowls the players must not touch the jack. Another difference is that bowling is an indoor game and bowls is played outdoors. Bowls is probably an older game than bowling.

boxer

The boxer is a dog whose name comes from its unusual way of fighting. When a boxer fights another dog, it strikes with its front paws as a man does with his fists. Boxers are sturdy and faithful dogs. They were first bred in England, about a hundred years ago, but were later developed in Germany. They are a mixture of mastiff, terrier, and bulldog. In the United States people keep them as watchdogs and as pets, because they can be trained easily. Boxers are often used as Seeing Eye dogs for the blind.

Gaines Dog Research Center
Two champion boxers in a friendly pose.

The boxer is a large dog. It stands about 21 to 24 inches high at the shoulders, and it may weigh between 60 and 65 pounds. The boxer's head is somewhat like that of a bulldog, but its muzzle is a bit longer, and the jowls are less drooping. The ears are clipped, which makes them stand up in small points close to its head. The tail is cut short.

The boxer's coat is smooth and shiny, with short hair. It can be light tan, reddish brown, or "brindle," which is a combination of black and brown hairs.

Boxer Rebellion

In the year 1900, when the Boxer Rebellion took place, China was a very poor, weak country, even though it was so large. Other countries owned large parts of it or had extensive financial interests there. Among them were Great Britain, Germany, France, Russia, the U.S., and Japan. China wanted to be fully independent, but the Chinese people did not agree on how to go about it. One group of Chinese wanted to modernize the country peacefully. Another group wanted to kill all the foreigners. In this group was a secret society, the "Order of Literary Patriotic Harmonious Fists," whom the English nicknamed "the Boxers." They attacked all the foreign people living in Peking (now called *Peiping*), which was the capital of China. The foreign powers sent an international army that stopped the rebellion and forced China to pay a great deal of money for the damages the Boxers had caused. The United States returned to China a large part of this money, to be used to give more Chinese children an education. The Boxers were disgraced, and the other group did a great deal to improve China in the years that followed.

boxing

Boxing means fighting with your fists, according to rules. This makes it a sport, instead of really fighting. There is a story that it got its name, boxing, from St. Bernard, when he was a young priest in Italy, seven hundred years ago. He was worried because the boys were fighting with knives, so he taught them how to use their fists. They would try to "box up," or corner, their opponents, so they called the sport *boxing.* Boxing is also called *pugilism,* because in the Latin language *pugil* means "a fighter with the fists."

BOXING IN ANCIENT TIMES

In ancient Rome and Greece, two thousand years ago and more, boxing was such a brutal sport that the fighters usually continued until one or the other was dead.

On one of his hands a fighter wore a leather strap studded with brass spikes. This was called a *cestus.*

Today the cestus is no longer used but boxing can still be a dangerous sport. A blow may land in a certain spot so that a nerve center, or the brain, suffers damage. Some consider boxing a brutal sport, but many people like it.

PRIZE FIGHTERS

In England, about two hundred years

ago, groups of men would sometimes put some money into a "purse," or prize, and then two fighters would compete for it. These boxers were known as prizefighters. People began to be interested in the sport, and soon there had to be rules. A fighter named Jack Broughton wrote up a set of rules, and later a group of officials had a meeting and adopted the "London Prize Ring Rules." They contained many rules that are in use today, such as "no hitting below the belt," and "no hitting a man who is down," and they had a referee in the ring to make the fighters obey the rules.

The first champion was James Figg, in England. He beat all comers, and eventually had to retire because no one would fight him. He opened the first gymnasium for boxers, known as "Figg's Academy for Boxing." About this time boxing began to be very popular, and spread from England to America.

BARE KNUCKLES TO GLOVES

For more than 150 years after James Figg's time, all the fights were with bare knuckles, and they were fights to the finish. You could not win except by a knockout, and the fight continued until a knockout was scored or one of the fighters gave up. When we read about those old-time fights that ran 50, 60 or 75 rounds, we must remember that a round in those days ended every time there was a knockdown, after which there was a 30-second rest period. So, if a fighter needed some rest, he simply dropped down, and then took his 30 seconds, and could repeat this any number of times. Today's fights, in which every round lasts three minutes, are much harder on the fighters.

Bare-knuckle fighting was illegal, and the police were always raiding the fights, arresting the fighters, and making the spectators go home. Then, in 1865, a rich English nobleman, the Marquis of Queensberry, introduced a famous set of rules, which are still the basis for all rules today. These rules include the use of boxing gloves, a limited number of three-minute rounds, no gouging or wrestling, and the rule that if a fighter is knocked down, and cannot rise within ten seconds, he loses the bout.

CLASSES ACCORDING TO WEIGHT

Boxers are classified according to weight as follows:

Professional:
Flyweight . . . not over 112 pounds
Bantamweight . " " 118 "
Featherweight . . " " 126 "
Lightweight . . " " 135 "
Welterweight . . " " 147 "
Middleweight . . " " 160 "
Light-heavyweight " " 175 "
Heavyweight, from 175 pounds upward.

Amateur:
The A.A.U. (Amateur Athletic Union) recognizes the following classes: 112, 119, 125, 132, 139, 147, 156, 165, 178, and heavyweight, anything over 178.

TRAINING

When a boxer has set the date for a fight, he goes into training. His success or failure will depend upon what condition he is in. Condition means good health and strength so that he will not get tired or slow down. The best boxer in the world is likely to lose unless he is in good condition.

First of all, training consists in getting plenty of good food and plenty of sleep, because the exercise is using up so much energy. A boxer in training avoids all tobacco and alcohol.

Boxers who can afford the cost, such as champions, set up their own training camps out in the country. Others find the necessary equipment at a local gymnasium, the Y.M.C.A., or a club or school. There are light and heavy punching bags, wall pulleys, weights, and a boxing ring.

The light bag is the one like a pear-shaped basketball, blown up with air. It is used to develop speed and to train the eye. With the light bag you learn to punch to the head.

BOXING

N.Y. Public Library

Univ. Museum, Phila.

The Bettman Archive

Standard Oil Co.

Wide World Photo

1. This 3,000-year-old piece of stone shows how old the art of boxing is.
2. The boxers who fought in ancient Rome wound strips of leather around their hands and arms.
3. Bare fists were used in the heavyweight championship bout between Paddy Ryan and John L. Sullivan, in 1882. Sullivan won this famous fight, which was called "The Battle of the Giants."
4. These boys are being given some lessons in boxing. Self-defense can be a skillful and enjoyable sport.
5. Challenger Ingemar Johansson nose dives into the canvas as he is knocked out in the sixth round of a title bout with heavyweight champion Floyd Patterson in 1961.

BOXING

The heavy bag is made of canvas and filled with sand or shot. It is used to develop power for body blows, and to hit fast in infighting (fighting close together).

Roadwork means running, to strengthen the legs. Many boxers time their roadwork like the rounds of a bout, 3 minutes running, and 1 minute walking, or rest.

Rope-skipping and shadowboxing are exercises to develop footwork.

Boxers are careful to avoid what is known as overtraining, which means that they have trained too hard, and are so tired that it will take them a long time to rest their hearts and muscles. Overtraining is just as bad for a boxer as undertraining.

After each training period, the boxer goes a few rounds with one or more *sparring partners*. These are fighters who are paid to give the boxer practice in actual boxing, and they must be very good themselves. Joe Walcott was once a sparring partner for Joe Louis, and then became world's champion himself.

GLOVES AND BANDAGES

Before putting on the gloves, or even before punching the bag, boxers usually tape, or "bandage," their hands. This protects the bones in the hand against breaking. The bandages are plain gauze, and they are wrapped loosely so as not to stop circulation, but not loosely enough to slip. They are never wrapped between the fingers or over the thumb. The thumb is used only to close the hand, and is never used in punching, as it is easily broken. All punches except the uppercut are delivered with the knuckles up and the thumb out of the way.

There are four different weights of gloves. For sparring and exhibition boxing, 14-ounce gloves are used. There are light gloves for punching the light bag, and heavy gloves for the heavy bag. Then there are the 8-ounce gloves for fighting, and 6-ounce for championship bouts.

Most boxers use a rubber mouthpiece during the fight, so that their teeth will not be knocked out or their lips cut. Head protectors are used in sparring, to protect the eyes and ears, but never in an actual fight.

Amateur (A.A.U.) rules require 8-ounce gloves for all classes below 147 pounds. In intercollegiate boxing, no glove lighter than 12 ounces is permitted, and interscholastic rules require 10-ounce gloves up to the lightweight class, and 12-ounce gloves in all heavier classes.

DEFENSE AND ATTACK

Scientific boxing consists of trying to protect yourself from being hit, and at the same time to hit your opponent.

Defensive tricks include *blocking,* by putting your arms and gloves in the way of a punch; *ducking* and *weaving,* so that the punch cannot land; *parrying,* which means to turn the blow with another blow, or ward it off; *sidestepping,* in which you avoid the blow, and at the same time surprise your opponent; and *slipping,* which means that you turn your head slightly, or move over a few inches, so that your opponent's blow misses its mark.

Offensive tactics are those of attack. They include: the *straight right* (or *left*), which is just what it sounds like, a straight punch to either the body or the head. It is usually used immediately after a left jab, and is the favorite knockout punch when it lands on the jaw. The *right cross* is a blow at about elbow height, with the elbow raised and bent. The body weight is thrown behind this punch, and it is a powerful punch when it lands right. The *left cross* is the same, but with the left arm. *Jabs* and *hooks* are most important, and a good boxer can be recognized by his use of these blows. The jab is a short, hard, poke with the arm almost straight out in front of you, and the power comes from the shoulder, as if to throw the shoulder a little to one side. You will notice that most boxers keep one arm slightly out, as a "lead," at all times, and jab with this arm. The hook is considered hard to learn, but is a knockout punch when it connects with the jaw. The *uppercut* is delivered by bringing your arm up close to your body, with the knuckles turned out. It is often used when infighting, and can be a knockout blow.

RULES USED IN BOXING

In the United States, most of the states have their own laws governing professional boxing, and this leads to a few special rules that apply in some states but not in others. Some of the principal rules may be described briefly as follows:

Each *round* is 3 minutes of fighting, with 1 minute between rounds for rest.

The *referee* is in complete charge while the fight is under way. He may award the fight to one of the fighters if he judges that the opponent has committed a foul, or is too badly hurt to keep on fighting without serious risk (called the *technical knockout*), or refuses to fight. There is usually a *timekeeper* who not only times the rounds but also counts off the seconds, up to ten, when a fighter is knocked down. When the fight ends without a knockout, there are usually two *judges* plus the referee, making three judges in all, who vote to decide which fighter has won, or if the fight was a *draw* (not won by either).

A *foul* includes hitting the opponent below the belt, or when he is down; using the knees to hit with; wrestling; and various other acts that break the rules.

A *knockdown* occurs when a fighter is lying on the floor of the ring, or when his weight is resting on any part of the body except his feet—for example, when he is kneeling. Technically, it is a knockdown even when a fighter slips and falls, so long as he is not on his feet. When a knockdown continues for 10 seconds, it is a *knockout,* ending the fight. But if the round ends before the count of ten is reached, it is not a knockout if the fighter is able to begin the next round.

Each fighter has one *corner* of the ring. Their corners are diagonally across from each other. The other two corners are *neutral corners.* When a fighter knocks his opponent down, he must go to the farthest neutral corner before the count begins, and must stay there until his opponent is on his feet again. Between rounds, the fighters go to their own corners, where their *seconds* (helpers) give them water and help them prepare for the next round.

A *clinch* occurs when either opponent is held so that he cannot move his arms freely. The referee taps both fighters on their shoulders and they must *break*—separate without any further blows, and be at arm's length before they start fighting again.

boxwood

Boxwood is a very strong, heavy, hard wood. It comes from a small tree called the box tree. There are several kinds of box tree, growing in Europe and Asia, but most of the wood comes from England. Because it is the smoothest, finest-grained wood known, it is the best wood for wood engraving. This means carving a picture on wood, then putting ink on the carving and printing a picture from it. Many pictures in books are made this way, and when boxwood is used the carving can be very delicate and show many details. Boxwood can be polished

BOYCOTT

beautifully, and it is used in making scientific and musical instruments.

The box tree grows very slowly, and it makes beautiful hedges. It can be clipped into all sorts of wonderful shapes. The art of training and clipping hedges in this way is called *topiary*. If you see a small tree that is the shape of a peacock, for instance, it may be a box tree. The box tree keeps its leaves in winter. They are small and glossy, but they are poisonous, so you should never put them in your mouth. The flowers are small and whitish. They can be seen near the ends of the branches when the tree is in flower.

boycott

When a group of people object to the way a person is acting or want to force him to do something, they sometimes get together and decide not to do business with him. This is called a boycott. If a group wants to boycott a store owner, they refuse to buy anything from him and try to keep other people from trading with him. In the early days of labor unions, the union members used to boycott certain employers when they thought the employers were being unfair to their workers or were not paying them enough for their work. Sometimes they even boycotted other businesses that dealt with their employers. They hoped to hurt these businesses and so to hurt their employers. This was called a *secondary boycott*, and in 1947 the United States passed a law making secondary boycotts illegal. But the boycott did not work very well, and the unions had to find other ways of trying to get the improvements in working conditions that they thought the workers should have.

Boycotts are sometimes political. A group of people who object to the policies and actions of a country will declare a boycott against the whole country. Some Americans and people of Allied nations boycotted German and Japanese goods during World War II by refusing to buy anything made in Germany or Japan.

The word boycott comes from a man's name. Captain Charles Boycott was the land agent for an English nobleman named Lord Erne, who owned a lot of property in Ireland about 75 years ago. A land agent is the man who collects rents and takes care of property for an owner. At that time Ireland was ruled by England, and English people owned much of Irish property and business. The Irish people did not like this. And the people who rented land from Lord Erne resented England and resented the way they were being treated by Captain Boycott. They thought he was unfair in evicting some of the tenants with hardly any warning. So they refused to work the farms for Lord Erne, and refused to pay their rent to Captain Boycott.

Boyne, Battle of the

The Battle of the Boyne was fought in Ireland on the Boyne River, about 250 years ago. It was a very important battle because it decided that the Protestants instead of the Catholics would rule Great Britain. James II was king of England, Scotland and Ireland in 1688. He was a Catholic. He was a very unpopular king, and some of his enemies asked the Protestant William of Orange and his wife Mary, who was the daughter of James, to be their king and queen. James was put off the throne, but he was allowed to escape to France. But the Catholics wanted him to be king again, and so James went to Ireland and got an army together to fight the Protestant supporters of William III, who were called Orangemen. James was beaten and fled to France, never to return. You can read about JAMES II and WILLIAM III in separate articles.

Boys' and Girls' Clubs

A boys' club or girls' club is a group of young people who meet to play or learn or work with one another. Members of a club learn how much better it is to be together than to live and play

BOYS' AND GIRLS' CLUBS

Left: Boys and girls of the 4-H Club meet to plan their various activities. *Right:* Fathers sometimes attend special meetings of their sons' clubs.

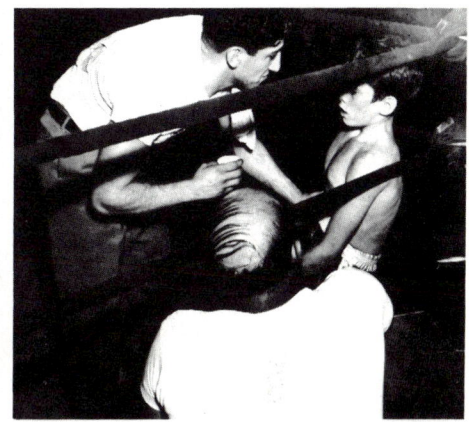

Left: The members of boys' clubs learn teamwork by playing basketball. *Right:* Many clubs have boxing tournaments. Boys of the same age and weight are matched.

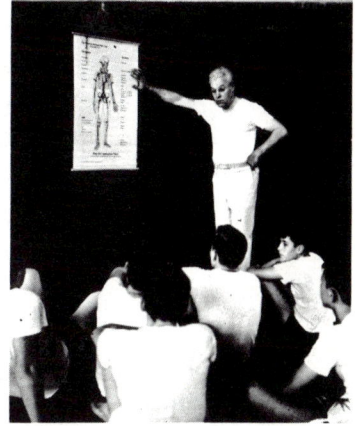

Right: Boys at the Y.M.C.A. are getting instructions in first aid so they will know what to do when someone is hurt. *Left:* Girls at a Y.W.C.A. club are making posters.

and work alone. They learn that two or more heads are better than one when there is a problem to be solved, a game to be played, or a camp to be set up. Young people all over the world join clubs. Usually they pay dues, a small amount of money each year that is used to buy equipment or pay for trips for the club members. They may have uniforms or dress alike. Their clubs may have special flags and mottoes. They may meet in their own clubhouses or in their school or church. Grownups' clubs, like the Lions Club or the Rotary Club, often help children's clubs by buying sports equipment for them or maintaining their summer camps.

Members of some boys' and girls' clubs meet only to play together. Others, like the Boy Scouts, go to camp together and study nature together. Members of 4-H clubs learn all about farming and homemaking. Many clubs are independent, which means they are not connected with other clubs. The Camp Fire Girls are a nationwide organization, with clubs all over the United States. The Boy Scouts and Girl Scouts are part of an organization that has spread all over the world. Boy Scout groups have been formed in about fifty countries. The World Association of Girl Scouts and Girl Guides covers thirty-two nations. There are Girl Scouts in Alaska, Guam, Hawaii, Puerto Rico, and the Canal Zone.

HOW CLUBS STARTED

Families used to be much bigger than they are today, and there would be so many children in each family that they always had someone to play with. But nowadays families are smaller and they are often far apart whether they live on farms or in city apartment houses. Farm children and city children do not meet each other very often. Sometimes they know only a few children of their own ages. Even children who go to school together may live far apart. Clubs bring all these young people together.

There is another good reason for boys' and girls' clubs. In a free country like ours, it is important for the children to learn how to get along with other children of different religions and races. It makes a country strong when its citizens get along well with all kinds of people. This is especially true in a country as large as the United States, where there are so many people of different regions, races, and religions.

In boys' and girls' clubs children learn to be good citizens in many ways. They learn to be "good sports," which means playing your best whether you win or lose. They learn to help others. In New York City recently 50,000 Girl Scouts gave about 170,000 hours of their spare time to hospitals, homes for the aged, and centers for child care. Perhaps the best way club members learn to be good citizens is by learning to talk over different ways of doing things and accepting the decision of the majority, which means doing things the way that most of the members think is best. They find out that this is the way to make their club a good and happy one.

There are many boys' and girls' clubs in the United States. The national ones are Boy Scouts, Girl Scouts, Camp Fire Girls, Boys Clubs of America, 4-H Clubs, the YMCA, YWCA, YMHA, YWHA, and many others. There are separate articles on each of these organizations.

Boy Scouts

The Boy Scouts are an organization of boys which was started in England in 1908 by an English general, Sir Robert Baden-Powell. In 1910, the Boy Scouts of America was founded by a group of men including Daniel Carter BEARD, about whom you can read in a separate article. Since then the Boy Scout movement has spread throughout the world and every four years scouts from many different countries come together for a two-week meeting called a World Jamboree. The aim of all Boy Scout organizations is to help young boys be good citizens and to train their minds and bodies while teaching them how to enjoy outdoor life. All scouts learn camping, woodcraft, nature lore, lifesaving, sports and good citizenship.

BECOMING A SCOUT

To become a scout a boy must be at least 11 years old. Usually he applies for membership in a neighborhood group of scouts called a *troop.* At the head of each troop is a scoutmaster, a man specially trained in scouting. The scoutmaster tells the boy what he must do to become a candidate scout. He must learn the scout oath, the twelve points of the scout law, the scout motto and slogan, and the scout sign, salute, and handclasp. Having learned these things, he becomes a member of a *patrol.* There are five to fifteen boys in a patrol, and two or more patrols make up a troop. Each patrol is named after a bird or animal and has its own flag or pennant and secret animal-call known only to its members. The patrol has a leader and assistant leader, a scribe who keeps a record of the patrol's activities, a treasurer who collects dues, and a quartermaster who has charge of equipment. The patrol is a small group which is part of the troop, or "big team." Each troop has its own flag with its colors and number.

Scouts wear uniforms that include a khaki overseas cap, shirt, and trousers, with brown shoes and a colored neckerchief. In the summer they wear shorts and short-sleeved shirts. They wear emblems and badges on their shirts which show their rank, patrol, troop number, and any honors they have won.

Boys Scouts are divided into three ranks or grades. The lowest is the *tenderfoot.* Next is *second-class scout* and the highest is *first-class scout.* Scouts must pass an examination to go into a higher grade. The candidate scout also must pass a test before he can become a tenderfoot.

WHAT SCOUTS DO

At the weekly scout meeting the boys play games, study to pass tests for the next rank, pay dues, make plans for hikes and camping trips and community events. They learn that the scout is expected to do his best at whatever he tries. He is expected to be faithful to his religion and attend his church or synagogue, and to respect the religion of others. He is taught to do a good turn every day and to be helpful to the people of his neighborhood. He takes part in parades with his troop, helps in safety drives, directs traffic in emergencies, plants trees to beautify his community, joins in all kinds of campaigns to help the poor and the sick, and is expected to be brave, courteous, loyal, obedient, thrifty, and clean.

As he works his way up through the ranks, the scout learns more and more about outdoor living. By the time he is a first-class scout he can take care of himself in the outdoors like an Indian scout of the old frontier days. He knows how to pack a knapsack expertly, what clothing to wear and what to take along when he goes camping or hiking. He can tie all sorts of knots that never untie or loosen and knows which one is best for any special use. He has learned all about the plants in his region of the country and knows which ones are poisonous and which can be eaten in an emergency. The scout learns all about different birds, snakes, animals, and insects.

SCOUTS AND WOODSMEN

The scout is trained in tracking and stalking. He can recognize and follow the tracks of wild animals. He can walk silently through the woods and can approach any animal or person without being seen. One of the tests he must pass is to trail another scout who knows he is being followed and keep up with him through woods and fields without being seen. A trained scout can find his way through unknown territory because he

BOY SCOUTS

knows how to use a compass, measure distances, read or make a map, keep on a straight course, and find his way at night by placing the North Star in the sky.

Knowing how to light a fire may seem like a simple thing, but scouts must learn to do it with only one match or with no match at all. If he has no matches he must be able to start a fire by striking a piece of steel against a hard stone called a *flint*. The scout learns that there are many different ways of building fires for cooking. Instead of building a huge bonfire, the scout knows how to broil, bake, or boil his food over the right kind of fire using only a small amount of wood. He knows how different foods can be cooked out of doors, what foods to take along, and how to work out a good menu. If he runs out of vegetables a well-trained scout knows which wild plants are safe to eat raw, boiled, steamed, or baked.

Camping outdoors can be fun but if you don't have a good shelter you can be very uncomfortable. The scout's shelter is his tent and he is taught how to set it up without poles inside and how to stake it down so that it will not blow over in a storm. He knows how to prevent water from seeping under it and how to keep dry while sleeping in rain or snow.

FIRST AID AND HOBBIES

Scouts are probably the youngest group

Standard Oil Co.

Boy Scouts of America

Boy Scouts of America

1. Boy Scouts attend weekly meetings in their club house. They begin each meeting by saluting the flag with the scout salute.
2. Every summer thousands of Boy Scouts go to camps near their homes. They go on hikes, swim, and enjoy the outdoors. These boys are chopping wood for an evening campfire.
3. Scouts have many hobbies. These boys have selected singing. Boys can win merit badges for good work in their activity.

1. Boy Scouts have all kinds of fun at troop meetings. These boys are having a rope-climbing contest to see who can reach the top of the rope first.

2. Many scouts enjoy making things out of wood. An older scout is showing two boys how to paint a totem pole that he has carved by hand. The boy on the left is a full scout. The boy on the right is wearing the uniform of a Cub Scout.

3. Older boys can become Explorer Scouts and take trips to all kinds of places. These boys are getting ready to take a cruise along the shore.

4. Many boys belong to the Boy Scout troop at United Nations headquarters. They come from countries all over the world. Here, some scouts are presenting a badge to the Assistant Secretary-General of the United Nations.

5. Hiking is one of the sports enjoyed by Boy Scouts. Sometimes they go on a trip for the day, and sometimes they take overnight hikes. They carry supplies in their knapsacks. These boys are climbing towards the hilltop where they will spend the night. The patrol leader, on the right, is in charge, and he is checking his squad as they pass.

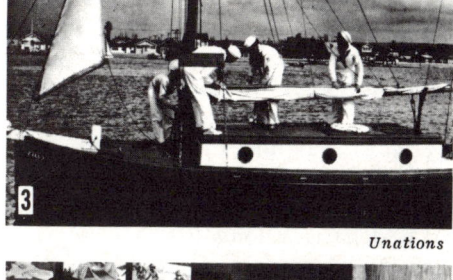

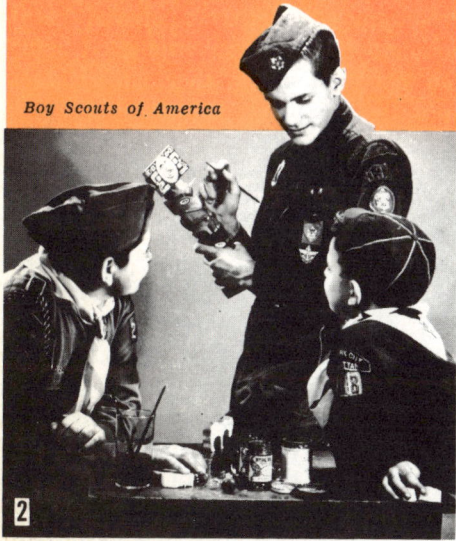

to be trained in first aid. They are taught first aid because when an accident happens on a hiking or camping trip there may be no doctor nearby, and quick first aid may be the difference between life and death. A first-class scout must know artificial respiration so that he can get a person breathing again, if he has stopped breathing. He also must know what to do about broken bones, serious bleeding, dog bites, snake bites, sunstroke, frostbite, heat exhaustion, fainting, and poisoning.

Not only must a scout learn swimming but he must also be able to get off his outer clothing in twenty seconds and rescue a drowning person. Scouts also learn how to rescue people who have fallen through ice.

Another unusual thing that scouts learn to do is to signal in Morse code by means of blinker lights at night and wigwag flags in the daytime. In Morse code each letter of the alphabet is made up of dots and dashes. At night a dot is a short flash and a dash is a long flash. In wigwag signaling a two-foot white flag with a red square in the center is waved to the left and right. A wave to the right is a dot, a wave to the left is a dash. In these ways scouts are able to signal emergency messages over long distances.

Scouts are encouraged to learn useful hobbies and to do them well. There are more than a hundred hobbies or skills from which a first-class scout can choose. After passing a test in his hobby, or skill, he is awarded a merit badge which he can wear on his uniform. Merit-badge subjects include such things as stamp collecting, plumbing, sheep farming, poultry raising, metalwork, music, art, dramatics, botany, insect life, chemistry, public speaking, athletics, horsemanship, farming, and aviation.

After a first-class scout has earned a number of merit badges, he may take tests to rise even higher and become a *Star Scout*, then a *Life Scout*, and finally the very highest rank—an *Eagle Scout*.

OTHER SCOUTS

For younger boys, aged 8 through 10, there are Cub Scout groups, called packs. When a Cub Scout reaches the age of 11, he can graduate to a regular Scout Troop. After 14, he can be a Senior Scout, a more advanced grade. Senior Scouts are also called Explorer Scouts, and some are Sea Scouts. They may go on trips in study and exploration groups either on land, on the water, or in the air. All are part of the general Boy Scout activities, from the Cubs to the Explorers.

Boys Town

Boys Town is the most unusual village in the United States. It is a school and home for boys who have no homes of their own. The only people who live in Boys Town, near Omaha, Nebraska, are the boys who go to school there and their teachers.

Boys Town has not always been a village. It started as just a small house in Omaha. This small house was rented by Father Edward J. Flanagan in 1917. Father Flanagan was a Catholic priest. He believed that all children should be given an equal chance, whether they were rich or poor, black or white, Catholic, Protestant, or Jewish. He believed that if homeless boys were given a good home and good schooling, they would grow up to become just as fine citizens as boys with homes and families of their own; but if they had no homes or were badly treated they might turn out to be very poor citizens, or even criminals. So Father Flanagan made up his mind to do everything he could to help homeless boys. He borrowed ninety dollars from some friends to rent the house, and he turned it into a home and school for boys who had no families of their own. At first only a few boys lived with Father Flanagan, but the news of his wonderful work spread very quickly and boys began to come to him from all over the

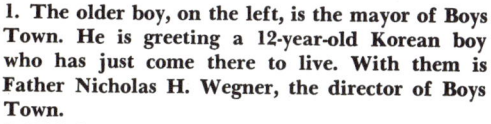

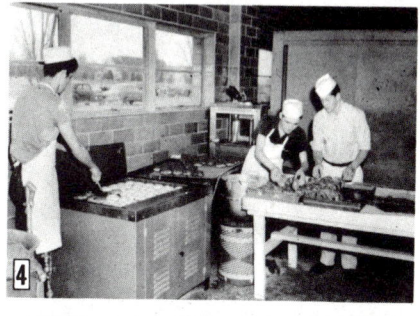

BOYS TOWN

1. The older boy, on the left, is the mayor of Boys Town. He is greeting a 12-year-old Korean boy who has just come there to live. With them is Father Nicholas H. Wegner, the director of Boys Town.
2. This is a statue of Father Flanagan, the founder of Boys Town, with some of the homeless boys he befriended. His kind and generous work helped boys grow up to be good citizens.
3. Boys do all kinds of work at Boys Town. Many work on the student farm, where they are taught the latest methods of farming. This fellow is giving one of the steers a good scrubbing. Some of the fine cattle raised by the boys have won prizes at cattle shows.
4. Some boys at Boys Town are learning to be bakers. They make all the bread, rolls and cake eaten in the community.   
5. The boys also learn printing, and put out their own newspaper.
6. Boys interested in carpentry are building a five-room house as a project.

country. Pretty soon the little house in Omaha was too small. Father Flanagan's friends decided to help him again.

They found a farm just outside Omaha, and gave it to Father Flanagan. The farm was very large, and soon enough buildings were built on it to take care of nearly five hundred boys. These boys come to Boys Town when they are very young, and live there until they are old enough to make their own way. At Boys Town they go to school, work on their own farm, and learn trades that will help them make their own livings when they are grown up. The farm at Boys Town grows nearly all the fruit and vegetables the boys need for their own meals. There are several school buildings in Boys Town, and a library, a gymnasium, dormitories, and an administration building. Boys Town has its own postoffice. The boys have their own orchestra and chorus. They have baseball and football teams.

Boys Town became a village in 1936. Since that time it has been governed by the boys themselves, just as any other village is governed by the people who live in it. The boys elect their own mayor and a council of six to help him see that everything is run smoothly and properly, and that Boys Town remains a good place to live in.

Father Flanagan was at Boys Town from the time he started it in 1917 until he died, in 1948. After he died, his wonderful work was carried on by Father Nicholas H. Wegner. People all over the United States think so much of Boys Town that they send money to support it, because they know that these boys will one day be among the finest citizens in the United States.

Bozzaris, Marco

Marco Bozzaris was a hero in the War of Greek Independence, when Greece freed itself from Turkish rule, about 125 years ago. Bozzaris was killed in the famous Battle of Carpenisi, when he led 350 Greeks against an army of 4,000 Turks and Albanians, and defeated them. His brother, Kosta, lived to become a senator in independent Greece.

Brabant, Duchy of

Brabant is a territory about the size of Connecticut and Rhode Island put together. It lies partly in Belgium and partly in Holland, and contains several large cities, including Brussels, Antwerp, and Louvain. It no longer has its own government, but hundreds of years ago it was an important and powerful duchy, which is a territory governed by a duke. From 1190 until 1430, when the last duke died, Brabant was one of the most

This great group of buildings is Boys Town, in Nebraska. It was once just a two-story house, but more and more boys came to enjoy the benefits of this community, and more buildings were needed. This large farm was finally bought to take care of all the boys who came there to live. In this view from the air, you can see the cottages where the boys live, the schools, post office, stadium, and student farm.

Boys Town Photos

prosperous states of Europe, famous for its fine wools and other cloths. The merchants of the towns became so rich by this trade that they were able to force the duke to agree not to make war or coin money without their consent. Today the eldest son of the king of the Belgians is called the Duke of Brabant, just as the male heir to the throne of England is known as the Prince of Wales.

bracelet

A bracelet is a band or chain of metal or stones or beads, worn around the wrist or arm as a decoration. Bracelets have been worn by men and women in every country as far back in history as we know. Three thousand years ago the Egyptians wore many gold and jeweled bracelets at the same time, several on each wrist and several more high up on their arms.

Today bracelets are mostly made for women. They are made of many materials, such as gold and silver bands or chains, diamonds and pearls and other jewels, and glass or plastic beads. Some chain bracelets have tiny ornaments made in various shapes, such as musical instruments, animals, coins, dice and other things that are intended as good-luck charms. These are called charm bracelets. During World War II every American soldier wore a chain around his neck with a tag on it giving his name, number, and army group. This was called an identification tag, and it started a fashion for identification bracelets on which the owner's name and sometimes his address were engraved. Identification bracelets are worn mostly by men, though some women and children like to wear them.

The handcuffs that policemen put on the wrists of persons they have arrested are sometimes nicknamed bracelets.

Braddock, Edward

Edward Braddock was a British general who came to America in 1755, when the states were still British colonies, to fight against the French. He led a force against the French fort called Duquesne, now Pittsburgh, Pennsylvania. George Washington was one of his officers. Near the fort, Braddock's troops were attacked by the Indians and French. The Indians hid behind trees, while Braddock's troops marched in columns. George Washington tried to tell him the proper way to fight Indians, but Braddock would not take his advice. More than half of Braddock's soldiers were killed, and Braddock was so badly wounded that he died.

Bradford, William

William Bradford was one of the Pilgrims who came to America on the Mayflower in 1620. He was the second governor of the Plymouth Colony (in what is now Massachusetts), which the Pilgrims started when they landed in America. He was a very good governor. He got along well with the Indians, and he knew how to guide the Pilgrims in all the problems of making their way in a new country.

The people thought so much of Bradford that they elected him governor over and over again. He was governor until just a short time before he died, in 1657. He wrote a book called *The History of Plimouth Plantation,* which tells the whole story of what happened in those exciting times. You can also read about the PLYMOUTH COLONY and the PILGRIMS in separate articles in this encyclopedia.

Bradley, Omar

Omar Bradley is the name of a great American soldier. Like General Eisenhower, he became a "five-star," or highest-ranking general. He was born in Missouri in 1893, and he married his childhood sweetheart. He went to West Point and to many other army schools. In World War II, he was in charge of all the American soldiers in the invasion of Europe. Field Marshal Montgomery was in charge of the other Allied troops in the invasion, and General Eisenhower was in command of the entire invasion. More than 1,300,000 men served under General Bradley. After the war, he was put in charge of the Veterans Administration, and then was made chairman of the Joint Chiefs of Staff, which is made up of representatives of all the armed forces of the United States. He resigned from that position in 1953 and retired from the Army.

Brady, Mathew B.

Mathew B. Brady was one of the earliest American photographers. He was born about 1823 and began experimenting with photography when he was sixteen. Very little was known about it then, but he was quick to use the discoveries of other inventors and often added his own improvements. Brady set up a studio in New York City in 1842. He photographed many famous and important people, including President Abraham Lincoln, and won World's Fair prizes in London and New York for his photography. Brady is best known for the wonderful pictures he took of officers, soldiers, camp and battle scenes during the American Civil War. Although Brady had only crude equipment, his photographs are considered to be some of the finest examples of craftsmanship in photography. Brady died in 1896.

Brahma and Brahmanism

Brahma is the name given to God in the Hindu religion, which is the chief religion of India. This religion has several other gods and goddesses, but the three most important are called Brahma, Vishnu, and Shiva. They make up what is called the Hindu *triad,* or group of three. Many of the Hindus do not believe these gods are real persons, but think that the names stand for ideas of what is true, or right and wrong.

Brahma is the oldest god in the Hindu triad. Hindus believe that he is the creator of the universe. Vishnu is the Preserver and Shiva the Destroyer. Of these gods, Vishnu is the most worshipped.

The Hindu religion is called *Brahmanism.* The priests of the Hindu religion are called Brahmans. They are the only ones who are allowed to preach and explain the scriptures. The Brahmans of India are the best educated, most intelligent and the strictest Hindus. They usually live fairly well, but often they become servants and do other things that bring them close to the common people.

The CASTE SYSTEM (about which there is a separate article) is an important part of Brahmanism. The Brahmans are the highest caste. Others are the *Rajanya* (warriors) and *Vaisya* (farmers and other workers).

HOW BRAHMANISM BEGAN

The ancient Hindu religion had many gods and goddesses. Some of these represented things in nature. There were gods of the sky, sun, light, fire, winds, heaven, and hell. Some of these were good and some were evil. There was even a goddess of luck. In fact, there were so many gods and goddesses that things were quite confusing all over India. Some Hindus worshiped certain gods in one part of the country, while in other parts different gods were worshiped. This ancient Hindu religion was written down in a book called the VEDA, and you can read about it in a separate article. The Veda goes back nearly 3,500 years, when India was invaded by the Aryan peoples from the north in about 1500 B.C.

Brahmanism began about a thousand years later, when the Brahmans wrote a book, called the *Brahmanas*. This book explains the other Hindu holy books and tells people how to worship the gods and also how to behave. Perhaps the most important thing that the Brahmans tried to do was to get rid of some of the old gods and persuade people to worship Brahma as the most important god of all.

The Brahmans were quite successful, though other forms of religion sprang up from time to time and challenged some of the things that the Brahmans believed. One of the most important of these other religions was BUDDHISM, which you can read about in a separate article. The Brahmans, however, wrote another book called the *Laws of Manu* which helped to make them almost as strong as ever. Today Brahmanism is believed by fewer people, but the Brahmans themselves are still considered the highest class of Hindus.

Millions of people in India come to worship at the statue of Brahma.

Many of the Brahmans in India are holy men who live very simply.

WHAT BRAHMANS BELIEVE

The Brahmans believe in the existence of one supreme god, whom they call Brahma. They do not believe he ever appeared on earth in human form, but they do believe there have been several men called "atavars," men with the spirit of Brahma, sent to earth to teach men something about God and His rules. Brahmans believe the human soul endures forever but that only those who repent their sins will be able to "join Brahma" (go to Heaven). Brahmans believe prayers to Brahma help them to become better people and they think it wrong to pray for such things as riches or happiness. They hold public religious services, but not on any special day, such as Sunday, nor at any special time of day.

The Brahmans have no Bible, but they do have several books that are holy to them, including the *Bhagavad-Gita*, the *Upanishads*, the *Brahmanas* (which has already been mentioned), and several others.

Brahmaputra River

The Brahmaputra River is one of the largest rivers in India. It is 1,800 miles long, but ships can sail on only 800 miles of it. The river starts high up in Tibet, in central Asia, flows down through India, and empties into the Bay of Bengal, which is an arm of the Indian Ocean. In the summer, the Brahmaputra River is filled with rushing water from the heavy rains. The river becomes so full that it overflows its banks, and floods hundreds of square miles of land. The flooding every year makes the soil very fertile, especially for rice-growing.

Brahms, Johannes

Johannes Brahms was a very great German composer, which is a writer of music. He was born in 1833. His father was a musician in Hamburg, and was his first music teacher, but later Johannes studied with a famous teacher named Eduard Marxen. When the boy was only 13 years old he began to play the piano at concerts and was very well liked by those who came to hear him. He began to write music before he was 20, and though other musicians liked his compositions, most people found them hard to listen to. Young Brahms could not make much money by writing music, but he got a job as teacher and choirmaster at the court of the Prince of Lippe-Detmold, a state in Germany.

When he was about 30 he went to live in Vienna, where he became very well liked and successful. He began to make more money and to write his most important music. Another famous composer named Robert Schumann, and his wife Clara, became his best friends. Brahms never married, and many people thought that he was in love with Clara Schumann, but they were only good friends. You can read about Robert and Clara SCHUMANN in a separate article.

Brahms is one of the "three B's." That is the way the great conductor Hans von Bülow spoke of the three greatest German composers, Bach, Beethoven, and Brahms. Brahms wrote all kinds of music except opera. As a composer of symphonies (music for a big orchestra) he ranks next to Beethoven (the greatest of all), and no one wrote better songs. The songs are in the German language and are called *lieder,* the German word for songs. One of the songs is "Wiegenlied," which means "Cradle Song." You may know it as "Brahms' Lullaby." Some of his best-known compositions are the *German Requiem,* the *Second Piano Concerto,* and a group of Hungarian dances. Brahms played in many taverns and cafes, and learned to use gypsy melodies in his music. He died in Vienna in 1897, at the age of 64.

Braille, Louis

Louis Braille was the inventor of a special system of writing for the blind. This system is called Braille, after him. There was a system of writing for the blind before Braille, but it was not easy to learn, and only a few people used it. With the Braille system, blind people can read and write almost as well as those who can see. In Braille, raised dots like little bumps are used for letters and numbers. There is a different pattern of dots for each letter and number. Blind people read Braille by running their fingers over these patterns of dots. They write by punching tiny holes in paper which is stretched across a frame. (See BLINDNESS.)

Louis Braille was born in France about 150 years ago, in 1809. He became blind when he was only 3 years old. When he invented Braille, he was only twenty years old. He was also a fine musician, and became known all over France for his organ playing. He died in 1852.

brain

The brain is the part of the body that we think with. No one knows *why* it works as it does, but scientists know

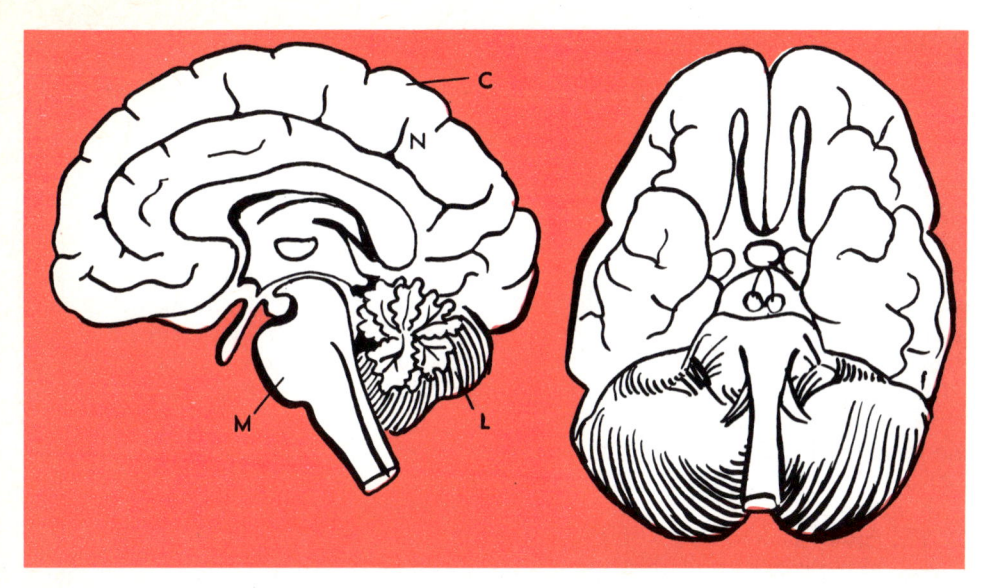

Left: A side-view of the brain. *Right:* A view of the brain from below. The human brain occupies almost the entire upper skull. The cerebrum (C) and cerebellum (L), each of which has two parts, and the medulla oblongata, or brain stem (M), direct all bodily activity. Voluntary motion and the senses are controlled by sections of the cerebrum called convolutions (N).

a great deal about *how* it works. It consists of a mass of nerve fibers, in the form of thin, white strands, at the top of the head. These nerve fibers connect with other nerve fibers that stretch from the brain to all parts of our bodies. They carry messages to and from the brain in less time than it takes to bat an eyelash.

Nearly all animals have some kind of brain. Some, like the ape, have brains which in many ways are like our own. Yet it is man's brain that puts him above all other animals. It enables him to think, to learn, to make decisions. It gives him knowledge of himself and the world in which he lives. In short, it makes him master of the earth. What is this amazing instrument that we call the human brain? How does it differ from the brains of all other creatures?

Let us look at the human brain. It is shaped somewhat like cauliflower, with ripples called *convolutions*. The brain has a coating of grainy gray stuff. This is called the *cerebral cortex*, or simply "gray matter." The gray matter is gathered into many dips and folds called *convolutions*, which give the surface of the brain a furrowed look, something like a walnut shell.

Let us also look at the brain of an animal, for example, the ape. Seen side by side, the two show a number of likenesses as well as differences. They are shaped the same, but the human brain is larger and heavier. Also, the human brain has more dips and folds than the ape's brain. Since each dip and fold is lined with gray matter, the human brain contains more gray matter than the ape's.

You may have heard the expression, "Use your gray matter." When you use your gray matter, you are *thinking*. At this very instant, as you read this article, you are using your gray matter. With the *cerebral cortex* or gray matter of the brain we do the complex things that are called perceiving, thinking, learning and forming judgments which add up to what we call our human intelligence. Special centers inside the cerebral cortex also control our senses, such as sight, hearing, taste, smell, and touch. When one of these senses is damaged by injury or disease, another usually takes over. For example, if a person goes blind, his hearing and touch become sharper to help him overcome his handicap. In this way the brain not only controls our actions, but also helps us to survive. We may say, therefore, that the most important part of the brain, the part that sets us apart from other animals, is the cerebral cortex or gray matter. The brain also contains a layer of *white matter,* consisting mainly of closely packed white nerve fibers. There is also a third or inner layer, which contains quantities of gray matter.

The brain itself consists of the forebrain, the midbrain, and the hindbrain. The forebrain is the largest of the three. It is divided into halves called the *right* and *left hemisphere.* Each of these controls the opposite side of the body, that is, the *right hemisphere* controls the *left* side, and the *left hemisphere* controls the *right* side. If the left hemisphere is injured, paralysis of the right side may take place. The paralysis, or inability to move, may be temporary or permanent, depending on the seriousness of the injury and on the amount of gray matter destroyed. Some parts of the brain control our muscles, and other parts control our various inner organs, such as the heart or lungs.

Nature has provided special protection for the brain by placing it in the skull, or brain case, which shields it from injury. In addition, the brain is covered by three sets of thin but strong sheaths called *membranes,* separated from each other by a liquid which also protects the brain by acting as a cushion against sudden shock. For example, if you bump your head, the liquid around the brain prevents it from being violently thrown against the bones of the skull.

The brain must have a constant supply of oxygen to keep up its many activities. This is ordinarily provided by the many blood vessels that pass through the brain. If the steady flow of oxygen is cut off for as long as three to four minutes, the brain can become severely damaged, and the body begins to come to a standstill. Death follows if all oxygen is cut off from the brain for ten minutes—sometimes less.

Brain Trust

When Franklin D. Roosevelt was elected president of the United States in 1932, he appointed a number of college professors as his closest advisers. This was considered very unusual, since most of the presidents before Roosevelt appointed businessmen and persons with experience in politics to help them run the country. James Kiernan, a writer for *The New York Times,* a newspaper published in New York City, jokingly called these college professors a "Brain Trust." A *trust* is a company or a group of companies that has a "monopoly" or complete control over the sale of some product. Brain Trust therefore meant a group of men with a monopoly of brains in the nation. The name Brain Trust was used to describe the president's advisers by people who felt he had made a mistake in appointing a group of men who were brainy or clever but had no practical experience in government or business.

brake

A brake is any device which is used to slow something down or to stop it from moving. All moving things need brakes to control their motion. Machines need brakes to stop them from turning or to make them turn slower. Automobiles need brakes; so do airplanes. Brakes may be of many different kinds. Most brakes work by rubbing against something. This is called *friction.* When you ride a scooter and let one of your feet drag along the ground, the friction of your foot against the ground slows you down.

Instead of a brake applied directly to the ground, it is much easier to rub something against the wheel of the scooter. This was how the first brake worked. It was used on old-fashioned wagons that were drawn by horses or oxen. A piece of wood was connected to a handle so that when the handle was pushed forward, the wood rubbed against one of the wagon wheels. This prevented the wheel from turning and stopped the wagon.

Such brakes were not good enough when the automobiles were first invented. A man was not strong enough to stop the fast and heavy car wiith a hand brake. Instead of a wood block rubbing against the outside of a wheel, a new kind of brake was developed. This brake applied pressure to the inside of the wheel. This prevented the tires on the outside of the wheel from being worn away. A hollow metal drum was fitted inside the wheel around the axle. Inside the drum were two metal bars lined with hard rubber or asbestos. They were called *brake shoes*. When the brake handle in the car was pulled back, or a pedal was pressed down, the brake shoes would press against the sides of the drum and slow down the wheel. The stronger the pull on the brake handle, the more the brake shoes pressed on the drum.

These brakes were called *mechanical* brakes. They depended on the strength of the driver's leg or arm muscles. They are still used as parking brakes on automobiles. They stop only the back wheels.

New brakes have been developed for trains and large trucks which relieve the engineer or driver of using his strength to apply the brakes. These brakes are called AIR BRAKES. You can read about them in a separate article. Most automobile brakes are operated by liquid pressure. These are called HYDRAULIC BRAKES, and there is also a separate article about them.

An airplane has brakes to slow it down when it is coming in for a landing. These are the flaps on the front of the airplane wings. When they are turned forward, air strikes against them and slows

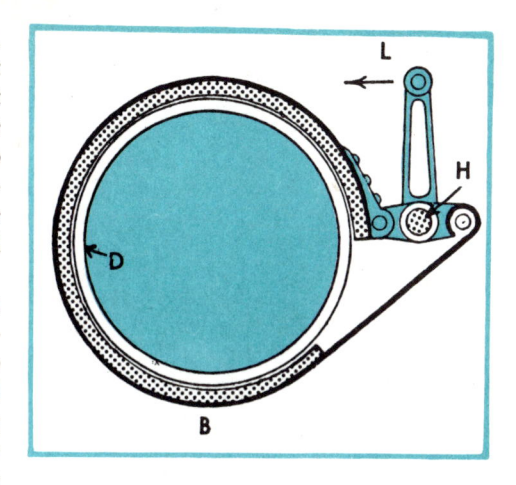

A band brake is used on heavy machinery and large trucks. When the lever (L) is pushed forward, it turns on a hinge (H). This tightens a leather or rubber band (B) around a moving drum (D). When the band is tight, the drum cannot turn.

the forward motion of the plane. A parachute is also a kind of brake. When a pilot jumps or bails out of a plane, he opens his parachute which balloons in the air like a giant umbrella. As it comes down, air is caught in the silk and slows the parachute. This prevents the pilot from hitting the ground at high speed and being killed. Parachutes are sometimes used as brakes on the airplane itself. They are attached to the plane and thrown out behind it. As they trail behind the plane, they catch air in their silks, thus slowing down the plane.

brake or bracken

Brake is a kind of fern with big, rough leaves that grow as high as a person's waist. It is found nearly all over the world, growing in open fields or in thin woods where there is plenty of light. Nearly everywhere it is regarded as a pest, because it chokes the grass and tree seedlings, and because cattle and sheep get sick if they eat too many of its leaves. In many places it is cut back each year and poisoned. Unless you dig into the ground, all you can see of the brake is its leaves. The main stem is underground, and grows as much as a hundred feet long, though it is always quite thin. The leaves are used as bedding for animals, and for making thatched roofs. In the fall the leaves turn golden, and hillsides are made beautiful by their color.

bran

Bran is the outer coat of cereal grains that is removed when the grain is ground into flour. Many people eat wheat bran as a breakfast cereal. It is rich in minerals and vitamin B, the energy-giving vitamin. Bran is also taken from rye, oats, and rice, but wheat bran is most commonly used. All brans are used as food for farm animals.

Brandeis, Louis D.

Louis Dembitz Brandeis was a great judge in the United States Supreme Court. He was born in 1856 in Louisville, Kentucky, and was graduated from Harvard Law School. He went into law practice in Boston, Massachusetts, and was very successful. Among the important cases he argued were cases for the people against big corporations and against states. President Woodrow Wilson made Brandeis a Supreme Court Justice in 1916. Brandeis knew a great deal about the United States Constitution, and he believed in it very deeply. He was greatly respected, and was known as the "people's attorney." He lived to be 85 years old, and he was in the Supreme Court until two years before he died, in 1941.

Brandeis University, in Waltham, Massachusetts, was named for Justice Brandeis. It was founded in 1947 and one of its principal objects was to provide a higher education for students regardless of their religious beliefs. In 1967 its enrollment was 2,504 students, men and women.

Brandenburg

Brandenburg is a part of Germany, and was once a province of Prussia, the biggest German kingdom. It belonged to the Hohenzollern family, from which came the kings of Prussia and then the German emperors until Germany lost World War I to the Allies in 1918.

Berlin, the biggest city in Germany, is in the Brandenburg territory, but the capital of Brandenburg is Potsdam, a famous old city, now a suburb of Berlin, where Prussia had its military academy for training officers in its army.

Brandenburg is now a part of East Germany and has a population of about 2,500,000. Brandenburg is also the name of a city in this province, with a population of about 87,700.

Brandt, Willy

Willy Brandt achieved world-wide prominence as the anti-Communist mayor of West Berlin. He was born Herbert Frahm in 1913 in Lubeck, Germany, but changed his name when he fled the Nazis in 1933 because of his activities in the Social Democratic youth movement. Taking refuge in Norway, he worked as a journalist for Scandinavian newspapers. He was active in German and Norwegian resistance movements during World War II and returned to Germany after the war. Elected Mayor of West Berlin in 1957, he became Vice-Chancellor and Foreign Minister of West Germany in 1966 when Kurt Georg Kiesinger replaced Ludvig Erhard as Chancellor.

brandy

Brandy is a strong alcoholic drink that is made from fruit instead of from grain (as whiskey is). Most brandy is distilled from wine, which is made from grapes.

The world's best brandy is said to come from grapes grown in the Cognac region of France. Other brandies are made from apples, cherries, apricots or peaches, and other fruits.

Brant, Joseph

Joseph Brant was a famous chief of the warlike Mohawk Indians. He fought on the British side in the American Revolution, but later became a good friend of the new United States.

Brant was born on the banks of the Ohio River in 1742, and was given the Indian name of Thayendanegea. Sir William Johnson, the British official in charge of dealing with the Indians, sent him to a school for Indians in Connecticut. When the colonies revolted, Brant became a colonel in the British army. He led Indian braves who came whooping down on New York settlements.

After the war Brant helped the new government make peace treaties with western tribes. He became a Christian missionary to the Indians, and translated the Episcopal Prayer Book and St. Mark's Gospel into the language of the Mohawks. He even went to England and raised funds to build the first Episcopal church in Upper Canada. The British government rewarded him with an estate on Lake Ontario, where he died in 1807.

Brasilia, see BRAZIL.

brass

Brass is one of the oldest metals that people knew about way back at the beginning of the BRONZE Age. (See the article on ARCHAEOLOGY.) They used to make it from copper and *calamine*, a kind of rock that is mostly zinc, and charcoal. About 175 years ago a man named James Emmerson found a way to make brass by melting copper and zinc and mixing them together. Then the brass is poured into a mold made of sand or iron, and when it gets cold it is ready to use. See the articles on BRONZE and COPPER.

Braun, Wernher von

Wernher von Braun, a brilliant physicist and rocketry expert, is Director of the George C. Marshall Space Flight Center of the National Aeronautics and Space Administration in Huntsville, Alabama. Born in 1912 in Wirsitz, Germany, Dr. von Braun attended various schools in that country since his father, Baron von Braun, was required to move from place to place as Secretary of Agriculture under President von Hindenburg.

In 1930, Wernher von Braun joined the German Society for Space Travel, a group of inventors who made and tested rockets. At the age of twenty, he received a bachelor of science degree in mechanical engineering from the Berlin Institute of Technology. Two years later he was awarded his doctorate in physics at the University of Berlin.

As a result of the experiments conducted by Dr. von Braun at the University, he was hired in 1934 by the German Ordnance Department as a rocket development engineer. By early 1937, his staff was developing a rocket designed to reach an altitude of 15 miles.

Dr. von Braun surrendered to the Allied Powers at the end of World War II and came to the U.S. to direct firings of captured V-2 rockets. He became an American citizen in 1955. In 1960, the Army Ballistic Missile Agency, under Dr. von Braun's leadership, became part of the National Aeronautics and Space Administration. Dr. von Braun's team launched the Western World's first satellites of the earth and sun, Explorer I and Pioneer IV, and performed the first successful recovery of animal life from space.

Brazil

Brazil

Brazil is a huge country that covers almost half of South America. Its coast, bulging out into the Atlantic Ocean, is thousands of miles long. Its boundaries touch every other country on the continent except Chile and Ecuador. Its population of almost 80,000,000 is equal to that of all the rest of South America. Although Brazil is bigger than the United States, it has only about a third as many people. The people of Brazil speak the Portuguese language. Almost everywhere else south of the United States, the language is Spanish.

Brazil was discovered more than 450 years ago. It has grown from a small colony of Portugal to a big independent republic. But Brazilians believe that their history as a great nation is only just beginning. Because of the enormous natural riches that lie in the earth and in the forests, waiting to be put to use, Brazilians speak of their country as "the land of the future."

During World War II the United States built several large airfields in Brazil. These were very useful in transporting men and supplies to North Africa and Europe, because Brazil is much closer to the Eastern Hemisphere than the United States is. The distance from Brazil to North Africa, across the narrowest part of the Atlantic Ocean, is less than 2,000 miles. In Italy, Brazilian troops fought side by side with United States soldiers against the Germans. Brazil was one of the first countries to join the United Nations. The United States of America and the United States of Brazil (for that is its full name) have always been good friends.

THE PEOPLE OF BRAZIL

The people of Brazil come from many races and origins. Probably no other country has so mixed a population. Brazilians are proud of this fact. They say that in Brazil they are gradually producing a new civilization, made up of all the races of mankind.

Before the Portuguese explorers came, the only people in Brazil were Indians. There were few of them and they lived in small villages far apart from one another. They wore very little clothing and painted their bodies. They lived mainly by hunting birds and wild animals in the forests, and fishing in the great rivers like the Amazon. Some were killed by the white conquerors, and some married whites or Negroes. But some others have been protected from change by the dense jungles around them. Even today there are Indians living in parts of the Amazon Valley exactly as their ancestors did hundreds of years ago.

When the settlers came to Brazil, they needed workers to clear the forests and farm the land. They made slaves of the Indians, but so many of them escaped or died in slavery that the settlers began to bring Negroes over from Africa as slaves. By the time the slaves were freed, more than fifty years ago, there were about two million Negroes in Brazil.

Meanwhile the white population was growing. French and later Dutch followed the Portuguese to Brazil to battle for possession of the country. Tales of Brazilian gold and diamonds brought adventurers from all over western Europe. In 1818 a large Swiss group arrived. From then on, the number of people who came to seek their fortunes increased steadily. Italians, Spaniards, and Germans came to settle the vast and empty land. From the Far East, Japanese, Chinese, and Malayans came or were brought in. Today the flow of people into Brazil still continues, particularly from southern Europe.

Because there have been so many marriages between members of one group and members of another, there are not very many "pure-blooded" people left in Brazil. About one Brazilian in every five is Indian or part-Indian; about one in seven is Negro or part-Negro; and the rest are white or nearly so, except for a small number of Orientals.

The great majority of Brazilians are Catholics. There are only about a million and a half Protestants in the country. Like Americans, Brazilians are free to follow the religion of their choice.

HOW THE PEOPLE LIVE

How people live in Brazil depends mainly on what part of the country they live in. In the vast Amazon region in the north, through which the equator passes, the weather is too hot and muggy for most white men, and there is little industry. Most of the people live by hunting and fishing. Some gather sap from the bark of rubber trees in the great forests and sell the crude rubber or exchange it for food. Others farm small patches of land on which they grow corn, sweet potatoes, and other vegetables. Products of the forests include tapioca from the cassava tree, the beautiful wood mahogany, indigo (used in making dyes), and quinine (a drug used to treat malaria).

Farther south, where the land is higher and it is not so hot, a number of crops are grown. Most of the Negroes of Brazil live in this central region, which in places is like the southern states of the United States. At one time sugar cane was the most important crop. Some sugar is still grown there, but most of the fertile land now is used to grow coffee. Brazil grows more coffee than any other country. More than a million Brazilians earn their living from coffee—raising it, harvesting the coffee beans, or transporting it to the coast to be shipped abroad. It is not surprising that coffee is Brazil's favorite drink.

Many thousands of Brazilians work in the fields growing cotton or rice; thousands of others grow oranges, bananas, pineapples, or corn. On many farms the tools are still very simple and old-fashioned, but many landowners have begun to use tractors and other modern machines.

About two Brazilians out of every three make their living from the land. Yet only a tiny part of the land has been put to use for farming. So you can see that Brazil can be very useful to grow food for people in countries where there are too many people and too little land to raise food for all of them.

Nobody knows how much iron, bauxite, gold, and other minerals will one day be dug from beneath the soil of Brazil. In the southern part of the central region, many Brazilians work as miners. Some work for themselves, panning the streams and rivers for gold and diamonds. This is a risky trade, but a man can become rich overnight if he is lucky.

In the southern part of the country

wheat is grown, as well as the crops already mentioned. The vast plains that stretch south to Argentina are like our old West. It is a frontier region where cowboys in colorful costumes watch over huge herds of cattle. But the most interesting part of the south is the cities. Here the weather is cooler. There are many more people here than in the other regions of Brazil, and most of them are white. They work at many businesses, trades, and industries. Outside the big modern city of Sao Paulo, for instance, are cotton mills and cement plants, and factories where tires are made and automobiles are put together. The people here look and dress much like people in American cities and towns.

Brazilians enjoy music and dancing. Some famous dances, such as the samba and others, originated in Brazil. The four days of carnival and the Mardi Gras celebrations in the big cities are famous all over the world. Opera, the kind of play that is sung instead of spoken, is very popular. Brazilians get very excited about their national sport, football, which is soccer, not the game that is called football in North America.

All boys and girls in Brazil must go to grammar school. In some areas there are not yet enough schools and teachers, but in the advanced states there are many elementary and high schools, and some universities. The University of Brazil, in Rio de Janeiro, is the biggest of these.

WHAT KIND OF A PLACE IT IS

Brazil is made up of three kinds of land. In the north is the vast, low Amazon Valley. In the center, spreading over half the country, is tableland crossed by chains of low mountains. This is the great Brazilian plateau. In the south, the land slopes down to form part of the La Plata River valley, along with the neighboring countries, Paraguay, Uruguay, and northern Argentina.

Counting the many rivers, small and large, that flow into it, the Amazon is the biggest river in the world. Most of it is very deep and wide. Where it empties into the Atlantic, it is 150 miles across. The land through which it flows is covered with dense jungle. Because all of the Amazon Valley lies on or near the equator, and is not very high above sea level, it is hot and damp all year round. It is a very rainy region.

The great Brazilian plateau in the central part of the country has a much more pleasant climate, partly because it is farther away from the equator, but mostly because it is higher. It is partly forest and partly open prairies. It makes a very fine place to live so that the plateau is often called "the real Brazil," meaning the place where Brazil's future lies. One reason why this region has been so little developed so far is that it is cut off from the coast by a chain of steep, high mountains, called the Serra do Mar.

Between the Serra do Mar and the Atlantic Ocean there is a long narrow strip of land. To the south, this strip widens out. All of Brazil's great cities are on this coastal plain.

The Pampa region of Brazil, at the southern edge of the great plateau, is much higher than the Amazon Valley. Its climate is healthful. Much of it is covered by grassy plains, ideal for cattle ranching.

Although Brazil lies almost entirely within the Torrid Zone, not all the country is hot. The height of the land above sea level makes a great difference. So do wind, rain, and distance from the sea. The climate of the Brazilian coastal plain and of parts of the great plateau is quite like that of the southern Atlantic States of the United States. Since Brazil is south of the equator, summer comes in December, January, and February, and winter—sometimes even with snow—comes in June, July, and August.

HOW THE PEOPLE ARE GOVERNED

Like the United States, Brazil is a federal republic. The country's first consti-

BRAZIL

Legend:
- Timber
- Rubber
- Veg. Oils & Nuts
- Quartz & Gems
- Cattle
- Sheep
- Coffee
- Manioc
- Cotton
- Maté
- Cacao

Cities labeled: BELEM (PARA), SAO SALVADOR, BELO HORIZONTE, SAO PAULO, RIO DE JANEIRO, PORTO ALEGRE

1. Brazil is rich in resources. This map shows some of the most important things that come from Brazil, and the section each comes from. Brazil ships coffee, cotton, and cacao, worth more than a billion dollars, all over the world.

2. On this map you can see how big Brazil is in comparison to the rest of South America.

3. Brazil is very big. It is almost 64,000 square miles larger than the United States.

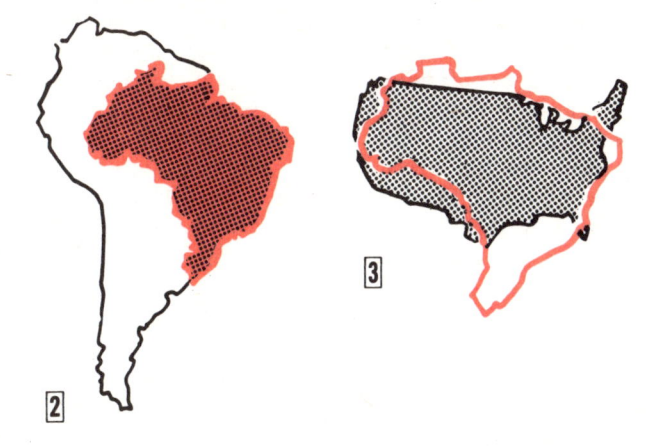

tution, issued in 1889, was written to be like the Constitution of the United States and the present Brazilian constitution is still like the United States one, though it has been changed several times. The President is elected by all the citizens over the age of 18. He serves for a term of five years. Laws are made by a National Congress, which has two houses, a senate and a Chamber of Deputies (like the U.S. House of Representatives). Senators are elected for eight years, Deputies for four years. In 1961 the constitution was revised to give all power to a Prime Minister elected by Congress.

The Brazilian constitution set up a Federal District, much like the District of Columbia, around the original capital, Rio de Janeiro, and a law passed in 1956 created a new Federal District around the new capital, Brasilia. The rest of the country is divided into twenty-two states and four territories. The states elect their own governors and their own law-making bodies, but the territories are ruled by governors appointed by the President. The territories are chiefly backward areas whose people have not yet learned how to govern themselves.

BRASILIA, THE NEW CAPITAL

In 1956 Brazil decided to build an entirely new capital city and move its government there, from Rio de Janeiro, in 1960 and 1961. The name selected for the new capital was Brasilia. The site selected was in the central part of the country, about 600 miles from the sea, on high ground (about 4,000 feet above sea level) overlooking the central jungle territory that has never been developed as other parts of Brazil have been.

Brazil is the third great country to build a new capital in this century, the others being India (New Delhi) and the Philippines (Quezon City); but both these other capitals were built in well-populated regions near the old capitals. Brazil placed its new capital so as to encourage development of a new region.

The planners of Brasilia estimated its population at 500,000. They designed the city to be the most modern in the world. The government provided $345,-000,000 to build Brasilia.

The chief cities of Brazil, with population figures from the United Nations, 1960, are:

Brasilia, the new capital, 130,968.

Rio de Janeiro, population 3,123,984, the original capital, the chief seaport and cultural center, and long the biggest city. It is in the southern part of the country, on the Atlantic Ocean. See RIO DE JANEIRO.

São Paulo, population 3,674,373, Brazil's leading industrial center and in recent years its biggest city, probably the fastest-growing big city in the world. See SÃO PAULO.

Recife, population 765, 305, an important seaport on the Atlantic Coast, in the north near the easternmost point of the bulge.

Salvador, population 571,101, an Atlantic seaport 750 miles north of Rio de Janeiro.

Porto Allegre, population 553,051, 750 miles south of Rio de Janeiro, a port on the Lagoa dos Patos, a large lagoon with an outlet to the Atlantic Ocean.

BRAZIL IN THE PAST

Brazil was discovered and claimed for Portugal by the explorer Pedro Cabral in 1500. In 1532 the first permanent settlement was established. The French and the Dutch controlled small areas for a short time, but Brazil remained a Portuguese colony until 1808. At that time Portugal was invaded by a French army under Napoleon. The King of Portugal and his family escaped to Brazil, and for a time Rio de Janeiro became the capital of the Portuguese empire. When Napoleon was defeated, the King returned to Portugal, but his son Pedro stayed behind, and in 1822 proclaimed the independent Empire of Brazil.

Dom Pedro I, as he was called, was not a popular ruler, and in 1831 he was forced to give up the throne. His son, Dom Pedro II, became ruler of the only kingdom in the western hemisphere (all the other Latin-American countries had become republics after revolting from

BRAZIL

Moore McCormack Lines

1. A cable car takes sightseers to the top of Sugar Loaf Mountain for a famous view of Rio de Janeiro. Part of the view can be seen in this picture, taken from the spot on Sugar Loaf where the cable car lands. On the peak in the distance is the statue shown in Picture 3.
2. The cable car between the city and Sugar Loaf. It frightens some tourists but is actually quite safe.
3. The huge statue of the Christ on Corcovado Mountain; see Picture 1 for a distant view of the mountain.
4 & 5. Rio de Janeiro has many mosaic sidewalks made with small bits of differently colored stones.

BRAZIL

Unations

Pan Am. World Airways

Pan Am. World Airways

Moore McCormack Lines

World Wide Photos

1. The people in Brazil have built large dams to increase the water power of the country. This dam supplies electricity to many homes and factories in the district.
2. Many people visit this beautiful church in Rio de Janeiro.
3. Rio de Janeiro has many very modern buildings. These tourists, standing on a mosaic sidewalk, have stopped to look at one of the most impressive of them.
4. In São Paulo, Brazil, is this beautiful city library, open to the public.
5. Modern government buildings rise toward the sky in the new capital city of Brasilia.

BRAZIL

Pan Am. World Airways

1. Rio de Janeiro has one of the most famous harbors in the world. Many people come to the fine beaches and hotels there.

Brazilian Inform. Bureau

Firestone Tire & Rubber Co.

2. The ant bear lives in the dense forests of Brazil. It is about four feet long. It eats ants with its long tongue.

3. One of the many Brazilian birds is the toucan, with its brilliant red, yellow and black feathers, and its large bill.

4. Rubber is one of the most important products in Brazil. These rubber molds have the shape of the containers they were in. They are called "biscuits."

5. You can pick papayas right off the trees in Brazil, and eat them.

Spain). Dom Pedro II was just and popular, and he reigned for fifty-eight years.

In 1888 Dom Pedro issued a royal decree freeing the slaves. The rich landowners and others who had supported him now turned against him. After a brief and bloodless revolution, Brazil was declared a republic. Since then, Brazil has had a peaceful existence compared to nearly all the other South American countries. The first president, General Fonseca, tried to become a dictator in 1891 but was overthrown in 1893. Brazil declared war on the side of the Allies in both World Wars but has settled all its disputes with its South American neighbors peacefully.

Coffee and rubber brought great wealth to Brazil around the beginning of the 1900s. But coffee sales dropped when other Latin-American countries produced more coffee, and the use of lower-priced rubber from the Far East almost wiped out Brazil's rubber trade. Since then Brazilians have learned not to depend on just one or two crops.

There was another revolution in 1930 when Getulio Vargas seized power (see VARGAS). But though Vargas ruled as a military dictator, he did not suppress all opposition as most dictators do. In 1934 he permitted elections and was himself elected president. He continued to rule as a dictator and the Army forced him to retire in 1945. In 1950 Vargas was elected president again and in 1954 the Army forced him to retire again. This time Vargas killed himself.

Since 1954 Brazil has had several political crises and a serious inflation (see INFLATION). In 1964 the Army, having forced two previous presidents to resign, made General Humberto Castelo Branco president. His moderate, anti-Communist government succeeded in reducing the inflation somewhat.

THE UNITED STATES OF BRAZIL *(Estados Unidos do Brazil)*. Area, 3,288,042 square miles. Population, 78,809,000 (1964 UN estimate). Capital, Rio de Janerio until 1960, thereafter Brasilia. Language, Portuguese. Religion, chiefly Roman Catholic. Government, federal republic. Monetary unit, *cruzeiro*, worth about 1/20 cent (U.S.). Flag, green, with twenty-two white stars forming the constellation of the Southern Cross on a blue circle superimposed on a gold diamond in the center; a white band running across the blue circle bears the motto "Order and Progress" in Portuguese.

Brazil nut

The Brazil nut grows on very tall trees in South America. These trees grow as high as 120 feet, and are found not only in Brazil, but in Venezuela and Guiana. The nuts, which are really seeds, grow in huge, round seed pods that are as large as basketballs. The pod is so hard that you have to hit it with a hammer to break it open. Inside the pod, there are fifteen to twenty nuts. The Brazil nut is white and very delicious, and it is sold to countries all over the world. The natives also get oil from these nuts, and they use it as fuel for their lamps.

Brazzaville

Brazzaville is the capital and largest city of Republic of the Congo. It lies on the northern shore of the Congo river. During World War II it was the African headquarters of the Free French, who continued to fight against the Germans after France had been beaten and occupied. Since the war it has grown bigger and more important. There are schools in Brazzaville in which the native Negroes learn to become teachers, factory foremen, and administrators. The town was named in honor of the French explorer Count Brazza, who founded it in 1880. The population in 1961 was 100,000.

bread

When grains, cereals, or seeds are ground or mashed into flour or meal, and then mixed with water and baked, we call it bread. Bread is made of many different things, such as wheat, corn, rye, oats, barley, millet, sesame, rice, potatoes, soy beans, and nuts. It may be that the first bread was made by pounding acorns or nuts and adding water to make a paste, which was dried by the fire. We don't know, because the first bread was made long before man had learned to write, and so there is no record of it. Some historians think it might have started in China, because they had underground "ovens" so long ago. In ancient Egypt bread was baked in ovens, and there were bakeries where people bought bread. Most historians believe that bread-making was invented in many parts of the world at about the same time, when our ancestors first learned to eat grains and cereals, and to plant crops.

Bread has been so important to people everywhere that sometimes the word is used to mean all food, not just bread itself. In the "Lord's Prayer," when we say, "Give us this day our daily bread," we surely do not mean bread alone.

At first every home made its own bread, but when bakeries started to sell bread in Europe, the first "pure-food laws" came into use. Pure-food laws regulate the sale of things we eat. All those who make and sell them must be clean, and must put in the right ingredients. A long time ago, when a baker made bad bread he was sometimes punished by being publicly whipped, or put in a pillory, a kind of wooden board with holes for his hands and feet, where people passing by made fun of him. Nowadays he may lose his license and not be allowed to make and sell bread for some time.

TYPES OF BREAD

There are two main types of bread, called "yeast breads" and "quick breads." The difference is in the speed with which the *leavening* takes place. Now let us see what leavening is and how it works.

In the Bible, "unleavened bread" is often mentioned. Unleavened bread is made of flour and water, and it is heavy and solid, instead of light and full of little air bubbles that make it porous. Most crackers are unleavened, also the *tortilla* Spanish people like, sea biscuit or hard tack, and the matzoth that is eaten by Jewish people on religious occasions. The Biblical meaning is that unleavened bread stands for purity. Leavened bread, on the other hand, is made by adding something to the flour and water, or dough, so that it will "rise" and become light and porous.

When yeast is used as a leavening agent, the bread is slow-rising, or yeast bread, and this group includes our fa-

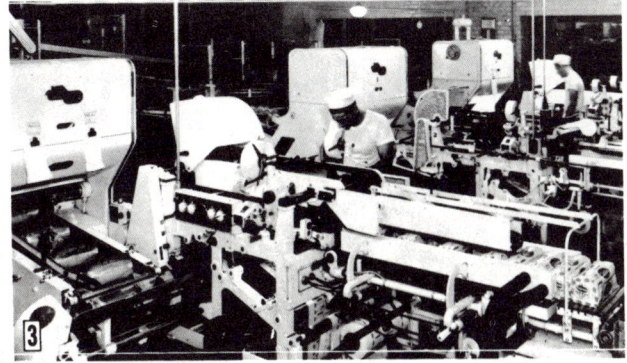

Taystee Bread

1. Thousands of years ago, the Egyptian people made flour for their bread by grinding the grain on a hard surface.
2. People in ancient Pompeii baked their bread in great stone ovens.
3. Modern machinery slices and wraps bread quickly.

BREAD

The first step in baking bread is to mix all the ingredients together into a dough. Bakeries use the same ingredients except in much larger quantities.

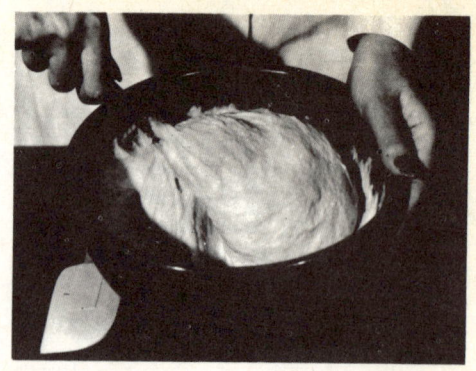

The dough has to be mixed thoroughly to get it smooth. If the dough is not well mixed it will be lumpy. An electric mixer is often used to save work and time.

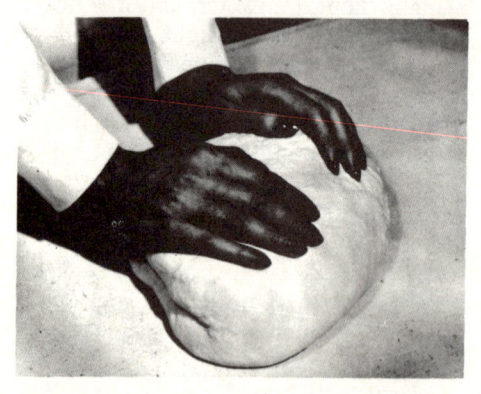

Then the dough is kneaded. The yeast in the dough causes air bubbles to form, and in a few hours the dough will swell up to twice its original size.

Now the baker must punch the dough hard to break up the air bubbles in the dough. If the bubbles are left, there will be big holes in the bread after it is baked.

Wheat and Flour Inst.

The dough is now shaped into loaves of bread or into rolls, and put into pans, ready to be baked. The bread has a delicious odor when it is baking.

The crisp loaves and rolls have come out of the oven and cooled off. The bread can now be sliced and eaten. It is one of our most delicious and nourishing foods.

miliar loaves of white or whole-wheat bread, rolls, coffee cake (really a kind of bread), pumpernickel (a slightly sour, dark rye bread), and many others.

Quick breads are made with baking powder, or soda and sour milk, and they rise very quickly. This group includes muffins, biscuits, gingerbreads, waffles, griddle cakes, and cornbread; and there are many, many varieties of all of these.

HOW BREAD IS MADE

1. *Yeast breads* are made in many sizes and shapes and flavors. For instance, there is raisin bread, bread with nuts in it, and other kinds. But there are some steps in the making of yeast breads that are the same for all of them. If you were a baker and were to bake some bread, here is what you would do:

First you would mix the flour, water, and other ingredients to make the dough. The flour might be the kind called "bread flour," or the kind known as "all-purpose flour." You would add the flour to water until the dough became rubbery and sticky. You might use milk instead of water, if you were making a special kind of bread.

Then you would add a little salt, and usually a little sugar and some fat, although not everybody uses sugar and fat. Next comes the yeast, called "bakers' yeast." It is sold in three forms, as a dry cake, or as a moist cake, but today almost all bakers use "crumbled yeast." Then you would start to knead the dough, or push, pull and squeeze it with your hands until it is smooth and all the ingredients are well mixed. In large bakeries a machine does the kneading, but at home it is done by hand on a board. As you kneaded the dough, you would see it changing. Little bubbles appear and the dough becomes less sticky and more rubbery.

After you had kneaded the dough, you would put it in a warm place, so that the yeast could begin to ferment. This is called "letting the dough rise." When it has become about twice the size that it was before, you would knead it again to break up the big gas bubbles, and shape it into loaves. Again it would rise until doubled in size. Then you would put it in the oven and bake it to a golden-brown color.

2. Quick breads can go into the oven as soon as the dough is well mixed. In most of these breads there is no kneading, although biscuits are usually kneaded slightly. The ingredients are almost the same as those used in yeast breads, except that some quick breads contain eggs and more sugar. They may also contain a large amount of fat, or shortening. This is also true of many cakes and pastries, so that sometimes it is hard to decide whether to call them bread or cake.

See also the articles on YEAST, BAKING POWDER, and FLOUR.

breadfruit

Breadfruit is a kind of fruit that grows on a big tree. The fruit is about as

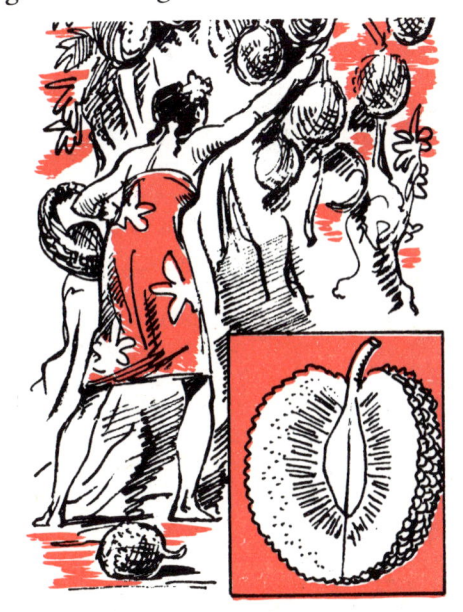

A native woman of Polynesia is picking breadfruit, which looks and tastes like bread when it is baked. *Insert:* This shows how the inside of a breadfruit looks.

big as a small loaf of bread, but it is egg-shaped. When the fruit is baked, it looks and even tastes something like bread, with a slightly nutty flavor. It is a very healthful food, and thousands of people in hot tropical countries raise breadfruit trees. These trees grow well in hot climates like Malaya, the South Sea Islands, and Indonesia.

You can bake breadfruit, or boil it, or dry it and grind it into flour, or cut it into slices and fry it. In the South Sea Islands the natives used to bake it in a hole in the ground filled with hot rocks. Then they would peel the breadfruit and eat it. There is a pit in the center that you throw away. The *jack fruit* tree often seen in Botanical Gardens is another type of breadfruit tree.

breakwater

A breakwater is a kind of barrier made of stones and concrete blocks that sticks out into the sea around a harbor. It protects ships and docks in the harbor by "breaking the water," that is, by checking the rush of waves during a storm. Some harbors, like San Francisco or New York, are almost entirely surrounded by land. In natural harbors like these, breakwaters are seldom needed. But other harbors, Los Angeles for example, have been made out of a straight shoreline by building breakwaters out into the water.

breast

The babies of certain animals live on milk provided by their mothers, and the special part of the body that gives the baby its milk is called the breast. The Latin word for breast is "mamma," and that is why this group of animals is known as "mammals." We human beings belong to this group, and so do horses, cows, dogs, and cats. Not every mammal lives on land; the whale is a mammal, with breasts to feed milk to its baby whale. Even though whales live in the sea and look like fish, they are not fish, because fish are not mammals. Fish come out of tiny eggs, and after they hatch out they must find their own food. Chickens and other birds do not feed their young on milk; their young are also hatched out of eggs. So neither fish nor birds have breasts.

A breast has one wonderful thing about the way it works; it never forms milk until there is a baby to need it. The female breast stays rather small until the female is ready to have a baby, and then the breasts get slowly larger. When the baby is born, the breasts of the mother are ready with the milk that the baby needs to grow on. The best milk for the baby is naturally the milk of its own mother, but if there is any reason why it cannot have its own mother's milk, some other can be used. That is why human babies are sometimes fed with cow's milk. A cow does not have any milk until it has had its own baby calf. But a cow is such a big animal and has so much milk, that its own calf does not need all of it and the farmer can sell the rest.

breastwork, a protective wall that is quickly put up: see FORTS AND FORTIFICATIONS.

breathing

You breathe when you take air into your lungs. This is necessary to life, because the air contains the gas called oxygen, without which you could not live. But one of the strange things about nature is that you do not have to try to breathe. You do it without thinking about it.

There are really two parts to breathing. Expanding the chest and allowing air to get into the lungs is the outside part, called *external respiration*. (Respiration is another word for breathing.) Lungs are like great sponges. If you squeeze a sponge and then let it expand under water, you can see how it soaks up the water. That is how the lungs soak up air when your muscles swell up your chest.

The second important part of breath-

BREATHING

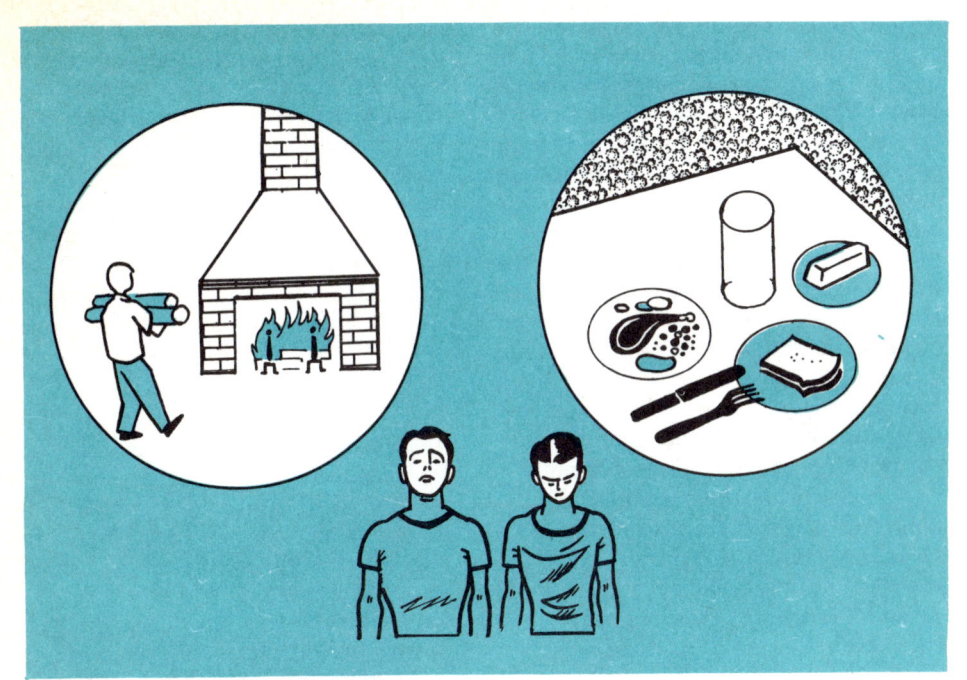

Above: For a fire to burn well it needs air and fuel. Your body needs air and food, which is the body's fuel. When you breathe in, your body gets oxygen to burn its fuel. When you breathe out, your body gets rid of waste carbon dioxide. *Right:* 1. This is the path breath takes from the mouth to the lungs. 2. A bronchial tube ends in many air sacs. 3. Air sacs swell when they are filled with air. 4. The air sac and capillaries exchange oxygen and carbon dioxide at the same time. 5. Lungs shrink when air is expelled, and swell like balloons when air is taken in.

ing is what takes place after your lungs are filled with air. This is the inside or unseen part of breathing, called *internal respiration*. The lungs are full of tiny tubes into which the air goes. At the ends of these lung tubes are tiny sacs called *alveoli*. Each sac is surrounded by a blood vessel that has very thin walls. The walls are so thin that the oxygen of the air can go right through them into the blood. The blood carries it to every part of the body. (See the article on BLOOD.)

The body does not use all the oxygen

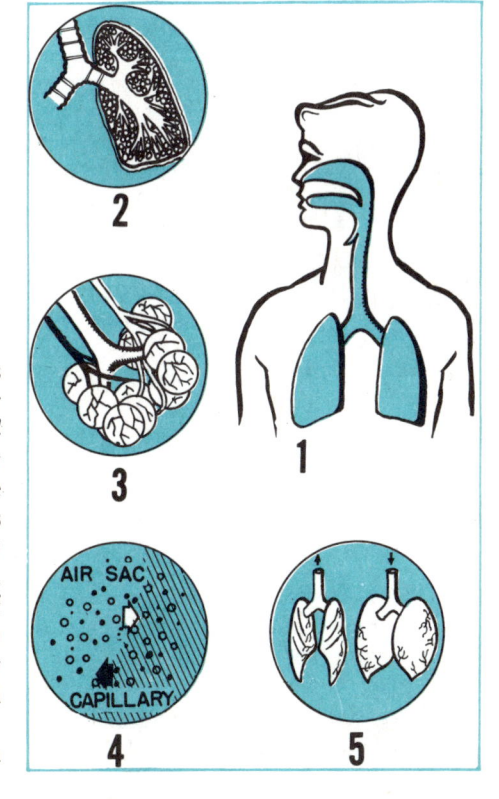

in the air we breathe in. Some of the oxygen combines with carbon from the body to form the gas called *carbon dioxide*. This gas is part of the air we breathe out. This is an equally important part of breathing, the same two steps only backward. The blood carries the carbon dioxide back to the lungs, to the thin-walled alveoli. It passes through the thin walls of the blood vessels, and back into the tubes. When you squeeze the air out of your lungs, out goes the carbon dioxide, and you are ready for your next breath, ready to take in fresh oxygen and start all over again. You do this, without thinking, about 20 times a minute.

A person who stops breathing for too long will die, but the articles on ARTIFICIAL RESPIRATION and IRON LUNG tell some of the ways that have been found to save the lives of those who have lost the power to breathe for themselves.

Breckinridge, John

Breckinridge is the name of a very prominent family of Kentucky. Several members have served as congressmen and senators. The most famous was John Cabell Breckinridge, who was the Democratic candidate for president in 1860 and lost to Abraham Lincoln. He then turned to the Confederate States, serving as a major general in the Confederate Army and (in 1865) was Secretary of War in the cabinet of President Jefferson Davis. He was born in 1821 and died in 1875.

Breda, Treaty of

Breda is the name of a city in Holland that is famous in history because many important political conferences took place there. One of these conferences was in 1667, at the end of a war between the Dutch and English. The treaty that they signed, together with France and Denmark, was called the Treaty of Breda.

Under the terms of the treaty, the Dutch kept Dutch Guiana in South America; the French got New Brunswick, Canada; and the English got the American colonies of New York (New Amsterdam), New Jersey and Delaware, and several islands in the West Indies. See the separate article on the DUTCH WARS.

breeding

Breeding is a way of making our plants and animals better by carefully choosing their parents. For example, if you are raising corn you want all of it to be good, with large, healthy ears of corn. You would save the seed from the plants with the best ears. Then the next year you would plant only that seed. It would grow into another crop of corn, and this time the corn would be better than the year before because the seed came from the best plants. This is called "selected seed." Now you would do the same thing again, so that the third season your corn would be even better, because it came from better seed. You could do this any number of seasons, and each time the seed would be taken from the best plants and your corn would keep getting better.

Now let us suppose that you live in a very cold country, and it is hard to grow corn because the frost kills it. But you notice that the frost does not kill all the corn; a few plants grow pretty well in spite of the cold. So you take the seed only from those hardy plants, and next season you plant that seed. Another crop grows, and this time there are many more plants that can survive the cold. You do the same thing again, and after a few seasons you have bred corn that will grow in a cold climate.

All living things, plants and animals and human beings too, inherit certain traits from their parents. In a family, some

BREEDING

INBRED PARENT STRAINS

B DETASSELED PRODUCES   **A** FURNISHES POLLEN   **C** DETASSELED PRODUCES   **D** FURNISHES POLLEN

SINGLE CROSS   SINGLE CROSS

(B x A) DETASSELED   (C x D) FURNISHES POLLEN

(B x A) x (C x D) PRODUCES

REPRESENTATIVE EARS OF THE CROP PRODUCED

U.S.D.A.

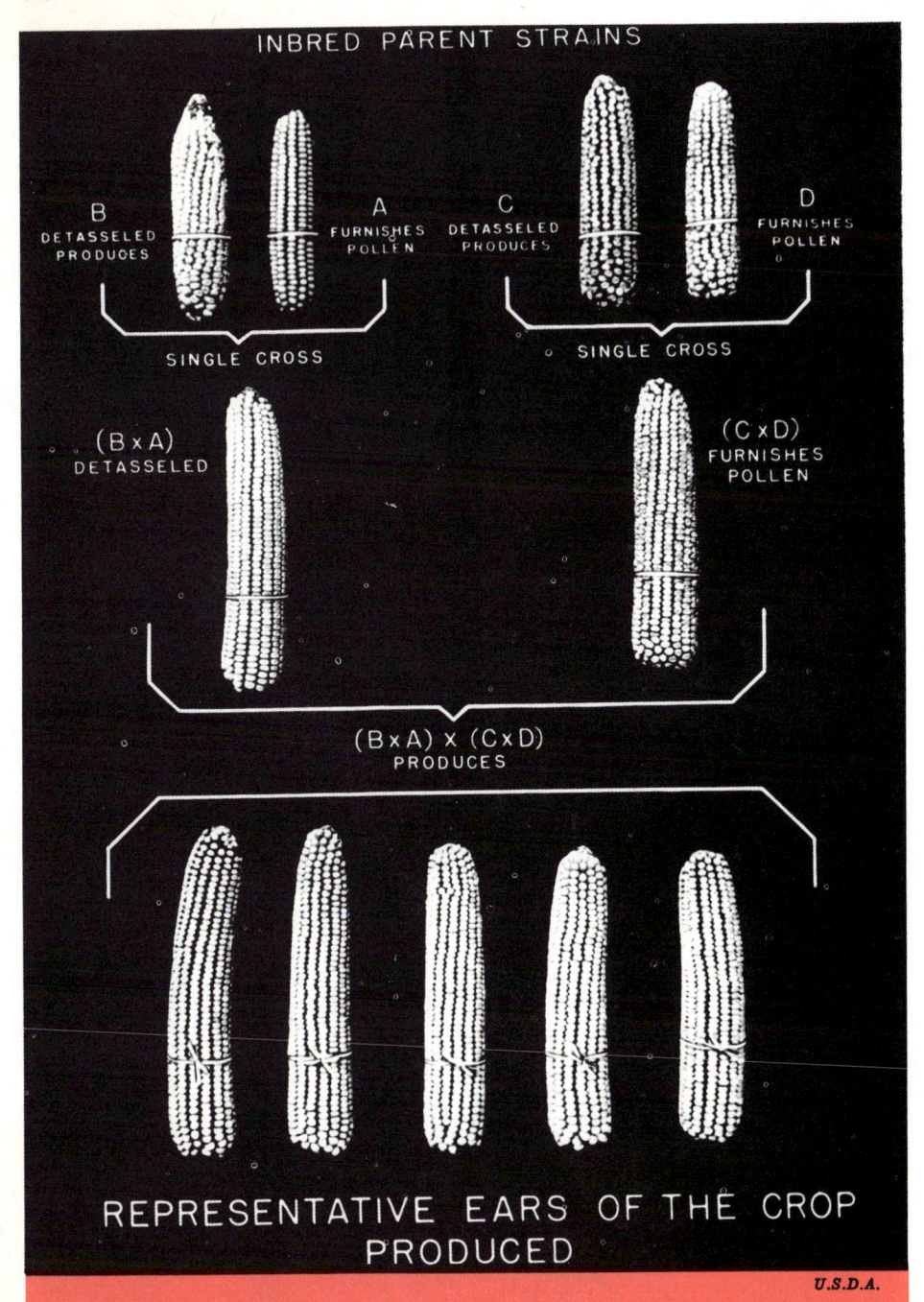

Crossbreeding of good corn has resulted in bigger and better crops. The two kinds of corn in the upper left were crossbred, as were the two in the upper right. Each crossbreeding produced a new corn (center). Then these two new corns were crossbred, and from that came the fine corn crop at the bottom. Hardier and better crops of all kinds have been developed by farmers through crossbreeding. It is a delicate process that farmers have learned through modern farming.

BREEDING

A crossbred calf poses with its mother (left) and its father (right). The parents come from two excellent breeds. The calf weighed 76 pounds when it was born, which is heavier than the average calf. It has the best qualities of both its parents.

U.S.D.A.

of the children look like the father, some look like the mother, and some look a little like each. See the article on HEREDITY.

Suppose you are raising horses, and you need two kinds. You want one kind to be very fast for racing, and the other kind to be big and strong to pull heavy trucks and wagons. You would see that the parents of the race horses were fast runners, and not too big and heavy.

You would want your truck horses to be heavy and strong, even if they could not run fast like the race horses, so you would select big, strong parents for them.

Now suppose you wanted a horse that had some of the qualities of the race horse and some of the qualities of the truck horse. You wanted a type of horse to pull a light wagon fairly fast. The race horse would be too nervous and high-strung, and not strong enough; and the truck horse would be too big and heavy and slow, and would not need half its strength. You would therefore breed horses from a combination of the race horse and the truck horse, so that some of the colts would inherit part of the speed and part of the strength of their parents. Then by breeding only those colts with the right combination of speed and strength, you would eventually get the kind of horse you wanted.

U.S.D.A.

A tomato that is excellent for canning and a tomato that can resist certain diseases were crossbred. It resulted in this big tomato that has both qualities.

WHAT BREEDING IS USED FOR

Breeding has been known since ancient times. Modern scientific breeding is based upon the discoveries of Gregor Johann Mendel, about ninety years ago, called the "Mendelian Law" of heredity. Today we breed sheep so that they will give us more and better wool, cattle for better milk and meat, and hogs, dogs, and almost every kind of domesticated animal. When no further change is wanted, the breeders keep the "strain" by always using the same type of parents. Then we have what is called a "pure-bred" strain of animals, or "pure-line" plants.

When we "crossbreed," or mix parents of pure strains, we have what is known as a *hybrid*. Hybrids can be stronger and better than either parent.

Bremen

Bremen is one of the largest, most important cities in West Germany. It has a population of about half a million. Bremen is chiefly a trade center. It is on the Weser River, which is not deep enough for big ships. Ocean freighters dock at the North Sea port of Bremerhaven, 46 miles away.

Bremen is more than 1,100 years old, and some of its streets and houses date back hundreds of years. In the Middle Ages it joined other towns in a strong trade association, the HANSEATIC LEAGUE, about which there is a separate article. Much of Bremen was destroyed during World War II, but it has since been rebuilt.

BREMEN, GERMANY. Population 546,107. Trade center on the Weser River.

Brenner Pass

For hundreds of years the Brenner Pass has been the most important route across the Alps, the highest mountains in Europe. Although it is 4,000 feet high, the Brenner Pass is the lowest gap in these great mountains. It connects Innsbruck, Austria, with Bolzano, in northeastern Italy. In 1772 a road for carriages was built across the pass, and in 1867 a railroad was opened.

In the village of Brennero at the top of the pass, Hitler and Mussolini, the German and Italian dictators, held a meeting on March 18, 1940. They met in a train standing in the railroad station, and agreed on plans for Italy to enter World War II on Germany's side. They held several other conferences in the Pass during the war.

Breslau

Breslau is the German name for the Polish city of Wroclaw in the region called Lower Silesia. It is now a city of about 450,000, on the Oder River. A thousand years ago Breslau was a Polish city; but many Germans settled there and in 1742 Breslau was made part of Prussia. It became almost entirely a German city, a large and important one. Just before World War II in 1939, Breslau had a population of more than 600,000; it was a manufacturing center for woolen and cotton goods, jewelry, machinery, and many other products, and it had beautiful churches and other buildings and a famous university.

In 1945 when Germany was losing World War II, Breslau was almost wholly destroyed by Russians attacking the city and Germans defending it. After the war the city was given to Poland and resumed its ancient name Wroclaw. Nearly all the Germans left the city and the population dropped to about 100,000. The Poles then rebuilt the city and nearly all of the present large population is Polish.

Brest

Brest is an important seaport city in France, on the tip of the peninsula of Brittany. It is on the Bay of Brest, which forms one of the finest harbors in the world. The only way ships can get from the Atlantic Ocean to this bay is through a narrow channel, scarcely a mile wide, called *Le Goulet*. More than 110,000 people live in Brest. Many of them work in factories, making paper, cork, candles, and soap. In World War II, the Germans captured Brest, and made it an important submarine base. The base was greatly damaged by bombings, and was recaptured by the Americans in 1944.

BREST, FRANCE. Population 110,713. In the department of Finistère.

Breughel

Three famous artists had nicknames which show how differently each one painted. Pieter Breughel, the father, was called "Peasant," because instead of painting pictures of important people, he painted farmers working in their fields and children playing games. His son Pieter was called "Hell" because his pictures were full of devils and witches. His son Jan was nicknamed "Velvet" because he painted beautiful flowers and garden scenes.

The Breughels are called Flemish artists. Flanders, where they lived, was a part of Holland, but now is a part of Belgium. Their three lives covered about a hundred years: the father lived from 1525 to 1569; Pieter the younger lived from 1564 to 1637; and Jan from 1568 to 1625.

Your museum has copies of Father Breughel's famous picture *Children at Play*. Look at this and see how many different games you can recognize, and which games children are still playing after four hundred years.

breviary

The breviary is a book of daily prayers that is used in the Roman Catholic Church. The book contains hymns, psalms, and prayers for each day of the year. The breviary is also divided into four parts for spring, summer, autumn, and winter. This book of prayers was once very long, but about seven hundred years ago, Pope Gregory IX ordered that it be made shorter. The Latin word for shortening is *breviary,* and that is how the book got its name.

brewing, a process for making ale or beer: see BEER.

Brewster, William

William Brewster was the religious leader of the Pilgrims, who came to America in 1620. He was born in England in 1566. In those days people who did not believe in the Church of England were not allowed to worship in their own way. When Brewster set up his own church, he was put in jail. Later he and others went to Holland, hoping to find religious freedom. When they did not find it there, these people, the Pilgrims, set sail for the New World. (You can read about the PILGRIMS and their ship, the Mayflower, in a separate article.)

In Plymouth Colony, Massachusetts, Brewster became the head of the church, and for nine years he was the only one to hold religious services. He was one of the most respected men in the community when he died in 1644. Many of his descendants are still living in New England.

Briand, Aristide

Aristide Briand was a French statesman famous for his work toward world peace. He suggested in 1927 that war be called an international crime, and that a nation which declared war should be treated as an outlaw. This idea became the Briand-Kellogg Pact, which by 1929 had been signed by 45 nations. Unfortunately, some of the nations later broke their word and started wars.

Briand was born in 1862. His first fame came in 1905, when he wrote the law separating church and state in France. The French government had favored the Catholic religion, but this new law gave a person of any religion, or none, the same rights as any other citizen.

Briand was French premier eleven times, more often than any other man of his time. He served twenty-five times as a cabinet minister. In 1926 he won the Nobel peace prize for his work on the Locarno Treaty, which was another attempt to prevent wars in Europe. Briand also suggested what the American patriot, Thomas Paine, had proposed a century before—a United States of Europe. Briand thought nations should settle their differences by discussion and cooperation, instead of by war. He died in 1932, at the age of 70.

bribery

Getting someone to do a wrong thing by offering him special favors or money is called bribery. The favor or money is called a bribe. Bribery is very wrong, and is a serious crime. Both the man who offers a bribe and the man who takes it are criminals. When people talk about "corrupt" men, they may mean that these men are willing to take bribes. A corrupt judge, for instance, would take a bribe to free a prisoner who is guilty and should be punished. A corrupt athlete would take a bribe to lose a game. The man who bribed him would probably be a gambler who had bet a lot of money on the athlete's opponent to win.

brick

A brick is a block of clay that has been baked to make it hard. Bricks have been one of the best and most popular building materials for thousands of years. First, men used sun-dried bricks, which you can read about in the article ADOBE. Then men learned that bricks would last hundreds of years longer if they were baked under great heat in an oven called a *kiln*.

Modern bricks are made by machinery, but the method is not much different from the one used for handmade bricks in past centuries. First, wet clay is pressed into the desired shape, which is usually 8 inches long, 3¾ inches wide, and 2¼ inches thick. Many of these bricks are put in the kiln and are baked for days or

People in the Near East and in the Orient still make bricks as their ancestors did thousands of years ago. A brick-maker packs mud and plant fibers into wooden forms. The soft mud bakes in the hot sun and hardens. The fibers help to make the bricks stronger by holding the clay together. This old-fashioned method is very slow but still works satisfactorily.

The first step in modern brick-making is to take the lumpy clay that has been dug from the earth, and feed it into a large crushing machine that breaks it up.

KIDC

A moving belt carries the crushed clay to another machine that grinds it into a fine dust. This finely ground dust, properly mixed with water and sometimes with coloring matter, is used for brick-making.

BRICK

Above: These bricks have been drying for 30 hours at 240 degrees. Now they are ready to be put into a kiln that has a temperature of 2,250 degrees.
Left: Bricks are sealed into the kiln for five and a half days. The doors are sealed up with bricks and cement. *Right:* The bricks then cool for three days before they are taken from the kiln.

even weeks at a temperature of 2000 degrees (on the Fahrenheit thermometer) or even higher. Different kinds of clay produce different colors of brick—red, yellow, brown, and other colors. Red brick gets its color from iron in the clay. This clay is the most plentiful, so most bricks are red. A brick weighs 4 to 5 pounds.

BRICKLAYING

Putting bricks together to make a wall or other structure is called *bricklaying*. A bricklayer is a skilled craftsman. He takes a brick, strikes it with his trowel to see if it "rings" (because a cracked brick will give a dull sound), and lays it in place. With the same trowel he spreads *mortar*, a kind of cement, which will harden and hold the bricks together. Bricklayers trying for a record have laid as many as two thousand bricks in a day, but usually a bricklayer lays about six hundred bricks a day.

Some of the earliest houses in America were made from bricks brought from Europe as ballast in the holds of ships.

It is easy to see how the camel-back bridge got its name.

bridge

A bridge is a roadway that goes over a body of water, a valley or ravine, or a highway or street. It is used by people on foot, in automobiles or on railroad trains. A bridge that is used by people only is called a footbridge. A bridge used by cars only is called a highway bridge. A bridge used only by railroads is called a railway bridge. Some bridges can be used by both people and cars, by people and railroads, or by all three.

Bridges are made of wood, stone, concrete, or steel. The first bridge that man ever used was a fallen log. Thousands of years ago a tree fell over a stream, connecting one bank with the other. A man probably saw it and found that he could go across the stream by walking on the log, instead of swimming or wading. He soon learned that he could chop down a tree and place it across a stream that he wanted to cross.

Then he learned that he could place logs across any stream. If the stream was very wide, he would place two or maybe three logs end to end, with large rocks in between them to hold them up. He would place a log from one shore to a rock or a pile of rocks in the stream, and a log from the rocks to the other shore. These rocks were the first bridge *piers.*

A pier is a stone, wood, concrete or steel structure placed in the middle or near the middle of a river or stream to support a bridge. The pier is usually sunk deep into the rock or earth beneath the water to hold it steady. The top of the pier sticks out of the water and holds up the bridge. By using piers, it is possible to make a bridge over a stream no matter how wide the stream is.

The first log bridges were sometimes difficult to walk over. A log is round, and can be slippery when wet. Many persons would tumble into the water when trying to walk over a narrow log. In order to make it safer to cross a stream, several logs were placed across the stream, side by side. This made the bridge wider and easier to cross. To keep the logs from slipping apart, pieces of wood were tied or nailed across them. This type of bridge is still used across small streams in the country. It is called a *girder bridge.*

At first, bridges were anchored to the shore by sinking them into the ground or fastening them to rocks. But when there were no rocks nearby and the ground was too hard to sink a log into, something else had to be done. Logs and rocks were placed near the edge of the water, against the bank. This kept the earth from sliding into the water, and made a firm support for the ends of a bridge. Such a support is called an *abutment*. An abutment supports a bridge at its ends. Nowadays it is made of concrete or stone, instead of logs.

All bridges that go across water have some kind of abutment at each end to support them. But only bridges that go across wide rivers and streams have piers. Very few of the bridges we see about us look like the first girder bridge that was made thousands of years ago. Since the first bridge was made, many different kinds of bridge have been built. Bridges must be strong enough to carry heavy loads, often hundreds of thousands of pounds. They must be able to stand up against high winds, and extreme changes in temperature. In order to do this, bridges are usually made of steel with a concrete or paved roadway. Different types of bridge have different ways of supporting the roadway. These types have different names. In the pictures with this article, you can see many types of bridge. The most important types will be described in the rest of this article.

Bridges are either *fixed* or *movable*. A movable bridge is one which can be opened in order to let high boats and ships pass beneath them. Bridges which do not open are called fixed briges. There are five types of fixed bridge.

INDEPENDENT SPAN BRIDGE

An independent span bridge is a fixed bridge which extends from one abutment to another without any pier to support it. The only supports for the bridge are the abutments at the ends. The span of a bridge is that part which is between two supports. An independent span bridge has a roadway supported by steel beams or trusses. Trusses are constructed in a crisscross fashion like a lot of x's next to one another. The trusses are usually above the roadway.

CONTINUOUS SPAN BRIDGE

The continuous span bridge is a fixed bridge with a long concrete roadway supported by several piers placed in the water between shores. These piers are long steel or concrete pillars or columns. They are sunk deep into the bottom of a river when the bridge is over a river. When the bridge goes across a highway, the piers rest on the highway below.

ARCH BRIDGE

The arch bridge is a fixed bridge, and is one of the oldest types of bridge in the world. It is also one of the most graceful. It was used as far back as the times of the Romans, more than two thousand years ago. It is made of steel, stone, or concrete. In concrete, steel, or stone arch bridges, the arch is underneath the roadway, and supports it from below. In some steel arch bridges, the arch rises into the air somtimes 500 feet above the water. The roadway is beneath the arch.

The George Westinghouse Memorial Bridge on the Lincoln Highway in Pittsburgh, Pennsylvania, is one of the best examples of a bridge with arches below the roadway. The Kill van Kull bridge, connecting Bayonne, New Jersey, with Staten Island, New York, is the longest arch bridge in the world. It has a steel arch above the roadway and is 1,652 feet long.

LONDON BRIDGE

In ancient times, the arch and the roadway were the same and were made of stone. They went over small bodies of water, and were usually less than 100 feet long. The Old London Bridge in England, built more than seven hundred years ago, was an arch bridge. It had towers at either end to prevent enemy soldiers from going across the bridge. Soldiers were placed in the towers to guard the bridge entrances. Homes and stores were also built on the bridge. In the middle of the thirteenth century, some of the homes caught fire and blocked both entrances to the bridge. To escape the fire about three thousand persons jumped off the bridge and were drowned.

BRIDGE

Below: The stone bridge is used to span narrow rivers. *Right:* Nature made this magnificent bridge in Utah, called Rainbow Bridge.

Santa Fe Ry.

Below: A swing or pivot bridge. *Left:* Coleman Bridge, in Virginia, is made of steel. The two parts of the bridge swing open and shut by machinery.

Va. Chamber of Comm.

Standard Oil Co.

Below: A vertical-lift bridge, used for carrying heavy traffic. *Right:* A tanker passes under a lift bridge at Newark, New Jersey.

BRIDGE

844

Below: The rigid-frame bridge, used over small streams. *Right:* A stone bridge of the same construction in Switzerland.

Below: The Roman arch or aqueduct bridge. *Right:* This railroad bridge in Pennsylvania is the longest of its kind.

Below: The primitive trestle bridge, supported by legs of wood. *Right:* A covered trestle bridge in Pennsylvania.

Below: A bascule or drawbridge. *Right:* The Burnside Bridge in Portland, Oregon, is raised to let a ship pass through.

Swiss Nat'l Travel Office

Pa. Dep't. of Commerce

Portland Chamber of Commerce

845 BRIDGE

Port of N.Y. Authority

Canadian Pac. Railway

Bethlehem Steel Co.

Below: A bridge with a steel arch and a roadway suspended from it. *Left:* Bayonne Bridge, New Jersey, the longest of this kind.

Below: A steel suspension bridge. *Left:* The George Washington bridge spans the Hudson River between New York and New Jersey.

Below: A cantilever bridge has a system of steel girders supported by steel beams. *Left:* The Quebec Bridge in Canada.

Below: A railroad trestle bridge supported by steel legs. *Left:* Chesapeake Bridge, Maryland, is of similar construction.

BRIDGE

CANTILEVER BRIDGE

The cantilever bridge is a fixed bridge with long steel arms extending outward from opposite shores. These arms or *cantilevers* are made of steel girders which support the roadway from above and below. The cantilevers rest on steel piers. The longest bridge of this type is the Quebec bridge in Canada over the St. Lawrence River. This bridge is 1,800 feet long.

SUSPENSION BRIDGE

The suspension bridge is a fixed bridge, and is the longest type of bridge in the world. It is made of long, strong, steel cables which are connected to the shore, and which rise up to high steel towers. These towers are supported by cables anchored in the banks. From the steel cables hang strong vertical steel cables which hold up the roadway of the bridge. The roadway hangs or is suspended from the cables, and this is why

Italian State Tourist Off.

San Francisco Chamber of Comm.

Roger Dudley

Italian State Tourist Off.

1. People in gondolas pass under the famous Bridge of Sighs, in Venice, Italy.
2. The Ponte Vecchio, in Florence, Italy, has many leather and jewelry shops right on the bridge over the Arno River.
3. The beautiful Golden Gate Bridge at San Francisco was the longest suspension bridge in the world when it was built. It is 6,400 feet long and has six traffic lanes.
4. Outside Seattle, Washington, is the Lake Washington Floating Bridge.
5. Many bridges cross the canals in Venice, where colorful events take place.

Cinerama

the bridge is called a suspension bridge. The longest suspension bridges are the Verrazano bridge over the Narrows between Brooklyn and Staten Island in New York City, with a span of 4,260 feet, and the Golden Gate bridge over the water separating the Pacific Ocean from San Francisco, California, with a span of 4,200 feet.

The largest bridge in the world is actually the Bay bridge that connects San Francisco with Oakland, California. It is a combination of suspension bridges and cantilever bridges. The entire bridge is 8 miles long. It was finished in 1936.

The George Washington bridge, spanning the Hudson River between New York and New Jersey, is another famous suspension bridge. It is 3,500 feet long.

There are three important types of movable bridge. None of these bridges is very long, the longest being about 500 feet.

SWING SPAN BRIDGE

The swing span bridge is a movable bridge with a large pier in the middle supporting it. When boats or ferries wish to pass beneath it, the bridge swings around in a semi-circle on the pier, like a swivel chair. The boats can then pass on either side of the pier through the section that the bridge previously occupied.

BASCULE BRIDGE

The bascule bridge is a movable bridge with two sections of roadway, separated at the middle and each half connected to opposite abutments. These sections are called *leaves*. The leaves can be raised straight up into the air. There is a famous painting by Vincent Van Gogh, called *The Drawbridge,* which shows an old-fashioned bascule bridge in Holland. A bascule bridge with only one section is called a drawbridge. It was used during medieval times to span moats surrounding castles. These moats were small streams that separated the castle from the surrounding land.

VERTICAL LIFT BRIDGE

The vertical lift bridge is a movable bridge which has a roadway that can be raised and lowered by an elevator at each end of the bridge. One of the most famous bridges of this type is the Buzzard's Bay bridge over the Cape Cod canal. It is 544 feet long.

MILITARY BRIDGES

When soldiers wish to cross a stream where there is no bridge, they put together a kind of floating bridge called a *pontoon* bridge. The pontoons are bags of rubber or skin filled with air so that they can float on the water. They are a kind of floating pier. Mostly, however, wooden or aluminum floats are used for heavy traffic. They are placed a few feet apart from one shore to the other. A wooden roadway is then set on them so that soldiers and equipment can be taken across.

Although such bridges are mostly used for military operations, there are a few which have been constructed for civilian traffic. The most famous is across Lake Washington, at Seattle.

The Bailey bridge, invented by Donald Coleman Bailey of England, is another type of bridge used in military operations. It can be easily put together and stretched across a stream. It is strong enough to carry heavy trucks and tanks.

bridge, a game of cards: see CONTRACT BRIDGE.

bridgehead

An army must often cross a river to attack an enemy. To do this, it must build a bridge. The engineers build the bridge, but other units of the army—the infantry and the artillery—must first control a place on both sides of the river, so that the engineers can build the bridge and the rest of the army can be safe when they cross it. A position on a river that is controlled by the attacking army is called a *bridgehead.*

Bridgeport

Bridgeport is an important manufacturing city in Connecticut, on Long Island Sound, 56 miles northeast of New York City. Bridgeport is the 2nd-largest city in Connecticut, with more than 156,000 people living there. Most of the people work in factories and plants that make more than five thousand different products. Bridgeport manufactures typewriters, sewing machines, electrical supplies, and many other useful things.

Bridgeport also has many beautiful parks and fine schools. One of the most interesting places to see there is the Barnum Institute, which is a museum filled with things that belonged to P. T. Barnum, the man who started the famous Barnum and Bailey circus. You can read about P. T. BARNUM in a separate article.

Bridgeport was settled more than three hundred years ago, and rapidly grew into a thriving town. In World War I and World War II it supplied the armed forces with guns and ammunition.

BRIDGEPORT, CONNECTICUT. Population, 156,748 (1960 census). On Long Island Sound. Settled 1639.

Bridges, Robert

Robert Bridges was an English poet. He was also a doctor, and he practiced medicine until he was 38 years old. Then he decided to spend the rest of his life writing poetry.

He was born in 1844. He went to school at Eton and to college at Oxford. His first poems were not very interesting to most people, but he later became more popular. Some of his best poems are very happy and lyrical, but others are also very difficult to understand. They are called "experimental," because in them he tried to work out new ways of writing poetry. They are also called "philosophical," because he tried to combine the ancient beliefs of religion with the new theories of science. His last poem is perhaps his greatest. It is called *The Testament of Beauty*.

Bridges became so famous before he died (in 1930), that his government made him the official POET LAUREATE, which is a very great honor that you can read about in a separate article.

brig

A brig is a small sailing ship with two masts. A two-masted ship of the same kind, but with a different arrangement of sails, is called a *brigantine*. A brig was considered a very fast ship in the days of sailing vessels, and was often used by pirates, who could use it to chase and catch the bigger ships they wanted to capture. The word *brig* is also used for a prison cell on any ship, where prisoners are kept until the ship reaches shore and they can be turned over to the police.

Bright, John

John Bright was a great English statesman, and a Member of Parliament. He fought against many injustices that rich and powerful men forced upon poor

The brig was a familiar sight on the high seas in the days before the steamship.

people during his time, which was about a hundred years ago. He is best remembered in the United States because during the Civil War he was for the North and against slavery. Most people in England favored the South. Bright was born in 1811 and was a Member of Parliament from the time he was 32 years old until he was a very old man. He died in 1889, at the age of 78.

Brisbane

Brisbane is the capital city of the state of Queensland, in Australia. About 578,000 people live there, and it is one of the most important cities in Australia. It is a large manufacturing center, as well as a port. The Brisbane River runs through the city and down to the Moreton Bay, about 15 miles away. Many beautiful bridges cross the river. One of the most beautiful is the Victoria Bridge. There are also many parks and impressive government buildings in Brisbane.

When Brisbane was first settled, in 1824, it was a colony for convicts. But the colony was broken up soon after that, and Brisbane became a city about thirty years later. Brisbane is very modern, and living there is much like living in any medium-sized city of the United States.

bristle

Bristles are short, stiff hairs from the back of a hog, from the manes and tails of horses, or from plants. They are used in paintbrushes, toothbrushes, and many other brushes. Artificial bristles are made of nylon. The United States uses millions of brushes every year, and imports tons of bristles to make them. One reason the United States does not raise its own bristles is that pigs are slaughtered for food before the bristles are long enough. At first, we imported them from Russia, but after the revolution there, the quality was not as good. We imported them from China after that.

Australian News & Inform. Bureau
The City Hall in Brisbane, Australia, has a tower 300 feet high. The palm trees show that the city has a warm climate.

The supply of bristles from China was cut off by World War II. The United States government declared bristles to be a strategic war material. The Air Force flew whatever bristles could be found in Free China over the mountains to India, then they were flown or shipped to America. But we still did not have enough. Horse hair from Argentina, plant hairs from Mexico, and nylon were used instead. After the war, the United States again imported bristles from China. The Korean war stopped this trade, so brushmakers again turned to substitutes. Shaving brushes and paintbrushes made of the finest bristles are very expensive.

Bristol

Bristol is one of the largest cities in England. It is an important port on the Avon and Frome rivers, 119 miles west of London. More than 436,000 people live there, working on the large docks and in factories. Bristol is a busy manufacturing center. It makes airplanes, chemicals, glass, and many other useful products. It is also a very old city, and you can see a cathedral there that was built eight hundred years ago. During World War II, the Germans bombed the large factories in Bristol many times, and many of its beautiful churches are still in ruins. The University of Bristol has a famous museum of English art.

Britain

The name *Britain* comes from the ancient name of the island that is now called Great Britain. The ancient name was *Britannia,* which is Latin. The Romans invaded the island in 55 and 54 B.C., and called it Britannia. Although the native British princes resisted bravely, the stronger Romans eventually succeeded in conquering the island. British culture was far behind that of Rome, but the Romans soon established their culture in the conquered land. The ruins of Roman roads, baths, altars, and houses can still be seen in many parts of England today. Christianity was also introduced by the Romans. Before that time the people had practiced Druidism. This pagan religion is explained in the article on DRUIDS. You can read more about the history of Britain in the articles on ENGLAND, SCOTLAND, IRELAND, and WALES, in other volumes of this encyclopedia.

British Columbia

British Columbia is the westernmost province of Canada. It is covered with great mountain ranges, and its beautiful scenery has made it a popular place for people to go on their vacations. British Columbia is the third-largest Canadian province, having 366,255 square miles, which is more than twice the size of California. In population it also ranks third in Canada, estimated in 1967 to be nearly two million. The province was given its name by Queen Victoria of England. It became a province in 1871. The capital is Victoria.

THE PEOPLE OF BRITISH COLUMBIA

The early settlers of British Columbia came from Great Britain, the United States, and other parts of Canada, to seek their fortunes. Others came from Europe, especially from Germany, France, and the Scandinavian countries. Today, most of the people are Canadian-born. There are about 25,000 Indians living there. Once the Indians were the only people living in British Columbia.

The people work in many thriving industries. More than half the British Columbians live in the cities, working in large saw mills, fish canneries, and in factories making wood and lumber products. Others cut timber in the great northern forests. Many are farmers and raise poultry, fruits and vegetables, and cattle. Still others work in the rich mines. The miners produce almost all the lead in Canada, and more than half the zinc. British Columbia ranks third among the provinces of Canada in the production of copper, gold, and coal.

The Anglican or Episcopal church is the largest church in British Columbia, but there are also United Church of Canada, Roman Catholic, and Presbyterian churches.

WHAT BRITISH COLUMBIA IS LIKE

British Columbia is very mountainous. The Canadian Rockies and the Coast Range and Cascades run through it. There are many towering peaks, vast forests, beautiful waterfalls, and swift rivers, including the Fraser, Columbia, and Peace rivers. Many tourists go to British Columbia to hunt moose, deer, and bears, which are found there. They also fish for salmon, which are caught in large quantities.

In the northeastern part there is a fertile plain where much farming is done.

The official buildings in Victoria, the capital of British Columbia, are all brilliantly lighted for a national celebration.

Canadian Nat'l Ry.

There are also irrigated sections in the central and southern parts where the people raise cattle and crops. Off the southwestern coast of British Columbia is Vancouver Island, which is rich in coal. Victoria, the capital city, is on the island and is an important industrial center. It is one of the busiest ports on the Pacific Coast. The Queen Charlotte Islands are also off the coast of British Columbia.

British Columbia has a warmer climate than any other Canadian province. This is because of the warm winds from the Pacific Ocean. At Victoria, on Vancouver Island, the temperature in summer is about 65 degrees; in winter, about 37 degrees. Flowers bloom there all year round. In the north, however, the climate is much more severe, falling way below zero in winter, and becoming very hot in the summer. There is a great deal of rain in the western part of the province, but little in the central or eastern regions.

There are railroads throughout most of British Columbia, and the rivers are an important means of transportation. There are also airports in most of the large cities. The Alaska Highway was built across the northeastern section in 1942.

HOW THE PEOPLE ARE GOVERNED

The head of the government of British Columbia is a lieutenant governor, who represents the British Queen. He is appointed by the Canadian federal government. The province is actually run by a premier. He is usually the leader of the political party which elects the most members of the legislature. The premier is assisted by an executive council or cabinet that he selects from among his supporters in the legislature. The premier and his executive council stay in office as long as they can keep the confidence of the majority of the legislature. The legislature is elected for a five-year term. Judges are appointed by the Canadian government in Ottawa, and hold office for life. The provincial government is in the capital, Victoria.

Everyone has to go to school between the ages of 7 and 15. Those children who cannot attend school can get instruction through the mail. Printed lessons are sent to them at home. The children study the lessons and answer the questions. Then they send them back for correction. There is one university, the University of British Columbia, at Vancouver. In 1961 it had 11,621 students. There are four affiliated colleges in various cities with a total enrollment of 1,073.

BRITISH COLUMBIA

Canadian Pac. Ry.

A train winds its way through the magnificent mountains that rise high in British Columbia.

Standard Oil Co.

People come to British Columbia on their vacations to enjoy the beautiful scenery.

Nat'l Film Board

Many bears live in the large forests, but this one is looking for new adventures on a highway.

Canadian Pac. Ry.

Vancouver, in British Columbia, is one of the most important ports on the Pacific coast. You can take a wonderful trip by steamer from there to Alaska or to cities along the coast of California.

Canadian Pac. Ry.

A big American Indian totem pole in Stanley Park attracts many tourists.

BRITISH COLUMBIA

Canadian Gov't Travel Bureau

Every year visitors come to British Columbia to enjoy the wonderful skiing on the snow-covered mountain slopes. Some of the slopes are very steep and fast.

Nat'l Film Board

Farmers raise good crops of winter wheat in the northern part of British Columbia.

Canadian Pac. Ry.

The forests of British Columbia furnish much timber for the busy sawmills.

Canadian Nat'l Ry.

Many people work in the large fisheries, and export tons of halibut each year.

Standard Oil Co.

The sawmills cut lumber that is shipped to factories in many places.

BRITISH COLUMBIA

CHIEF CITIES IN BRITISH COLUMBIA

The leading cities of British Columbia, with population figures from the 1967 estimate, are:

Vancouver, population 410,375, the largest city, a shipping center, in the southwestern part of the province.

Victoria, population 175,000, the capital and second-largest city, trading and manufacturing center, in the southwestern part of the province.

New Westminster, population 38,000, third-largest city, manufacturing center, in the southwestern part of the province.

Trail, population 11,600, fourth-largest city, mining center, in the southern part of the province.

BRITISH COLUMBIA IN THE PAST

When Captain James Cook and his men landed on Vancouver Island more than 175 years ago, they found friendly Indians living there. They exchanged blankets and other articles for furs, and a flourishing British fur trade began at Nootka. However, the Spanish claimed that this part of the coast belonged to them, and they took possession of Nootka in 1789. This almost brought about a war between Great Britain and Spain, but it was finally settled peacefully, and both countries were given equal rights to trade there.

Other trading posts were started by Canadians and men from the United States, and settlers began to come to this region. Arguments sprang up between the British and Americans about who had the right to this territory. Many Americans felt that the United States had the right to the western coast of Canada up to the line on the map marked 54 degrees 40 minutes latitude. The cry in the United States was "54–40 or fight." However, the matter was settled peacefully. In 1846 the boundary between British Columbia and the Oregon Territory was fixed, and British Columbia became a British possession.

Very few settlers came to this territory until gold was discovered in 1858. Then people began rushing to British Columbia to seek their fortunes. The population grew so quickly that it became a British colony in the same year. Vancouver Island was joined to it eight years later, and in 1871 it became a province. However, British Columbia agreed to become a province only on condition that the Canadian government would build a railroad to the Pacific coast. It was very difficult to build the railroad, because of the high mountains, but finally it was completed in 1885.

More people now came to the province, and its mining and lumber industries grew rapidly. British Columbia also became important for its salmon fisheries. Trade flourished and cities grew. In World War II, the province supplied many valuable products to the war effort. Today British Columbia ships products from its mines, factories, and farms to places all over the world.

PLACES TO SEE

Glacier National Park, 521 square miles, in southeastern British Columbia, in the Selkirk Mountains, west of State Highway 95. Snow-capped peaks and glaciers; contains Nakimu Caves and Mt. Bonney, 10,194 feet high.

Kootenay National Park, 543 square miles, in southeastern British Columbia, in the Canadian Rockies, on State Highway 1B. Forests and deep canyons, including Marble Canyon.

Mount Revelstoke National Park, 100 square miles, in southeastern British Columbia, in the Selkirk Mountains, on State Highway 1. Large forest of virgin timber.

Yoho National Park, 507 square miles, in eastern British Columbia, in the Canadian Rockies, on State Highway 1. Waterfalls and lakes, including Emerald Lake; Mt. Gordon, 10,346 feet high.

Mount Fairweather, in the northwest, on the boundary between British Columbia and Alaska. The highest point in the province, 15,318 feet high; slopes covered with glaciers.

Water Route from Vancouver to Alaska, off the west coast of British Columbia. One of the most beautiful boat trips in the world.

[British] Commonwealth

The Commonwealth is the official name for a large group of nations that coöperate in trade and financial matters. It was formerly called the Commonwealth of Nations, and most people call it the British Commonwealth because its members were once part of the British Empire.

Members of the Commonwealth are independent nations, but the Commonwealth also includes *dependencies*. A dependency usually governs itself locally but in some matters is controlled by one of the independent nations.

The Commonwealth is a vast thing, covering one-fourth of all the land and also one-fourth of all the people on earth.

In 1966 twenty-seven nations were either members or had agreed to join the Commonwealth during the year. Twenty-two of them were already members at the end of 1965: the United Kingdom (England, Scotland, Wales, and Northern Ireland, often simply called "Britain"); ten other countries that recognize the same queen as Britain: Canada, Australia, New Zealand, Jamaica, Trinidad and Tobago, Ceylon, Malta, Sierra Leone, Malawi and the Gambia; ten republics: India, Pakistan, Singapore, Cyprus, Ghana, Nigeria, Kenya, Uganda, Zambia, and Tanzania; and one monarchy, Malaysia, that elects its own king. The five newly independent nations becoming members in 1966 were Botswana (former Bechuanaland), Lesotho (former Basutoland), Swaziland, Guyana (former British Guiana) and Mauritius.

Member nations of the Commonwealth insist that Southern Rhodesia is still a member, because, they say, it was illegal for Southern Rhodesia to declare itself independent in 1965. See RHODESIA.

The British queen (or king) is the head of the Commonwealth. She is the head of the state in the member nations of which she is queen, but except in the United Kingdom she is represented in each of these nations by a Governor General selected by the country's government. The position of the Queen or Governor General is called "the Crown." The parliament of each country has all the actual power and the Crown must be neutral in politics, but the Crown can often have great influence as an impartial and respected guide when the country's political leaders cannot agree.

DEPENDENCIES

There are several kinds of dependency, and since most of the dependencies within the Commonwealth are those of the United Kingdom, it is easiest to describe the British dependencies first.

A *Crown Colony* is a possession, just like part of the home country. In a *Protectorate* the British government has considerable power. A *Protected State* has made a treaty giving the British government certain rights, especially in foreign affairs and in wartime. A *Trust Territory* is administered (governed) by the British or other Commonwealth nation but under the rules agreed upon with the United Nations.

United Kingdom dependencies are:

ISLANDS *(all colonies except as stated)*: St. Helena, Ascension, Tristan da Cunha, South Georgia, and the Falkland Islands, in the South Atlantic; Bermuda, the Bahamas and the British West Indies, in the Western Atlantic; Pitcairn, the Gilbert and Ellice Islands, Fiji, the Solomons *(Protectorate)* and Tonga *(Protected State)* in the Pacific, plus the New Hebrides Islands, ruled jointly with France (this is called a *condominium*); Seychelles, Socotia, Chagos and Rodriguez, and Christmas, in the Indian Ocean.

IN ASIA *(all colonies)*: Aden, in South Arabia; Hong Kong, off the China coast; the Protectorate of South Arabia and Bahrain, Qatar, and the Trucial States of the Persian Gulf *(Protected States)*.

IN AFRICA. *Protectorates:* parts of Kenya, and Gambia. *Colonies:* parts of Kenya, and Gambia.

OTHERS *(colonies)*: Gibraltar and British Honduras.

BRITISH EMPIRE

COMMONWEALTH DEPENDENCIES

AUSTRALIA'S colonies include: Antarctic Territory; Territory of Ashmore and Cartier Islands, including Heard and McDonald Islands; Norfolk Island, Cocos-Keeling Islands, Christmas Island, and Papua. Trust Territories are New Guinea and Nauru Island.

INDIA has Sikkim (protectorate). Also claims the disputed state of Kashmir-Jammu, on the border with Pakistan.

NEW ZEALAND has Ross Dependency in Antarctica and the Union or Tokelau Islands.

British Empire was the name given to the part of the world ruled by Great Britain before the formation of the Commonwealth. See BRITISH COMMONWEALTH.

British Guiana (Guyana)

Guyana, a new nation that achieved independence as of 1966, was called British Guiana during the many years (since 1783) that it was a colony of Great Britain. It is in South America, on the Atlantic Ocean between Venezuela and Surinam. The area is 82,997 square miles and the population in 1964 was 628,000.

Most of the people are East Indians (originally from India) and Negroes. They live along the coast, the most modern part, where the capital, Georgetown (population 148,000 in 1960) is. Most of the people are farmers. They raise sugar, rice, and coffee. Bauxite is mined, and also gold and diamonds in the mountains. In the interior there are large tropical forests, where savage American Indians and Negroes live. The climate is very hot and damp.

British Honduras

British Honduras is a colony in Central America that belongs to Great Britain. It is on the Caribbean Sea, east of Guatemala. It is 8,867 square miles in size, and more than 103,000 people live there. Most of the people are Negroes and American Indians, and they grow bananas, sugar, and fruits. Parts of British Honduras are low and fertile, and much of it is covered with forests of valuable mahogany and logwood. Off the swampy coast there are dangerous reefs that were used long ago as hideouts for pirates. The climate is hot and damp; often the temperature goes over 100 degrees. The British have ruled British Honduras since 1783. Belize, the capital, is the largest city and most important seaport. About 33,000 people live in Belize.

British Isles

The British Isles lie northwest of France, a few miles off the mainland of Europe. There are many small islands in the group, but the two chief islands are Ireland and Great Britain. The island of Great Britain includes England, Scotland, and Wales. The island of Ireland contains the Irish Republic, also called Eire, in southern Ireland, and Northern Ireland. Northern Ireland is part of the United Kingdom. You can read more about the countries and divisions of the British Isles in the article about each one in this encyclopedia.

There are several smaller island groups surrounding the British Isles, and they are all associated with the United Kingdom. The Channel Islands are between England and France, in the English Channel. These are the islands of Alderney, Guernsey, and Jersey. The Scilly Islands are southwest of the southwest tip of England. In the Irish Sea, between England and Ireland, is the Isle of Man. Off the northwest coast of Scotland are the Outer Hebrides, Skye, and Mull. To the north and east of Scotland are the Orkneys, and still farther to the northeast are the Shetland Islands.

British Museum

The British Museum in London, England, is one of the biggest, best, and most famous museums in the world. It is the official place where the British government collects treasures of art, literature, and science. These treasures include printed books and manuscripts (which are books that are written by hand), drawings and printed drawings of all kinds, old coins, medals, and statues. However, there are not many paintings.

In 1753 the British Parliament passed a special law establishing the British Museum. For many years the Museum was made up mostly of books and art objects that had been given by King George II and other private collectors. These were kept in Montague House. One part of

Brit. Inform. Service

The great library at the British Museum is used by people from all over the world.

the present building was begun in 1829. But the central part, which is the reading room of the library, was only completed in 1857. It is a great circular room many stories high with an enormous glass-domed roof.

The book collection is one of the largest in the world. There are more than six million books. These include a copy of almost every book printed in the English language. The library gets more than fifty thousand new books every year. Many of these books are received free, because the copyright law in England requires publishers to give the library a copy of every new book.

The museum also owns some of the most famous art treasures in the world. There are the ELGIN MARBLES from ancient Greece, and the ROSETTA STONE from Egypt. (You can read about these treasures in separate articles.) Admission is free to the whole museum, but whoever wants to read the books in the library must first get special permission.

Brittany

Brittany is a section in the northwest part of France. Its French name is *Bretagne*. Many English (British) people moved to this part of France about 1,500 years ago, and that is how it got its name. The country is very beautiful, with many rough hills, and rich, fertile valleys. The people of Brittany are not like the rest of the French people. They even speak a different kind of French. It has many words that were once a part of the Old English or Anglo-Saxon that was spoken by the British settlers there. The costumes of the "Bretons," or people who live in Brittany, are quaint and old-fashioned. In some country districts, people look almost the same as their ancestors looked three and four hundred years ago. They kept their old ways and customs longer than the people of any other part of France. Breton fishermen have been famous sailors; one of them was Jacques Cartier, the great explorer.

Brno

Brno, or Brünn, is a city in Czechoslovakia. It is on the Svartka and Svitavy rivers, at the foot of Mt. Spielberg. At the top of the mountain is a castle that is nine hundred years old. More than 306,000 people live in this old city. They work in factories, making woolen goods, leather, machinery, and many other products. Brno is the capital of the province of Moravia, which became part of Czechoslovakia after World War I. In World War II, the Germans captured the city, but it was retaken by the Russian army in 1945.

broadcasting, sending out radio programs from a transmitting station: see RADIO.

Broadway

Broadway is the main street in New York City. More than three hundred years ago, when the city was founded by the Dutch, Broadway was only a cowpath that ran through the "bouweries," or

Every visitor to New York knows the Times Square district of Broadway, with its bright lights and entertainment places. Thousands of people come here every year. Most sections of Broadway are quieter and not so brightly lit.

Outdoor Advertising, Inc.

farms, at the lower part of the island of Manhattan. But as the city grew, more fine houses were built along Broadway than any other street. Broadway got longer, too—so long, in fact, that it is sometimes called the longest street in the world. It ends officially where it crosses the city limits at 263rd Street, but it really goes the whole way north to the city of Albany, 150 miles away. There are only two other longer streets in the world. One is the Appian Way in Italy and the other is Watling Street in England. But both of these are very ancient Roman highways, and neither is a modern street like Broadway.

Broadway today is mostly a business or commercial street, and very few of the beautiful old houses remain. Downtown, however, there are several fine old churches, including St. Paul's Chapel, which is the oldest church building in New York. Broadway also crosses Wall Street, which is the financial center of the country. Farther uptown, Broadway runs through the clothing manufacturing district until it comes to 42nd Street and Times Square.

This section is the theater district known as the "Great White Way," because there are so many big electric signs. The theaters themselves are no longer on Broadway, as they used to be. They are on the nearby side streets. Broadway is lined with big movie houses, restaurants, and nightclubs that are visited more by tourists than by native New Yorkers. However, New Yorkers still think affectionately of Broadway, especially when they are away from home. A famous New Yorker named George M. Cohan once wrote a popular song about Broadway in which he "sent his regards" to the street!

Throughout the United States and the world, people often speak of "Broadway" to mean the entire New York theatrical business.

brocade

Brocade is a cloth, usually made of silk, that has rich, colorful designs woven into it or embroidered on it so as to make a raised pattern. The raised design may be of silk, silver, or gold threads. People have been making brocade for more than two thousand years. The damask used today in the finest tablecloths and napkins is a kind of brocade. Until about a hundred years ago, all brocades were made by hand. Then the invention of a special loom, called a Jacquard loom, made it possible to weave complicated designs by machine.

broccoli

Broccoli is a popular vegetable that is closely related to cauliflower. It looks like a small, dark green bush, with a stalk one to two feet high. It has many short branches, each ending in a cluster of little flower-buds surrounded by leaves. When broccoli is ready to be eaten, these tiny buds are green. If the plant is left in the garden, the buds turn yellow and coarse.

Broccoli was brought to the rest of Europe and to America from Italy. Its name in Italian means "little sprouts."

Brock, Sir Isaac

Sir Isaac Brock was a British general who won the title "hero of upper Canada" for his defeat of the United States forces at Detroit, during the War of 1812. When this war between England and the United States broke out, Brock was in charge of the government and the armed forces in Canada. He quickly organized Canada's defenses, and drove back an invasion by the American general, William Hull. On August 16, 1812, with only 730 men and 600 Indians, Brock captured Detroit and forced Hull and his 2,500 men to surrender. After this, Brock was a popular hero, and was made a knight. He was killed two months later in the Battle of Queenston Heights. A monument to his memory was erected at Queenston, and the battlefield is now a public park.

Brodie, Steve

Steve Brodie was a saloon-keeper in New York City. He was not an important man at all, and the only reason he is remembered is that in 1886 he said he had jumped from the Brooklyn Bridge into the East River. The Brooklyn Bridge is 140 feet above the river. Very few people believe that Steve Brodie actually made this jump, but taking a big chance on something is still called "pulling a brodie."

broker, a person who buys and sells stocks and bonds, or grain or cotton, or real estate or insurance, or a number of other things, for his customers and not for himself. He charges his customers a *brokerage fee* for his work. See COMMODITY EXCHANGE and STOCK EXCHANGE.

Bromfield, Louis

Louis Bromfield is the name of an American novelist who was born in Mansfield, Ohio, in 1896. He attended Columbia University, but gave up his studies during World War I in order to serve with an American ambulance corps attached to the French Army. He lived in France for a long time after the war, but in 1939 returned to America to live on a farm near the town where he was born. One of his greatest interests was farming and country life. His first novel and one of his most famous is called *The Green Bay Tree*. He died in 1956.

bromine and bromide

Bromine is a chemical that has many uses. It is a dark brown liquid, but when left standing in a room it turns into a red gas. It smells very bad, and is dangerous because as a liquid it will burn your skin if you touch it, and as a gas it will make your eyes water and give you a sore throat. However it is useful in making certain dyes and drugs. Bromine can be made from salt water by the process called ELECTROLYSIS, about which there is a separate article. Almost all the bromine used now is used in the making of the "ethyl fluid" that is added to gasoline.

The drugs made from bromine are called *bromides*. A bromide is a mixture of bromine with a metal, such as silver, calcium, mercury, sodium, or potassium. A bromide tastes like salt. Most of the drugs that are bromides are used to quiet people's nerves, to put them to sleep, or in some cases to make them stop vomiting. Bromides should never be taken unless they are prescribed by a doctor. Too many of them can cause skin irritations or extreme weakness.

bronchi

The bronchi are two tubes in your body. They carry air from the back of your throat into your lungs.

The main tube from your lungs to your chest is the *trachea*. The trachea divides into two tubes, one for each lung, and these tubes are the bronchi. The bronchi divide again into many tiny tubes called *bronchioles*. The whole structure looks like a tree with many branches, and so is called the *bronchial tree*.

The inside of the bronchial tree is kept comfortably moist by a thin fluid. That is why breathing is such a pleasant and easy thing to do when we are well. Sometimes germs get into the bronchial tree and this fluid gets thickened and makes us uncomfortable. It might even stop up some of the little tubes, and make breathing difficult. This is called *bronchitis*, and without medicine it can get worse and last a long time. In order to get rid of this thickened fluid, the lungs squeeze violently and suddenly, hoping to throw this thickened material up into the throat. That sudden movement is called a cough.

Bronchitis usually starts with what seems to be a simple cold. Also, smoking

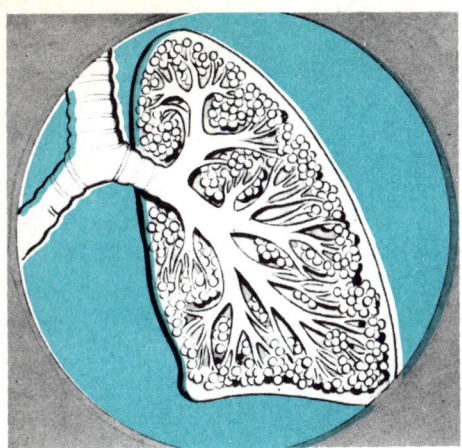

The smallest bronchial tubes in your lungs end in tiny bags called air sacs, which fill with air when you breathe in.

can irritate the bronchi, and this can start a chronic (lasting) bronchitis. Workers who have to breathe in a lot of dust also have trouble in the bronchial tree. Nowadays people who work in certain trades wear masks over their mouths and noses to filter out the harmful dust or fumes.

Brontë

There were three famous sisters named Brontë. Their names were Charlotte, Emily, and Anne, and they were all writers. They lived in England about a hundred years ago. They were daughters of a clergyman, and had two older sisters and a brother. They went to a very strict school when they were girls, and later they became teachers and governesses. Charlotte's most famous novel was *Jane Eyre*, a story of some of her experiences in school and as a governess. Emily wrote *Wuthering Heights*, a tragic love story that describes the countryside and moors in which the girls were brought up. Anne wrote two good novels, *Agnes Grey* and *The Tenant of Wildfell Hall*, but neither was as great as her sisters.' All the sisters wrote under "pen-names," calling themselves Currer, Ellis and Acton Bell, and for a long time not even their publishers knew who they really were. Charlotte, Emily and Anne all died of tuberculosis at an early age.

Charlotte Brontë was born in 1816 and died in 1855. She was the only sister who married and she lived longest, though she was only 39 when she died. Emily, born in 1818, died in 1848, when she was barely 30, and Anne, born in 1820, died in 1849, aged 29. Their brother Branwell Brontë, whom they loved and admired very much, was born in 1817 and died in 1848.

brontosaurus

The brontosaurus was a huge dinosaur that lived about 130 million years ago. It weighed about 20 tons, and walked on all four feet. Its footprint covered one square foot of ground. It had a thick body, a long neck and tail, and a very small head. Its great weight and its small brain show that it was a slow-moving beast, with not much intelligence. The brontosaurus was a reptile, related to the lizard. It ate plants and spent much of its life in the water. The bones of the brontosaurus have been found in the United States, in Wyoming and other western states.

Bronx

The Bronx is one of the boroughs of New York City. It lies between the East

River and Long Island Sound. Nearly one and a half million people live there. Most of the people do not work in the Bronx, but travel by subway and automobile to offices and factories in the borough of MANHATTAN, about which there is a separate article. Most of the people live in large apartment houses, though in the northern part of the Bronx people own large homes.

Attractions in the Bronx include the huge Yankee Stadium, which is the home of the New York Yankees, and one of the world's finest collections of wild animals at the Bronx Zoo. There are many fine parks and universities, and people have called the Bronx "the borough of universities." Among the more famous are Fordham University, one of the largest Catholic universities in the United States, and New York University with its Hall of Fame for great Americans. Another interesting place is Poe Cottage, the house where the noted author Edgar Allan Poe lived and wrote some of his poems.

The first settler of the Bronx was Jonas Bronck, from whom the borough gets its name. For a very long time the Bronx was made up of large farms, and until fifty years ago a trip to the Bronx was like taking a trip out into the country. Today, more people live there than in most cities of the world. The Bronx became part of New York City in 1898.

BRONX, NEW YORK. Population, 1,424,815 (1960 census). On the East River and Long Island Sound; settled in 1641.

bronze

Bronze is an "alloy," or mixture, of copper and tin that is used for making statues, church bells, and medals. Bronze is also made by mixing copper and other metals, such as aluminum and nickel, and this is used in machinery, telephone wires, and nuts and bolts. Bronze is a dark, rich, golden brown in color. Men have used it since ancient times to make weapons, household articles, and monuments. In the Middle Ages, about six hundred years ago, it was used to make the great bells and doors of cathedrals. Today, many artists still use bronze for making statues because it is lighter than stone, and it lasts longer than wood. When bronze stands out-of-doors for a long time, it becomes discolored with patches of green, blue, or black. This is called verdigris.

Bronze Age

Bronze Age is the name of a period in history when man first learned to use metals, and to make tools and weapons of them. See the articles on AGE and ARCHAEOLOGY in other volumes of this encyclopedia.

Brook Farm

Brook Farm was a famous community in West Roxbury, Massachusetts, more than a hundred years ago. The small group of people from New England who started Brook Farm hoped that it would become an ideal place, where everybody could live and work together in harmony. Everyone was to share the farm work, and also have time to read and study. Brook Farm was started in 1841 by George Ripley and his wife, and many important people joined them. The most famous was the American novelist Nathaniel Hawthorne. The community lasted for only six years. Some people found the farm work too difficult, and some did not get along so well with the others. Brook Farm was finally given up, but it is remembered as a place where people honestly tried to live cooperatively. Many other cooperative communities like Brook Farm were established in the United States, but few of them succeeded.

Brooklyn

Brooklyn is one of the five boroughs of New York City. It is on New York Bay and the East River at the west end of Long Island. It has the largest population of all the five boroughs of New York with almost three million people living there. Many of them work in factories that make shoes, chemicals, and paints. Others work in the shops and department stores. Still others travel by subway and automobile across the East River to offices and factories in the borough of Manhattan. (There is a separate article about MANHATTAN.) Brooklyn is connected with Manhattan by three large bridges. The most famous is Brooklyn Bridge, which was opened in 1883.

Brooklyn is a borough of homes and churches. People have called it "the city of Churches," and one of the most famous is Plymouth Church, where Henry Ward Beecher preached for forty years. Also in Brooklyn is Prospect Park, one of the most beautiful parks in the United States. On the southern shore of Brooklyn is Coney Island, the most famous amusement park and beach in the country. On a hot summer day, there are more than one million people on Coney Island's beach and boardwalk. Brooklyn also has several colleges and universities. Brooklyn College has an enrollment of more than 19,000 students.

Brooklyn is a very old region. It was settled more than three hundred years ago by the Dutch, and later by the English. During the American Revolution, General Washington fought the battle of Long Island where Prospect Park now stands. Until 1898, Brooklyn was a separate city. Then it became part of New York City.

BROOKLYN, NEW YORK. Population, (1968 estimate) 2,650,000. Settled in 1636.

Brooks, Phillips

Phillips Brooks was a very famous minister in the Protestant Episcopal Church. He was born in 1835 in Boston, Massachusetts. He graduated from Harvard College, then studied for the ministry at Alexandria, Virginia. He was for many years the rector at Trinity Church in Boston, a very beautiful church that was built especially for him. He wrote many books on religious subjects, and also wrote the beautiful Christmas hymn, *O Little Town of Bethlehem.* Phillips Brooks was made Bishop of Massachusetts in 1891, two years before his death.

broom

A broom is a brush that is used for sweeping dust or dirt off surfaces. Brooms usually have long handles, which make them easier to use. Most of the brooms we use are made of the stalks of a plant called *broomcorn,* that grows in the Middle West. Cattle eat the flowers of the broomcorn, and the stalks are used for broom-making. The stalks are tied together at the top, so that the broom is shaped like a cone. Then it is put in a vise, and flattened out by being squeezed.

In early days, people used a broom called a *besom.* It was made of the stalks of a plant called *broom* that grows in England and Europe. The broom plant has very short leaves and bright flowers. It grows in sandy soil where other plants cannot grow. It is a wildflower, and is very hardy.

Brown, John

John Brown was a man who lived more than 100 years ago, when Negroes were slaves in the southern states of the United States. He hated slavery and finally gave his life and the lives of his sons in trying to do away with it. Brown was born in New England in 1800, but spent most of his life in the West. In Kansas, he kept a station on the "underground railroad," which was not a real railroad but a secret method of getting Negroes north into Canada where they could be free. John Brown and his sons fought the men who wished to have slavery in Kansas. One night he killed five such men at Pottawatomie. Several months later, he made a heroic stand against pro-slavery forces at Osawatomie, and from then on he was called "Old Brown of Osawatomie."

Lake Placid Chamber of Commerce

The tomb of John Brown at Lake Placid, New York, where he lived part of his life. Many people visit his house and grave there. *Above, right:* A picture of John Brown.

Then John Brown had a plan to free the slaves: give them guns and ammunition and let them fight to free themselves. He rented a farm near the town of Harper's Ferry, in the part of Virginia that is now the state of West Virginia. The night of October 16, 1859 (less than two years before the Civil War began) Brown led a party of his sons and friends and captured the arsenal (a kind of fort) at Harper's Ferry. The slaves did not revolt and a company of Marines led by Robert E. LEE (later a Confederate General) killed or captured Brown's whole party.

While the entire nation shook with excitement, John Brown was convicted of treason and hanged at Charles Town (not at Charleston, the capital of West Virginia) near Harper's Ferry on December 2, 1859. In the trial he defended himself calmly and walked bravely to the scaffold to be hanged. His name became a watchword to anti-slavery forces and in the Civil War the Union soldiers marched to the song "John Brown's body lies a-molderin' in the grave..."

Browning

Robert Browning and Elizabeth Barrett Browning were English poets who lived about a hundred years ago. They are remembered almost as much for the true love story that led to their marriage as for the great poetry they wrote.

Robert Browning was born in 1812, of a rich family. He became a successful poet and playwright while he was still in his twenties. Elizabeth Barrett was born in 1806, so she was six years older. From girlhood she was an invalid, so she could not go out, and her very strict family did not let her meet men she might marry. She too wrote poetry and had it published while she was in her twenties.

In the years 1841 to 1846 Browning wrote some of his best poems and plays, published under the title *Bells and Pomegranates*. In 1845 Elizabeth Barrett wrote him a letter praising them and he called to see her. They fell in love and, defying the strong opposition of Elizabeth Barrett's father, they were married in 1846. They lived together happily, chiefly

Robert Browning   Elizabeth Barrett

in Italy, until Mrs. Browning died in 1861. Browning lived much longer, dying in 1889.

Mrs. Browning's most famous poems are a series of love poems, *Sonnets from the Portuguese,* which she wrote to her husband. (She was nicknamed "the Portuguese" because she was very dark in coloring.) Browning wrote many famous poems and is now generally considered the greatest of the Victorian poets, those who wrote during the reign of Queen Victoria of England.

Bruce, Robert

King Robert I of Scotland is also called Robert Bruce, or Robert the Bruce. He lived more than 600 years ago, but he is still famous because he was one of the Scottish leaders who would not let their country be made part of England. Robert Bruce was born in the year 1274. As a young man he was the Earl of Carrick and supported the English king, Edward I. In 1306 he became king of Scotland, and he carried on constant warfare with England to make them allow Scotland to be independent. He won a great battle over the English in the Battle of Bannockburn, in 1314. At other times the English were winning and he had to hide. On one of these times, according to an old story, he was hiding in Ireland and had almost given up hope of beating the English. He had tried and failed six times. Then he happened to notice a spider trying to spin a web on the ceiling over his head. Six times the spider tried and failed. But the spider tried a seventh time and succeeded. Bruce decided that he too should try a seventh time. He went back to Scotland and led another army against the English. This time he was successful, and in 1328 the English recognized Scottish independence. Less than two years later, in 1329, Robert Bruce died. He is buried at Dunfermline, in Scotland.

Brueghel, another spelling for the name BREUGHEL.

Brummell, Beau

"Beau" Brummell was an Englishman who lived about 150 years ago, and who did much to create the style of men's clothing that is still followed. His real name was George Bryan Brummell and he was born in 1778. He was neither a nobleman nor a rich man, but he went to the best English schools—Eton and Oxford—and made friends with many important people. These included the Prince of Wales, who later became King George IV. At that time men's clothes were changing greatly. The old style had been knee-breeches, very frilly shirts, and bright-colored coats. Young men who were fashion leaders were called *beaus,* or *dandies.* Beau Brummell became the prince's adviser on correct dress. He favored styles that were not too fancy, and he taught many good habits, such as daily baths. Later, Beau Brummell quarreled with the prince and went to France, where he lived in poverty. He died in a charity hospital in 1840, when he was 62 years old.

Brunswick

Brunswick is a district of about 1,400 square miles in West Germany. It is a rich district, with copper, lead and iron mines, fertile farms where cattle, fruits and vegetables are raised, and several manufacturing cities. The German name is Braunschweig. In former times Brunswick was an independent duchy, ruled by a royal duke, and after World War I it became a state in the German Republic. After being in the British zone of occupation following World War II, it became part of the new German state of Lower Saxony.

Brunswick is also the name of the principal city of the district and the former capital. The city is more than a thousand years old and has been an important trading center for centuries. Now it is a manufacturing city where canned goods, cameras, clothing and machinery are made. Many of the historic buildings and monuments were destroyed by bombs in World War II, but some remain.

BRUNSWICK, GERMANY. District, area, 1,379 square miles; population 782,950. City, population 245,983.

The famous Town Hall is one of the many old buildings in Brussels. People shop in the square at stands set up on market day.

Brussels

Brussels is the capital of Belgium and is one of the richest and most beautiful cities of Europe. It is in the central part of the country, on the Senne River, which carries shipping to the sea through Antwerp, 27 miles to the north. Almost 1,500,000 people live in Brussels.

Though Brussels has been a famous city for hundreds of years, in 1958 it became better known than ever to the rest of the world by holding a great world's fair, called the Brussels Universal and International Exposition. Fifty nations built displays of their national life and products at the exposition. The United States pavilion, which cost about $12,500,000, was one of the most popular with the 35,000,000 tourists who visited Brussels to see the exposition. (See the article WORLD'S FAIR.) The Belgian government spent $300,000,000 on the exposition and an additional $400,000,000 was spent on improvements and modernizations in Brussels.

Brussels is a great manufacturing city. It is famous for carpets and lace, but there are many other important products, including cotton and woolen goods, automobiles, and bicycles. Most of the people speak French but many speak Dutch.

Most of Brussels is modern, but some parts are very old, with narrow, winding streets and churches and houses that are more than 500 years old. In the modern part there are fine hotels and shops, the royal palace where the Belgian king lives, the government buildings, and the University of Brussels. Brussels has been called "the Little Paris" because it resembles the French capital.

Brussels was founded more than 900 years ago. It was an important commercial city in the Middle Ages and has been the capital of its region for more than 500 years. In 1830, when Belgium became independent, Brussels was made the capital. One of history's most famous battles was fought at Waterloo, a few miles to the south. In both World Wars the Germans captured and occupied Brussels but little damage was done to it.

BRUSSELS, BELGIUM. Population 170,409; with suburbs, 1,398,326. Capital of Belgium.

Brussels sprouts

Brussels sprouts look like tiny cabbages, only an inch or so thick instead of seven or eight inches. They are members of the same family of plants as cabbage, but they are not the same plant. Brussels sprouts are really buds that grow close together on a thick stem that is usually 2 or 3 feet high. They start to appear as little buttons at the bottom of the stem; then more buds, or sprouts, come out all the way up the stem. Each stem grows about a quart of sprouts. They can be picked all fall, since frost improves their flavor. Brussels sprouts get their name from the city of Brussels, the capital of Belgium, where they were grown and sold more than seven hundred years ago.

Brutus, Marcus Junius

Marcus Junius Brutus was a statesman and general in Rome two thousand years ago, when it was the greatest nation on earth. We remember him best because he was one of the group of Roman senators who killed the Roman leader, Julius Caesar, on March 15, in the year 44 B.C. Before that, Brutus had been considered one of Caesar's best friends, but his group had decided to kill Caesar because they thought he was trying to make himself the emperor of Rome. In one of William Shakespeare's best-known plays, *Julius Caesar,* it is to Brutus that Caesar speaks his last sad words, when Brutus stabs him: "You too, Brutus!"

Brutus was born in 85 B.C. There was a civil war in Rome in 49 B.C., and Brutus fought for Pompey, the general who was Caesar's rival; but Caesar won, and Brutus then joined his side. After Caesar's death, Brutus fought against Mark ANTONY and Octavian, who later became the emperor AUGUSTUS (there are separate articles about both these men). Brutus lost to them in a great battle at Philippi, in Greece, in 42 B.C. When he saw that he had lost the battle, he killed himself by falling on his sword. Brutus was the name of a great family in Rome, and several of Marcus Brutus's ancestors were also famous men.

Brussels sprouts look like rosebuds, and are called "rose cabbages" in Germany

Bryan, William Jennings

William Jennings Bryan was one of the most famous public figures of the United States in the years from 1896 to 1925. Three times he was the Democratic candidate for president, in 1896, 1900, and 1908, but each time he was beaten by the Republican candidate. He was considered one of the greatest orators, or public speakers, who ever lived.

His most famous speech won him the nomination for the presidency. Bryan was born in Salem, Illinois, in 1860. After he finished college and became a lawyer he moved to Nebraska, served in Congress, and in 1896 went as a delegate to the Democratic convention where the candidate for president was to be nominated. At that time the United States, like most countries, was on the "gold standard," which means that the government guaranteed that an ounce of gold would always be worth a certain number of dollars. In Nebraska and other western states where silver was mined, people wanted the government to guarantee the value of silver, too. As a Nebraskan, Bryan made a speech in which he said, "You shall not crucify mankind upon a cross of gold." His "Cross of Gold" speech made such an impression that he was nominated. Bryan was often called "the great commoner."

When Woodrow Wilson was elected president in 1912, Bryan was made Secretary of State. He resigned in 1915 and after that he lectured and wrote until his death in 1925. Bryan was a very religious man and was a leading "fundamentalist," which means he believed that every word of the King James version of the Bible should be accepted as literally true, not merely as a story told to teach a lesson.

Bryant, William Cullen

William Cullen Bryant was a famous American poet who was best known for his lovely nature poems. He was born in 1794, in Cummington, Massachusetts. Even as a boy, he wrote and published poems that were so good that people found it hard to believe that such a young boy had written them. When he was nineteen, Bryant wrote one of his most famous poems, *Thanatopsis,* a beautiful poem on death. Although he had studied to become a lawyer, Bryant practiced law for only a few years, and then became editor of the New York *Evening Post.*

Most of Bryant's poems are about flowers and wild animals, such as *Death of the Flowers, To the Fringed Gentian,* and *To a Waterfowl.* William Cullen Bryant died in 1878.

Bryce, James

James Bryce was a great British lawyer and statesman who is remembered in the United States because he wrote a book, *The American Commonwealth,* which told how the American government works. This book was written in the year 1888, when a great many people in Great Britain did not know much about the United States, and it helped to make the English-speaking peoples more friendly. Later, from 1907 to 1913, Bryce was British ambassador to the United States. He was born in Belfast, in Northern Ireland, in 1838, but lived most of his life in England, and served as a cabinet minister and as professor of law at Oxford University. In 1914 he was made a viscount and became Lord Bryce. He died in 1922.

Bryn Mawr

Bryn Mawr is a famous college for women, at the town of Bryn Mawr, Pennsylvania, a suburb of Philadelphia. It was founded in 1885 by the Quakers, but today it is nonsectarian. About 1,000 young women attend it.

Buchan, John

John Buchan was a British statesman and writer. His best-known novel was *The Thirty-Nine Steps,* an exciting story about spies. Buchan was born in Scotland, in 1875. Although he held many important government jobs, he always found time to write, not only stories but also history. In 1935 he became governor general of Canada. Shortly before he died in 1940, he was given the title Baron Tweedsmuir.

JAMES BUCHANAN

James Buchanan was the fifteenth President of the United States. He was born in 1791 near Mercersburg, Pennsylvania, and was a lawyer before he entered the field of politics. During his early years as a lawyer, Buchanan was saddened by the death of the girl he was engaged to. He wanted to keep busy in order to overcome his grief, so he decided to become a politician. He never married, and was the only president of the United States to remain a bachelor.

Buchanan became president at a time when the country was faced with the question of slavery and other great problems. His administration did not succeed in straightening out the problems that were facing the country, and Buchanan has often been blamed for many of the events leading up to the Civil War.

When Buchanan was elected president in 1856, the disputes between northern and southern states over slavery had become violent, and feelings were strong. Many people in the North were bitterly opposed to slavery, and wanted to abolish it. Most people in the South wanted slavery to continue.

There were many southerners at the time who resented the Federal government's control over an individual state's government. Some of these people went so far as to say that if the Federal government interfered too much, a state had a right to resign or secede from the Union. These people were known as secessionists. Buchanan appointed several men to his cabinet who were active secessionists, and throughout his administration his feelings were divided between the North and the South. Since he was elected by the Democratic Party, Buchanan tried to be fair to all members of the party, but he seemed to favor the hotheaded southern members.

Any president at that period would have had a very hard time, but a stronger man might have been able to do more than Buchanan. Buchanan could do nothing and the country became more and more divided. In November, 1860, Abraham Lincoln was elected to succeed Buchanan as president. Buchanan, in a last message to Congress, tried to blame the North for what was happening to the country. He did this even though he knew that the southern states had begun to break up the Union by seceding from it.

Although Buchanan said that no state had any right to secede, he also said that Congress, on the other hand, had no right to try to stop secession. Most people thought that he could not make up his mind as to what was right and what was wrong. As a result, states went on seceding, and the war was finally touched off by the Southerners firing on Fort Sumter. You can read about this in the article on the CIVIL WAR.

After his term as president was over, Buchanan supported the Union side in the war. He felt, however, that it was necessary to explain his presidential policy, and wrote a book called *Mr. Buchan-*

an's Administration. His life has been the subject of considerable discussion by students of political history ever since he died in 1868.

HIS EARLY YEARS

James Buchanan was born on April 23, 1791, in Mercersburg, Franklin County, Pennsylvania. It was a small country town about ninety miles west of Gettysburg. When he was only eighteen, he was graduated from Dickinson College in Carlisle, Pennsylvania, and he became a lawyer at the age of twenty-one. Buchanan was considered a handsome young man, with thick, wavy hair, and heavy eyebrows.

As a young lawyer, Buchanan was interested in politics but did not become active in this field until after the death of his fiancée. He grieved for her so much that he wanted to keep busy every minute, and working in politics seemed like a good idea. He worked so hard that he became a member of the House of Representatives on the Federalist ticket in 1820, and served for ten years. When Andrew Jackson was a candidate for the presidency in 1828, Buchanan became a Democrat and supported him. After the election, Buchanan became U.S. Minister to Russia, and did very well in that position. He arranged the first commercial treaty between Russia and the United States. It gave the United States important rights concerning American ships entering the Black and Baltic Seas, both of which were entirely controlled by Russia at that time.

When Buchanan returned to this country, he ran for the United States Senate, and became a member of that body in 1834, and served in it until 1845. While he was in the Senate, he argued frequently in favor of allowing each state to choose whether it wanted to have slavery. He said that the national government had no right or power to interfere with the states where people had slaves.

Buchanan was offered the Democratic nomination for president in 1844, but he refused to accept it, and James Polk was chosen instead. Buchanan was Secretary of State during the Polk administration, and he was responsible for many things during that period which have greatly influenced the country's history. They are described in the article about James POLK, in a later volume of this encyclopedia.

When Polk was succeeded by Zachary Taylor as president, Buchanan retired to his farm near Lancaster, Pennsylvania. During this time he adopted his niece and nephew, whose parents had died. In 1853, Franklin Pierce was the new president, and he appointed Buchanan ambassador to England.

In 1856 Buchanan was nominated for the presidency on the Democratic ticket, and he was elected. After his inauguration in the spring of 1857, he announced the names of the men he had chosen for his cabinet. This immediately caused trouble with northern Democratic Party members, because Buchanan had chosen men who were active secessionists, and many Northerners thought secessionists were not loyal to the United States. It was unfortunate that Buchanan had such people in his cabinet, because it caused him to be accused of failing to do his best to preserve the Union. During the four years that Buchanan was president, he accomplished very little, and his weakness as a leader caused much trouble. Instead of uniting the country, Buchanan's policies helped to divide it even more.

By the time Buchanan's term was over, the Civil War seemed certain to be fought, although most people still hoped it could be avoided. James Buchanan left office with his country turned against him.

HIS LATER YEARS

He retired to private life and wrote a book explaining his policy during the time he was president. He attempted to justify his actions in this book, and some people think that he did all that he possibly could under the circumstances. On the other hand, many people think that he could have been more determined to preserve the Union, and could have made decisions that might have helped to prevent the Civil War, although the causes of that war had existed for a long time.

James Buchanan died at the age of 77 at Wheatlands, his farm near Lancaster, Pennsylvania, on June 1, 1868.

Bucharest

Bucharest is the capital and largest city in Rumania. It is on the Dambovita River, and is one of the most important manufacturing centers in the Balkan Peninsula. More than one million people live there, and they work in factories, making furniture, leather goods, machinery, paper, soap, and many other products. The Dambovita River runs through the city. The part of the city that is on the right bank of the river is very old, and has narrow, winding streets. The part of the city that is on the left bank is modern, and here you can see beautiful gardens and fine buildings.

Bucharest was founded more than six hundred years ago. A Roman fortress had probably stood on the spot where the city was built. In 1861 Bucharest became the capital of Rumania. In World War II, it was taken by the Germans. The city was taken from the Germans by the Russians in 1944.

BUCHAREST, RUMANIA. Population, 1,291,351. Capital of Rumania. On the Dambovita River.

Buck, Pearl Sydenstricker

Pearl S. Buck has been famous as an American novelist, and she became best known for her book *The Good Earth*. Thousands of people have read this story of a Chinese family and millions have seen the motion picture that was made from the book. In 1932, *The Good Earth* won the Pulitzer Prize that is given every year to the best novel written by an American. Pearl Buck was the daughter of an American missionary. She was born in Hillsboro, West Virginia, in 1892, and spent her childhood among the Chinese people. Later, she taught at several Chinese universities. Most of her stories are about these people she knew so well. In 1938, Pearl Buck was given the great Nobel Prize which is awarded each year to the most outstanding people in many fields. She was given the prize for her fine writing.

Buckingham Palace

Buckingham Palace is the London home of the British royal family. It was built about 250 years ago by the man who was the Duke of Buckingham at that time. When George III became king soon after, he liked the palace so much that he bought it, and English kings and queens have lived in it ever since. Buckingham Palace is attended night and day by special troops of the British Army. These troops work in shifts, like all guards. Each time a new shift comes on, there is a very colorful ceremony called the "Changing of the Guard." The bugle call at this time suggested the music for the song that starts, "They're changing Guards at Buckingham Palace, Christopher Robin went down with Alice."

Buckner, Simon Bolivar

Simon Bolivar Buckner was a Confederate general in the Civil War. He was born in Kentucky in 1823. He graduated from the United States Military Academy at West Point. When the Civil War broke out, he joined the Southern army, but in 1862, he was forced to surrender to General Grant. Many years later, he became governor of Kentucky. His son, Simon Bolivar Buckner, was a famous general in World War II. He was born in 1886, and became an army officer like his father. He was the commanding general in Alaska during part of World War II. In 1945, he was made the commanding general in the invasion of the island of Okinawa, in the Pacific. The invasion was successful, but General Buckner was killed only a few day before the Japanese surrendered the island.

buckskin

Originally buckskin meant a soft leather that was made from the skin of a buck, or male deer. American pioneers and frontiersmen wore buckskin breeches and buckskin shirts. Many American soldiers wore buckskin clothing during the Revolutionary War, and those soldiers were often called "Buckskins." Most buckskin is now made by softening sheepskin in oil instead of tanning it in the usual way.

buckwheat

Buckwheat is a plant that is grown in many parts of the world for grain. It does not grow very high, but it grows very thickly and chokes off anything else where it is planted. Farmers often plant buckwheat to choke off weeds. They use the buckwheat seeds to feed cows, pigs and chickens. They also make buckwheat flour by grinding the seeds. The flour is used mostly for pancakes. The buckwheat plant first grew in Asia, and it was brought to Europe in the Middle Ages. It grows in many parts of North America. Buckwheat usually grows about two feet high, and it has heart-shaped leaves and pale red flowers.

bud

A bud is the part of a plant from which a new flower grows, from which a new plant may develop. A bud, therefore, is a very valuable part of the plant, and in cold climates the trees usually have bud scales which protect their buds from frost in the winter. From the shape of the bud scales, particularly those at the tips of the branches, you can nearly always tell what sort of tree you are looking at, even in midwinter.

With special care, gardeners can grow a whole new plant from a single bud, by "budding," or cutting off pieces which have several buds on them. The "eyes" of potatoes are buds, and you can plant a piece of potato that has two or three eyes, and grow a new potato plant. Some plants, like palms and lilies, have only one bud, and all their growth takes place from it. Palms hold their bud high in the air, and they are easily killed by frost, but lilies, onions, and many other plants with only one bud, keep it safely underground, where it can live through the coldest winter. For more on this subject, see the article on BULB.

The lower kinds of plant, such as seaweeds, and of animals, such as jellyfish, also have buds; from their buds a whole new plant or animal may develop. This is often their chief way of reproducing themselves.

Budapest

Budapest is the capital and most important city in Hungary. It is one of the most beautiful cities in Europe. Almost two million people live in Budapest. They work in the large mills and factories, making flour, metal products, tobacco, textiles, dishes, and many other important articles. Budapest is also the greatest railroad center in Hungary, and the farmers ship most of their crops through this city.

Budapest is really two old cities that grew upon opposite sides of the Danube River, and were finally joined together in 1872. Buda was on the right bank of the Danube, and Pest was on the left bank of the river. When one city was made from these two places, the new name came from joining the two old names. These two parts of the city are joined by many fine bridges. Buda is on high ground, and is built around a great rock called the *Varhegy* (Castle Hill).

BUDAPEST

Alfred Markus Travel Agency

Top: A beautiful night view of Budapest shows the bridges across the Danube River that connect Buda and Pest. **Right:** Matthias Church on Castle Hill.

On this hill is the splendid royal palace, now in ruins, and a cathedral where the emperors of Austria were crowned as kings of Hungary.

Pest is on a sandy plain, so low that walls had to be built to keep the waters of the Danube out. This part of Budapest is very beautiful. Here you can see many fine boulevards, parks, and buildings. People who visited the city before World War II called the *Andrassy Ut* one of the most beautiful streets in the world.

The towns of Buda and Pest are very old. They were both probably founded by Slavic tribes more than 1,500 years ago. The Magyars, who now are the largest group in Hungary, conquered the two towns about a thousand years ago. Buda and Pest were under Turkish rule for almost 150 years during the Middle Ages; when the Turks were driven out in 1686, they left the two towns almost completely destroyed. Then Buda and Pest were rebuilt and were finally joined together.

During World War II the Germans controlled Budapest. They defended it against advancing Russian armies in 1945 and many of the beautiful buildings were damaged before Russia captured the city. The Russians set up Communist rule in Hungary and in 1956 the people of Budapest led the nation in fighting to become free again, but they were suppressed by the Russian army. See HUNGARY.

BUDAPEST, HUNGARY. Population, (1960 estimate) 1,807,299. Capital of Hungary. On the Danube River.

Buddha and Buddhism

Buddha is the name of a great teacher who founded the religion called Buddhism. Buddha lived in India 2,500 years ago. His name was originally Siddharttha Gotama (or Gautama). By this name he was known until he was 29 years old. Then he took the title of "Buddha," meaning "the enlightened one." A Buddha is a sort of prophet. Followers of Buddhism believe such Buddhas are born every few generations, to keep the faith of the people alive. Gotama, the Buddha, taught people the meaning of reverence, the love of truth, and the evils of superstition. His followers today number 450 million people, scattered over India, China, Burma, Ceylon, Tibet, Siam, and Japan. He is also honored in the Western World as one of the greatest teachers of all time.

Legend says that Gotama was born the son of a king. When he was 19 he married a beautiful princess, and they had a son. But Prince Siddharttha had seen visions that showed him how vain and useless was the life of a prince. Taking a last look at his young son in the arms of his sleeping mother, he departed from the palace, leaving behind his royal name and all the splendor that had gone with it.

He did not return until seven years later. This time he was dressed in a coarse, yellow robe, and begged for food in the streets. He had come back because his father, wishing to see him once more, had sent for him. But the king was ashamed of his son's begging, and ordered him to stop. Buddha replied, "My noble father, you and your family may claim the privileges of royal descent; my descent is from the prophets of old, and they have always acted so; the customs of the law are good, both for this world and the world that is to come."

He left his home again, and took five pupils with him to study and pray in the wilderness. He fell ill and was believed dead, but he recovered when the kind daughter of a villager brought him food.

His pupils left him, and Buddha himself was tempted by thoughts of his past life, but the religious side of his nature won out in the end. Instead of returning to his old ways, he made up his mind to leave the wilderness and preach to the people. We are told he came to this decision as he sat in the shade of a big tree, eating the food the village girl had brought him. The people of India call this tree the sacred *Bo Tree of Wisdom.*

WHAT BUDDHISM TEACHES

Like all great religions, Buddhism teaches the importance of spiritual or holy values. This religion teaches that if a person has a pure mind everything he does will be pure and decent, and that if he has a pure heart all happiness will come to him. The highest virtue, according to Buddha, is *universal charity*—giving all you can to anybody who needs help.

Buddhists believe in *reincarnation.* This is a religious belief that is common in the East. It means we are born many times, and in each new life we are better than we were before. According to the teachings of Buddha, the good are rewarded by being born into higher forms of goodness, and those who achieve the highest form of goodness finally escape both life and death. These people, having reached their final stage of goodness, are not born again and therefore do not die again, but remain forever and ever in the Buddhist heaven, called Nirvana.

Buddha taught and preached for many years, wandering from city to city. Many noble youths went with him, including his own son and his brother.

He died at the age of eighty, preaching and teaching to the end. He left behind many notable sayings which his followers faithfully wrote down and passed on to others. On one occasion, for instance, Buddha was asked what is the

BUDDHA

C. T. Loo, N.Y.

1. Many Japanese come to pray in front of this great bronze statue of Buddha. It is 50 feet high and 96 feet around. Its eyes are made of gold.
2. A prayer wheel that contains written prayers is used by Buddhist monks.
3. The Buddhist priest blows the ceremonial trumpet during a religious ritual.
4. There are many beautifully carved figures of Buddha throughout the Orient.
5. In many Eastern countries, you will find Buddhist temples like this one, just as you find churches in the Western world. This beautiful temple is in Cambodia.

greatest blessing. He listed ten different blessings, some of which follow:

"To serve wise men, and not to serve fools, to give honor to whom honor is due, this is the greatest blessing. To dwell in a pleasant land, to have done good deeds in a former birth, to have the right desires for one's self, this is the greatest blessing. To succor father and mother, to cherish wife and child, to follow a peaceful calling, this is the greatest blessing. To give alms and live righteously, to help one's relatives and do blameless deeds, this is the greatest blessing. They that act like this are invincible on every side, on every side they walk in safety, and theirs is the greatest blessing."

budget

A budget is a way of putting down on paper the total amount of money that comes in, and then putting down how that money will be spent. One person may make a budget for himself, or a family may make a budget. The governments of cities, states and countries all make budgets. Government officials make a new budget each year to show how much money the government will have to spend, and what the money will be spent for. A personal, or family, budget is usually made for a week, a month, or a year.

A budget helps people to live within their income, which means they plan their expenses so that they do not pay more for food, clothing, entertainment, or other things, than they can afford. People who live on a budget usually do not run out of the money they earn in a week before the week is over. People who do not have a budget sometimes spend all their money before they have bought some things they need. They either have to borrow money (which they have trouble paying back) or they have to go without things until they get their next salary for the work they do.

If you spend all your allowance a few days after you receive it, and then find you need money for something important to you, then you should plan a budget for yourself. Put down the amount you receive as allowance. Then write down all the things you want to spend money on until your next allowance. When the total amount you plan to spend is equal to, or less than your allowance, then you have a good budget. You should always try to save a little money in your budget —it helps take care of things that you may need to do, but had not thought of.

A government budget is a bit different from a personal one. Much larger sums of money are involved. Each year the person in charge of a government budget plans what shall be done with the government's money during the coming year. The budget for the government of the United States is prepared by a man called the Director of the Bureau of the Budget. He meets with the heads of all government departments and they tell him how much money they will need to run their departments during the coming "fiscal" year. A fiscal year starts on July 1 and ends the following June 30. It is the same length as a regular year, but the government finds it more convenient to have its fiscal or money year start at the beginning of July instead of January.

The Director of the Budget sends his finished budget to Congress. The members of Congress study this budget, and then vote on accepting it. Sometimes Congress makes changes in the budget before it is voted on. Many billions of dollars are spent in a government budget, and Congress must find ways to save money. The income side of a government budget comes mostly from taxes that people pay to the government. Most of the money spent by the government goes for defense (Army, Navy, and Air Force), national parks, aid to veterans, farmers, and friendly nations, and for many other things, including the salaries of all government officials from the president on down to thousands of clerks. In the early days of the United States, the Director of the Budget had to plan for the spending

Pan American-Grace Airways
The Avenue of the 9th of July in Buenos Aires may be the widest street in the world.

of just a few hundred thousand dollars a year. Since the start of World War II, he has had to account for more than fifty billion dollars a year.

Buena Vista, Battle of

The Battle of Buena Vista was one of the hardest-fought battles in the war between Mexico and the United States. It took place on February 22 and 23, 1847. It is important because the American force of only 5,000 men won against 20,000 men in the Mexican army.

The battleground was a plateau (a high flat piece of ground) with mountains rising on two sides. The Americans were commanded by General Zachary Taylor. After he won this battle he became so popular in the United States that he was nominated and then elected president. The Mexican army was under General Santa Anna, who was also the president of Mexico. Taylor's army was made up mainly of men who had volunteered and who were not trained soldiers. During the fighting on the first day the Mexicans attacked fiercely and almost drove the American army into a full retreat. But the Americans fought back bravely until the Mexicans retreated in confusion on the following night. The Americans lost only 749 men, while the Mexicans lost more than 2,000.

Buenos Aires

Buenos Aires is the capital of Argentina and one of the biggest cities in the Western Hemisphere, with about four million people living there. It is a historic city, founded by Spanish settlers in 1536.

Buenos Aires is on the wide La Plata River, which is the baylike mouth, or *estuary*, of the Panama and Uruguay Rivers. The city is the commercial and industrial center of Argentina and also of a vast area that includes parts of Paraguay and Uruguay. Many people work in the city's factories, which turn out automobiles, paper, cloth, and chemicals. Others work in meat-packing plants, printing plants, metalworks, and oil refineries.

Buenos Aires (which means "Good Airs" in the Spanish language) is a modern city. It has many fine parks and squares. The best known square is the Plaza del Mayo. Around it stand several impressive buildings, including the official residence of the president of Argentina. The president of the United States lives in the White House, but the president of Argentina lives in the *Casa Rosada,* or Pink House. If you were to visit Buenos Aires, you would see the Avenida del Mayo, a beautiful, broad boulevard lined with trees, that runs about a mile from the Plaza del Mayo to the Plaza del Congréso, where the National Congress meets to make laws. You would also see the Avenue of the 9th of July, which is said to be the widest street in the world.

You can travel to Buenos Aires by railroad, ocean steamer, or airplane. In the city, you could ride on subways, buses, streetcars and taxis. You would find the climate there much like that of most American cities, except that it would be winter in Buenos Aires when it is summer up north, and so on through the year.

BUENOS AIRES, ARGENTINA. Capital city of Argentina. Population, 3,845,279.

buffalo

The buffalo is an oxlike animal with long horns that is found in Asia and Africa. The Asiatic buffalo, or *water buffalo,* is a large and powerful animal. It is about 7 feet long and 5 feet high at the shoulder, and it has great curving horns. It is an excellent animal for farm work, and it can haul great loads. The tamed water buffalo is gentle and very different from the wild water buffalo, which is savage and fierce and will even attack tigers and elephants. Many of these animals are hunted from the backs of elephants in India. It is called the water buffalo because it loves the water. Its favorite spot is a muddy water hole, where it lies hidden among tall grasses. Another name for the water buffalo that is found in the Philippine Islands is the *carabao.*

The buffalo that is found in southern Africa is called the *Cape,* or *black, buffalo.* It is larger than the water buffalo, and very fierce. It is eight feet long and almost six feet high at the shoulder. Its great horns often measure seven feet from tip to tip. Like the water buffalo, it also enjoys lying in marshy swamps.

The American "buffalo" that once roamed the plains of North America is really a *bison.* You can read about the BISON in a separate article.

Buffalo

Buffalo is an important port at the eastern end of Lake Erie, where the waters of this Great Lake flow into the Niagara River to form, at this point, the boundary between the United States and Canada. Buffalo is the second largest city in the state of New York. It was laid out as a frontier village in 1803 and burned by the British when they tried to conquer the United States in the War of 1812. Buffalo began to grow rapidly when the Erie Canal was opened in 1825, and it became possible to ship furs and forest products eastward by barge to the cities of the Atlantic coast. Settlers thronged through the town on their way west—and a good many of them stayed on.

Today, the people who live in Buffalo include many whose families came from European countries, particularly Poland. They work in huge plants producing steel, pig iron, flour, rubber goods, airplanes, automobiles, plastics, cloth goods, and lenses for cameras and telescopes. On week-ends they often take their children to visit nearby Niagara Falls, the world-famous waterfall.

BUFFALO, NEW YORK. Population 532,759. County seat of Erie County. On Lake Erie at its Niagara River outlet.

Buffalo Bill, a famous American scout and showman. See CODY, WILLIAM F.

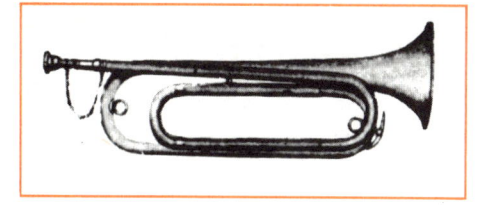

Left: A United States bugler blowing a call. *Upper right:* A regulation bugle. *Lower right:* An American Legion bugle.

U.S. Army Photo

buggy

In the days before automobiles, the buggy was one of the best-known types of carriage that people used to ride in. An American buggy had four wheels, but some English buggies had only two wheels. Some buggies were pulled by two horses, but most of them needed only one horse. Two or more people rode in a buggy, and they sat under a top, but the sides were open. The best American buggies were made by a man named Carter, who lived in New Jersey more than a hundred years ago. His buggies were much lighter and stronger than other buggies. Carter used light hickory wood instead of the heavier oak that other buggy-makers used. He made his buggies more comfortable by putting very good steel springs between the wheels and the body.

By 1890, hundreds of thousands of buggies were manufactured every year by such companies as Studebaker and Fisher. These companies are now in the automobile business. People called the first automobiles "horseless buggies." When people began to ride in automobiles, the buggy and other horse-drawn carriages began to disappear. Some buggies reappeared during World War II, when gasoline rationing limited the use of automobiles. You may sometimes see farmers driving buggies on dirt roads in the country, or you may see them at a county fair. The word buggy is sometimes used, like jalopy, as a slang word for automobile.

bugle

A bugle is a kind of coiled horn. Its sound is loud and can be heard a long distance away. It is made of brass, and has a separate mouthpiece that fits in the front end of the bugle. There are only a few notes that you can play on a bugle. You play them by changing your lip pressure as you blow into the mouthpiece. A bugle has no keys or valves like a cornet or trumpet. Armies have always used "bugle calls" to signal the troops.

Soldiers learn the tunes of the various calls so that they recognize them and know what they mean. Soldiers get up in the morning when the bugler blows *reveille;* they go to eat when he blows *mess call;* they gather for information when he blows *assembly;* they stand at attention and salute the flag as it comes down, when the bugler blows *retreat;* and they know it is "lights out" and time for bed when they hear the lovely notes of *taps* on the bugle. The Army officially uses trumpets instead of bugles, and the calls are now trumpet calls, but unofficially the soldiers still refer to them as bugle calls.

Building

building

Building is one of the oldest and most important activities of man. It is the way man has used his intelligence, imagination, and strength to put things together to make his life safer and more pleasant. Man has built houses to live in, churches to meet and worship in, theaters and stadiums to be entertained in, and factories, mills, barns, and offices to work in. He has built hospitals, garages, railroad stations, warehouses, and airplane hangars. All of these buildings are shelters. They all have a foundation, floor, ceiling and roof, although what a building looks like depends on what it is used for, and of what materials it is made.

Man also builds many things for purposes other than shelter. He builds ships and railroads, airplanes and bridges, canals and tunnels and docks for transportation purposes. He builds aqueducts to carry water, and pipe lines to carry oil and gas. He builds mighty dams to hold back rushing water, and he builds great monuments, like the pyramids in Egypt, and the Lincoln Memorial in Washington, D.C., to honor famous people. He also builds tremendous atom smashers to make atomic energy and atomic bombs. You can read about most of the things that man has built in separate articles about each of them.

Man is the greatest builder of all the animals, but he was not the first. When early man was still living in caves that he found, or sleeping in treetops, other animals had been building things for millions of years. Birds had been building many kinds of nests. Ants were building anthills with marvelous rooms and tunnels, wasps and bees were building hives, and beavers were building their wonderful dams and lodges. Man probably first began to build by watching some of these other animals, and he soon began to do things better than any of them.

HISTORY OF BUILDING

The first building man did was to make a place to keep himself warm and dry, and he used whatever materials he could find most easily. If he lived where there were many stones, he used them to build a shelter. If he lived in a forest, he used the trees and leaves. He made homes out of dried clay if he lived near a river bank, and if he lived in the far north he made his house of ice and snow. Then when man had a safe, warm place for himself and his family to live in, he wanted company, and soon he began to build larger shelters. He built meeting halls where he and his neighbors could get together to talk things over and have a good time, and he built churches where men could come together to worship God.

Then about 150 years ago man began to build factories and other buildings where many men could work together.

Before that most men worked at home. Shoemakers made shoes, and weavers wove cloth, and doctors took care of sick people in the houses where they lived. But when man's busy mind began to discover new and better ways of doing things by machine instead of by hand, he needed buildings large enough to hold the machines and the people to run them. With the INDUSTRIAL REVOLUTION (you can read about this important event in another volume), man started working together with many other men, and so he had to build places to work in—factories, offices, and places to store the things that he made.

With his new machines, man could build things much better than ever before, and he came to have even more respect for the wonderful builders of ancient times. The people of Egypt had no steam shovels to help them carry the huge stones to build the pyramids. We know that some of these great pyramids were built almost four thousand years ago, and all the work was done by the strong arms of men. The Romans had no bulldozers to help them build their roads, and the Greeks had no complicated machinery to make the temples and other buildings that we can still see standing in magnificent ruins. We know that the Romans found a way to bring water through pipes into their houses, and they built huge aqueducts and public baths. With all this new knowledge and fine equipment, modern man still honors the mighty builders of the past and wonders at their skill. These ancient men knew how to make a building strong and beautiful. You can read about some of the ways they did this in the article on ARCHITECTURE in another volume. You can also read how man's idea of what is beautiful changes all the time, and how he changes the way he builds and develops new styles of architecture.

CHANGES IN BUILDING

Modern man builds higher and faster than the early builders did. He can use the machines he has made to do easily and quickly things that would have taken his great grandfather many hours of hard work to do. Modern man has trains and airplanes to help him and this has made an important change in the way he can build. Long ago, the workmen had to be wherever the building was going on. Now, a man in St. Louis may work on the pipes for a new office building that is being put up in New York City. A man in Seattle may make the nails, and someone in Wisconsin will make the glass. Nails, glass, pipes, and all the other things that are needed for the building can be shipped to New York City by plane or train in just a few hours.

Machines and transportation have made it possible for houses and even huge buildings to be built in factories. Walls and floors and roofs are made in the factory and then sent to the spot where the building is to be put up. Buildings that are made in the factory are called *prefabricated.* Recently in New York City two sides of a tremendous skyscraper were put up in one day in this way, and during World War II whole towns of prefabricated houses were built very quickly and cheaply for men who needed a place to live while they were working in war factories.

One big difference between the way a big city like New York looks now and the way it looked a hundred years ago is that the buildings are very tall. The first modern skyscraper was built in Chicago about seventy years ago. Two important things had happened that made the modern skyscraper possible. Steel and reinforced concrete were two new materials that made a lot of difference in building. (Reinforced concrete is ordinary concrete with steel rods inside of it so that the concrete is much stronger and will not crack.) Before man learned to make steel he could not make his buildings very tall because the walls had to be thick enough to support the weight of

BUILDING

Oregon State Highway Comm.

N.Y. Public Library

Am. Museum of Nat. Hist.

3. Many Indian tribes killed the buffaloes roaming on the plains, and sewed the hides together into sturdy tepees. A tepee had an air hole at the top and a floor made of hard earth.
4. The cliff-dwelling Indians in the southwestern United States made their homes in the stone cliffs. This ancient "apartment house" had 60 rooms.
5. In the southwest, there are many adobe Indian villages. An adobe house was made out of blocks of mud that were hardened by being left to dry in the hot sun.

The houses people have built, and the ways they have built them, have changed through the centuries. Once, men depended on the materials they could find close at hand. In some places they still do. For a long time, people had only crude tools to work with, and building a house was a slow and difficult task for everyone.
1. American pioneers built their houses out of logs that they cut down in the great forests. This is a large modern log cabin.
2. The Wichita Indians made their houses out of grass and branches.

Nat'l. Park Service

BUILDING

Standard Oil Co.

Ezra Stoller

Modern skyscrapers could not be built until men developed special materials and machinery, and most important of all, the elevator.
1. An outside work elevator is built to bring materials to the top of a skyscraper under construction.
2. A construction gang swings the heavy steel girders into place.
3. The 38-story Seagram Building in New York City, the world's first bronze building.
4. A workman at his job 30 stories up.

Standard Oil Co.

BUILDING

the whole building. But when he learned how to use thin, strong steel he found he was able to build as high as he pleased.

One more thing was necessary before man could make high buildings. If you have ever walked up four or five flights of stairs, maybe you can imagine what it would be like to walk up twenty or ninety flights. Man needed some way to get up and down in these very high buildings, and then about a hundred years ago the first elevator was tried out in New York City. Now man had a way to go up and down, and materials strong enough to hold the weight of many floors. This was a good thing, because with more and more people living together, there was not very much room on the ground any more. One way to go was up, so cities began to climb up into the sky.

Man is finding new kinds of glass, aluminum and many other materials to make his offices and apartment houses, factories, and farms as beautiful and comfortable and safe as possible. Gas, electricity, and now air conditioning, are being used in buildings. Modern homes have been changing too. You may think the newest houses with all glass walls and screens that move in place of any inside walls may look a little funny, but they are designed to make life as healthy and happy as can be for the people who live in them.

THE MEN WHO BUILD

A man can build a little house all by himself, and many men like to do this. But to build the Empire State Building, which is more than 1,200 feet high, many men had to work together. Everyone likes to watch the men who build. The steam shovels pick up large pieces of rock, the bulldozers smooth the ground, men shovel and hack and weld and split and hammer and work machines. It seems that no one pays any attention to what anyone else is doing, and yet you know that out of it all the men who work so busily on some special part of the building are working according to a plan. The architect has made the plan, and everyone else carries it out. The contractor is the man who has to see that the building is done exactly the way the architect planned it. Then there are the bricklayers, the ironworkers, the steamfitters, the plasterers, plumbers, and electricians. All of these men have been trained to do their special work, and all of the work has to be done just right. Every part is important.

First, the foundation of the building must be strong. The Empire State Building is built so solidly that if a wind blew 100 miles an hour against one side, and it blew for two hours, the building would move only 1½ inches. The frame of the building is made of steel columns and crossbeams. The ironworkers have to weld the crossbeams to the columns, and this is dangerous work because it has to be done many stories above the ground. Men are working on all parts of the building at the same time. While the ironworkers are doing their job, bricklayers are laying bricks; on another floor steamfitters are busy, and other men are cutting glass, laying floors, and doing all the things that must be done to make the building grow. When the building is ready the painters and plumbers go to work, and even these are not all the men who have to do with the building. Other men, maybe in other cities, are making bathtubs and sinks, light bulbs, paint, chairs and screws. All of these things are part of the building.

Bankers and government officials are interested in the building too. The banker may lend the money to the builder, and the government may promise that if the builder cannot pay back the money, the government will. The builder has had to file plans for his building with the government and the local government must decide whether the plans meet all the safety requirements, and whether it is all right to build in that location.

SOME FAMOUS BUILDINGS

Some of the buildings that man has made are famous all over the world. One is the Pentagon Building in Washington, D.C. Another is the group of buildings called Rockefeller Center, in New York City. The tallest building in the world is the Empire State Building, in New York City. It has 102 floors and is more than 1,200 feet high. The oldest building still standing in the United States is the Palace of the Governors in Sante Fe, New Mexico, which was built about 350 years ago.

bulb

A bulb is a plant bud that develops underground. Like all buds, it is the part of a plant from which a flower, or a new plant itself, will grow. Many kinds of plants grow from bulbs. Some of these bulbs are used by man for food, and some are used to grow beautiful flowers. The onion is the best known food bulb along with other members of its family —garlic, shallot, leek and scallion. Many of our most beautiful garden flowers are grown from bulbs, such as the lily, tulip, daffodil, hyacinth, narcissus, and snowdrop.

Bulbs vary in size, but they are all somewhat round in shape, and they are all hard and tightly packed. Some bulbs, like the onion, are made up of many complete coats, or layers. You can see this by counting the rings of an onion that has been cut in two. Other bulbs, like the lily, are made up of many leaves that are tightly packed together like a firm rosebud. Both the layered and the leaf bulbs contain the life of a new plant. When winter comes, or a dry season sets in, and a plant has withered and died above the ground, the bulb underground still has life. The bulb sleeps in the ground until the warm weather and water comes to awaken it. Then it sends out roots deeper into the ground, and pushes a new plant up through the soil to the surface. In its "sleeping" state a bulb looks dry and lifeless, but it can be taken from the ground, and then when it is replanted it will grow and bloom.

U.S.D.A.

Beautiful flowers will bloom from these narcissus bulbs in the spring.

Bulfinch, Charles

Charles Bulfinch was one of the first American architects. He was born in Boston, Massachusetts, in 1763, and after he was graduated from Harvard College, he traveled in Europe and studied architecture there. He learned to plan and design beautiful buildings. Bulfinch came back to Boston where he built the first theater in all the New England States. He wanted Boston to be a beautiful, clean city so he had the streets made wide and designed a new way of lighting them at night. In 1795, he made the plans for the new State House in Boston, and later designed many other important buildings.

Bulfinch began his most important work in 1818, when he was chosen to be the architect for the national Capitol in Washington, D.C. The work had been started by another architect, but Bulfinch did much of the important work on this great domed building. He died in 1844.

Bulganin, Nikolai

Nikolai Alexandrovich Bulganin is the name of a Russian Communist leader who became premier (head of the govern-

BULGARIA

ment) of the Union of Soviet Socialist Republics.

Bulganin was born in 1896 and joined the Communist Party in 1917. During World War II he was in charge of Russia's armed forces and was made a marshal, the highest rank in an army. After serving several years as Commissar of armed forces (like the United States Secretary of Defense), he was made premier in 1955. However, this was only to win the support of the Soviet Army for the Party Secretary, Nikita Khrushchev, who held the real power. Bulganin and Khrushchev made several "good will" trips together to foreign capitals in the years 1955 to 1957. In 1958 Bulganin was forced to resign as premier and nominate Khrushchev, who was elected premier in his place.

Bulgaria

Bulgaria is a small country on the Balkan Peninsula in southeastern Europe. It is about 43,000 square miles in size, not quite as large as Wisconsin, and more than eight million people live there, about twice as many as live in Wisconsin. For centuries Bulgaria was ruled by Turkey. In 1908 it became independent, but since 1946 it has had a Communist government controlled by Soviet Russia.

THE PEOPLE WHO LIVE THERE

Most of the Bulgarian people are a mixture of two groups of people that settled there many years ago. The first group were Slavs, who came from the north more than 1,700 years ago. The other group were Bulgars, who came from the east about 1,300 years ago, and conquered the Slavs. Both groups of people then lived together peacefully. The Bulgars started doing many things the way the Slavs did them, and they even began to speak the Slav language instead of their own. Many Bulgars married Slavs, and that is why most Bulgarians today are the descendants of this mixture of Bulgars and Slavs. There are also some Turks, Greeks, and Gypsies living in Bulgaria.

The people of Bulgaria are not very tall, but they are very strong and healthy. They are known for their strength and for the fact that many of them live to a very, very old age. Most Bulgarians belong to the Greek Orthodox Church, to which a great many of the people of Eastern Europe belong. Their language is called Slavonic, and it is something like Russian.

Nowadays, Bulgarians wear clothes very much like ours, but for special occasions they dress in the costumes their ancestors wore. The women wear hand-embroidered blouses and skirts that are colorful and very attractive. The men wear beautifully embroidered shirts and loose pants like knickers.

All Bulgarian children have to go to school from the time they are seven until they are fourteen. Some of them get a chance to continue their education at one of the eleven colleges in Bulgaria.

HOW THE PEOPLE LIVE

Most of the people of Bulgaria are farmers. Many of them live and work on farms that are owned by the government. Almost half of them own their own farms. The farmers raise wheat, rye, oats, corn, barley, cotton, flax, and many kinds of fruit. They also raise cattle, pigs, sheep, goats, horses, oxen, and chickens. The soil is very fertile, but not all of it is used for farming. There are long stretches of countryside where nothing is grown, and there are many forests. The Bulgarian horses are smaller than the horses we see in America, but they are very strong and sturdy. The Bulgarian people get most of their milk from their sheep, instead of from cows, and they make a sheep's-milk cheese that some people think is very delicious.

The Bulgarian people have been trying to become more modern. Since the end of World War II, they have tried to build more factories and to produce better crops on their farms. Some of the people who work in factories make modern farm equipment. Other factory workers make machinery, textiles, clothing, and metal products. Most of the houses are old and do not have modern plumbing, heating, or lighting.

The biggest city in Bulgaria is its capital, Sofia. About 674,000 people live there. This is about as many people as there are in Dallas, Texas. The biggest university in Bulgaria, the University of Sofia, is in that city. The next biggest city is called Plovdiv. About 172,000 people live there, which is somewhat fewer than there are in Springfield, Mass. There are two main seaport cities in Bulgaria. These cities are on the Black Sea, and are called Stalin and Burgas.

WHAT KIND OF PLACE IT IS

There are many mountains, rivers, and forests in Bulgaria. The main mountains are the Balkans and the Rhodope Mountains. The Danube River separates Bulgaria from its neighbor, Rumania, in the north.

The weather in Bulgaria is usually pleasant. The summers are very hot, but very dry, and the winters are short, cold, and dry. It rains a good deal in the autumn and the spring. The rainy spring and hot, dry summers are very good for flower gardening. Roses grow all through Bulgaria. They are very beautiful and very fragrant. The Bulgarians crush the petals to make a perfume called attar of roses.

There is much coal in Bulgaria, and there is some copper, zinc, and lead. But Bulgaria does not have as many natural resources in proportion to its size as many other countries of the world.

BULGARIA

More than one-third of Bulgaria is covered by forests. All kinds of animals live in these forests. There are bears, deer, wild goats, and squirrels. In the marshes near the river banks there are many kinds of wild birds.

HOW THE PEOPLE ARE GOVERNED

Bulgaria has had many different kinds of government. Since 1946, it has been a republic. It has a constitution that was made up in 1947. This constitution is very much like the constitution of the Union of Soviet Socialist Republics (Russia). Bulgaria is actually controlled by the U.S.S.R. in all important matters.

The main governing body of Bulgaria is the National Assembly, which is made up of representatives elected by the people. The National Assembly is elected every four years, and the members of the National Assembly elect the prime minister and the other ministers, who form a body somewhat like the cabinet in other countries.

Since the republic was established in 1946, the government has taken over the operation of most of the industry and farms of the country, but there are still some businesses and farms that are owned by private citizens.

All the men in Bulgaria have to serve in the army. They can be called into the army any time between their eighteenth and sixty-fifth birthdays, and they usually must serve for two years. The Bulgarians have fought in many wars, and although their army is not very big, the men are fierce and good fighters.

BULGARIA IN THE PAST

Bulgaria was part of the Roman Empire nearly 2,000 years ago. It was called Moesia at that time. After the Roman Empire fell, the Slavs came into Bulgaria. Then the Bulgars invaded the country and established a kingdom about 1,300 years ago. The people of Bulgaria became Christians about 1,000 years ago, when they were converted by missionaries of the Greek Orthodox Church. The Turks invaded Bulgaria about 550 years ago, and for the next five hundred years they ruled the country. The Turks were not Christians, and the Bulgarians were, so there was much bad feeling between the two peoples. The Turks treated the Bulgarians very badly, and their cruelty to the Bulgarians made every one in Europe very angry. Late in the nineteenth century, the Russians went to war against the Turks, and when the peace treaty was signed between the two countries, in 1878, the Turks were made to treat the Bulgarians better. In 1908, a revolution in Turkey gave the Bulgarians the chance to become independent. They established their own kingdom and chose a German prince named Ferdinand as their king.

In World War I, Bulgaria fought on the German side. When the war was over, Bulgaria had to give up some of her territory.

In World War II, Bulgaria once again was on the side of the Germans. Two days before Russian troops entered Bulgaria in 1944, Bulgaria declared war on Germany. Shortly after that the Bulgarians made peace with Russia, Great Britain, and the United States.

After the war was over, the Russians forced the Bulgarians to get rid of their king, and establish a government like the Russian one. This form of government is called a republic, but it is not a democracy like that in the United States. The Bulgarians were allowed to vote, but they could vote only for the candidates selected by the Communist party. Thus Bulgaria, instead of being independent, became very much dependent on the Communist country of Russia.

The United States and Bulgaria did not get along very well after that, and relations between the two countries reached a low point in 1950 when Bulgaria accused the American Minister and members of his staff of spying. The U.S. was so angry that it broke off diplomatic relations with Bulgaria and withdrew its

BULGARIA

1. People in Tirnovo live in houses built on the sides of steep hills. The city was the ancient capital of Bulgaria.
2. When the famous Bulgarian roses bloom, the blossoms are picked. The oil pressed from the petals is called attar of roses, and is used to make perfume.
3. This is the beautiful Valley of Roses, where these lovely flowers bloom each spring.
4. Bulgarian farmers use oxen to do the heavy farm work.
5. The farmers' daughters help with the spinning and weaving.

BULL

1. A peasant girl in southern Bulgaria wears a typical native costume with beautiful embroidery and bright colors.
2. The cathedral at Sofia, the capital of Bulgaria, is the largest in the Balkans. The big dome is covered with gold.
3. There are many fine buildings to see in the capital city. This is the University of Sofia, built about 70 years ago.

Bulgarian Nat'l Comm. Photos

representatives. Diplomatic relations were finally resumed in 1959 when Bulgaria apologized for the unfounded accusations.

BULGARIA. Area, 42,796 sq. mi. Population (1964 U.N. estimate) 8,144,000. Capital, Sofia. Language, Slavonic. Chief religion, Greek Orthodox. Government, republic. Monetary unit, lev, worth about 8½ U.S. cents (free rate). Flag, white, green, and red bars across the flag; canton (shield shape) with coat of arms on it.

bull, the male animal of the bovine family: see CATTLE.

bulldog

The bulldog is a ferocious-looking dog but it has a gentle, kind disposition. It has great courage, and is a brave protector and watchdog. Originally the bulldog was bred in England for bull baiting. Bull baiting was a cruel sport in which a bull was tied up on a short rope, and the dogs were supposed to jump up and get a grip on the bull's nose. At that time the bulldog was a strong, stubborn, tough animal, and seemed to feel very little pain, even when badly hurt. When bull baiting became illegal, the bulldog was bred to be the gentle, easygoing dog that it is today. It is a dog of medium size, but heavier than average for its height.

A bulldog stands about 18 to 20 inches high at the shoulder, and weighs between 40 and 50 pounds. Its head is large, and

Milsande's Scotch Lassie, a champion bulldog, winner of many first prizes.
Milsande Kennels

the teeth on its lower jaw show, because the lower jaw juts out quite a bit in front of the upper jaw. Its face is full of deep wrinkles, and its ears are small, lying close to its head. A bulldog looks slightly bow-legged, but that is only because it has heavy muscles on the outside of its legs, and not because the legs are actually crooked. A bulldog's short tail is sometimes straight, and sometimes crooked. Its coat is smooth, short, and soft, and may be solid white, reddish brown, light tan or yellow, or with large splashes of different colors.

bulldozer

A bulldozer is a large and powerful kind of tractor that is used in building or construction work. Most tractors are used to pull loads, but a bulldozer is used to push things. A bulldozer has a great curved blade mounted on its front end. This blade is used to scrape dirt and to push it into large piles. The blade is also used to knock down trees and push aside rocks.

Bulldozers make it possible to do many construction jobs much more quickly than they could be done before. That is why the army uses bulldozers to make airports, and why people who build bridges, roads, dams, houses, and athletic fields, all use bulldozers.

bullet

A bullet is a piece of metal that is fired from a pistol, rifle or machine gun. The first bullets were small, round balls of lead that were dropped in the barrel of the gun after the powder charge had been put in the gun. Modern bullets are usually long with a sharp, pointed nose. Bullets for CARBINES (which you can read about in a separate article) have rounded noses. They are made of lead, with an outside jacket of copper and zinc over steel plating. They are held, at the bottom, in a brass case that contains the powder charge. The case, or cartridge, is placed by hand, or fed automatically into the breech of a gun. The breech is the opening at the back end of the gun barrel. You can read more about bullets in the article on AMMUNITION.

bullfighting

Bullfighting is the national *fiesta* (entertainment) of Spain and some Latin-American countries. It is more popular there than baseball or football in the United States. Thousands of people go to watch the bullfights in Spain, Mexico, and other places. The fights are held in large circular fields, called arenas, that are completely surrounded by rows of seats. These arenas are very much like the football stadiums in the United States. Before a bullfight begins, there is a wonderful parade of all the men who take part in it, all dressed in beautifully colored costumes.

After the bullfighters have paraded, the arena is cleared, and the bull is let loose. He comes charging out, snorting and pawing the dirt. Then several men called *picadors* come into the arena. They are mounted on horseback and they carry long, sharp lances. Their horses are covered with a thick padded coat to protect them from the bull's horns. The picadors charge the bull and attempt to stick it

BULLFIGHTING

with their lances. Sometimes the maddened bull charges the horses, and wounds them with his horns, even though the horses have the padded coats. When the picadors have stabbed the bull three times and weakened it, they leave the arena, and men on foot called *banderilleros* come in. The banderilleros wave bright-colored capes at the bull, and try to get close enough to stick sharp darts into the bull's shoulders. The darts have

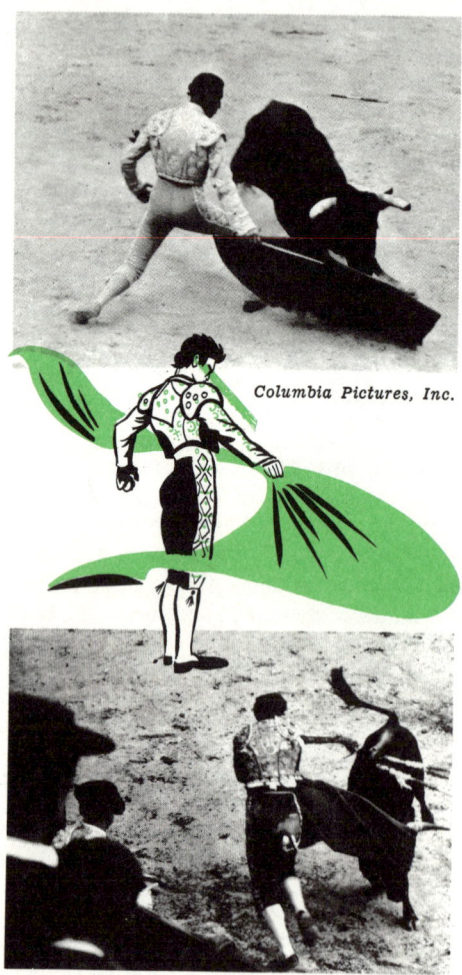

Columbia Pictures, Inc.

Standard Oil Co.

Top: The matador avoids the charging bull with a graceful movement that takes great skill. *Bottom:* The bull has been maddened by the sharp darts stuck into him. *Right:* Bullfights are as popular in Mexico as baseball games are in the United States.

brightly colored ribbons attached to them. When the bull chases the banderilleros, they jump over a low fence to get away.

When the bull has three pairs of darts, which are called *banderillas*, stuck in his shoulders, the master bullfighter, the *matador*, enters the arena. He carries a sword and a *muleta*, a stick which has a piece of red silk attached to it. The muleta is sometimes called a cape. It is waved at the bull to attract its attention. Bulls, like all animals, are colorblind. They are not maddened by seeing something red, but by movement. Besides, the bull is now furious because of the darts sticking in his shoulders.

The matador tries to make the bull pass as close to him as possible. Sometimes he misjudges the distance, and he is gored by the bull's horns. Some matadors have been killed in this way. Finally the matador gets set for the last charge. He holds his sword up and when the bull comes close, he plunges the sword into the bull's shoulders.

The art of bullfighting is very complicated, just as complicated as baseball or football and many other sports. Bullfight fans argue with each other about the best ways of doing things and about who is the best matador. Bullfighting is more than just a sport to see who will win or lose. First of all, it is far more dangerous than most sports, because the matador himself is often hurt badly, and sometimes dies. Also, there are rules in bullfighting, just as in other sports, but it is not enough for the bullfighter merely to obey the rules. Bullfighting is also an art, like dancing or acting, and the best bullfighter must also be the most graceful.

Bullfighting began in ancient times, in Rome and Greece. It was probably introduced into Spain by the Moors of North Africa. Today, it is more popular in Spain than anywhere else. In southern France and Portugal, there is a special type of bullfighting in which the bulls

Am. Museum of Nat. History
Someone has left food for these bullfinches.

are not killed. But in Mexico and in some other Latin-American countries it is the same as in Spain. The largest bullfighting arena in the world is in Mexico City. It is so big that it holds 47,000 spectators.

bullfinch

A bullfinch is a small bird that lives in Europe and Asia. There are many different kinds of bullfinch. One of them, called Cassin's bullfinch, sometimes flies to Alaska from Asia. All bullfinches look very much alike. Mostly they are about the size of a canary, with the same shape of beak—pointed, but stout and strong for eating seeds. The commonest sort lives in woods and is a very pretty bird. It is soft and blue above, with a brick-red breast. Bullfinches make very good pets, and can be taught to whistle tunes. They are often kept in cages, but less often than years ago, because many people think it is cruel to keep a wild bird a prisoner.

bullfrog, a large American frog. See FROGS and TOADS.

bullion

Bullion is gold or silver that has been made into solid bars. The bars are made by melting the gold or silver and pressing it into molds. In some countries you may buy gold or silver bullion if you are going to make some jewelry or use it to fill teeth. In the United States the word bullion is used only for the bars of gold and other precious metals that are security for money. (There is a separate article on MONEY.) These bars are kept in the vaults of the Treasury Department. A *gold certificate* is paper money you can exchange for gold, but it is now against the law to keep gold money or gold certificates. When you need gold for making things you must apply to the government for a special license.

Bull Moose Party

The Bull Moose Party was the nickname of the Progressive Party, founded in 1912, that nominated Theodore Roosevelt for the presidency. At the Republican convention that year, President William Howard Taft was nominated for reëlection, and almost immediately Roosevelt's followers organized the Progressive Party, and nominated Roosevelt to run for the presidency. He and Taft were both defeated by the Democratic candidate, Woodrow Wilson. The name of the party was taken from a remark of Roosevelt's during the campaign. He said, "I feel as fit as a bull moose."

Bull Run, Battle of

Bull Run is a small stream in Virginia, near where two important Civil War battles were fought. The first Battle of Bull Run took place on July 21, 1861. The Union army, under General Irvin McDowell, was defeated by the Confederate army under General P. G. T. Beauregard and General J. E. Johnston. This victory at the beginning of the war gave the South great hope, and showed the people of the North that the war would not be over in a few months as they had thought.

The second Battle of Bull Run was fought on August 29 and 30, 1862. A

N.Y. Public Library

The Union Army suffered a great defeat at the first Battle of Bull Run early in the Civil War. Many soldiers on both sides were killed or wounded.

Union army of 70,000 men attacked a smaller number of Confederates under the famous General "Stonewall" Jackson. Jackson's troops held off the Union soldiers for one day until fresh troops were brought up by the Southern leader, General Robert E. Lee. Then they counterattacked and defeated the Union army. This battle was considered one of the important military victories of Jackson and Lee. In the South, the Battles of Bull Run are called the Battles of Manassas, because they were both fought near the railway junction at Manassas.

bull terrier

The bull terrier was the fiercest fighting dog when dog fighting was a popular sport. At that time it was called the "pit bull" because dog fights were held in deep pits. This was years ago, however, and now bull terriers are kept both in Europe and America as pets. They are strong and courageous as watchdogs, but are also usually friendly and playful pets. Very rarely will a bull terrier fight another dog unless the other dog attacks first. Then it will do its best to tear the other dog to pieces.

The bull terrier is a medium-sized dog. It stands about 18 to 22 inches high at the shoulder, and weighs anywhere from 25 to 60 pounds. The bull terrier's eyes are of an unusual triangular shape, and are set very close together. Its tail is short and straight, and slightly pointed. Sometimes the coat is pure white, sometimes it is brown, tan, or black, and sometimes it is one of these colors with white markings. The hair is coarse, and lies flat against the body.

bulrush

The bulrush is a reedlike plant that grows in marshes along the edge of lakes and ponds. It can be found all over Europe, and in parts of the United States. The bulrush grows as high as 9 feet, and is almost leafless. Its stem is the most useful part of the plant. It is used to make mats and the seats for chairs; and, in California, it has been used in packing, to protect wine bottles. The most famous story about this plant can be found in the Bible. The baby Moses was found hidden in the bulrushes in Egypt. The Egyptians used bulrushes to make the paper called papyrus. You can read about MOSES and PAPYRUS in separate articles.

Bulwer-Lytton

Sir Edward George Earle Bulwer-Lytton was a famous English writer. Most of the novels, plays and poems he wrote had historical backgrounds. His most famous book was *The Last Days of Pompeii* which is still very popular today. It tells about the Roman people who lived in the city of Pompeii. The city was at the foot of a volcano called Vesuvius. When the volcano erupted and shot out melted rock and fire, all of Pompeii and the people in it were destroyed. Sir Edward was born in England in 1803 and died there in 1873.

bumblebee, a large, fuzzy, humming bee. See BEE.

Bunche, Ralph Johnson

Ralph Bunche became famous as a peacemaker for the United Nations. He

Silverwood Kennels

The white bull terrier is a terror in a fight. It gets a grip and hangs on.

received the Nobel peace prize in 1950, for the work he did to stop a war between the Israeli and the Arabs. Bunche was the first Negro ever to win a Nobel Prize. He was born in 1904, and when he grew up, he became a teacher. During World War II and for about ten years after it, Bunche held important positions in the United States government, including presidential appointments as a delegate or commissioner to international meetings. He was an Assistant Secretary of State and a delegate to the United Nations. In 1958 Bunche accepted a position in the Secretariat of the United Nations, rather than live in Washington, D.C., where his children might suffer from discrimination against Negroes.

Bunker Hill

The Battle of Bunker Hill was the first real battle of the American Revolutionary War. It took place on Breed's Hill, near Bunker Hill, in Charlestown, Massachusetts, June 17, 1775. The battle was between 2,500 British soldiers commanded by General William Howe and 1,500 Americans under Colonel William Prescott. The Americans defended the hill against the British. The British attacked the hill three times, and twice they were thrown back by the Americans. The third time they reached the top of the hill, but more than a thousand of their men had fallen. The British losses were so high because Colonel Prescott told his men, "Don't shoot till you see the whites of their eyes." [That is, let the enemy get very close before you shoot.] Some historians believe the American commander, General Israel Putnam, and not Prescott, gave this order. Whoever said it, Americans have remembered it ever since.

The entire town of Charlestown was burned to the ground after the battle. By capturing Bunker Hill, the British were able to capture and hold Boston. The battle, however, raised the spirits of the Americans, who had shown the British that they could put up more of a fight than the British thought they could.

Bunsen, Robert Wilhelm

Robert Bunsen was a German chemist who became famous for inventing the *Bunsen Burner*. Burners very much like his original invention are still used in every science laboratory. Bunsen was born in 1811, and he had a long and busy life as a scientist, dying in 1899. He made many important discoveries in chemistry and invented scientific appliances that are known by his name. The Bunsen Burner is a metal tube in a holder that burns gas with a very hot, smokeless flame. The high heat is produced by mixing air with the gas. The more air that can be brought

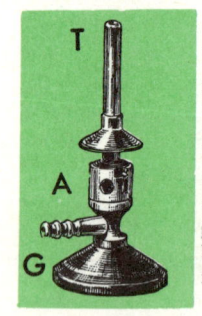

In a Bunsen burner, the gas pipe (G) is connected to a gas jet by a rubber tube. Gas goes into the burner and mixes with air that comes in through the air hole (A). This mixture goes up the tube (T), and burns with a very hot blue flame.

to a flame, the hotter the flame will burn. The Bunsen burner makes it possible to heat things more quickly and to a higher degree of heat. It is used to heat things in glass flasks and test tubes.

bunting

A bunting is a bright-colored bird which looks a little like a finch. Various kinds of bunting are found mostly in England and sometimes in other parts of Europe, Asia, Africa, and America. The *snow bunting* breeds in the north. The *cirl bunting* has a dark-green head. It stays farther toward the south.

The *yellow bunting* is found all over,

and the *reed bunting,* which has a black and white head, stays mostly in the marshes.

In America, the *black-throated bunting* lives in the open country of the middle west, and the *bay-winged bunting* lives in the eastern part of Canada and the United States.

The *lark bunting* lives in the far west, and has a brilliant song, unlike some of the other buntings, which have harsh voices.

Bunyan, John

John Bunyan was an English preacher and writer who became famous for writing a great book called *Pilgrim's Progress.* He was born in 1628 in the little town of Elstow, about 90 miles northwest of London. As a boy he worked at his father's trade of pot-mending or tinkering. After Bunyan was married, he became very religious. He gave up swearing and all kinds of amusements to devote himself to preaching and writing religious books. His first book was published in 1656.

Four years later he was arrested for preaching without a license, which was at that time against the law in England. He was sent to prison for twelve years, and during that time he wrote nine books, and preached to the others in prison with him. He was released in 1672, but five years later he was again arrested, and imprisoned for a short time. During this second time in prison he wrote the great book, *Pilgrim's Progress.* After his prison term was over, Bunyan spent the rest of his life preaching and writing. He died in 1688.

Bunyan, Paul

Paul Bunyan was an imaginary hero who is supposed to have lived about a hundred years ago in the lumber camps

Hakkerup Studio

Paul Bunyan and his blue ox, Babe, were supposed to have been as large as these statues of them in Minnesota.

of the northwestern part of the United States. The men who worked in these camps were called loggers or lumberjacks, and they used to sit around their campfires at night and tell "tall tales" about Paul Bunyan and Babe, his great blue ox. Paul was a great giant, the biggest lumberjack of all, and he did many wonderfully impossible things. Babe, the blue ox, was so big that they said it "measured 42 ax handles and a plug of chewing tobacco between the horns."

Nobody knew just exactly when Paul Bunyan lived, but they said that he lived in the imaginary period between the Winter of the Blue Snow and the Spring That the Rain Came Up From China. The character of Paul Bunyan is probably based on a French-Canadian lumberjack with the same name, who became famous fighting against the English and working in the lumber camps. But almost everything in the stories about him is made up. You can read these stories in two exciting and amusing books, each called *Paul Bunyan,* one by James Stevens, the other by Esther Shephard.

buoy

A buoy is a marker that floats in the water to show sailors where there is

1. A can buoy. 2. A nun buoy. 3. A spar buoy. 4. A bell buoy. 5. A light buoy.

danger, and where to steer their ships safely. If a ship or boat is going along in a river, bay, or harbor, it might run into rocks, sand bars, cable-crossings, mine fields, and other things, if it were not for buoys. A buoy is held in place by an anchor which is attached to it by a steel cable.

All buoys are not alike, and if you were sailing a ship through a passage marked by buoys, you would have to pay attention to the "markings" and also to the type of buoy. By looking at your chart (a map of the waters through which you are sailing), you would see such marks as "S" meaning a "spar buoy," "N" meaning a "nun buoy," and "C" meaning a "can buoy." Then there are different colors and numbers on the buoys themselves, which mean something to the navigator. Let us see what types of buoy we may find:

(1) *Spar buoys* are made of wood or iron plates and stick up out of the water like poles. The wooden ones are generally cedar, spruce, or redwood logs, bound together by heavy iron bands. Wooden buoys are painted with special paint so that the water and animal life in the water will not damage them. They vary in size from about 20 to 50 feet. The other type of spar buoy is made of iron plates riveted together. They vary in length from 30 to 50 feet. They are cigar-shaped. More of the length of spar buoys is under water than the part that sticks up out of the water.

(2) *Nun buoys* are made of iron plates riveted together. Inside there are two or three airtight compartments, so that the buoy will not sink if it is broken in one place. Nun buoys are of two types, short ones shaped like pears, and tall ones shaped like cigars. They are generally painted red, and have even numbers (2, 4, 6, etc.) painted on them. Short nun buoys sometimes have hollow balls attached to their sides so that they will float upright.

(3) *Can buoys* get their name because the part that sticks up out of the water is shaped like a tin can that food comes in. The part under water is either rounded, if it is a short can, or cigar-shaped, if it is a tall can. They are generally painted black, and have uneven numbers (1, 3, 5, etc.) on them.

Can buoys and nun buoys are also painted with stripes at times, for different signals, and if they are placed to show a channel or obstruction, there are no numbers.

WHISTLING BUOYS

At some important places it is desirable to have a light or sound to guide vessels at night, or in a thick fog. For these places, there are buoys with lights, bells, or whistles. Here is how they work:

(1) *Light buoys* have lights that burn all the time. Some still have oil lamps, but most of them work on an electric battery. Some have bells or whistles.

(2) *Bell buoys* have a bronze bell. Most of the buoy is a big steel float, under water. The bell part is built over the buoy, and when the waves rock it, the bell rings.

(3) *Whistling* buoys are shaped like short nun buoys, with the upper end more pointed. A tube runs through the buoy from top to bottom. At the upper end of the tube there is a whistle. When the buoy rises and then falls in the waves, the air in the tube (which is open at the bottom) is compressed, as in a pump, by the water pushing up from below. There is no place for the air to go, except up through the whistle, which makes a loud sound.

This bell buoy is being repaired by sailors of the Coast Guard.

Burbank

Burbank is a city in southern California. It is a suburb of Los Angeles. More than 90,000 people live there. There are important motion-picture studios and aircraft factories there.

Burbank, Luther

Luther Burbank was a scientist who experimented with plants and became famous for developing new kinds of flowers, fruits, and vegetables. He was born near Lancaster, Massachusetts, in 1849, and grew up on a farm. As a young boy he became interested in working with plants to see if he could make them grow bigger and better. He learned to select the seeds of the best plants to grow new ones, and when he was 24 years old he had developed the Burbank potato that is still one of the best. Soon after this he moved west for his health. He went to Santa Rosa, northwest of San Francisco, California, which he said was the "chosen spot of all this earth as far as Nature is concerned." There he set up his experimental farm, where he worked for the next 50 years, until his death in 1926. He became famous all over the world, and he inspired many other people to take up plant breeding.

Burbank grew over a million plants a year. Sometimes he had several thousand experiments going on at once—all different. He used both *crossbreeding* and *grafting*. In *crossbreeding* a berry, for example, he took one kind that had a fine flavor but was small in size and mated it with another that was larger. When the result was good, the fruit of the *hybrid,* or new plant, was both large and full-flavored. Burbank made 40,000 hybrids by crossing blackberry and raspberry plants. He also developed a thornless blackberry.

Grafting is a way of giving a weak plant a strong root system. An apple that is good for both eating and baking may grow on a frail tree. Another apple tree may have a strong, healthy growth, but its fruit may be small, bitter, or taste-

BURBOT

Stark Bros. Nurseries

Luther Burbank's experiments in crossbreeding have made it possible for farmers to grow giant peaches that are many times larger than those grown in the past.

less. Burbank would take a cutting, or branch, from the frail tree and graft it into a slit in the branch of the sturdier tree. The pieces grew together, and the new branch bore its own fruit. In Burbank's tests, a single tree sometimes carried 600 different grafts. You may have seen flowering trees that have been grafted so that several different kinds of blooms appear on the same tree.

Burbank's work on a single fruit or vegetable might extend over many years. His new varieties included the Gold and Bartlett plums and the Splendor and Sugar prunes. He developed better apples, cherries, peaches, and nectarines, as well as tomatoes, sweet and field corn, squash, and peas. He also grew new kinds of lilies, roses, and the famous Shasta daisy.

burbot

The burbot is the only freshwater fish belonging to the same family as the cod. It is large, shaped like an eel, and has very long fins above and below that extend from its middle to its tail. It has a soft, slimy skin in which there are tiny scales, and a long fleshy feeler under its chin. The burbot is found in deep, cool water in lakes or big rivers in the northern parts of America, Europe and Asia. Some burbots have been caught in Alaska that were five feet long and weighed about sixty pounds. Some people say the burbot is good to eat, but most do not like the way it looks, and refuse to eat this fish.

The burbot is sometimes called *ling* by Americans.

burdock

Burdock is a big, coarse weed. It originally grew in Europe and Asia, but it was brought to America where it now grows wild. It has large, soft leaves, and pink or purplish flowers. These grow in large "heads," like the flowers of a thistle or a dandelion. When they go to seed, this head becomes a big round mass of burs. In Japan the root of burdock is cooked and eaten as a vegetable, which is called *gobo*.

You can see great patches of burdock growing along the sides of roads and in uncultivated fields.

bureaucracy

A government is called a bureaucracy when it is run by many minor officials, or heads of "bureaus" (smaller divisions of the big government departments). When a person says a government is a bureaucracy, he means that he disapproves of the way it is being run. The idea is that minor officials follow the law strictly even when it is unfair, while higher-ranking government officials would use the law more intelligently. Another criticism of a bureaucracy is that all these officials try very hard to keep their jobs, because they could not get better jobs anywhere else. Therefore they look for ways to make more work for their bureaus, instead of less, and this costs the taxpayers money. The very big men in a government are not usually interested in the salaries they get in their jobs, because most of them have made or could make bigger salaries working for privately owned companies.

The word *bureaucracy* means, literally, "government from a desk," or "from an office."

Burgess, Frank Gelett

Gelett Burgess was an American writer who was born in 1866 and died in 1957, more than 90 years old. He never used his first name, Frank. He wrote more than thirty books, and drew the pictures for many of them himself. He wrote things like the *Burgess Nonsense Book,* and *Goops and How To Be Them,* but he is best-known for a little four-line jingle called *The Purple Cow.*

> I never saw a purple cow,
> I never hope to see one;
> But I can tell you anyhow,
> I'd rather see than be one.

burglary

Burglary is the crime of breaking into or entering a person's home with the idea of stealing something. Some states have laws that say burglary can only take place at night. If the same thing takes place in the daytime these states call it *housebreaking.* When the police arrest a burglar they sometimes say that he is guilty of "breaking and entering," because they can put him in jail for breaking and entering if he opens a closed window or forces a door to get into a house, whether he steals something or not. Some burglars climb up to a porch or window on the second floor of a house because the ground floor is more often locked up. These burglars are called "second-story men."

Burgos

Burgos is a historic city in northern Spain and also the name of a large inland province of which the city is capital. The province is about the size of the state of Georgia and about 400,000 people live there. Most of them are farmers. The city of Burgos is on the Arlanzón River. About 70,000 people live there, working in factories that make woolen and leather goods, and paper. Farm products from the province are shipped from the city by river boat and railways.

Burgos was already an important city

Spanish Tourist Office
Most of the buildings and sculpture in Burgos are hundreds of years old.

more than a thousand years ago. It was the capital of Castile and León for about 500 years until that kingdom became part of the Spanish kingdom in 1560.

During the Spanish Civil War of 1936 to 1939, Burgos was the headquarters of the forces under General Francisco Franco. At Burgos you can see one of the most famous and beautiful cathedrals in Europe. This cathedral was built in 1221, and one of the most important Spanish heroes, the Cid, is buried there. The Cid lived at Burgos, a fact that still makes the people of Burgos very proud.

BURGOS. Province: Area, 55,350 square miles. Population 390,058. Capital, Burgos, population 69,789.

Burgoyne, John

John Burgoyne was a famous English general during the American Revolution. He was born in 1722 and went to school in England. After graduation, he entered the army. In 1774 he was sent to America, and in 1777 he was a leader in the fight against the American colonists.

General Burgoyne is shown as he surrendered to General Gates at Saratoga, in 1777.

With several thousand English soldiers and a few hundred Indians, he captured Fort Ticonderoga, in New York State. He then lost battles at Bennington, Vermont, and Stillwater, New York, and was badly defeated by the Americans under General Gates at Saratoga, near Stillwater, in October, 1777. Burgoyne and his whole army were captured. He was later allowed to return to England, and he became commander in chief of the English army in Ireland. His last days were devoted to writing plays and histories. He died in 1792.

Burgundy

Burgundy is a region in eastern France that was formerly a large province. It is now divided into four departments, which are something like states. The departments are Ain, Yonne, Saône et Loire, and Côte d'Or. Burgundy is a rich agricultural country that is especially famous for the wines made from the grapes grown there.

The ancient Burgundians were a German tribe who lived more than 1,500 years ago and formed themselves into a kingdom. Then the kingdom became a duchy, which means that it was ruled by a duke. The dukes of Burgundy were very powerful, more powerful even than the kings of France itself. One of the dukes fought with the English against the French King Charles VII and his army which was led by Joan of Arc. However, the duke was finally beaten and Burgundy became a province of France under King Louis XI. All this happened about 500 years ago.

The largest city in Burgundy is Dijon, which is also the historical capital of the province. There are several beautiful churches and palaces in Dijon as well as in the other towns of Burgundy. In the countryside, there are some very big and famous castles in which people still live.

burial

Burial is the way in which mankind disposes of the bodies of people who have died. Throughout history different peoples in different places have had different ways of disposing of dead bodies. The earliest savage wanderers probably just left bodies lying on the ground. Only when men began to settle down and stay in one place did they probably dig holes and bury the dead. They did this because they found that they could not keep dead bodies lying around to rot away and smell, and attract wild animals. Man also began to bury the dead because he had become religious, and even in his primitive religion, he believed that some respect had to be shown to those who had died.

Many primitive groups believed that people make a long journey after death. So they put certain kinds of tools, or weapons, or food, in the grave when they buried a dead body. When men became more civilized, they still continued to do this. The ancient Egyptians even killed the dead person's horse and pet animals, and buried them with him. Some Eskimo tribes still bury a dead man's dog with him, so that the dog can make this long journey with his master.

There have been tribes throughout history that believed that birth and death are alike in some ways, and that the earth is the mother of all people. These tribes arranged the bodies of their dead in the same position as the unborn child has in the mother, and then buried the bodies in the ground.

People in some parts of the world do not bury the dead in the ground, but build platforms above the ground to hold the bodies. Many Indian tribes have done this, particularly those that lived in the north where the bodies would not rot away so quickly in the cold. Some South American Indians buried their dead high up in the mountains where the ice and snow never melt. In this way, the bodies were kept in a sort of deep freeze and never rotted away.

Many early tribes and many civilized people *cremate* dead bodies. You cremate a body by burning it until nothing is left of it but ashes. The ashes are then either placed in a jar and buried or put in a tomb or place of honor, or they are scattered so that they may mix with the earth from which people believe all life originally came.

Man learned very early in his history how to keep dead bodies from rotting. The Egyptians developed a way of preserving dead bodies, called *embalming*, by injecting certain chemicals into the bodies. They put the bodies in stone tombs. The embalmed bodies of Egyptian kings and queens (called "mummies") were buried in huge tombs called pyramids, that took thousands of workmen years to build. The mummies of some of the kings and queens have been discovered by scientists recently, and these mummies are unusually well preserved. The Greeks and Romans also embalmed their dead before they buried the bodies. In modern countries the law requires that a doctor make out a paper stating what a person died from, before the body can be embalmed and buried.

Most people today bury their dead in the ground or cremate them. Sometimes, if a person dies while he is at sea, his body is sewed in a weighted canvas sack and dropped into the sea.

Burke, Edmund

Edmund Burke was a great British statesman and orator at the time of the American Revolution. He was born in Dublin, Ireland, in 1729. He planned to become a lawyer, but changed his mind and became a writer instead. He lectured on political matters, and wrote many articles about political issues of his day. Burke believed that the American Colonies were being treated unfairly by King George III, and he made a speech before Parliament, the English legislature, in which he said that more justice should be shown to the American colonies. The Americans thought Burke was their best friend in the British government. Burke made many stirring speeches in Parliament, and he was always on the side of the people who were being unjustly treated. He also wrote several books that helped win sympathy for American colonists. He is best remembered for *American Taxation* and *Conciliation with America,* which most students read in high school. Burke died in 1797, at the age of 88.

burlesque

Burlesque is the name given to any exaggerated way of making fun of somebody or something. Whenever you see someone imitate another person's actions in a funny, clownish way you are watching a burlesque. When you read something that makes something seem ridiculously funny, you are reading a burlesque. A burlesque show is one in which the actors make fun of serious things, other shows, or very important people. In John Gay's *Beggar's Opera* produced in London more than 200 years ago, the actors and singers made fun of royalty. For about 75 years, starting about 1850, burlesque shows were musical comedies, or revues, almost like modern musical comedies. In the 1920s they began to use so many naughty jokes and scenes that most people disliked them, and now most places have laws against these burlesque shows.

Burma

Burma is a country in eastern Asia, about halfway around the world from the United States. It is south of China and east of India. It is about 260,000 square miles in area, which is about the size of Texas, and has about 25,000,000 people living in it, which is more than twice as many people as there are in Texas. Life in Burma is very different from life in the United States. The Burmese civilization is very old and is highly developed, but the people of Burma do not have the modern things that we have.

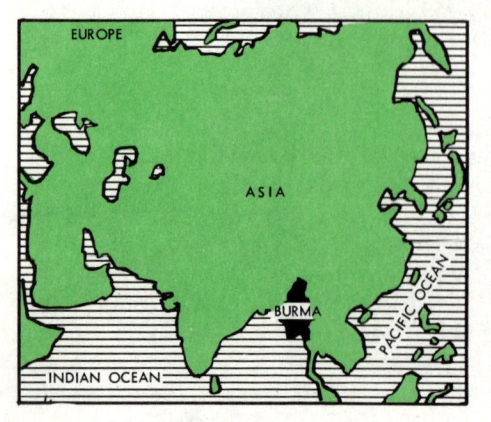

THE PEOPLE WHO LIVE THERE

Most of the people of Burma belong to the Mongolian race, to which the people of China, Japan and Korea also belong. They came to Burma several thousand years ago from China. There are several different peoples in Burma. The largest and most powerful is the Burmese. Most Burmese believe in the Buddhist religion. (You can read about this religion in a separate article on BUDDHISM.) They are not very tall, and most of them are stocky. They are very cheerful, peaceful and even-tempered people. Although they are not very rich or modern in their ways, most Burmese can read and write, and they learn a lot from the Buddhist priests who live in each village. The Burmese are very polite and kind, and the Burmese men treat their women much better than women are treated in most eastern civilizations.

The next most important group of people in Burma is the Karens, who live in the section of Burma which is near the mouth of the great Irrawaddy River. Other Burmese groups are the Chins, the Kachins, the Shans, the Kayaks, and the Nagas of the wild North. Some of these tribes were very primitive until just a short time ago. The Nagas were once head-hunters, and it was dangerous for a stranger to enter their territory. The head-hunting tribes lived by themselves in the hills.

Many Chinese and Indians live in Burma. They went there because their own countries have so many people that it is hard to make a living. Many of the

BURMA

Unations

1. Burmese craftsmen make beautifully decorated pottery in their homes.
2. Many people in Rangoon go to the public pump to wash and do their laundry.
3. Young boys in Burma learn how to do block printing.
4. This ruined Burmese temple, or pagoda, is at Pagan.

Indians in Burma became rich and powerful because they became bankers and landowners. When Burma separated from India in 1937, most Indian merchants returned to India. The Chinese who live in Burma are mostly craftsmen and merchants.

HOW THE PEOPLE LIVE

Most of the people of Burma are farmers. Their main crop is rice. They live mostly in small villages, and it is not easy to get from one village to another. Not many farmers have automobiles as American farmers do. Very few of them know how to farm in a modern way.

There are only two big cities in Burma. Rangoon is the capital city. About 740,000 people live there, which is about as many as live in New Orleans. There is a very fine university in Rangoon and also one at Mandalay, and many young Burmese study modern ways of doing things and to become scientists, doctors, engineers, and modern farmers. The other big city in Burma is Mandalay. About 186,000 people live there, just about as many as there are in Worcester, Mass. If you were to visit Rangoon or Mandalay you would see many beautiful temples and palaces in both of these cities. Most of the people who live in the cities are tradesmen. Some of the city people work in the different industries the government is trying to develop.

Burma is just beginning to be a modern country. It does not have many big factories or modern plants. But the Burmese government has started on plans to make Burma more modern. Burma can become very rich if the Burmese people learn to take advantage of all the things that can be found there. For instance, there are many rich tin and silver mines in Burma. The most beautiful rubies, sapphires and jade in the world come from that country. A very beautiful tree called teak grows in Burma. Its wood is valuable and is used for making fine and expensive furniture.

WHAT KIND OF A PLACE IT IS

Burma is a very hilly country. It has many high mountains, some of them so high that their tops are covered with snow all year round. Many rivers run through Burma and most of them run from the north to the south. The largest river is the Irrawaddy, and many boats carry goods on it for almost a thousand miles. There are only two seasons in Burma— a wet season and a dry season. In the wet season, there are very heavy rains, and many rivers are flooded. The people who live in villages near the rivers protect their homes from the floods by building them on stilts. It gets quite hot in Burma from February to October. The temperature sometimes goes as high as 100 degrees, but the evenings are usually pleasantly cool. There are many wild animals in the forests of Burma. There are elephants, rhinoceros, and a strange animal called the tapir. There are some very dangerous snakes in Burma, too, such as the cobra and the python.

HOW THE PEOPLE ARE GOVERNED

Burma is a republic. It used to be part of the British Empire, but it became independent in 1948. Under its constitution, Burma is to be governed by a president, a parliament, and a premier. The premier is the real head of the government. The president just has the honor of leading the government. The parliament is made up of representatives of the different sections of the country. Members of the parliament are elected by the people, and the president is elected by the parliament. But during much of the time since 1958, the Burmese people have actually been governed by military dictators.

BURMA IN THE PAST

For many centuries the Burmese had their own government. This government was ruled by a king, who was very powerful. Burma had very little to do with the Western World until the 18th century, when the British and the Dutch discovered that Burma was rich in precious gems and other things. The British took over the Burmese government in 1885, and Burma became a British colony. The British continued to rule Burma until World War II. In 1942, Japan conquered Burma and held it until the Allies won it back in 1945. After the war was over, Burma became part of the British Empire again, until 1948.

When Burma became independent it had many problems. The Karens wanted to set up their own government, and the Communists were trying to seize power.

A man named U Nu ("U" is a title of respect, just as we might say "Mr. Nu") was premier from 1948 to 1958. In 1958, when the Communist danger became too great, U Nu asked the head of the Burmese Army to run the country. Free elections were held in 1960 and U Nu was again elected premier. But in 1962 the Army took control for a second time, dismissed U Nu, dissolved the parliament, and set up a military government.

Burma is a member of the United Nations. In 1961 a Burmese statesman, U Thant, was selected to act as Secretary-General of the United Nations.

THE BURMA CAMPAIGN

When the Japanese took over Burma in World War II, the Allies lost a very important supply route to China. The Burmese people did not like the Allies but they were not happy under Japanese control, either. The Allies were able to work with Burmese patriots to drive the Japanese out of the country. The British did most of the fighting in Burma. American and Chinese soldiers fought with the British.

The war in Burma was very hard to fight. Most of it took place in the jungle and in hilly places. The soldiers had to fight in heavy rains and in great heat. But the Allies finally drove out the Japanese armies in Burma, and in April, 1945, retook the country.

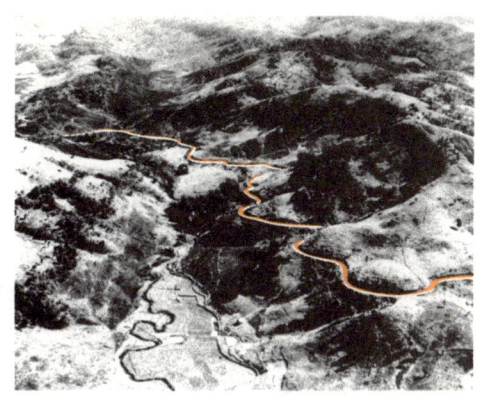

British Inform. Service
An aerial view of the winding Burma Road.

BURMA. Area, 261,789 square miles. Population (1964 estimate), 24,229,000. Chief language, Burmese. Chief religion, Buddhism. Government, republic. Monetary unit, the kyat, worth 21¢ (U.S.). Flag, red with dark blue shield; white five-pointed star in center of shield, with a smaller star between each two points of the big star.

Burma Road

The Burma Road was built and became known all over the world during the early days of World War II. The Chinese people were fighting a desperate war with the Japanese armies that invaded China, and they could not get supplies from other countries because the Japanese controlled the coasts and ports of China. The only way the Chinese could get supplies was from Burma in the south, and there were no roads leading over the mountains between Burma and China. So the Chinese decided to build a road. While the road was being built, American airmen flew supplies over "The Hump," the name they gave to the high mountains between Burma and China. They flew in many supplies but not nearly enough to help the Chinese in the war.

The Burma Road was begun in 1937, and it took 200,000 workers, both Chinese and Burmese, more than a year to complete it. The men who worked on the road had very little equipment. They did not have any bulldozers or other necessary machinery. Almost all the work was done by hand labor under very primitive conditions, and many of the workers became sick and died.

The Burma Road is 800 miles long. It is very winding, and coils like a giant snake through forests and over mountains. More than 300 bridges were built to carry the road across rivers. The air distance between one end of the Burma Road and the other is less than 400 miles, so you can imagine how the road twists and turns. The Burma Road is not a modern paved highway. It is made of earth and crushed stone, and is difficult and dangerous to travel on.

The Burma Road continued to be an important Allied supply line until the Japanese captured Burma in 1942. Then the road was closed. But early in 1945, the Allies recaptured Burma, and the Burma Road became an important route for supplying ammunition and other war materials to China and other Allied soldiers in China. It is now closed and there is very little traffic on it.

burn

A burn is an injury caused by heat. The heat can be an open flame or a very hot object like the unprotected handle of a pot. When the heat is a very hot liquid, the burn is called a "scald." Like any other injury, a burn can be small, in which case it is no more serious than any other small injury like a bump or bruise. But if the burn covers a large part of the body, it can be serious enough to send the patient to a hospital for many weeks.

Sometimes a burn, even one that covers a large area, is only on the very top of the skin, like a sunburn. That is a burn too, but it does not actually destroy any of the skin, and it is called a *first degree* burn. If the burn is deeper and the outer layer of the skin is really burned off and a great many blisters are formed, it is a *second degree* burn. This, of course, is much more serious and takes longer to heal. The worst kind is a *third degree* burn, when the skin and perhaps the muscles and other layers underneath are hurt. If this third degree burn is wide enough, it can sometimes cause death.

All burns are very painful. Even a bad sunburn is painful. For first degree burns there are a number of cooling and soothing ointments that can be put on at once. Burns should always be kept clean and covered. More serious burns must be treated by a doctor, as quickly as possible, because patients with serious burns go very quickly into a state of "shock" (see the article on BIOCHEMISTRY), and the doctor must do other things to the patient besides treating the burn itself.

There is an old proverb that says, "Never play with fire." While fire is the most useful of all our natural servants, it can get beyond control very easily and then it can cause a great deal of harm. Always be very careful to keep smaller children away from the stove or the fireplace. You show good sense when you are careful with lighters and matches.

Burnett, Frances Hodgson

Frances Hodgson Burnett was a famous writer who was born in England in 1849. She had her first story published in that country when she was only sixteen years old. The Civil War had just ended in America and she and her parents came to live in Tennessee. Frances Burnett went on writing stories and novels for grownups and children for the rest of her life. Her most popular book, *Little Lord Fauntleroy,* was about a little boy who wore velvet suits with white silk blouses, and always behaved himself and had perfect manners. Many other stories were made into plays that were very popular both in England and America.

Burns, Robert

Robert Burns was a great Scottish poet who lived about 200 years ago. He became famous for his songs and poems that were written mostly in the Scottish dialect, the form of English that people of his country spoke. He wrote *Auld Lang Syne*, the song we all know and often sing when we want to say goodbye, or at the end of the year. The words are Scottish and mean simply "old long since." Burns wrote about ordinary everyday things in a wonderfully simple and beautiful way. The people loved his poems so much that they called him by the affectionate nickname of Bobbie, or Robbie.

Robbie Burns was born in 1759 at Alloway, Scotland, near the town of Ayr. His father was a peasant and so poor that he could not afford to send his Robbie and the six younger children to school. But he was a very fine and intelligent man who taught Robbie almost as much as he would have learned in school. They all worked so hard on the farm that Robbie's health was almost ruined. His early life was so hard that his only amusements were reading books and writing songs and poems. When he was older he began to live in a reckless way that caused people to criticize him.

Robert Burns loved three different girls, Elizabeth Patron, Jean Armour, and Mary Campbell. He was going to marry Mary Campbell, but she died just after his first book of poems was published. He married Jean Armour and they had four children. He tried to make a living as a farmer, but failed. He then became a tax inspector, and kept this job until he died in 1796 when he was only 37 years old.

Not until after he died did everyone realize how great he really was. He made almost no money from his poems and was so poor that just before he died he had to borrow money from his cousin to pay some debts and save himself from spending his last days in jail.

Burnside, Ambrose

Ambrose Burnside was a general in the Union army during the Civil War. He became better known for the kind of whiskers he wore than for anything he did on the battlefield. He was born in Liberty, Indiana, in 1824. He went to the United States Military Academy at West Point.

He resigned from the army, but he rejoined it when the Civil War broke out. He held several important commands in the Union army, and the soldiers easily recognized him because of the special kind of whiskers he wore, which became known as "burnsides," or "sideburns," after him. Sideburns are whiskers that grow on the side of the face. Burnside died in 1881.

Burr, Aaron

Aaron Burr was Vice President of the United States from 1801 to 1805, during Thomas Jefferson's first term as President. Burr was born in 1756, and studied to be a lawyer. He liked politics and soon became leader of a political party that opposed the election of George Washington as President of the United States.

However, Burr is best remembered as the man who shot and killed Alexander Hamilton in a duel, July 11, 1804. Burr and Hamilton were members of two different political parties. They were bitter enemies. After Burr lost the election for governor of New York, he challenged Hamilton to a duel with pistols. He blamed Hamilton for helping to defeat him in the election.

The two men met in Weehawken, New Jersey, across the Hudson river from New

York City. When the signal was given to fire their pistols, Hamilton aimed his pistol into the air to avoid hitting Burr. Burr aimed directly at Hamilton, and wounded him so severely that Hamilton died.

Shortly after this, Burr was accused of plotting to take over Mexico and the western part of the United States, and set himself up as a king. Jefferson had him arrested and brought to trial three times for treason, but each time Burr was found not guilty. Burr then went to Europe. He returned to the United States in 1812 very poor and without friends. He opened a law office and was a lawyer until he died in 1836, at the age of 80.

Burroughs, John

John Burroughs was a famous American writer who wrote many books about nature. He was born in 1837 on a farm near Roxbury, N.Y., and did not receive much education, but he learned much by himself, especially about the wonders and beauties of nature. As a young man, he met the great American poet, Walt Whitman, who became his greatest influence and a very dear friend. Burroughs wrote several books about Whitman and he helped to make the poet popular. Burroughs was also a teacher, a magazine writer, and a treasury official in Washington. But about 1871, he settled on a farm on the Hudson River, in New York, and wrote the first of his twenty nature books. He died in 1921.

Burroughs was a keen observer and a delightful writer. He told of his adventures with birds, fish, flowers, trees, and the seasons of the year and made his readers see things they had never noticed. Many people came to visit him and join his walks through the countryside. Burroughs could show them that "the most precious things in life are near at hand, without money and without price."

Burundi

Burundi is a small kingdom in east central Africa. It became independent on July 1, 1962. Before World War I the territory was part of German East Africa and was called Urundi. Later it became part of the Belgian United Nations Trusteeship territory of Ruanda-Urundi. In area Burundi is about the size of Maryland and has almost the same number of people living there. The chief products are coffee, cattle, and animal hides. The government consists of a king called the Mwami, a premier who acts as head of government, and a legislature. The capital is Bujumbura, a city of 50,000.

The people of Burundi are Negroes belonging to the Bahuto and Watusi tribes. There are also some Pygmies of the Batwa tribe. Most of the people are Bahutos, but for centuries the Watusi have ruled the country. The king is a Watusi. In neighboring Rwanda, the Bahutos drove out the Watusi leaders and gained control of the government; but in Burundi the Watusis kept power. In both countries there has been constant fighting between the two groups and many people have been killed. (See also RWANDA.)

BURUNDI. Area, 10,744 square miles. Population (1964 estimate), 2,780,000.

bus

A bus is a long motor vehicle that carries paying passengers from place to place. It is much longer than a taxicab and carries ten times as many people. Buses that carry passengers within a city or town are called *local buses*. Those that travel from city to city are called *intercity buses*. The word *bus* is from the Latin *omnibus,* meaning "for all."

Kings and nobles began to use private horse-carriages more than three hundred years ago. Ordinary people could not afford such luxury, so they demanded public vehicles to carry them about their

1. Buses in 1902 looked very different from those of today, but they could get just as crowded during the rush hour.

2. Before going on a bus trip, you must buy your ticket at the ticket office. You can go all the way from New York to California by bus.

3. If your bus is not ready to leave, you go to the waiting room. Here grandma is reading a story until bus time.

4. Finally everyone gets on board. You may get a seat by the window if you are lucky.

Standard Oil Co.

business. One of the first horse-drawn coaches to carry passengers belonged to the borough of Hackney in London, England. That is where our word "hack" comes from. The French king issued a license for a public coach service in 1662. New York had this kind of bus about thirty years later. It was owned by a Bowery saloonkeeper who gave his patrons special transportation. In 1719, an intercity line started between Philadelphia, New York, and Boston. It took four days to go from New York to Boston. The buses you see today make the same trip in half a day.

THE MOTOR BUS

The first automobile appeared around 1900. Within 25 years, motor buses were

BUS

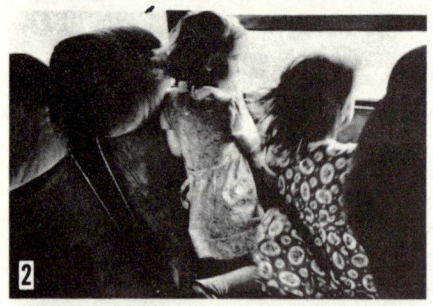

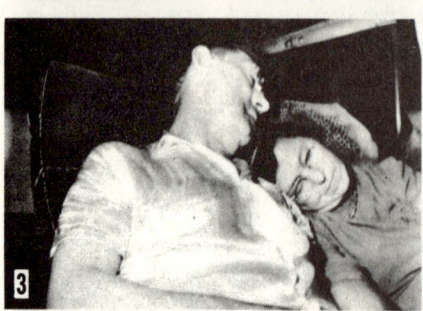

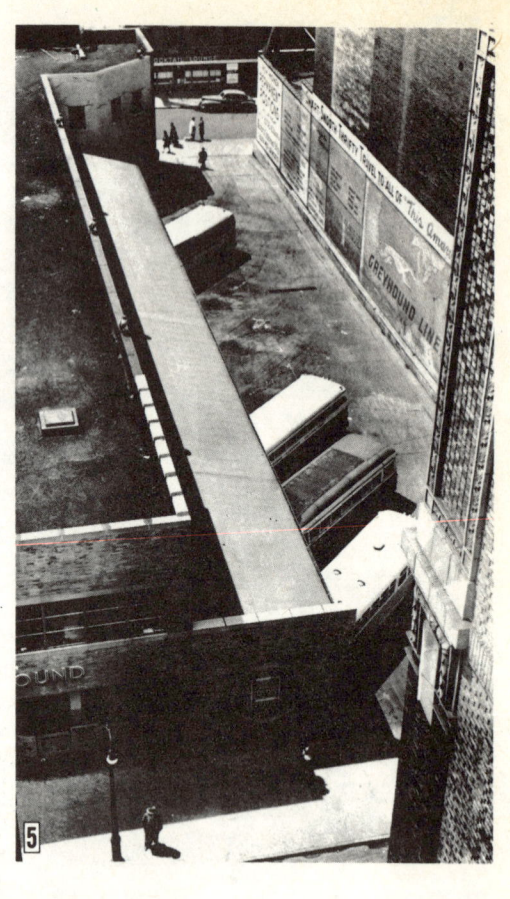

1. As you get on the bus, the driver checks your ticket to make sure you are on the right bus. The bus driver has to be experienced because all the people in the bus depend on him to get them safely to their destination.

2. You can see many interesting things through the window during a bus trip. You may pass by fields and farms and through towns and cities that you never saw before.

3. While you are looking out the window, mom and dad may take a nap. When they wake up, maybe you can tell them about some of the interesting things you saw along the way.

4. On a long trip, the bus usually stops a few times to let everybody get out and stretch his legs. At these bus stops, you can eat, drink and buy candy before you start off again.

5. At last you arrive at the end of your trip at the bus terminal building.

Standard Oil Co.

replacing streetcars in the cities and had begun to carry passengers who had previously ridden from city to city on railroad trains. The bus lines began to use diesel engines in 1938. These engines give more miles for each dollar's worth of fuel than gasoline engines. (Both engines are described under INTERNAL COMBUSTION ENGINE.)

In 1944, one American bus line alone had 65,000 miles of route, five times more than any railroad. There were more intercity buses on the highways of America than there were passenger coaches on rails. In 1960 there were about 72,850 local and intercity buses in the United States. They carried more than five billion passengers that year. Some cities like San Francisco, Chicago, and Honolulu have trolley buses. Trolley buses, like streetcars, receive their power from overhead electric lines. They are better than streetcars because they do not have to stay on tracks or rails. The coast-to-coast buses go from New York to Los Angeles in three and a half days. They are very comfortable. They are air-conditioned and they have rest rooms. The latest models cost twenty times as much as most new automobiles. There are so many buses going in and out of New York City every day that the world's largest bus terminal was built for them. It is called the Port of New York Authority Bus Terminal. About 180,000 passengers and 6,200 buses use it each weekday.

OTHER USES

Buses are also used for sightseeing. Every day you may see them in great cities like New York, driving slowly past places of interest like the Empire State Building and Grant's Tomb.

In 1960 there were about 178,440 school buses in the U.S. They carried 12,310,000 children to and from school every day. North Carolina has more than 6,000 school buses, the largest fleet in the world. Many parents want their children to ride on these buses because they are sure the children will get to school safely and on time. School buses are usually painted yellow and marked with large signs that warn other drivers to be careful. In many communities, the law forbids drivers to pass a school bus when it is taking on passengers or letting them off.

Bush, Vannevar

Vannevar Bush became famous as the American scientist who was the head of atomic research during World War II. He was one of the most important people in the development of the atomic bomb. Bush was born in 1890, and became an electrical engineer. In 1932, he was made dean of engineering at the Massachusetts Institute of Technology, and later he became the head of research at the Carnegie Institution of Washington. After World War II broke out, he was made the head of the government Office of Scientific Research and Development. He supervised all the nation's scientists who worked on the atomic bomb, radar and the other inventions that helped America and its allies to win the war.

bushido

Bushido is a set of unwritten Japanese rules on how to behave. It was first used in Japan more than seven hundred years ago. It was like the code of honor that the Knights of the Round Table lived by. Every Japanese noble and warrior in the Middle Ages lived by these rules. They taught him how to live with honor, and also how to die to save his honor. The code covered everything in life, from courage and loyalty to handling a sword and how to dress.

Some of the laws are still lived up to in Japan today. During World War II many pilots of Japanese planes and many soldiers in the Japanese army killed themselves because they thought it was dishonorable to be captured. This was a part of law of bushido. The act of *harakiri* is another part of the same law. This is suicide by cutting open one's own stomach and bleeding to death. Although some of the ideas of bushido still exist today, most of them disappeared after the defeat of Japan in World War II.

bushman, one of the backward peoples of Africa. The natives of Australia are also sometimes called bushmen. See the articles on AFRICA and AUSTRALIA.

bushmaster

The bushmaster is a large poisonous snake that lives in South and Central America. It is known as "the silent rattler," because it vibrates its tail when it is angry, but the sound produced is no more than a low buzz. The bushmaster is about nine feet long, though some have been found that are twelve feet long. It is pale brown, with large black and brown patches. This snake is dangerous and will attack anything that comes close. It has poison glands in its head and long fangs through which the venom is injected into the creatures it bites.

Am. Museum of Nat. History
Would you believe that this bushmaster, curled up in the sun, is nine feet long?

bushrangers

The bushrangers were a band of thieves and escaped convicts who terrorized Australia about 150 years ago. They got their name because they used to hide in the scrubland, or bush, after their raids. They would raid farms and villages and rob travelers on the roads and highways. When gold was discovered in the southern part of Australia, they used to rob the prospectors and the wagons that carried the gold. They became so bold that in 1815 Australia declared martial law. (That is, the army and the police joined forces to protect the people.) By 1830 laws had been passed against the activities of the bushrangers and to punish them when they were caught. It still took many years to wipe out the last of them, and it was not until about 1870 that the Australian people were sure there were no more of these highwaymen and robbers.

business

Business is any one of many things that people work at to earn money and to do things for other people. It actually comes from the word *busy* and means "being busy with." You would hardly ask a person what he was busy with when you wanted to know what kind of work he did, but you would ask what business he was in.

Business is everything people do that concerns making and selling things. Manufacturing is business, and so are all the other kinds of work concerned with the things that are manufactured—advertising, building, banking, and selling. A *wholesaler* is a businessman who buys large quantities of a product from a manufacturer or producer and sells it to a retailer. A *retailer* is a businessman who sells what he buys to all of us who are customers.

Business really started with the first man who produced more of something than he could use, and then traded it to neighbors who gave him something in return. Perhaps this early businessman had more stone arrowheads than he needed, and his neighbor had an extra piece of fresh meat. When the trade was made the two cavemen had become the world's first businessmen. From that time on business grew. As men produced more and more of a particular thing and built wagons and ships to carry their products, they engaged in bigger and bigger businesses. Modern business has grown from the first simple swap to a point where billions of dollars change hands each year. The more money that is spent in business, the more money there is on hand to pay all the people who work in the many businesses we now have.

Business has grown so big that governments now have laws to control it. Not too long ago, some businessmen used to be greedy, and they took advantage of everybody they did business with. Government rules now prevent businessmen from taking unfair advantage of the people who work for them, of the people who buy from them, and of the people who are in the same business—their competitors.

Modern business is one of mankind's greatest activities. It provides us with food, clothing, shelter, medicines, transportation, and entertainment. It also provides us with the weapons with which we can defend ourselves when we are threatened or attacked by other countries. Modern business is highly specialized. This makes it possible to produce many things more cheaply and more quickly than they could be made in any other way.

Specialization makes it possible for men to learn to do one thing well, instead of doing many things poorly. It makes us dependent on many people for all the things we need for good living. It also gives jobs to many millions of people. The more people there are working, the more there are with money to buy the things that business provides, and the more jobs there are for other people. Business is good when people are working, earning good wages, and buying many things. Business is bad when fewer people are working, and fewer people have money to spend on the things they need and want.

Busoni, Ferruccio Benvenuto

Ferruccio Busoni was a famous Italian pianist and composer, or writer of music. He was one of the greatest pianists who ever lived, and many people think he was the best of all time. Busoni was born in Italy in 1866. His father and mother were both musicians, and they were his only teachers. When he was seven years old he played in public for the first time, and for the rest of his life he played the piano before audiences all over Europe and America. He composed many things, including a concerto for piano and orchestra, a violin sonata, and a fine opera, *Doctor Faust*. He was also famous for his arrangements of other composers' music so that it could be played on the piano. Busoni's name is often mentioned with that of Johann Sebastian BACH, about whom you can read in a separate article. Busoni took music that Bach had composed for the organ and arranged it to be played on the piano. He died in Berlin in 1924.

butane

Butane is a gas that is found in oil and gas wells. It is a mixture of hydrogen and carbon, and for that reason it is called a *hydrocarbon*. It belongs to the family of hydrocarbons called METHANE, about which there is a separate article.

Butane is very unusual. It boils at the temperature at which water freezes. This temperature is 32 degrees Fahrenheit (32° F.). It is hard to believe that something could boil at such a low temperature. When a liquid boils, it changes into a gas or vapor. The temperature in oil wells and swamps is usually very much above 32° F., causing butane to boil and become a gas. If the temperature were lower, butane would be a liquid.

Butane can be changed into a liquid

by a process called *condensation*. To condense butane, the temperature must be brought below 32° F. A special kind of butane, called *isobutane,* boils at an even lower temperature: 13° F. To change isobutane into a liquid, the temperature must be below 13° F.

Butane is often mixed with *propane,* a similar gas. This mixture is used as fuel for heating homes, and in gas stoves.

There is another gas which is similar to butane. This is *butylene*. Butylene is made by the removal of hydrogen (called "cracking") from butane. Butylene glycol is a compound made from butylene and other chemicals. It can be changed into a gas called *butadiene*. Butadiene is used in making artificial rubber, which you can read about in the article on RUBBER.

Butler, Nicholas Murray

Nicholas Murray Butler was a great educator and worker for world peace. He was born in Elizabeth, New Jersey, in 1862, and was graduated from Columbia University in New York City. He became a teacher and professor at Columbia, and in 1901 he was chosen to be president of that great university. Butler thought that the more educated people there were in the world, the better chance there would be for peace in the world. He worked very hard for peace, and he was given the Nobel peace prize in 1931. He was also a politician. He was a leader of the Republican Party for many years and when William Howard Taft was chosen by that party to run for president, in 1912, Butler was chosen to run for vice president. They were not elected, and Butler continued as president of Columbia University until 1945. He died two years later at the age of 85.

Butler, Samuel

Samuel Butler was the name of two great English writers. One of them lived about a hundred years ago. He was born in 1835. His grandfather was a bishop and his father a clergyman, so it is not surprising that his family expected him to become a minister too. But at the last moment Butler refused, saying that he was not sure he was fit for the duties of a minister. Instead he went to New Zealand to operate a sheep ranch.

He earned a small fortune from his ranch, and after five years he returned to England. He never married. He was the author of several books. His novel *The Way of All Flesh* tells about a young man who suffers from the cruelty of his minister father. People who knew Butler knew he was writing about himself and his father in this book. Another book he wrote, *Erewhon,* is a long account of a voyage to an imaginary country cut off from the world. As you see, "Erewhon" is close to being "Nowhere" spelled backward. Butler died in 1902.

The other Samuel Butler lived nearly three hundred years ago. He was born in 1612 and died in 1680. His famous work was a long poem called *Hudibras*. We still quote some of the famous lines from *Hudibras*. One of them is, *"Don't count your chickens before they are hatched."*

butte

A butte is a hill with steep sides, that rises sharply from a plain. Another name for a butte is a *knoll*. In the United States, buttes are usually found in dry regions in the western part of the country. Many buttes are found in the Rocky Mountains, in Montana and North Dakota. In Canada and England, a butte usually means a high mountain peak that is set apart from other peaks.

butter

Butter is a pale- to golden-yellow substance made from the fat in milk or

BUTTER

Butter has been an important food for many centuries. Until the invention of modern machinery, it was made at home by women. Above and below, you can see old-fashioned butter churns. Today, huge quantities of butter are made in large plants under sanitary conditions.
1. Large storage tanks churn the butter at the right temperature.
2. The butter is cooled in vats.
3. Salt is added to the butter.
4. The butter is removed from the churns and put into cartons. Before the day is over, the butter will be ready for shipment to cities all over the country.

Nat'l. Dairy Council

cream. It is one of the most prized of all foods because of its pleasant taste. It is a healthful food, as it contains vitamins and the fat in it is easy to digest. If you shake milk for a long time it will separate into two parts—a layer of butter made by all the tiny drops of fat in the milk joining together, and a thin watery part called BUTTERMILK, which you can read about in a separate article.

Until about a hundred years ago butter was made only on farms or in people's homes, but now most butter is made in factories called creameries. These creameries must be kept very clean and cool, so the butter will be of good quality and safe to eat.

In making butter, the milk is first whirled round and round to extract the cream. The cream is then allowed to stand for a while; it slightly sours and gets the flavor it will have as butter. The flavor is caused by bacteria, which are living organisms so small they can be seen only through a microscope. To make sure the right bacteria are present in the cream, some are usually added to the cream. After the cream has been standing for a while, it is churned to separate the butter. The butter is washed, and usually a little salt is added to it. Then it is stirred to make it smooth.

The natural color of butter depends on what the cows have eaten. When the cows eat lots of fresh grass, their milk makes rich yellow butter. When they have to eat dry hay through the winter months, the butter made from their milk is almost white. If the butter is too pale, artificial coloring is added so that the butter will be yellow.

Butter is then packaged in pound "prints" that are often divided into two or four parts. Some butter is packed in large containers and sold as "tub" butter to large users such as hotels, restaurants, and so on.

There are many different kinds of butter. In some countries it is made from the milk of goats, sheep, and mares. Butter has been made for more than two thousand years, and was known in ancient Egypt and Greece. At first it was used as fuel in lamps, as medicine, and as an ointment for the skin. Today the countries which produce the most butter are the United States (chiefly in the northern Midwest), Russia, Denmark, Australia, and New Zealand.

buttercup

A buttercup is a kind of wild flower which grows mostly in meadows, though some grow floating in slow-moving streams. They have shiny yellow flowers, the color of butter, with round petals. Their leaves are very pretty—dark green, and deeply cut up into the shape of a tiny hand. Buttercups have sharp, acid juice, so they are not eaten by cows, horses, or other grazing animals. Some people think that if cows eat buttercups, they will give bitter milk. Some buttercups have juice that will blister your skin. Some are so beautiful that they are grown in gardens. One of these is the turban buttercup, which comes in many colors and has "double" flowers.

butterflies and moths

Butterflies and moths are small animals that fly about with big, colorful wings. They are *Insects,* which means that they have six legs and their bodies are divided into three parts—a head, a middle part called the thorax, and a tail part called the abdomen. But they are different from all other winged insects because their wings are covered with scales. If you touch a butterfly's wings, your finger becomes dusty. Under a powerful magnifying glass, this "dust" can be seen to be thousands of flat, wedge-shaped scales. These scales give the butterfly or moth its beautiful colors. Sometimes this is because the scales themselves are colored, but more often it is because they reflect light, in the same way that light is reflected from oil on water. Be-

BUTTERFLIES

Margot L. Wolf

This beautiful thistle butterfly is feeding on the nectar of a flower.

cause of these scales, butterflies and moths are grouped together to form a class of insects called *Lepidoptera,* which means "scaly-winged."

HOW TO TELL THEM APART

There are many ways in which you can tell butterflies from moths. Nearly all butterflies fly only during the day; most moths come out at night. When resting, butterflies usually fold their wings together overhead; moths spread their wings flat, either wide apart, or with the front pair of wings covering the hind pair. The antennas (feelers) of a butterfly end in little knobs; the antennas of a moth are pointed or feathery. Certain butterflies, called *skippers,* are halfway between butterflies and moths.

WHERE THEY ARE FOUND

There are many more kinds of moths than butterflies. About 120,000 kinds of moth are known in the world, about 8,000 kinds in North America alone. Only about 16,000 kinds of butterfly are known in the world, of which only 700 are known in North America.

The most beautiful butterflies and moths of all are found in forests in hot, tropical regions. In Brazil there are giant butterflies with wings of a brilliant flashing blue that measure ten inches across. Other kinds have wings that are as transparent as glass, and there are lovely green-and-white swallow-tailed moths that fly about in the day and behave like butterflies. In Malaya there are giant bird-wing butterflies, and in India is found the largest of all butterflies and moths, the Atlas moth. The smallest moth, the British golden pygmy, is only one-fifth inch in wingspan.

Here in North America there are

BUTTERFLIES

many beautiful butterflies and moths—the pale-green Luna moth, the rich-colored, brown-and-red Cecropia moth, the graceful swallowtail butterflies, and many others.

THEIR STRANGE WAYS

If you watch a butterfly or moth as it sits on a flower you will see a strange thing. From under its head a long coiled tube, which looks at first like a watch-spring, unwinds itself and begins to probe about in the flower. This tube is the butterfly's mouth, through which it sucks all its food. Butterflies and moths live entirely on liquids, such as the nectar, or sweet liquid, found in flowers; the juice of fruits; or honeydew (a sweet liquid that oozes from the leaves of some plants). A few butterflies and moths have "spines" on the tips of their mouth tubes, and with these they can dig into ripe fruit.

As the butterflies and moths move from one flower to another, feeding on nectar, they also carry pollen from one to the other. This helps the flowers produce their seeds and fruits.

Most butterflies and moths visit many different kinds of flowers, as each kind opens, but sometimes a moth or butterfly will drink the nectar of only one particular plant. The moth or butterfly depends on that plant for its food, and the plant depends completely upon the moth or butterfly for its pollination. Only the yucca moth, for instance, has a feeding tube long enough to get into the flower of the yucca plant to get at the nectar, and to carry the pollen. After the moth has sucked up the nectar from one flower, it goes on to another flower carrying pollen from the first, and so on. In each flower the moth lays some of its own eggs. When these hatch, the *caterpillars,* as the young of butterflies and moths are called, feed on some of the seeds of the plant.

Butterflies and moths have many enemies, such as birds, wasps, flies, mantises, and spiders, but they have many different ways of protecting themselves. The Indian Leaf butterfly is colored so that it looks just like a leaf. The owl butterflies have markings on their wings that look like huge staring eyes, probably to frighten away birds. When a swallowtail butterfly is at rest its "tails" look like antennas, to fool an attacker into thinking that the butterfly is facing the wrong way. The little hairstreaks rub their two hind wings together, so that they look like waving antennas. Some butterflies are both evil-tasting and brightly colored; once a bird has eaten one it will never touch another one. The monarch butterfly has this kind of "warning" coloration. The viceroy butterfly protects itself by looking like the monarch, even though it is actually good to eat.

Some butterflies and moths "migrate," that is, they move from one part of the country to another regularly, according to the seasons of the year, just as birds and some fishes do. The painted lady, for instance, spends the winter in southern Europe or North Africa, and in the spring flies north again, often as far as Iceland. The monarch butterflies appear in large numbers in Canada and the northern part of the United States and then, usually in early fall, they all begin to fly south, to Florida, California, or even to the West Indies. More often, however, butterflies and moths will migrate in huge numbers at irregular times and seasons, for no reason that is known. In many parts of the world large numbers of a certain kind of butterfly or moth will be born year after year in one area, and then suddenly start moving in millions to some other part of the country. This may happen at regular intervals of years, such as every four years, or it may happen once a year.

Some butterflies and moths pass the winter asleep in sheltered places such as hollow logs, or even inside houses. Others die when winter comes, leaving their eggs or caterpillars. The bagworm moth

BUTTERFLIES

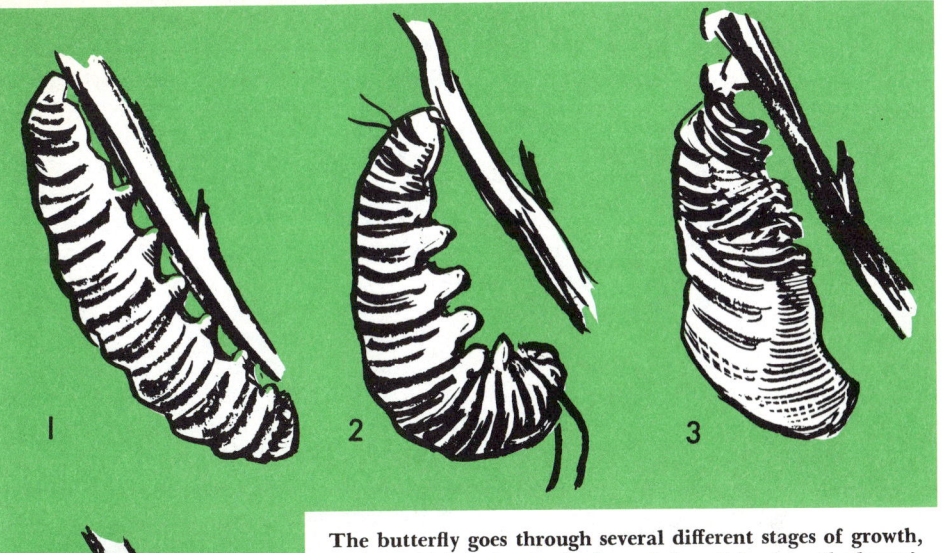

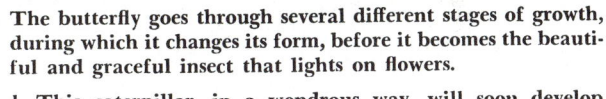

The butterfly goes through several different stages of growth, during which it changes its form, before it becomes the beautiful and graceful insect that lights on flowers.

1. This caterpillar, in a wondrous way, will soon develop into a brilliant monarch butterfly.

2. It attaches itself to a twig, and is ready to start spinning a cocoon around itself.

3 & 4. The caterpillar completely encloses itself in the cocoon, and sleeps inside the cocoon for several weeks or months depending on the weather.

5. In the spring, something comes out of the cocoon that does not look anything like a caterpillar.

6. The caterpillar has turned into a butterfly.

7. It dries its wings and is now a full-fledged monarch butterfly, ready to fly off into the air.

BUTTERFLIES

White Peacock butterfly

Minois Semele

Pearly-eyed butterfly

Monarch butterfly

Tiger Swallowtail

lays its eggs in a silken bag at the tip of a branch. The caterpillars of the viceroy butterfly live through the winter in a rolled-up leaf, those of the cattail moth inside the stalks of the cattail plant, and those of the apple codling moth inside the core of an apple.

The eggs of the butterfly or moth are often so tiny that they can be seen only under a magnifying glass. They may be round little balls, or cores, or rods; they may be egg-shaped, or flat. Whatever their shape, they are nearly always covered with ridges or networks of raised lines in beautiful patterns. Usually the eggs are carefully laid on the leaves or twigs of the kind of plant the caterpillars will feed on. A single butterfly or moth may lay as many as a thousand eggs.

CATERPILLARS

Quite soon after they are laid, the eggs begin to hatch. Out crowd the baby caterpillars, which begin eating at once. The caterpillars have jaws for biting solid food. They feed mostly on the leaves and soft parts of the plants on which they hatched. Some caterpillars eat other insects, such as aphids or ant grubs.

Caterpillars, like the adult butterflies and moths, have many enemies, and have their own ways of protecting themselves. The caterpillar of the hawk moth has a long horn at its rear end, and frightens its enemies just by looking horrible. The "looper" caterpillar disguises itself by looking like a twig. Some caterpillars can throw out jets of acid when attacked, or give off poisonous fumes. The tiger moth caterpillar is so covered with hair that it makes an unpleasant mouthful. Some caterpillars even have hairs that sting. Caterpillars protect themselves best by feeding only at night, and hiding during the day in rolled-up leaves or in special "tents" made out of silk. Caterpillars, like spiders, have special organs in their bodies that produce silk. It comes out as a liquid, hardens at once in the air, and is drawn out into a thread. The "tent" is made of this silk, and caterpillars often use the silken thread as a life-line, dropping off twigs when disturbed and hauling themselves back again later.

A caterpillar's skin cannot stretch, except when new. As a caterpillar eats, it cannot get very much larger unless it gets out of its skin, which is exactly what it does. A new, soft skin forms under the old one. The old one bursts and rolls off like a pullover sweater, while the caterpillar swells rapidly inside the new one before it hardens. In this way a caterpillar grows larger and larger until it has grown as large as it can. Then, if it is a butterfly caterpillar, it sticks a small button of silk under a twig, attaches itself to this button, and casts its skin for the last time. What appears now is a strange object, pointed at both ends, with a hard, smooth skin. This is a resting stage in the life of the insect and is called a *pupa*. The pupas of moths are different from

Clothes moth

Ruiner moth

Adult case-bearer moth

Clearwing moth

Sphinx moth

BUTTERFLIES

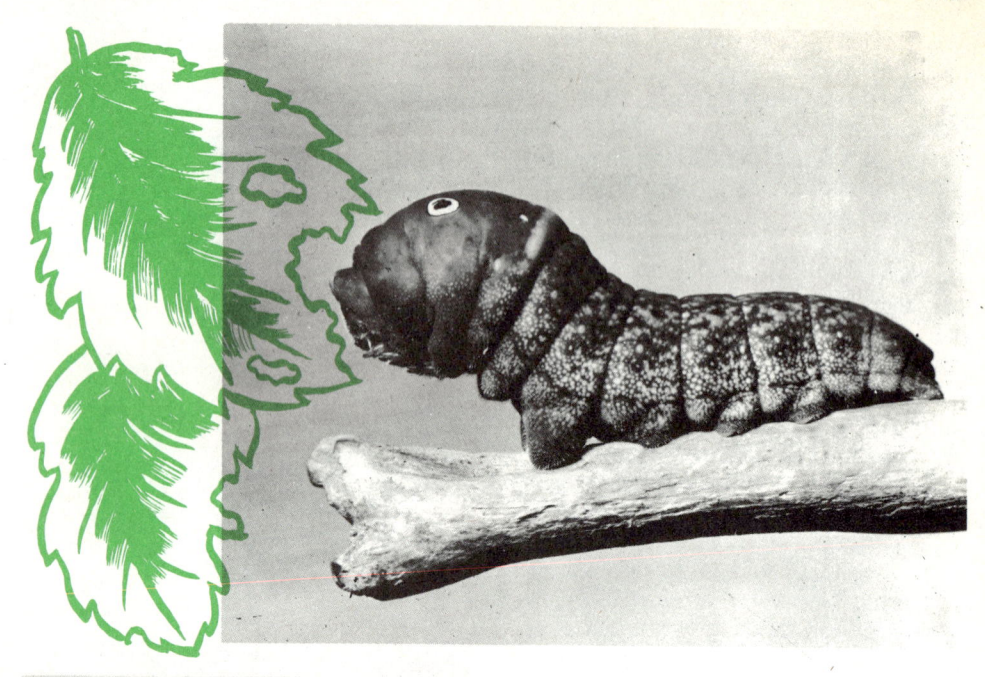

N.Y. Zoological Society

Top: The tiger swallowtail caterpillar. *Bottom:* The Persian silkworm spins its cocoon. At the top, it has just started. In the center, it is half through, and at the bottom, the cocoon is all finished, with the insect tucked safely inside it.

those of butterflies. The moth caterpillar usually weaves a fluffy case of silk, called a *cocoon,* around itself. From one such cocoon comes the silk used in clothing; see the article on SILKWORM.

The moth or butterfly may spend weeks or even months as a pupa, but all this time marvelous changes are taking place inside the case. All the organs of the caterpillar become liquid and change into the organs of an adult butterfly or moth, complete with wings, sucking mouth and so on, hardening again as soon as the new organs are formed. Then the pupa splits near one end, and the insect drags itself out. It is still rather soft and damp, and its wings are crumpled. It rests a while, fanning its wings and pumping air into its veins. Then it flies away. Every butterfly or moth that you see has been through these wonderful changes.

BUTTERFLIES, MOTHS, AND MEN

Adult butterflies and moths are completely harmless. The caterpillars of butterflies, too, are harmless, except for a few that feed on cabbage leaves. The caterpillars of moths, however, do millions of dollars of damage each year. Various caterpillars bore into wood; eat clothing, hair, carpets, and wool; and infest grocery stores, flour mills, and grain stores. Army worms, leaf rollers and loopers are caterpillars that eat the leaves of fruit trees; cankerworms, cutworms and many kinds of borers are caterpillars that attack the roots and stems of food crops; codling moth caterpillars bore into apples; and peach moth caterpillars attack apples, plums, cherries, and peaches.

On the other hand, moths and butterflies may almost repay man by their valuable work in pollinating flowers, eating other insect pests, and giving him silk.

AS PETS

Butterflies and moths are very easy to raise as pets. You may try hatching a pupa, burying it in a jar of earth if you found it underground, or hanging it up in a warm dry place where it can get plenty of air. If you try to raise caterpillars, you must note carefully the plants on which you found them and the part of the plant on which they were feeding, so that you will be able to feed them properly. They must be kept in a warm, dry place from which they cannot escape, but where they will get plenty of air. If you have both males and females of the same kind, and can find out what plant their caterpillars eat, you may be able to watch the whole life story from egg to caterpillar, to pupa, and to adult once again.

buttermilk

Buttermilk is the liquid that is left after butter has been removed from regular milk or cream by churning. Although most of the fat has been taken out, buttermilk is very good for you because it still contains vitamins and other important foods that are in whole milk. Buttermilk has a slightly sour taste that many people like better than fresh milk. Years ago it was thrown away or fed to animals, but nowadays buttermilk is used as a drink, or dried, or condensed, which means boiled down until it is thick. It can then be used in ice cream and custard powders, in chicken feed, and in baking. Sometimes you may be sold a kind of buttermilk that is full of white lumps. This is called *cultured buttermilk* and is made by curdling, or souring, fresh milk with bacteria.

butterwort

The butterwort, or *bog violet,* is a small, pretty, wild plant which grows in damp places. There are many kinds, found in Europe and Asia as well as in North America. They have long, pale green leaves, held flat against the ground in a circle. These leaves are very wonderful things, for with them the plant catches insects and eats them. The leaves

BUTTON

are sticky on top, and insects which settle there are caught. Then the edges of the leaves roll in and give off a juice that digests the insect. When the leaf has absorbed the juice, it unrolls again to wait for another insect. From the center of the circle of leaves the plant sends up a long thin stem, on which there is usually one flower. This is usually purple or white, but one kind of butterwort, which grows in the southeastern United States, has a yellow flower.

button

Buttons are mostly used to fasten or hold different parts of our clothing together. Sometimes they are used just for ornament. Buttons are of many sizes and they can be of different shapes too, but ordinarily buttons are round. Since buttons usually have to be attached to clothing, they are made either with little holes in the middle, or with a piece of metal called a shank on the back, so they can be sewed on with thread. Buttons have been made from metals like steel, brass, iron and even silver and gold. They have also been made from wood, paper, cloth, glass, ivory, bone, horn, paste, celluloid, plastics, pearl and pottery clay.

Buttons are manufactured in many countries, but most of them are made in England and America. Buttons have been made in England for over three hundred years, but they did not become important until about two hundred years ago. At that time, the English button makers covered round metal buttons with cloth. These cloth-covered metal buttons are still made in England and the United States. Brass, steel, gilt, ivory, horn and bone buttons were made in Birmingham England, before the American Revolution. When the Puritans came to America they felt that buttons were too fancy and bright to go with their plain dark clothes, so they decided to wear little hooks and eyes instead. The Amish people who live mostly in Pennsylvania still use hooks and eyes rather than buttons.

Buttons were made by hand at first. Each button was shaped and decorated by a skilled button maker, but gradually people invented ways of making many buttons at one time all looking exactly alike. There are different methods for making buttons of each different kind of material. In Czechoslovakia for instance, glass buttons are made by pressing the heated and softened end of a glass rod into a mold. The glass hardens in the

Cooper Union Museum

Buttons were once very beautiful works of art, as you can see above. They were often hand-painted and very decorative. Today, buttons on clothing are useful but much more simple. *Right:* The buttons being sewn on this dress were manufactured by machine in large quantities.

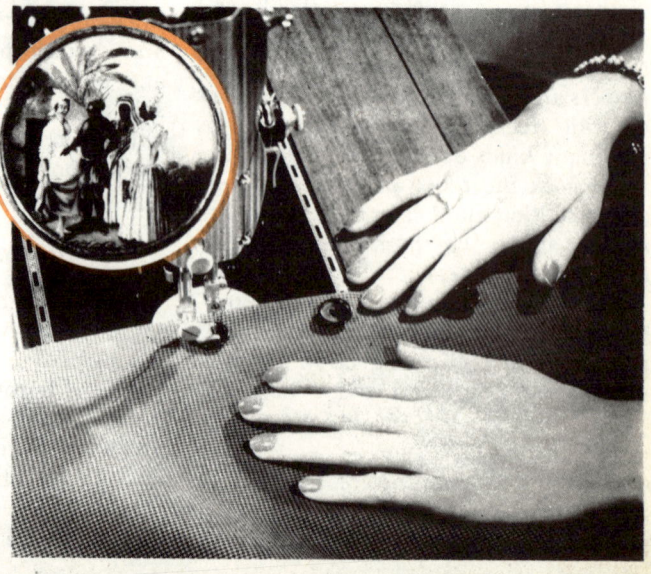

Singer Sewing Centers

mold and sticks to a shank that has been placed there.

In America the center of the button industry is in Connecticut. Metal, bone, horn, vegetable, ivory, and pearl buttons have been made there a hundred years or more. Pearl buttons are made out of a certain kind of mussel shell which is found in the Mississippi River. These are called fresh-water pearl buttons. Mother-of-pearl buttons are called ocean pearl buttons, and are made from oyster shells. Some of the bone buttons are made from the horns and hooves of cattle and other animals.

Buttons have been found that were made by men who lived many thousands of years ago. Buttons were used as decorations by the Greeks, Romans, and the Chinese who wore them as a sign of high position, but they were first used as fastenings in about the 15th century in Europe. Buttons with special colors and patterns are still worn as decorations or as a sign of membership or high rank in some organization. They are also used in political campaigns so that people can show which candidates they favor in an election.

buzzard

Buzzard is the name given to more than thirty different kinds of hawk. They are all fairly large birds, with long, narrow wings, sharp hooked beaks, and strong, cruel "talons," or claws. European buzzards are mostly brownish-black on top and grayish-white underneath. American buzzards are about the same, except for the buzzard that is also called the *red-tailed hawk*. This bird is also brownish-black with a gray belly, but it has a red tail that is tipped with white. Buzzards build rough nests of sticks in the tops of the highest trees. Three or four white eggs speckled with brown are laid in the nest each spring. Buzzards eat small animals such as field mice, squirrels, chipmunks, smaller birds, and reptiles.

Some people call the vulture a turkey buzzard. Vultures feed on dead animals, and are not at all like the real buzzards. (You can read about the VULTURE in a separate article.)

Am. Museum of Nat. History
The red-shouldered hawk, with a mouse in its talons, is a true buzzard.

bylaw

If you join a club or an organization, or work for a company, you have to obey certain rules and regulations that have been passed by these groups. These rules and regulations are called bylaws, because they are not the laws of the country. They do not affect everybody, but only those people who belong to, or work in, the organization that has made the bylaws.

Suppose that you and some of your friends decide to form a club. You may vote on a set of rules and regulations as to how many members your club will have, how often it will meet, what dues will be paid, and so on. These are written down and they become the bylaws of the club. When similar rules and regulations are written into the organization of a town or city, they are sometimes called bylaws.

Byng, Julian

Julian Byng was a British soldier and statesman, who became famous as one of the most important Allied generals in World War I. He was born in England in 1862 and entered the army after his education was completed. He served as an officer in India and Africa, and in World War I he was made commander-in-chief of the British 3rd Army. He led his men to several important victories, and when the war was over he was made a baron by King George V of England. In 1921, the king chose him to be governor-general of Canada, and Byng held this post until 1926. The king made him Viscount Byng when he returned to England. Lord Byng was the head of Scotland Yard, the famous London police headquarters, from 1928 to 1931. He died in 1935.

by-product

A by-product is anything that can be made from the leftovers of an industry. Sometimes a by-product can be used just as it is when the leftover itself is gathered, as in the case of sawdust. As lumber is sawed, the sawdust falls to the ground, and it is collected and used for many things as a by-product of the lumbering industry.

Other leftovers must be manufactured in order to make useful by-products. This is true in the case of soap. Soap is a by-product of the meat-packing industry. The animal fats are used to make soap, and soap has become just as important an industry as meat-packing itself. This is often true of by-products. Many plastics are by-products of lumbering. The resins from lumber are used to manufacture many kinds of plastics, and the plastic business is now a very important industry that started with a by-product of another. Cotton-raising has the by-product cottonseed oil. Flax gives us the by-product, linseed oil.

See the articles on COTTON, FLAX, and PLASTICS.

Byrd, Richard Evelyn

Richard E. Byrd was a famous explorer, the first man who ever reached both the North and South Poles by air. He established the LITTLE AMERICA settlement (about which there is a separate article) on the Antarctic continent. He was a United States naval officer, rising to the grade of rear admiral in the United States Navy. He died in 1957.

Byrd was born in Winchester, Virginia, in 1888, and was graduated from the Naval Academy at Annapolis in 1912. While he was at the academy he injured his left leg, and for this reason was told that he could not pilot a plane, but he persuaded the Navy doctors to let him try, and he became a famous aviator, one of the first men to fly over the North Pole (in 1926) and one of the first men to fly nonstop across the Atlantic Ocean (in 1928). In 1929 he flew over the South Pole, and in 1933 and 1939 he led big expeditions by ship to Antarctica. In his flights across the Atlantic and across the South Pole he had with him another famous explorer, Bernt Balchen.

The Byrd family has been a prominent one in Virginia for many years. Admiral Byrd's brother, Harry Flood Byrd, served as governor of his state and as United States senator.

Official U.S. Navy Photograph
Rear-Admiral Richard E. Byrd, snug in his hut in the snow on an expedition at Little America near the South Pole.

Byron, Lord

George Gordon Byron was one of the greatest English poets. He lived about 150 years ago. During part of his lifetime he was the most popular English poet. He lived a very interesting life, and died when he was only 36 years old, trying to help the Greek people win their independence from the Turks who had ruled them for hundreds of years.

Byron was born in 1788. When he was 3 years old his father died, and his mother, who brought him up, was not a very sensible person. She would sometimes scold him angrily and then treat him with a great display of love, so that he grew up very confused. When he was 11 years old, the death of his great-uncle gave him the title Lord Byron, which meant that when he grew up he could sit in the House of Lords as a member of the British peerage. He was very proud of being a lord.

As a boy, Byron was not happy. He was born with a deformed foot, and limped when he walked. He was fat, and most of his life he almost starved himself to keep his weight down. But he tried very hard at whatever he did. At Cambridge University, he became an excellent swimmer and boxer, in spite of his lameness. His first book of poems was published while he was at the university, and most people did not like it, but he did not give up. He kept on writing poems.

After he left school, Byron took a trip through Europe for two years. While he was away he wrote the first part of a long poem called *Childe Harold's Pilgrimage*. This was published in England when he returned, and was a great success. Byron wrote, "I awoke one morning and found myself famous." This was the first of many successful poems by Byron. He made a great deal of money by writing poems. Many consider another long poem, *Don Juan* to be his best.

Byron was a very handsome man, and many women loved him, but when he married, at the age of 27, he and his wife had an unhappy life and separated. This caused a scandal, and everyone blamed Byron. He never went back. He lived most of the time in Italy, where he saw much of Shelley and other famous English poets of that time.

In 1823 he went to Greece to help the people there, but he died of a fever in 1824, before he could join the fighting. He was buried in England, near Newstead Abbey, the house in which he spent his boyhood.

Byzantine Empire

The important city that is now named Istanbul, and is the biggest city in Turkey, was named Byzantium when it was first built, more than 2,500 years ago. It is on the Greek side of the Bosporus, a narrow channel of water that separates Europe from Asia, and for many years it was part of Greece. Then the Roman Empire, which ruled all the civilized world two thousand years ago, took it over. About 1,600 years ago, in the year 330, a great Roman emperor named Constantine changed its name to Constantinople (which means "city of Constantine") and made it the capital of the Roman Empire.

Later in that same century, in the year 395, the Roman Empire was divided into two parts: the West Roman Empire, with its capital at Rome, and the East Roman Empire, with its capital at Byzantium. The East Roman Empire was often called the Byzantine Empire, because its capital had been called Byzantium for so long. The East Roman, or Byzantine, Empire lasted nearly a thousand years longer than the West Roman Empire. Western Rome fell to barbarian armies in the year 476, while the Byzantine Empire finally fell in the year 1453,

BYZANTINE

1. Some of the finest mosaics were made by Byzantine artists. A mosaic looks like a painting, but it is made of many colored stones pasted together.
2. Beautiful and brilliantly colored enamel work like this was done on large medals and tablets.
3. The top of this Byzantine chest was carefully carved out of ivory. It took a skilled artist a long time to do this.

when Constantinople was captured by the Turks.

The Byzantine Empire had a very stormy history during the period of more than a thousand years in which it existed. The emperors and the men who ran their governments were usually evil men, who did not hesitate to murder and steal for their own benefit. The empire was constantly under attack by Mohammedans from the east and savage tribes of Germans and Russians (Slavs) from the north. At first, the empire owned a great part of Asia Minor and some of North Africa, but these territories were taken away from it by losses in wars, and it shrank until it was not much larger than the modern country of Greece.

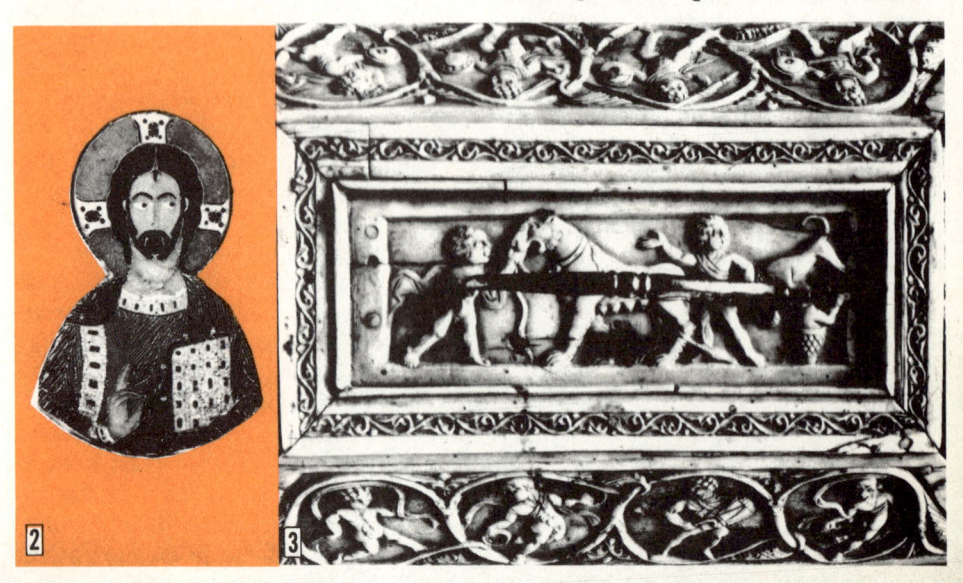

But even while it was so bad, the East Roman Empire did much to keep culture alive during the Dark Ages (the period of about a thousand years, from the fall of Rome to the beginning of the Renaissance, when learning was nearly forgotten in Europe). The designs and paintings and sculpture of that period are called *Byzantine art,* and although it was quite fancy when compared to the art of today, it created some great masterpieces that can still be admired for their beauty. The buildings of that period are described in the article in this encyclopedia on ARCHITECTURE.

The East Roman Empire also did much to keep Christianity alive in a large region that would otherwise have become Mohammedan. Russia became a Christian country because of the influence of the East Roman Empire, and so did some other parts of eastern Europe. The church of the East Roman Empire became what is now known as the Orthodox, or Greek Orthodox, Church.

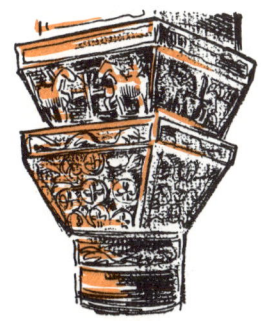

Top: The columns of Byzantine buildings were decorated with colorful scenes and figures that tell us much about this period in history. *Bottom:* This is how a Byzantine building looked 600 years ago.

Top: The remains of this Byzantine arch still stand in Athens, Greece. It was named after the Emperor Hadrian. *Bottom:* Important Byzantine buildings were decorated with beautiful sculpture. There were full-length figures and busts carved out of stone, both inside and outside the buildings. This is the head of a fine piece of Byzantine sculpture. If you visit the city of Istanbul, you will see many fine examples of Byzantine art.

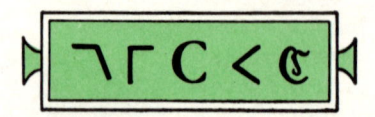

C or c

The letter C, the third letter of our alphabet, came to us as most of our letters did: First, thousands of years ago, it was one of the symbols used by the ancient Egyptians in their system of "picture-writing," or *hieroglyphics*. In this system a picture of something, instead of a letter, finally came to stand for a single sound. Most scholars believe that the letter C began as a picture of a camel. In the Hebrew language, the word for camel was *gimel,* and the sign for it was the one shown at the far left in the box at the top of this page.

Next the ancient Greeks used this letter. But the Hebrews read from right to left, while the Greeks read from left to right, as we do. So the Greeks turned the letter around, and then it looked like the one shown next to the *gimel*.

The Romans were the next to use this letter, and they gave it the rounded form that we use. The Romans had two ways to pronounce C. One way was like the G in *game*. Later on, they put a little tail on the C, and made our present G out of it. The other way the Romans pronounced C was like K. We still do that, in such words as *cave,* and we also pronounce it like S, in such words as *center*. We usually pronounce C as K when the next letter after it is *a, o,* or *u,* and as S when the next letter after it is *e* or *i*.

In the illustration above, at the right of the capital C is the "small c" that the Romans used, and at the far right is the "German black-letter" C that is used in many German books.

Read also the article ALPHABET.

cabal

A cabal is a group that gets together to plot against others and to work out secret plans for its own benefit. These plans are secret because they are usually against the law, or dishonest. Sometimes the word *cabal* is used to mean the plot or the plans themselves. The name was made up from the initials of five men who were ministers to the English king, Charles II. During King Charles' reign there were many plots, and these men, whose names were Clifford, Ashley, Buckingham, Arlington, and Lauderdale, were often behind the plots.

cabbage

On the coasts of Europe there grows a scraggly-looking wild plant with tough leaves; you would never think so, but it is the ancestor of all the many different kinds of cabbage that we eat. In the common form of cabbage we eat the leaves, which are big and grow packed together in the shape of a ball. Some cabbages have smooth leaves, and some have crinkly leaves. There are red and green varieties of cabbage. They are eaten in many ways. They may be cooked, or pickled, or made into cole slaw. There are also many other vegetables that look and taste quite different from each other but that are of the cabbage family. Among these are: *Brussels sprouts,* in which small edible buds grow along the stem; *cauliflower,* of which the part eaten is the mass of dense white flower buds; *broccoli,* a kind of cauliflower with a looser head of purplish-green buds; *kale,* of which the curly leaves are eaten, and which is also used as a cattle food; and *kohlrabi,* of which the swollen stem is eaten.

Cabell, James Branch

James Branch Cabell was an American writer who wrote a great deal about real and imaginary characters in history. He was born in Richmond, Virginia, in 1879, and was graduated from the college of William and Mary. Many of his stories take place in an imaginary kingdom called *Poictesme,* during the Middle Ages when knights in armor were supposed to have fought dragons, defended beautiful princesses, and searched for such legendary things as the Holy Grail. Cabell described these adventures in an exciting way, but at the same time he made fun of his characters for doing many things that seem silly to us today. For this reason he is called a satirical novelist. His best-known novel is called *Jurgen.* He died in 1958.

cabinet

A cabinet is a committee made up of the heads of the chief departments of a government. In most countries the cabinet is made up from the leaders of the political party that controls the parliament, or lawmaking body. Members of the cabinet are called ministers. Its head is called the prime minister, or premier, and he and the ministers actually run the government.

In the United States government, the cabinet is a group of men who advise the President. The President is the head of one part of the government, called the executive branch, the branch that carries out the laws. To help the President, the Congress set up ten executive departments. Each department takes charge of a certain part of the job of putting the laws into effect. These ten departments are: State, Treasury, Defense, Justice, Post Office, Interior, Agriculture, Commerce, Labor, and the combined Health, Education and Welfare Departments. At the head of each is a person who is called the Secretary of that department (except that the head of the Justice Department is called the Attorney General, and the head of the Post Office Department is called the Postmaster General). Together these ten department heads are called the cabinet, when they meet to advise the President.

The cabinet was not set up by the Constitution, as were the Congress and the office of the President. In fact, it has no official place in the government. It is only a matter of custom, but it has a long history as a part of the government. The first President, George Washington, started this custom by asking the department heads to discuss certain problems with him, and every President since then has continued the custom. Today the cabinet meets regularly, usually once a week, and discusses whatever the President suggests. The meetings are private. The members of the cabinet tell the President all they can about the business of their departments. They also discuss many important decisions with the President. It is up to the President to make the final decisions, but he is glad to have help from the people who know most about the different parts of the government.

cabinetmaking

Cabinetmaking is the trade of building wooden furniture. A cabinetmaker builds many things. The word comes from a French word meaning a "collection of fine things," and a cabinetmaker is one who builds fine things. That is how he differs from a carpenter, who usually does a rougher type of building, such as building houses or repairing them. (See the article on CARPENTRY.) Cabi-

Left: The cabinetmaker carefully examines wood before he uses it. When he builds a piece of furniture, he makes joints to fit the pieces of wood together. *Right:* The dovetail (above) and the mortise-and-tenon (below) are two joints he uses.

netmaking includes making furniture, wooden wall paneling, built-in bookcases or shelves, and floors of patterned wood.

A cabinetmaker must know a great deal about the woods he uses and how to match and select them. Mostly he uses hard woods, such as mahogany, walnut, oak, and fruit woods. When a cabinetmaker puts pieces of wood together to make something, he *joins* them instead of nailing them as a carpenter would. This means that he fits the parts together by cutting them with interlocking notches, and then glues the joint. Sometimes you can see the *dovetails* where drawers are put together. Another kind of joint is called a *mortise and tenon*. The mortise is a square hole that is cut into one piece of wood, and the tenon is a tongue cut at the end of another. The tenon fits tightly into the mortise, and they are glued together. There are many other kinds of joints for different purposes.

Nowadays cabinetmakers use electric tools for most of their work, but until about thirty years ago everything was done by hand. Many famous cabinetmakers were also designers. Some of the best known are Thomas Sheraton and Thomas Chippendale, who lived in England about 150 years ago; Jean Henri Riesener, who lived in France about the same time; George Hepplewhite, who lived in England about 200 years ago, and Duncan Phyfe, who lived in the United States 100 years ago. You can read more about cabinetmaking in the article on FURNITURE.

cable

A cable is a rope or chain. There are many different kinds of cable, and each kind has a different use. The length and thickness of a cable, and the material it is made of, depend on the use for which it is intended.

The first cables were simply ordinary ropes used by seamen to lower anchors into the water or to tie a ship up to a dock. About 150 years ago iron chains began to be used with anchors because they were less likely to break and lasted much longer. Later, wire ropes (cables made up of a number of wires braided or twisted together) came into use for mooring ships. Today all three types of cable are used on ships.

Modern bridges of the type called suspension bridges hang from cables, which in turn hang from bigger cables that are several feet thick. Bridge cables are made up of a great many wires, twisted or straight, and are covered with a casing which protects them from rust. They must support extremely heavy loads, so they have to be very strong. See the article BRIDGE.

Smaller cables are used to carry electrical current. In many cities and towns they are strung overhead to supply power to the streetcars or buses that run beneath them. These are called *trolley cables*. Another example are the cables by which elevators move up and down. The lines that carry electricity from the generator where it is produced to the home or factory where it is used are also cables. Like telegraph cables and telephone cables, power transmission cables are buried underground in most cities and towns, but out in the country they are usually strung on poles.

LONG-DISTANCE CABLES

Most electric cables are made of copper, which bends easily, and aluminum, which is the lightest metal in general use. The light weight of aluminum makes it particularly useful for overhead lines. These cables are often very long. A single telephone cable, for instance, stretches from New York to Chicago for 861

Standard Oil Co.

The men on this barge are laying a telephone cable across the Mississippi River. *Below:* **This is how an underwater cable rests on the rocky and hilly bottom of the Atlantic Ocean.** *Bottom:* **Men are attaching one end of a transatlantic cable to the shore.**

Western Union Telegraph Co.

miles. Most of it is strung aboveground on telephone poles. Like almost all overhead cables, it is covered with a sheath of lead to protect it from the weather.

The most famous cable in history was laid between Europe and North America in 1866, after four earlier attempts had failed. Under the leadership of an American, Cyrus Field, the cable-laying group sailed from Ireland on July 13, 1866, aboard the steamer *Great Eastern.* All the way across the ocean the cable unwound from huge drums on the deck, without breaking once. The *Great Eastern* reached Newfoundland on July 28, its job done. On the way back, Field's group found the end of a cable that had been lost in an attempt the year before. They attached it to a new cable and on September 8 they brought the second cable ashore. Since then the number of transatlantic telegraph cables has risen to twenty-one and there are cables across the Pacific and South Atlantic Oceans and nearly every sea and channel in the world. In 1955 the first telephone cable was laid across the Atlantic.

A special kind of cable that has recently become important is the *coaxial cable.* By means of the coaxial cable a number of telegraph signals, telephone conversations, and television pictures can be sent at the same time in both directions, along each of the several cables of which it is made. This makes it possible to send television pictures across the country, which could not be done before.

cable car

A cable car is a kind of streetcar that is pulled by cables or ropes over ground that is too steep for walking or driving. Most cable cars ride high above the ground, and it is very exciting to ride in them.

The cable car that gave men the idea for all others is used in mining. It is made of buckets attached to a circular chain, or cable, which goes around all the time. The miners put the gold or coal or whatever they are mining into these buckets. The cable pulls them up from the pit, or down from the mountain. The second kind, for carrying people, is a streetcar attached to an underground cable. It was first used in San Francisco in 1873. Before then, horses had pulled the heavy streetcars up the steep hills. The man who invented it, Andrew Hallidie, was in the business of making cables. He put

Austrian Tourist Bureau
Cable cars like this one are used by sightseers. Although they seem to hang dangerously, they are quite safe.

Southern Pacific Co.
This cable car is clanging merrily up a hill in San Francisco. It is pulled by a cable underneath the ground.

strong clamps or grips under the streetcar and a circular cable underground between the tracks. The conductor attaches clamps on the streetcar to the moving underground cable when he wants the car to move. He releases the clamps when he wants to stop. The third kind of cable car is called an *aerial tramway*. It carries passengers, but it is attached to an overhead wire instead of to the ground. It is like an elevator that goes up at an angle. There is one at Franconia Notch, New Hampshire. Another, called the Cog Railway, runs up Mount Washington. To get to the top of Lookout Mountain, near Chattanooga, Tennessee, you ride in a car that is partly pulled up by the weight of another car that is going down. Most aerial tramways and ski-lifts are pulled up and let down by machines that turn big drums. The turning of the drum winds and unwinds the cable, which is attached to the cable car.

Cabot, John and Sebastian

John Cabot and his son Sebastian Cabot were explorers who lived during the time of Columbus. The Cabots were Italian, but they moved to England when Sebastian was still very young, and they were in England when Columbus made his famous discovery of America in 1492. Columbus had not set out to discover new lands but to find a way of going by sea from Europe to Asia. When John Cabot heard about Columbus' trip, he made up his mind that he would go farther than Columbus and actually find a sea route to the East. In 1496, he and his son sailed all the way from Bristol, England, to the land we now call Nova Scotia, and took possession of the Cape Breton Islands for the British. The Cabots were really the first to set foot on the mainland of North America, because Columbus had landed only on islands up to that time.

In 1498, the Cabots made a second trip. This time they landed in Greenland and traveled south by ship along the Atlantic coast all the way to Chesapeake Bay. The second trip was very difficult, and the crew mutinied.

After John Cabot died, Sebastian went into the service of the Spanish king. He made a trip to South America, and spent three years there exploring the La Plata River. Sebastian made excellent maps of the routes he and his father had taken to North America, and of his own discoveries.

Cabrini, Saint Frances Xavier

Mother Frances Xavier Cabrini was the first citizen of the United States to be canonized (declared a saint) by the Roman Catholic Church. Mother Cabrini spent her whole life trying to help unfortunate people, especially orphans and the sick. She was born in Italy in 1850, and christened Maria Frances Cabrini. She wanted to be a nun from the time she was a little girl, but she was not very strong, and twice when she tried to become a nun she was refused. Finally she succeeded and was put in charge of a church orphanage in Italy. She came to the United States when she was 38 years old. She died in 1917 and was canonized by Pope Pius XII in 1946. Her title, "Mother," means that she was a nun.

cacao

The cacao is the tree from which we get chocolate and cocoa. It is found in Central America, the West Indies, and the tropical, or hot, parts of South America and Africa. On the trunk of the cacao tree grow large pods, shaped like cucumbers and as much as 12 inches long. These pods are cut off with long knives. Inside there are rows of "beans," from which the chocolate and cocoa are made. When the beans have been cleaned and roasted they are known as *nibs*. Other parts of the tree and its fruit are used as cattle food, and to make *cocoa butter,*

Right: The giant saguaro cactus grows in the deserts of the Southwest, and often reaches a height of 60 feet. *Top:* When it blooms, it has beautiful large flowers.

Tucson Chamber of Commerce

which is not really butter but a kind of ointment.

See also the article CHOCOLATE AND COCOA.

cactus

Cactus is the name of a family of about a thousand different plants. Most kinds of cactus have no leaves or very tiny ones. The stem is flat and green, and inside it is often fleshy and full of water. The plant is covered with sharp spines, which are arranged in rows or in small clusters. Sometimes the spines are several inches long, and often they are bright red, purple, yellow, or some other color.

Cactuses grow in very strange shapes. Some look like pincushions, others like footballs, candelabra, or long leathery whips. Some kinds even grow into quite big trees. Their flowers are almost always large and very beautiful. They may be red, yellow, pink, or white. One of the most beautiful is the *night-blooming cereus*, which is a climbing cactus that flowers once a year and then only at night. The flower of the *giant cactus* is the state flower of Arizona.

Although cactuses can be found growing in places as far north as Canada, and in the dense, steamy forests of the Amazon, most of them grow in deserts or other very dry places where you can find few other plants. Cactuses can live in these places because they store water in their plant tissues. The sharp spikes prevent animals from eating them.

Cactuses are popular as house plants. They also are grown as hedges. The big ones can be used as wood. The fruit and stems of some cactuses, such as the *prickly pear,* are very good to eat. Cactuses grow wild only in America. The plural of the word *cactus* is often spelled *cacti.*

caddis fly

The caddis fly is a small insect that lives near water. It looks like a moth, but it has hairy wings and its young live underwater. There are about 4,500 kinds of caddis fly. They lay their eggs in the water, and the young are called *caddis worms*. Some caddis worms are almost four inches long.

The best-known kinds of caddis worm build cases round themselves and crawl around inside them. They build the cases out of bits of twigs, grains of sand, pieces of grass, and so on, bound together with strands of silk which they make themselves. The caddis worms that live in rapid streams make silken cases and attach them to a stone. They also make a silken net with which they catch their food. Some, if they lose their hold on the stone and get carried downstream, can spin out a lifeline and crawl back along it to their homes.

When it is fully grown, the caddis worm closes its case at both ends or spins a cocoon. Inside this it changes to a *caddis fly*. It bites its way out of the case, comes to the surface of the water and flies away. Both caddis worms and flies are eaten by fish.

Cadillac, Antoine de la Mothe

Antoine Cadillac was a French colonial governor who founded the city of Detroit more than two hundred years ago. He was born in 1658, and came to the New World as a young man. Cadillac was in charge of a frontier post at Mackinac in what is now northern Michigan. He thought a post on the Detroit River would be a better place to defend against the British. So he got permission from King Louis XIV to open a post and trade with the Indians. The settlement started with only fifty people, but Cadillac managed so efficiently and got along so well with the Indians that in two years more than two hundred settlers had come to Detroit. Later Cadillac was made governor of the huge Louisiana territory. In 1716 he returned to France and died there in 1730, at the age of 72.

Cadiz

Cadiz is a city in Spain on the Atlantic coast near the western end of the Mediterranean Sea. It was from Cadiz that Columbus sailed on his second voyage to America. Though most of its buildings are fairly new, the city itself is very old. It was founded eleven hundred years before the birth of Christ by the early Mediterranean traders called Phoenicians. Later Cadiz was ruled in turn by Carthaginians from North Africa, by Romans, Barbarians, Moors, and finally by the kingdom of Castile which became Spain. When Spain was a great world power Cadiz was its chief seaport. Today Cadiz is a clean city of sun-baked white buildings, with straight streets all leading to the sea. It is also a naval base.

CADIZ, SPAIN. Population (in 1960) 113,749. Capital of Cadiz Province. Major seaport on Atlantic Ocean.

cadmium

Cadmium is a metal that has many uses. It is found in ore with the metal ZINC (about which there is a separate article), and it is somewhat like zinc. It can be made very smooth, and it can be polished until it gleams like silver. It does not rust, and so it is often used for plating iron and steel, which do rust. Cadmium melts at lower temperatures than many metals, so it is mixed with lead and tin to make solder, which is used to fill holes in metal containers, or to fasten pieces of metal together. Cadmium is also used in the fuses that protect electric wires against becoming too hot, and in television tubes. Cadmium mixed with sulfur is used in making yellow paint. But cadmium is poisonous, and so there is a limit to the number of things it can be used for.

Most of the cadmium in the world is mined in Pennsylvania and in Scotland. In Scotland it is often called *greenockite* because it is found in a place named Greenock.

Cadmus

Cadmus was a character in Greek mythology, the stories the ancient Greeks told about their gods and goddesses. He is famous for having founded the city of Thebes. According to the legend, Cadmus killed a sacred dragon and then pulled out the dragon's teeth and sowed them in the ground like seeds. From these teeth there sprang up soldiers who were ancestors of the later people of Thebes. But Ares, the god of war, became angry because Cadmus had killed the sacred dragon and caused many unfortunate things to happen to him and his family.

Cadmus is also famous because he is supposed to have invented the alphabet. Of course, this is only a story; see the article on ALPHABET.

Caedmon

The first Christian poet who ever wrote in the English language was named Caedmon. He was a servant who took care of the cattle at a monastery in Whitby, England, more than twelve hundred years ago. One night, as Caedmon slept in a shed, a man appeared to him in a vision and commanded him to sing, and he did. When he woke up, he remembered the words of a poem he had sung in praise of God. After that he composed many more poems. Others wrote them down for him, as he could neither read nor write. These poems are written in Old English, or Anglo-Saxon, which is not very much like the language we know today.

Caesar

Caesar was the name of a famous family in ancient Rome. Its name has come to mean an emperor, because of the first Roman emperor, Augustus Caesar, who was the adopted son of Julius Caesar. *Czar* in Russian, and *Kaiser* in German, mean "emperor" or "Caesar."

Caesar, Gaius Julius

Julius Caesar was a very great Roman statesman and soldier. He was born about a hundred years before Christ. Caesar's family was rich and powerful, and had always taken a leading part in Roman politics. When Caesar became interested in government, he found that Rome had a very corrupt government that was in need of reform. He was an honest man.

He held various important positions in the Roman government while he was still quite young, but he wanted to be even more important so he could do more for his country.

In Rome in those days the best way to do this was to become a military man as well as a politician, so Caesar got himself appointed governor of two Roman provinces, Cisalpine Gaul and Transalpine Gaul. *Cisalpine Gaul* was the Latin way of saying "Gaul on this side of the Alps," and *Transalpine Gaul* meant "Gaul on the other side of the Alps from Rome." These provinces form what is now France. The Germans were trying to take these provinces from the Romans, and the Gauls themselves were trying to win their independence from Rome. But Caesar defeated their armies. He kept Gaul for the Romans after many great battles. He wrote the whole story of his campaigns in Gaul in a book called *The Gallic Wars*, which is still studied by all schoolboys and girls when they learn the Latin language.

When Caesar got home from Gaul, he found that some of his friends were trying to take away his military power in Rome. That would have left all the power in the hands of another Roman general, Pompey, who also had a big army. Caesar had trained and equipped his army so well that it was the greatest fighting force the world had ever known. Caesar found it hard to decide on war against another Roman army, but he finally made the decision. With his army he crossed the Rubicon river in North Italy and marched on Rome. This was in 49 B.C. Pompey also brought his army to Rome, and the two armies fought. Pompey was beaten and fled to Egypt. Caesar followed him there, but before he arrived Pompey had been murdered. Caesar stayed in Egypt for a while, partly because he was in love with the Egyptian queen Cleopatra, and he helped her get firmly established on the throne. While he was in that part of the world he fought battles with many enemies of Rome. One of them was Pharnaces II, king of Pontus, who was threatening to take over some territory of Rome. When Caesar fought this army he defeated it so easily that he told all about the battle by saying: "I came, I saw, I conquered."

All during this time, Caesar's political power had been growing greater and greater, and when he returned to Rome he was made dictator for ten years. He was given the greatest honors. He was called "Father of his Country," his statue was placed in the temples, coins were made in his likeness, and a month was named for him—Julius, the month that we still call July. But some of the Roman politicians, including his friend Brutus, were afraid that he was becoming too powerful and doing too much for the common people. They plotted to murder him. He was killed on March 15 (which the Romans called the Ides of March) in front of the Senate. Caesar was born in 102 B.C. and died in 44 B.C. One of the greatest things he did was to change the calendar. See the article CALENDAR.

Caesarea

In ancient times there were several very important cities named Caesarea. Two of the most important were in Palestine. One of these, Caesarea Palestinae, was a seaport built by Herod the Great about twenty-five years before Christ was born. During the time of the Crusades, there was a large fort in this city held by the Crusaders. The fort was destroyed by the Moslems in 1265. When Palestine became the new state of Israel, a modern village called Sdot-Yam was founded on the site of ancient Caesarea Palestinae.

The other Caesarea in Palestine was Caesarea Philippi, which was founded by Philip the Tetrarch, ruler of part of the realm of his father, King Herod the Great. This city was in Syria. It is mentioned several times in the Bible. It was also an important city for the Crusaders. A small village called Baniyas now stands where Caesarea Philippi used to be.

cafeteria

A cafeteria is a restaurant where the food is displayed on long counters and the people who come to eat choose what they want and carry it to a table themselves. Cafeterias are so common now that it is hard to believe the first one was opened only a few years before 1900. Before that time, anyone who wanted to eat away from home had to go to a restaurant, and most of the restaurants were very expensive. Many working people could not afford to eat in them, and had to prepare their lunches at home and take them to work.

Then in 1891, a man named H. S. Thompson got the idea for a self-service restaurant. He knew he could serve good food for less money if he did not have to pay waiters or waitresses. He opened a cafeteria in Chicago, Illinois, and it soon became very popular. Many other cafeterias were opened after that. The Young Women's Christian Association (YWCA), for instance, began to operate cafeterias for its members who worked in offices and could not afford to eat in expensive restaurants. Nowadays, many big factories and industrial plants have cafeterias for their workers, and there are cafeterias in many schools and colleges.

The Automat is a kind of cafeteria where foods like salads, sandwiches, and desserts, which can be prepared in advance, are kept in little glass cases against the wall. The customer puts coins in a slot and turns a handle, and the glass case opens so that he can take out the food.

caffeine

Caffeine is a chemical substance that is found in coffee, tea, cola, and other drinks. (In tea it is called *theine*.) Caffeine is a stimulant, which means that when you are tired it makes you feel brighter and stronger. Of course, this can be overdone, but in small amounts caffeine does no harm. Tea contains more caffeine than coffee, but more coffee is used per cup, so it evens up. In its pure form caffeine is a crystal, belonging to a group of chemicals called *alkaloids*. It is used as a medicine, and can be made from tea dust and the soot from ovens in which coffee is roasted. Caffeine is also extracted or removed from coffee, which is then sold as "caffeine-free coffee."

Caiaphas

Caiaphas was the high priest of the Jews during the time of the trial and crucifixion of Jesus. In some of the books of the New Testament of the Bible, the story is told of how Jesus was betrayed by Judas Iscariot, and how he was brought before Caiaphas for preaching things that the Jewish priests did not believe. Caiaphas condemned Jesus to death, but the sentence had to be approved by the Romans, who were the rulers of Palestine at that time. Pontius Pilate was the Roman governor, and Caiaphas brought Jesus before him. At this trial the death sentence was confirmed.

Cain, brother of Abel: see ABEL.

cairn

A cairn is a cone-shaped pile of stones, sometimes surrounded by a circle of larger stones set upright in the ground. Cairns are not much used any more except as decorations (in rock gardens, for instance), but at one time they were often put up to mark boundaries. Other uses were to show where an important person was buried, or where a battle had been fought. Many cairns have been found in Ireland and Scotland, and in Norway and Sweden. Mounds of earth found in England and Denmark are the same shape and size as cairns, and served the same purpose. There are many mounds in the United States; see the separate article on MOUNDS.

Cairn terrier

The Cairn terrier is a small dog with a big dog's loyal and protective spirit, and a willingness to work hard at its specialty of catching rats and mice. The breed originated on the Isle of Skye, off the coast of Scotland, and it was originally called the short-haired Skye terrier. It was renamed Cairn terrier because its rough coat and stocky body made people think of a rocky cairn (see the article CAIRN above this one). Cairns are often kept as hunting terriers today, and they can hunt in all kinds of weather because of their coats. The coat is thicker and deeper than that of most terriers. In the United States, the Cairn is usually kept as a house dog and pet.

The Cairn terrier stands about 9½ inches high at the shoulder, and weighs about 14 pounds. Its coat is heavy and coarse, with a soft thick undercoat, and it may be any shade of gray, brown, tan, or black, but it is never white. Its front legs are very straight and stiff, and its tail stands up straight, at right angles to its back.

Cairo

Cairo is the capital of Egypt and the largest city on the continent of Africa. The city lies on the banks of the Nile River, partly on level ground and partly on a rocky range of hills. On top of one

B.O.A.C.

In Cairo, the past and the present meet. *Above:* Two Egyptians in the desert near Cairo watch a plane flying over the pyramids, built thousands of years ago. *Below:* 800 years ago, this fortress was one of the chief defenses of Cairo. It was built by a ruler in Egypt, named Saladin. *Right:* In the modern city of Cairo, craftsmen, like this coppersmith, still work in the streets as they have for centuries.

of these hills there is a fortress called the citadel, from which there is a very wide and beautiful view. Below lies the city with its strong walls and high towers. There are gardens, squares, palaces, mosques (the churches of the Moslem religion) with carved domes and minarets, or towers. You can see the broad river Nile with its many islands and the river valley dotted with groups of date trees and palms. Near the city are the great pyramids; to the northwest are fields, villas, and gardens; to the east are barren cliffs and behind them, like a great ocean of sand, lies the Sahara Desert.

Cairo today has a population of almost three million. Most of the people are native Egyptians, but there are also many Copts, Negroes, Jews, Turks, Greeks, Armenians, French, and English. Part of Cairo is a modern city with wide streets, but the most famous palaces and mosques are to be found in the older sections. One of the most famous mosques, called El Azhar, is nearly as old as the city itself. In this mosque is the most important Moslem university in the world, with more than 34,000 students. There are many other wonderful things to see in Cairo, such as the Arab and ancient Egyptian museums and the national library. One interesting thing is an instrument more than a hundred years old called the Nilometer. This is a column marked off like a great yardstick. It is used to tell how high the water is in the Nile river. It is on Roda Island, where the baby Moses is believed to have been found in the bulrushes.

Cairo was founded nearly a thousand years ago by a Fatimite general named Jauhar. The Fatimites were descendants of Mohammed the Prophet through his daughter Fatima. You can read about MOHAMMED and the religion he founded in another volume of this encyclopedia. Cairo was attacked many times during the centuries that followed, beginning in the 12th century with the Crusades. The citadel was built to defend the city against the Crusaders, who were Christian soldiers trying to take the Holy Land back from the Moslems. During the 15th century, the city was ruled by the MAMELUKES, whom you can read about in a separate article. Cairo then was one of the busiest and richest cities in the world. Later it became less important and was occupied by the French under Napoleon and after that by the English until 1922, when Egypt became fully independent.

CAIRO, EGYPT. Population (in 1961) 3,-100,000. Capital of Egypt. On the Nile River.

caisson

A caisson is a big box, as big as a room, in which men can work under water when they are building a tunnel or the foundations for a bridge. The caisson is a box with sides and a top but no bottom. It is usually made of concrete and steel. The reason it does not have a bottom is that the men in the caisson are going to dig at the bottom, to make room for the tunnel or the bridge foundation.

One section of the caisson is called the *cofferdam*. This section is filled with rocks or other heavy things, called *ballast*. The ballast makes the caisson heavy enough to sink into the water. (There is a separate article about BALLAST.)

First, the caisson is allowed to sink to the bottom of the water. It is connected with the surface by a shaft, usually with an elevator in it. The men who work in the caisson (and who are called "sandhogs") will enter it through this shaft.

Next, all the water is pumped out of the caisson and compressed air is pumped in. In the article on AIR COMPRESSION you can read how compressed air can be so strong that it will keep the water from flowing back into the caisson. But the men who work in the caisson could not stand such high air pressure without becoming used to it gradually. So they pass through chambers called *air locks* when they go to work and when they leave work. An air lock is airtight, and whatever air pressure is pumped into it, it will

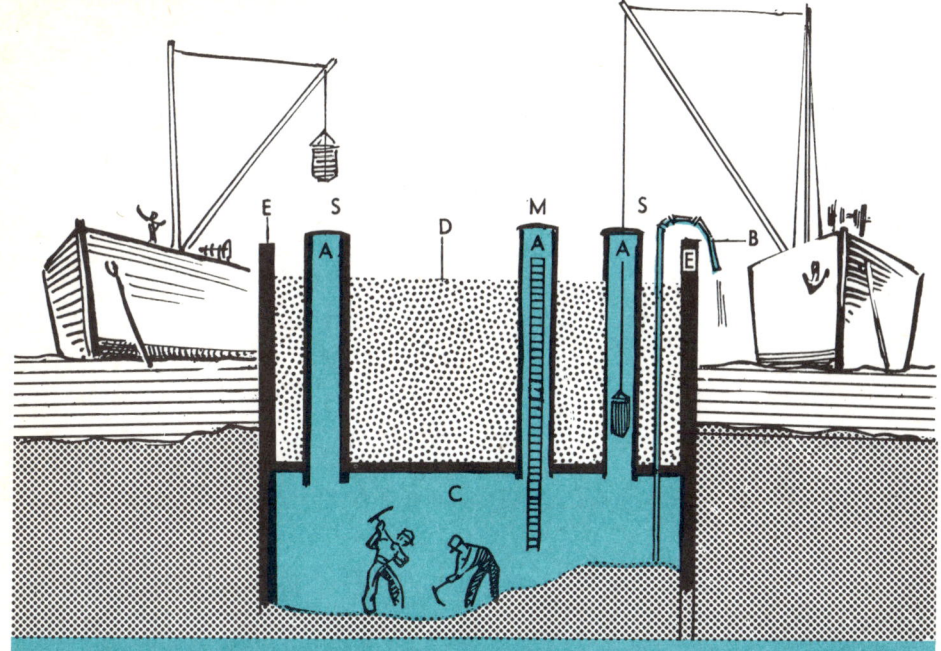

This compressed-air caisson is being used to lay a bridge foundation or pier. The caisson has not yet stopped sinking. As the men dig into the floor, the sharp side edges (E) sink into the bottom, forced downward by the concrete load in the cofferdam (D). The men in the working chamber (C) are protected from high pressure by compressed air in the airlocks (A) and in the chamber. The shafts (S) on either side of the main shaft (M) are used to remove soil that has been dug out. The blowout tube (B) removes sand and other materials.

stay that way. Sandhogs going to work stay in the air lock while the pressure is gradually increased. When they have become accustomed to the normal pressure of the outside air, they leave the air lock.

The men working in the caisson dig away the mud and rock beneath them. What they dig away is removed from the caisson through the shaft, or through "blow-out pipes" that dump it into the water around the caisson. The sides of the caisson sink deeper as the sandhogs dig. When they have dug enough, concrete is poured onto the bottom. This will be the bottom of the tunnel, or the foundation of the bridge.

There is a disease called "caisson disease," or "the bends," that men sometimes get when they do not wait long enough in the air lock. This disease can be very dangerous. Divers sometimes get it from going too deep in the water. Sandhogs very seldom get it now, because they are careful to use their air locks.

Ammunition wagons for artillery are also called caissons. The official song of the U.S. Field Artillery was named "The Caissons Go Rolling Along."

calabash

A calabash is the dried shell of the fruit of the calabash tree. Calabashes become very hard when they are dried, which makes them useful as dippers, bottles, bowls, or even cooking pots. They often grow as big as footballs. Sometimes they are carved and painted, and used as ornaments. Small ones are filled with seeds and used as rattles or "shak-shaks" by native orchestras.

The calabash tree is a low, spreading tree with very twisted branches, that grows in the West Indies. Its flowers are white, and grow on the branches and trunk. From the flowers grow the huge fruit, full of yellowish juicy pulp which is not very good to eat. The fruit of various kinds of cucumber or pumpkin vine are also sometimes called calabashes, but the real name for them is *gourds*.

Calais

Calais is a seaport on the northern coast of France, just across the English Channel from Dover, England. During the Allied invasion of northern Europe in World War II Calais suffered severe damage from both sides. Since the Germans had strong forces there, the English and Americans bombed the city many times. When the Germans finally retreated they blew up the docks and harbor buildings so that Calais would be useless to the Allies as a port. The old town was completely destroyed. Thousands of people were killed.

Calais was a fishing village until the tenth century. It was fortified by the French about six hundred years ago. Not long afterward the city was besieged and finally captured by the English, who held it for two hundred years until the French retook it. Up to 1940 it was France's greatest center for the making of lace. Although ferry service to Dover and Folkestone across the English Channel started again after the war, Calais found it hard to recover from the effects of being a battleground. The population in 1936 was more than 65,000. The present population is about 60,340.

calamine

Calamine is an ore from which the metal zinc is obtained. (An ore is rock that has a metal in it, mixed with other substances.) The article on ZINC tells how it is taken from the ore. In the United States, calamine is found in New Jersey, Pennsylvania and Virginia in the East, and in Missouri, Utah and Montana in the West. We also hear the word *calamine* in *calamine lotion,* a white liquid that is spread on skin that is red and itchy from poison ivy or from other causes. Calamine lotion is made with a chemical called zinc oxide, but it is not the same substance as the ore.

calcium

Calcium is a silver-white metal that is found in most rocks and also in the ground. We see calcium every day, but we do not think of it as a metal. Calcium occurs in many compounds. One of them is the hard substance in our bones and in our teeth. It is found in chalk, and got its name because in the Latin language *calx* means "chalk." In one form, calcium carbonate, it makes limestone and marble, and also the pearls found in oysters.

Though calcium is found nearly everywhere, it is never found by itself. It is always combined with other chemicals. Calcium carbonate, mentioned above, is one of these compounds—calcium and carbon. In its many mixtures, calcium is one of the most useful things we know. It prevents water from freezing in the winter; it fertilizes fields for farmers; it makes ACETYLENE, about which there is a separate article; and it is used in dozens of other ways.

Calcium is important to the human body, not only in the bones but also in the blood, where it helps to stop bleeding. Mothers who are expecting babies often take special calcium pills so that the babies will have strong bones. Some salts containing calcium are taken for an upset stomach.

calculating machines

A calculating machine solves problems of arithmetic and saves you the trouble of doing them in your head. It also prints both the problem and the answer, saving you the trouble of writing them down. Some machines can only add. Some can add and subtract. Some can also multiply and divide.

CALCULATING MACHINES

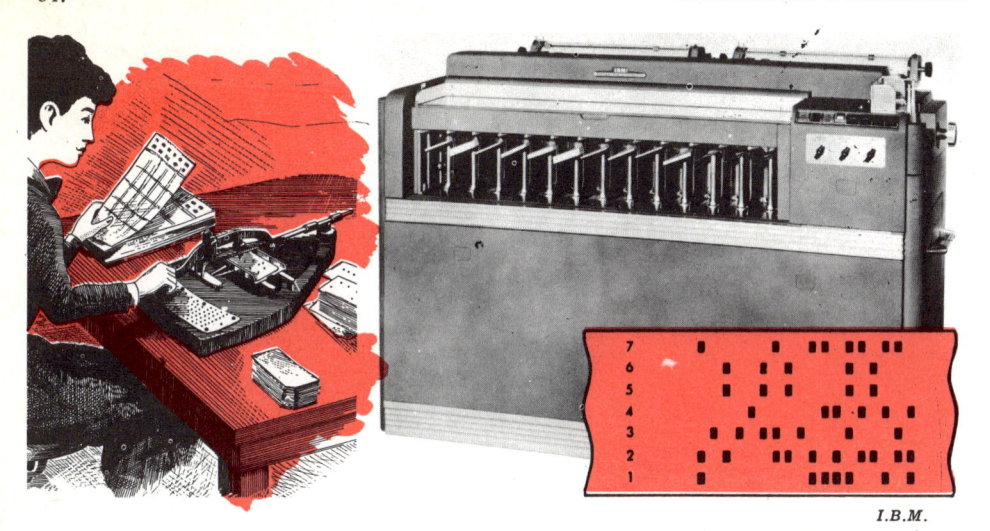

Left: The earliest card-punching machines were operated by hand. Modern calculating machines are run by electricity. *Right:* Automatic machines like this one do several jobs at a high rate of speed; 450 cards a minute are printed, sorted, and counted. *Insert:* The latest calculating machines use a tape with magnetized spots instead of punched holes. One reel of tape may contain thousands of facts.

There are hundreds of different kinds of calculating machines, and they are useful in many different businesses and sciences. In the articles on BOOKKEEPING and ACCOUNTING you can learn how important it is for business firms to keep track of how much money they have earned and how much they have spent. Bookkeepers used to have to add up long columns of figures. Now machines do it for them—and the machines do not make mistakes. Scientists use calculating machines to multiply figures so huge that you can hardly even imagine them. Banks use calculating machines to show quickly how much money a person has deposited. The Army uses calculating machines to keep track of millions of soldiers. These are only a few of the uses of calculating machines.

Thousands of years ago, men used pebbles to help them do arithmetic. They used the pebbles in a device called the ABACUS, about which there is a separate article. The word for "pebble" in the Latin language, which was used in ancient Róme, is *calculus,* and that is where we get our word *calculate.*

The first modern calculating machine was an adding machine, invented about three hundred years ago (in 1642) by a French scientist named Blaise Pascal. About fifty years after that a German scientist named Gottfried Leibnitz made a machine that could also multiply.

ADDING MACHINES

The calculating machine that is used most often is the adding machine. An adding machine looks like a small typewriter. Some adding machines have even more keys than a typewriter, and the keyboards look more like the fronts of cash registers. In fact, every cash register has an adding machine built into it.

Besides the keys with numbers on them, an adding machine has keys to press when you want to add, or to subtract, or to correct a mistake made by pressing the wrong key, or for other special purposes.

The numbered keys have the figures from 0 to 9 on them. Each key is connected with a little metal bar with the same figure on it. This metal bar will print the number you want on a roll of

CALCULATING MACHINES

Friden Calculating Machine Co., Inc.

This machine can give you the answers to difficult mathematical problems.

paper at the back of the machine. After you have pressed the keys you want, you make the number print by pulling a handle on what is called a *manual* machine, or by pressing a button on an electric machine. For instance, if you want to add 963 and 754, first you press the keys for 963 and pull the handle or press the button to print it; then you press the keys for 754 and print that in the same way.

Each time a number is printed on paper, a small wheel is turned inside the adding machine. There is a wheel for each column of numbers. (The meaning of the columns of numbers is explained in the article on ARITHMETIC.) The wheels are lined up next to each other, like small circles side by side. Each wheel has ten little metal points sticking out of it. Each of these points stands for a number from 0 to 9.

After all the numbers you want to add have been printed on the roll of paper, you press a button marked TOTAL. Then you pull the handle or press the button the same as to print a number. The answer you want will then be printed on the roll of paper.

Here is how the adding machine adds: when a column of numbers adds up to more than 9, the wheel attached to that column turns the wheel at the left a certain number of points forward. For instance, if the column adds up to 23, only the 3 is printed, and the wheel at the left is turned 2 points forward. If the column adds up to 56, only the 6 is printed, and the wheel at the left is turned 5 points forward. This goes on, with each wheel turning the wheel to the left of it, until all the columns have been added, and the answer printed.

On machines that multiply as well as add, there is a special key marked MULTIPLY. When you press this key, a number will be printed as many times as you wish to multiply it. Then the column will be added. For instance, to multiply 7 by 5 (5 times 7), you first press the key marked 7, then you press the multiplica-

Left: **More than twelve million mathematical steps were used to describe how an atom is split. This is the keyboard of the calculator that was used.** *Right:* **The huge machine itself fills a large room, and is like a giant mechanical brain.**

Internat'l News Photos

CALCULATING MACHINES

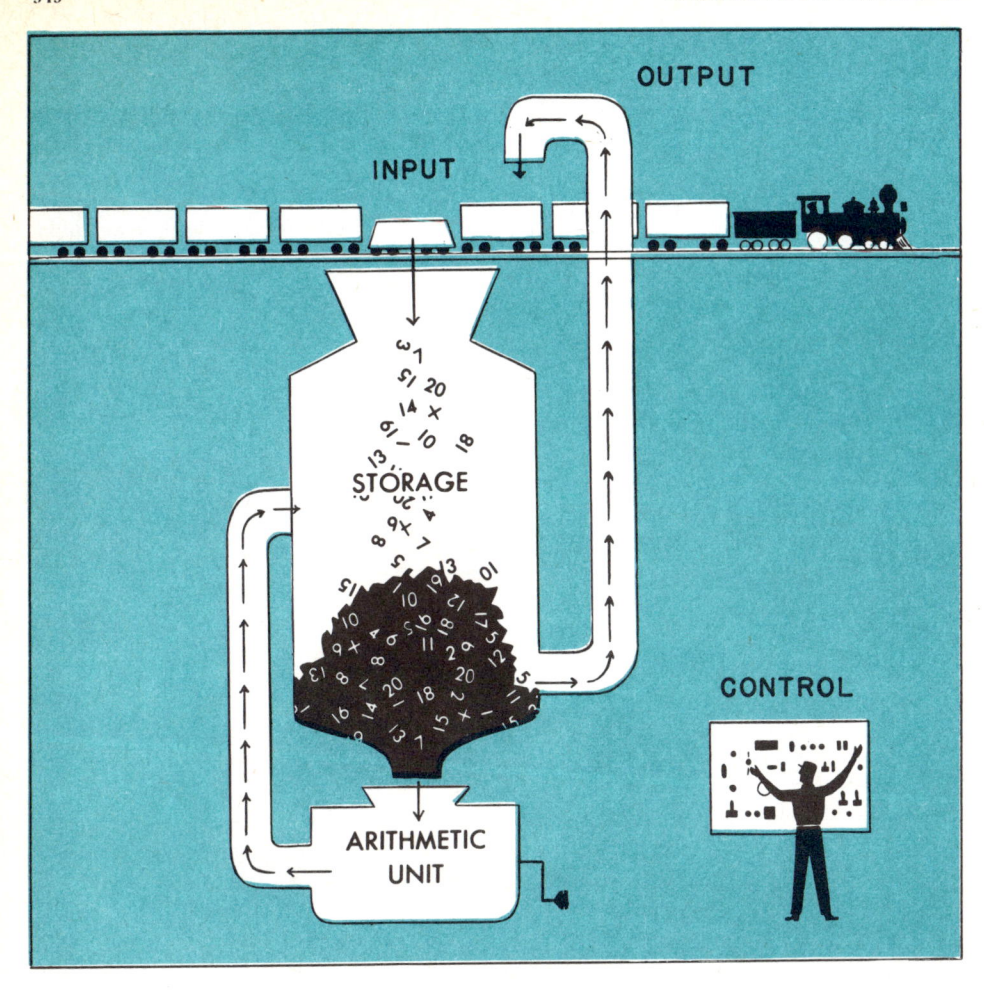

A calculating machine can be compared to a freight train. The problem you want to solve is in one of the cars. It is dumped into a bin, called the *input*. The problem goes into the arithmetic unit, where the problem is solved. The answer comes out at the *output*, on a piece of paper. The man at the controls works the buttons of the calculator as an engineer controls a train. Now he is ready for the next problem.

tion key until 7 has been printed 5 times. The column of 7's will then be added, and your answer, 35, will be printed underneath it.

ELECTRONIC COMPUTERS

There are other calculating machines that can solve problems in science. Some of these problems are so complicated that it would take a man with only a pencil and paper many weeks and even months to solve. Even after he had solved the problem, he would not be sure that his answer was right. A calculating machine would give him the right answer the very first time, and he would not have to check it.

The calculating machines that are used in science are worked by electronic tubes, tubes like the ones used in radio and television sets. These machines are called electronic computers. *Computer* is another name for *calculating machine*. Such machines sometimes have more than

CALCULUS

18,000 electronic tubes inside them. They are as big as small houses and weigh more than one hundred tons (200,000 pounds). Some electronic computers can do more than a million problems of multiplication in only one hour.

Most of these big machines are called *data-processing* machines. Data (information or facts) is fed into them and they calculate the correct results. Some of these machines work from *punched cards*. Holes are punched into certain places on a card and the machines will sort thousands of the cards in a minute and perform complicated mathematical processes depending on where the holes are punched. In the *mark-sensing* process, magnetic ink is used to record the data on the card. In the most modern calculating machines, the information is first recorded on tape (as in a tape-recorder that reproduces sound) and the tape then controls the machine. All these machines are being used more and more in business, science, and industry.

calculus

Calculus is one of the ways in which the science of mathematics is used to solve problems. It is such a difficult form of mathematics that no one studies it until he is in college and has already studied the other branches of mathematics, such as arithmetic and algebra and geometry. Calculus has two main

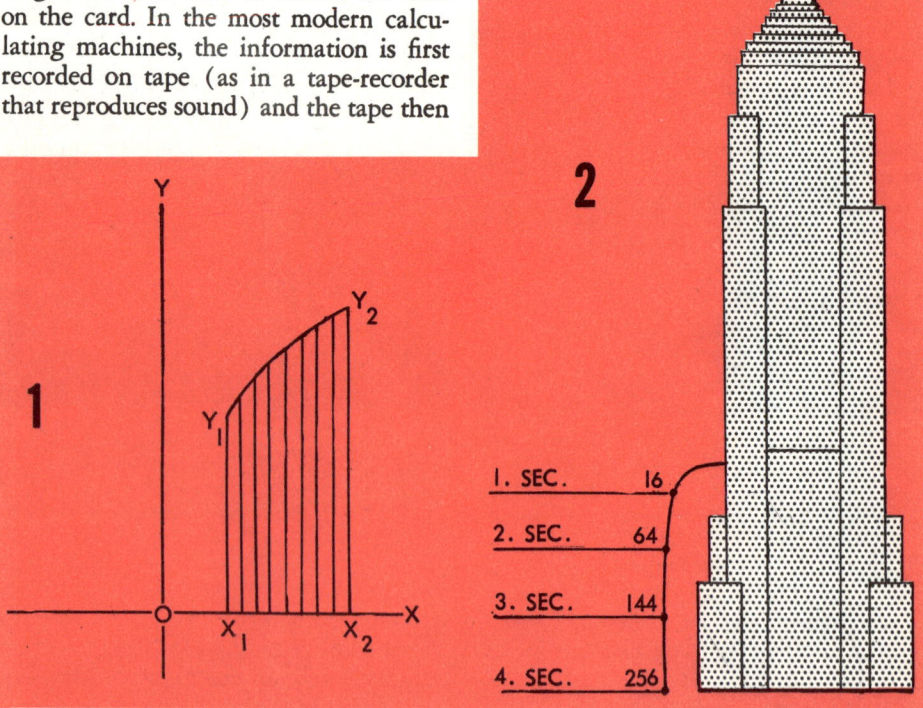

1. By using integral calculus, mathematicians can find the areas under curves such as Y_1Y_2. First, they draw small strips or rectangles between the lines Y_1X_1 and Y_2X_2. By finding the area of each strip and adding, or integrating, these, they find the entire area.
2. Using differential calculus, mathematicians are able to figure out how fast a ball would fall if it were dropped from the 20th floor of the Empire State building. At the end of the first second, it would be falling with a speed of 32 feet per second; at the end of the next second, 64 feet per second; at the end of the third second, 96 feet per second; and as it hits the ground after the fourth second, its speed would be 128 feet per second. The numbers on the picture show how many feet the ball will have fallen after 1, 2, 3 and 4 seconds.

branches, called *differential calculus* and *integral calculus*.

Differential calculus is used to solve problems about things that are moving or changing. In simple arithmetic, as when you add 3 and 4 to make 7, there is no change; 3 is always 3, and 4 is always 4, and 7 is always 7. Then suppose a ball is dropped from a building 256 feet high and strikes the ground 4 seconds later. You can divide 256 by 4 and find out that the *average* speed of the ball was 64 feet per second. But how fast was the ball going at the end of the third second? Just before the ball was dropped, it was going zero feet per second, because it was not moving at all. It must have gone faster and faster as it fell; this is called *acceleration*. Differential calculus is used to solve such problems.

Integral calculus is used to find a total that is made up of things that cannot be measured in the same way. The simplest example is finding the area of a big field with edges that are all kinds of curves and angles and irregular shapes. First the big field is divided into many smaller spaces, all with regular shapes. Geometry teaches how to find the area of each of those regular shapes. When they are added together, the area of the whole field is known. The great Greek mathematician, Archimedes, first used this method more than two thousand years ago, to find the area of a circle. Differential calculus was not used until nearly three hundred years ago.

Calcutta

Calcutta is a city in India. It is the capital of West Bengal state, and lies on the Hooghly River 65 miles from the Bay of Bengal, which is an arm of the Indian Ocean. Calcutta is one of the two largest cities in India and is a modern and beautiful city, especially along the river. There are many fine buildings, including the University of Calcutta, and a large park on the river where people take walks or drive in carriages in the evenings. There is also another large park in which

Black Star

At an election in Calcutta, a woman has a special ink mark put on her finger after she has voted. This is a way of knowing who has already voted and who has not.

is a giant banyan tree whose branches and leaves extend 300 feet across.

Calcutta is one of the biggest manufacturing cities of India. It has a population of more than three million. The people who live there work in factories that make cloth and jute. From Calcutta, rice, oils, jute and shellac are sent abroad.

The city was founded only about 250 years ago by the British East India Company. For many years it was very unhealthy because of bad water, bad sanitation, and large swamps that bred mosquitoes. Hundreds of English colonists and thousands of natives died of malaria and other diseases. The city grew, however, and the bad conditions were corrected until Calcutta became the healthiest city in India. From 1772 to 1911, Calcutta was the capital of all India, but in 1911 the capital was moved to Delhi.

Calcutta is chiefly famous in history because of something that happened in 1756 when the city was captured from the British by the nawab of Bengal. A *nawab* is a Mohammedan prince. The British soldiers who had been taken prisoner were put overnight into such a small, hot, and airless room that most of them died just in that short time. This terrible thing shocked people all over the

CALCUTTA

Left: People in Calcutta dress in thin clothing because of the hot weather. They often gather together in the squares to discuss the latest news. The building in this picture leads down to the water's edge, and it is very old, like many of the buildings in Calcutta.

Ewing Galloway

Right: The modern traveler arriving at the airport in Calcutta may be surprised to see an Indian performing the ancient art of snake charming. He plays on his odd pipe, and the snake in the basket sways to the music. You can see snake charmers perform in many parts of the city. *Below:* Calcutta has many beautiful buildings. One of the most famous is the Victoria Memorial. It is built of marble, and contains important books and documents that tell about the history of India.

B.O.A.C.

world, and the room was called the "black hole of Calcutta."

CALCUTTA, INDIA. Population (1960 est.) 3,040,000. With suburbs, 5,909,000. On the Hooghly River. Capital of West Bengal state.

calendar

A calendar is a way of dividing time so that all people in a group or country can keep count of it in the same way. There have been many different calendars used at different times in history, but all of them have been based on what we call natural divisions of time. Days, and years are natural divisions of time. The day is the length of time it takes the earth to turn completely around; for example, the time from one sunrise to the next. The year is the length of time it takes the earth to travel all the way around the sun and back to the same place again. The *lunar month* is a natural division of time, from one "new moon" to the next; but the month as actually used in calendars is not a natural division of time, because in most calendars the month averages about thirty days, while the lunar month is closer to twenty-nine days.

The difficulty in making calendars has always been that the year is not an even number of days or an even number of months. A year is about 12⅓ lunar months. It is about 365¼ days. So calendar-makers throughout the ages have added a few days to months, or an extra month every few years, or an extra day every few years (as we do when we have *leap years*) to make things come out even.

EGYPTIAN CALENDAR

The ancient Egyptians had a calendar that was made up of 12 months of 30 days each. That left 5 extra days each year and 6 extra days every fourth year. The Egyptians counted in the extra 5 days each year, but they paid no attention to the extra day in the fourth year. After a long time of ignoring that extra day, they found that there was something wrong with their seasons. It was dry during months that were supposed to be wet and wet during months that were supposed to be dry. But they did not know how to correct this mistake.

ROMAN CALENDAR

The next important calendar was invented by the Romans many hundreds of years ago. That calendar is the one on which we base our own calendar. The Roman calendar had 12 months, with either 29 or 30 days. The year was 355 days long, instead of 365 as it should have been. In order to correct this, a 13th month of 22 or 23 days was added every other year, and still another extra month was supposed to be added once in twenty-four years. But the officials in charge of making these changes in the calendar were lazy and sometime forgot to do it. Before long the Romans found themselves in the same kind of trouble the Egyptians had been in earlier. Julius Caesar corrected this after consulting with an Egyptian astronomer named Sosigenes. Caesar and Sosigenes worked out a calen-

An old Roman stone calendar had three months on each of its four sides.

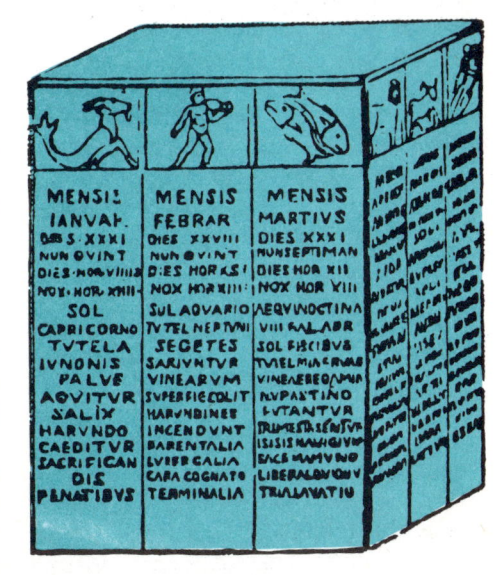

CALGARY

dar made up of three years of 365 days and one year of 366 days. The year began with the month of January, and went through all the months as we know them today.

We call this calendar the Julian calendar (for Julius Caesar). A few hundred years later, when Christianity had become the official religion of most of Europe, the Church began to date everything from the year when it was estimated that Jesus was born. This estimate was wrong by a few years, but we still follow it.

Unfortunately, the Julian calendar had a mistake in it. There are about 11 minutes each year that were not taken care of by the Julian leap year. After about 1,600 years, the Julian calendar was wrong by about ten days.

Pope Gregory XIII, who was Pope from 1572 to 1585, made another change in the calendar, to correct the mistake in the Julian calendar. His calendar, the Gregorian calendar, is used in nearly every part of the world. In this calendar, years ending in even hundreds (1700, 1800, 1900) are *not* leap years unless they can be evenly divided by 4. The year 1600 was a leap year, and the year 2000 will be. Dates in the Julian calendar are called "Old Style," or O.S., and dates in the Gregorian calendar are called "New Style" (N.S.).

Many churches have their own calendars by which they date Church holidays. The Julian calendar is still used in the Orthodox Catholic Church, which is the official church in Greece and was in Russia before the Communist rule.

JEWISH CALENDAR

The Jewish year begins in the fall, in their month of *Tishri*. They number their years from the date of the Creation, which they estimate to be October 7, 3760 B.C. The date September 27, 1954, was the beginning of the Jewish year 5715. Another difference is that the Jewish year has twelve months of alternately 29 and 30 days. Seven times in every nineteen years they add a thirteenth month, to make their calendar come out even.

MOHAMMEDAN CALENDAR

The Mohammedan calendar starts from a different time than either the Gregorian or Jewish calendars. The first year of the Mohammedan calendar was the year of a very important event in the Moslem religion. In that year, our year 622, Mohammed was forced to go from the city of Mecca to the city of Medina. In the Mohammedan calendar, there are 12 months. Some have 30 days and some have 29 days. There is a leap year in 11 out of every 30 years. The Mohammedan year does not have the same number of days as the solar year, and so the different seasons do not fall in the same month every year.

This calendar shows a recent attempt to make each quarter of the year have the same number of days. There would be two special holidays each year, one at the end of June, one at the end of December (marked by W on the calendar).

Calgary

Calgary is the second-largest city in the province of Alberta, in western Canada. Only eighty years ago, Calgary was just a small fort for the Northwest Mounted Police. Now 181,780 people live there, and it is the most important trade and industrial city in all southern Alberta.

Calgary is near the foothills of the Rocky Mountains and it is surrounded by wide plains and rich mountain valleys. Products from hundreds of miles around are sent to Calgary to be shipped out to all parts of the world. Calgary has meat-packing plants, oil refineries, grain elevators, lumber mills, steel-rolling mills, and iron foundries. Its factories produce machinery, chemicals, food, and clothing.

Calhoun, John C.

John Caldwell Calhoun was the most famous statesman on the Southern side in the argument that led to the Civil War in the United States, more than 100 years ago. John C. Calhoun was a Senator from the state of South Carolina. When he was alive, Negroes were slaves in South Carolina and other states of the South. Most of the people in the North thought that slavery was wrong and wanted the United States Government to set the slaves free. The Southern states insisted that "States' Rights," according to the Constitution of the United States, left it up to them to decide what would go on in their own territory. There were constant arguments in the Senate about matters connected with this idea. Calhoun always led the Southern senators.

In 1828, when he was 40 years old, Calhoun wrote the most famous argument of its time for States' Rights, and this caused South Carolina to pass a *nullification act* in which the state tried to nullify, or cancel, two tariff (customs tax) laws that Congress had passed. Congress compromised by passing a different law. Calhoun won many honors in the United States Government. He was born in 1782, while the Revolutionary War was still being fought. He served first in the House of Representatives, from 1811 to 1817. He was Secretary of War under President James Monroe. Then he was vice-president of the United States from 1824 to 1832, and Secretary of State under President John Tyler. Nearly all the other years of his life he was a senator. He wanted most of all to be president, and was very disappointed that he could not be, but the people would not elect a man who was so strongly for slavery and who thought the states should be stronger than the Federal Government. Calhoun died in 1850, nearly eleven years before the Civil War began.

calico

Calico is the name of a flowered cloth first brought from India to Europe in the 17th century. Calico is woven with unbleached cotton threads and then the cloth is bleached, dyed or printed, usually in a small flowered design. The weaving is done in a special way so that there are the same number of threads going up and down and across. After a while all smooth cotton materials woven with an equal number of warp (lengthwise) and filling (crosswise) threads were called calico. Some of the calico weaves we know today are chintz, cretonne, canvas, muslin, chiffon, and challis.

When people in England and France saw the beautiful calico cloth that had come from India they started to make it themselves. At first the pattern was put on the cloth with a blockprint. (See BLOCKPRINTING.) Later the block was changed to a roller, so that yards and yards of material could be printed and rolled out as if they were going through a clothes wringer. There are other ways of printing calico material too, such as BATIK and STENCILING, which you can read about in separate articles.

California

California

California is a state in the far western part of the United States. Its nickname is "the Golden State" because of the gold that is mined there, and because of the great wealth of golden harvests it produces each year. The name *California* comes from an imaginary island mentioned in a Spanish novel that was written in 1510. It represents an earthly paradise. The state flower is the golden poppy, and the state tree is the redwood.

More people live in California than in any other state in the United States. There are nearly nineteen million people living there. In area California ranks third, covering almost 160,000 square miles. Only Alaska and Texas are bigger.

California became a state in 1850, and was the 31st state admitted to the Union. Its capital is Sacramento.

THE PEOPLE OF CALIFORNIA

The people of California came originally from all parts of the world. Until a little over a hundred years ago, most Californians were Spanish and Mexican, with just a few Americans from the East who worked as fur trappers or traders. After the discovery of gold, thousands flocked to California from everywhere to seek their fortunes. This was followed by the building of cross-country railroads, which drew many thousands more to the state. There were Chinese laborers on the railroads, and most of them remained. When the tracks were finished and trains began to run across the continent, large groups of Europeans settled in California. The Italians began raising grapes for wine, and also went into the fishing trade off the Pacific coast.

Portuguese, Swiss, and Germans joined the Italians, Chinese, Spanish, and Mexicans already there, and California became a land of many nationalities living together. Japanese and Filipino laborers came in considerable numbers, and became farm workers. Now all these different nationality groups have been settled for so long that they have families and homes in all parts of the state, and today almost nine-tenths of the people living in California are native-born Americans.

There are still about 39,000 Indians in the state, though fewer than 9,000 of them live on reservations, where they work chiefly as farmers and cattlemen.

Although almost a third of the state is used for some form of agriculture, more people live in cities than live in rural or country districts. Only about one-fifth of the population lives in the coun-

CALIFORNIA

Above: The large white building with the dome is the state capitol of California, in Sacramento.

try. The people in the cities work in stores, offices, and factories. Since World War II there have been many large aircraft and machine factories in California, and almost all the cars sold west of the Rocky Mountains are assembled from factory parts in the state of California. The people in rural districts work on farms, in the oil fields, or in the lumber industry.

WHAT CALIFORNIA IS LIKE

California is a state where there is almost every kind of land and climate. It is so big that the different sections might almost be different countries.

Along the northern part of the Pacific coast section there is a double chain of mountains, and the valleys between are rich in all kinds of fruits and vegetables. There are also fine grazing lands in these valleys, where cattle raising and dairy farming are profitable. Toward the border of Oregon, at the far north, are mountains heavily wooded with redwood trees, the state tree of California.

East of the coastal ranges, but still in the northern part of the state, are the beautiful Sierra Nevada mountains. These are rugged peaks with snow caps all year round. One section of these mountains is called the Lava Plateau, where the only active volcano in the United States is located. This is the famous Mount Lassen, which erupts occasionally but not very violently.

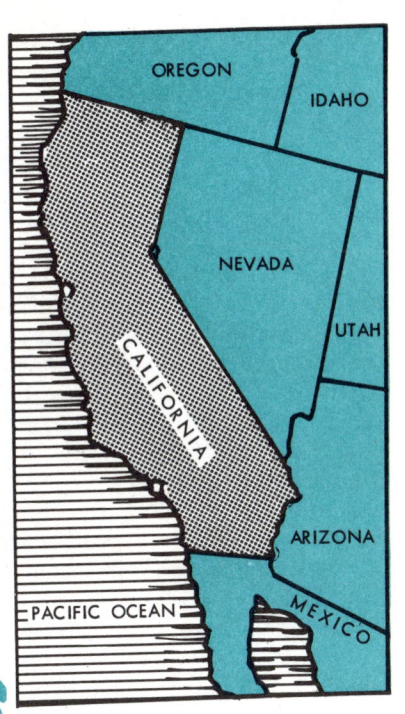

It is in the Sierra Nevadas also that the largest gold deposits in the state are found.

The Central Valley of California runs between the coastal ranges and the Sierra Nevadas. It is this rich valley that produces the biggest part of California's important agricultural output. This is the northern and central section of the valley. In the southern section are oil fields and plentiful sources of natural gas.

Moving south, you would notice a great deal of difference in the countryside as you went along. There is even a big difference between the eastern and western parts of the state, in the southern section. From fertile coastal plains, the traveler in California can go east over

CALIFORNIA

the mountains to the desert country of Death Valley, where nothing is cultivated. Within a few miles of this desolate stretch is the luxuriant Imperial Valley, where huge crops of melons, fruits, and vegetables of many different kinds are harvested each year.

Still farther west, on the other side of the Sierra Nevadas' southern reaches, there is the extremely hot Colorado Desert, where the temperature often reaches 120 during the day. Farther north, in the mountains, the climate is totally different from that of the southern part of the state. The winters are very cold, and long. It is not unusual for freezing temperatures to occur occasionally, even in summer. This kind of weather contrast, and sharp differences in climate, hold true all over the state.

California has a large number of rivers, fed by the mountain streams which start in the many mountain ranges throughout the state. Modern roads have formed a network over the state, and it is no longer a problem to cross either the highest mountain passes or the scorching deserts. Good highways, and ample railroads, go everywhere.

Tourists have found that California is a fine vacationland. There are so many different kinds of climate and so many different kinds of countryside, it is possible for almost everyone to find the recreation he likes, in the type of country that appeals to him.

THE GOVERNMENT OF CALIFORNIA

California, like most other states, is governed by a Governor, a Senate, and an Assembly. The Governor and the Senators are elected to serve four-year terms, and members of the Assembly are elected to serve two-year terms. Judges are elected and serve twelve years. The capital is Sacramento. There are 58 counties in the state. All children have to go to school full-time from the time they are eight years old until they are sixteen and part-time from sixteen to eighteen. The schools provide textbooks free to pupils. There are about 5,700 public schools.

There are 122 colleges, universities, and technological and professional schools. State, county, and city governments support 61 of these. Among the largest colleges and universities are:

University of California, with branches at Berkeley, Los Angeles, San Francisco, Santa Barbara, Davis, Riverside, La Jolla (Scripps Institution of Oceanography), and Mt. Hamilton (Lick Observatory). Enrollment 47,539 in 1961. The largest enrollments are at Berkeley (about 20,000 students) and at Los Angeles (about 17,000 students). The medical school is at San Francisco.

California State Polytechnic College at San Luis Obispo. Enrollment 6,468 in 1961.

Los Angeles State College of Applied Arts and Science, at Los Angeles. Enrollment in 1961, 14,642.

University of San Francisco, at San Francisco. Enrollment 4,009 in 1961.

Stanford University, at Palo Alto. Enrollment 8,560 in 1961.

University of Southern California, at Los Angeles. Enrollment 15,932 in 1961.

California Institute of Technology (men only), at Pasadena. Enrollment 1,224 in 1961.

California Western University, at San Diego. Enrollment 1,512 in 1961.

CHIEF CITIES OF CALIFORNIA

The leading cities of California, with 1960 census figures, are:

Los Angeles, population 2,479,015. Largest city in the state, and home of the great moving picture industry. There is a separate article about LOS ANGELES.

San Francisco, population 740,316, city of the famous Golden Gate. There is a separate article about SAN FRANCISCO.

Oakland, population 367,548, across the bay from San Francisco, and connected with it by the Bay Bridge.

San Diego, population 573,224, the closest to Mexico of all the important cities in California. There is a separate article about SAN DIEGO.

Long Beach, population 344,168.

Sacramento, population 191,667. There is a separate article about SACRAMENTO.

San José, population 204,196.

CALIFORNIA

Right: Los Angeles is one of the most beautiful cities in Southern California. It is a favorite vacation spot with its sunny climate, palm trees, fine hotels and boulevards. This scene shows a part of the famous Wilshire Boulevard. *Below:* The home and gardens of Luther Burbank at Santa Rosa. The great plant scientist is buried under the 100-foot cedar of Lebanon tree, at the left, that he planted when he came there to live.

All-Year Club of Southern Calif.

Below: People from many places spend their vacations at the many fine beaches in California. One of the most popular is at Catalina Island, off the southern coast. Here people lie in the hot sun and swim in the blue Pacific Ocean. In the evening they go to the Casino (the building in the background), and enjoy dancing and entertainment.

Redwood Assn.

Below: The second-largest city in California is San Francisco. This aerial view shows its beautiful modern skyscrapers and many piers. In the foreground is the San Francisco Bay Bridge. In the background is the famous Golden Gate Bridge.

San Francisco Chamber of Comm.

Santa Fe Ry.

CALIFORNIA

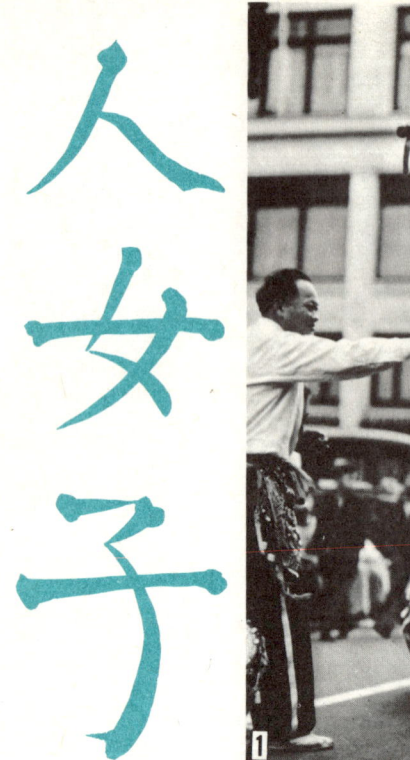

人女子

Redwood Empire Assn.

Santa Fe Ry.   San Diego Chamber of Comm.

1. This great dragon is part of a colorful parade celebrating the Chinese New Year in San Francisco's Chinatown. Thousands of Chinese live in this section.
2. Near Carmel, you can see one of many missions built by Spanish priests who settled California hundreds of years ago.
3. This monument in San Diego is in honor of Cabrillo, the Spanish explorer, who discovered part of California in 1542.
4. Long ago, American Indians in northern California built their houses from slabs of the giant redwood trees.

Copyright Curriculum Films, Inc.

CALIFORNIA

1. Many of the buildings in California, built in the style of the Spanish missions, show the influence of the earliest settlers in this state. This is San José State College, in San José. It is the oldest public college in California, and was built in 1857.

2. Many Russians settled in California more than a hundred years ago. If you visit Fort Ross, you can see the church where they worshipped. The cross on top of the church is that of Russia's Greek Orthodox Church.

3. This old Spanish lighthouse stands at the entrance to San Diego Bay. It is not used any more, but is still a place of interest.

4. For four years before California became a state, it was an independent republic. In June 1846, the flag was raised at this spot in Sonoma, at the home of General Vallejo. This property is now owned by California, and attracts many visitors every year. *Insert:* The Bear Flag of the California Republic.

5. San Gabriel Mission, nine miles from Los Angeles, is one of the oldest Spanish settlements in California. It was founded in 1771, and is known as the "Queen of all the Missions."

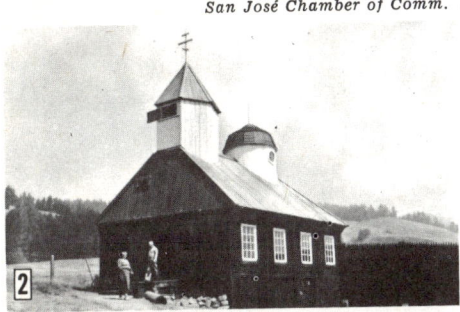

Redwood Empire Assn.

San José Chamber of Comm.

Redwood Empire Assn.   Southern Pac. Co.

Los Angeles Chamber of Comm.

CALIFORNIA

All-Year Club of Southern Calif.

Above: California is a state of magnificent blooming flowers. The blossoms of the Joshua tree are as big as your head.

Below: One of the most wonderful places to see in California is Yosemite National Park. The Yosemite Falls, tumbling from the cliffs, is a beautiful sight.

Santa Fe Ry.

CALIFORNIA IN THE PAST

The land that is now California was discovered by a Spanish explorer named Hernando Cortez in 1534. No one settled in the new land until 1683, when some missionary priests moved to the part now known as Lower California. Upper California, or the part that is now the state, was first settled by the Spanish in 1768. They built a mission at San Diego, and began to convert the Indians to Christianity.

Although a great many Indians made trouble for the Spanish missionaries, the Spaniards did not give up their efforts to convert the Indians. They built many more missions up and down the coast. The first mission on the shores of San Francisco Bay was established in 1776, the same year that the colonies in the East published the Declaration of Independence.

California was a Spanish colony, however, and was not connected at all with

Below: The redwood forests of California are world famous. The mighty tree in this photograph is taller than a 28-story building and is 21 feet thick at the base.

Redwood Empire Assoc.

CALIFORNIA

Nat'l Highway Users Conf.

Many modern highways run through California, carrying people and products to and from the state. Here two main highways cross in a "clover leaf," near San Diego.

California has not only high mountains but great deserts that stretch for many miles. The Imperial Valley sand dunes are an important point of interest to visitors.

All-Year Club of Calif.

People catch many kinds of fish in California's thousands of lakes and streams. In the background, you can see some of the state's beautiful snow-capped peaks.

All-Year Club of Southern Calif.

CALIFORNIA

the original thirteen colonies that were engaged in the American Revolution.

It remained a Spanish colony until 1822, when Mexico revolted from Spanish rule. California declared its own independence from Spain at that time, and joined with Mexico.

About twenty years later, thousands of easterners moved to California, making the long, dangerous journey by covered wagon. This divided the population of California between eastern Americans and Mexican or Spanish Californians. California was such a rich land that both Mexico and the United States wanted to own it, and in 1846 war broke out between the two countries. The United States won within a year. A few months after the war ended, gold was discovered in California, in February, 1848, and the famous gold rush started.

This drew many thousands of people to California, both from the eastern part of the United States and from Europe. Many of them were lawless and wild. At the time when California was admitted to the Union, in 1850, there was a great deal of trouble in the state because of criminals and outlaws who had been attracted by the promise of great wealth in gold. It was necessary to do something to protect the good citizens, and so a "Vigilance Committee" was organized to restore law and order. Before long, California was again a quiet, peaceful place.

The quiet did not last, however. When the gold rush died down, and people were finding it hard to earn a living because prices were so high, and there were so few jobs, California again went through a hard period. There was plenty of land, but there was a lot of trouble about getting land legally. The Spaniards and Mexicans of California owned great ranches, and they found that squatters were taking this property from them. A squatter was a man who simply settled down on a piece of land and started to live there. Many people settled on land that seemed to belong to no one, and that was all right. But sometimes they settled on land that was part of someone's ranch, and the real owner of the ranch objected to losing good land that way. If they threw the squatters off, that

California is not just a vacation spot with beautiful scenery. If you travel through the state, you will see many valuable oil fields like this one.

CALIFORNIA

M.G.M.

1. The huge logs from the California forests are shipped to sawmills to be cut into lumber. This is the largest sawmill in the world, at Scotia.

2. One of the greatest industries in the state is the motion-picture industry.

3. Equally noted are the famous orange groves. California is one of the largest orange-growing regions in the world.

4. Farmers grow large quantities of delicious grapes in the fertile valleys.

5. Another important product is cotton. Here, bales of cotton are being loaded to be shipped to cotton mills.

6. This canal is one of the many used to irrigate the soil and make it fertile.

All-Year Club of Southern Calif.

Redwood Empire Assn.

Southern Pacific Co.

Ets. Boy-Landry, Saigon

CALIFORNIA

did not help much, because those people had to live somewhere, and a lot of people with no homes can cause trouble any place. Eventually this was all settled, however, by passing many land laws, so that everyone was treated as fairly as possible, and so that everyone had at least a place to live.

The motion-picture industry made the town of Hollywood famous. Hollywood is a part of greater Los Angeles, and it became the center of the motion-picture industry when small independent producers moved away from New York to avoid legal troubles. A movie trust in the East tried to keep small film companies out of business. There were lawsuits, raids, and riots. To escape from this trouble, one man fled to Los Angeles and made the first commercial motion picture ever produced in California. His name was William Selig, and the picture was *The Count of Monte Cristo,* made in 1908 at Los Angeles. Three years later, the first movie studio in Hollywood was opened. The film company originally went to California just to get away from trouble in New York, but soon the business grew so large that Hollywood suddenly became the movie capital of the world. There is a separate article about the MOTION PICTURES.

During World War II, California became an important war production center, as well as a point of embarkation for the war in the Pacific. Many large aircraft manufacturers established plants in the state, and remained there after the war was over. This increased California's population again, and also added to its importance as a production center.

PLACES TO SEE IN CALIFORNIA

Lassen Volcanic National Park, 163 square miles, in Lassen National Forest, at the northern end of the Sierra Nevada Mountains. It is the area around Lassen Peak, the only active volcano in the United States. It can be reached by State Highways 89 and 44.

Sequoia and General Grant National Parks, the wildest country on the western slopes of the Sierra Nevadas, about 53 miles east of Fresno. It was named for the giant sequoia trees found there. It can be reached by State Highways 32, 180, and 198.

Kings Canyon National Park is directly north of Sequoia National Park, and it can also be reached by State Highway 180.

Muir Woods is a grove of giant sequoias on the west central edge of Sequoia National Forest, on Route 32.

Lava Beds National Monument, in the Modoc National Forest, north central California, an area of about 80 square miles of strange lava formations. There are many caves and frozen underground streams in the area, and lava that hardened into unusual shapes, some of which resemble crude animals. It can be reached by U.S. Route 97.

Yosemite National Park, 752,744 acres, 429 lakes inside the park, and numerous rivers. This national park has accommodations for visitors all year round, and many kinds of sports and entertainment are available at all times. There are hotels, restaurants, cabins, tents, and camping grounds. There is a hospital, and ambulance service. There are even doctors and dentists. Yosemite National Park is so large it is almost like a huge, sprawling, spread-out town.

Death Valley, in the Colorado Desert, has been made a national monument. Although the section that is the actual Death Valley of covered wagon days is comparatively small, the general area covers about 1,500 square miles that have been set aside as a national monument. It extends several miles over the Nevada border. A highway travels the full length of the Death Valley National Monument, and passes through the center of Death Valley proper. In addition, the center of the Death Valley National Monument is crossed by State Highway 190.

FAMOUS PEOPLE FROM CALIFORNIA

Many very famous people have made California their home. Among the famous writers from California are Gertrude Atherton, Jack London, William Saroyan, John Steinbeck, Kate Douglas Wiggin, and L. Frank Baum.

In the music field, there is the composer, Charles Wakefield Cadman, and Lawrence Tibbett, the singer.

The poet Robert Frost also lived in California, and so did the famous publisher, William Randolph Hearst.

Will Rogers, the humorist, Luther Burbank, the plant wizard, and Vice President Richard M. Nixon were also residents of California, and the most famous of all was Herbert Hoover, President of the United States.

CALIFORNIA. Area 158,693 square miles. Population (1960 census) 15,717,204, (1965 estimate) 18,605,000. Capital, Sacramento. State flower, California golden poppy. State tree, the redwood. Admitted to the Union in 1850. Official abbreviation, Calif.

California, Lower, and Gulf of California

Lower California is a part of Mexico, south of California in the United States. The people who live there call it *Baja California,* which is the Spanish way of saying "Lower California." It is a long, narrow peninsula, which is a piece of land almost entirely surrounded by water. It is about 760 miles long from north to south, with the Pacific Ocean on the west and the Gulf of California on the east. Two ranges of mountains extend the length of the peninsula, one on the east coast and one on the west. The coastline itself is very irregular, with hundreds of bays cut into it. Many small islands dot the shoreline on both the gulf and the ocean sides. The northern section has dense woodlands, the central part has rich, fertile farmlands, and there is a large desert in the south. If you were to visit that desert, you would see enormous cactus plants growing there. Over on the gulf coast you would probably see native pearl divers at work. You might also feel the tremors, or quivering, of a slight earthquake, because Lower California has a great many light quakes.

The people of Lower California are mostly Mexicans who speak the Spanish language and belong to the Roman Catholic religion. In the wild valleys in the middle of the peninsula there are still many very primitive and backward Indians.

Spanish explorers first reached Lower California in 1538, about four hundred years ago. They began to build settlements there and in what is now California in the United States. It was not until about two hundred years ago that the two Californias were separated. The Spanish explorer Hernando Cortez discovered the Gulf of California, and it was first named the Gulf of Cortez in his honor. The gulf is about seven hundred miles long and about a hundred miles wide. In addition to pearl diving, the Gulf of California has a great deal of deep-sea fishing for sharks, whales, barracuda, and other fish.

Lower California is almost equally divided into two sections, Northern and Southern, each with its own capital. The area is not thickly settled. There are only about two people per square mile. Since there would naturally be families of five or six living in one place, you can see that there are large areas with no one at all living in them.

LOWER CALIFORNIA. Region in Mexico. Area, 55,629 square miles. Population (1960 census) 605,000. Divided into two sections. Northern section (a state): area, 27,653 square miles; population, 522,000; capital, Mexicali. Southern Territory: area, 27,967 square miles; population 83,000; capital, La Paz.

Caligula

Caligula was a famous Roman emperor who lived more than 1,900 years ago. He was born A.D. 12. His real name was Caius Caesar Augustus Germanicus, but he was given the nickname of *Caligula,* which means "little boots," because he wore military boots when he was a child.

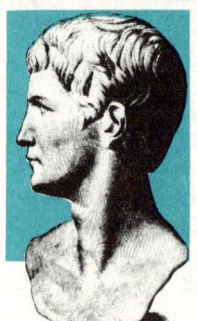

When Caligula grew up and became emperor, he was so evil that people thought he was insane. He may very well have become insane during an illness. At any rate, he did many mad things. Some of the things that he did were funny. On one occasion he made his horse a consul. But he also had many people tortured and executed. He is supposed to have said that it was too bad everybody did not have the same neck so that it could be chopped off at one blow. All this made the Roman people very angry and he was finally murdered in the year 41, when he was only 29 years old.

caliph

The head of the Mohammedan religion was at the same time a great ruler. He was called the *caliph.* His position was called the *caliphate,* just as the Pope's position is called the papacy.

When Mohammed the Prophet died more than 1,300 years ago, he did not leave any sons, so his followers had to choose a *calif,* or "successor" (which is what the word means). The first caliph they chose was Mohammed's father-in-law, Abu Bakr. He and the caliphs who came after him became also the rulers of the Arab empire and their capital was the city of Damascus. As the empire grew, there were many quarrels over who would become the caliph. At one time there were three caliphs, one in Baghdad, one in Cairo, Egypt, and one in Cordova, Spain. The most recent caliphs were the sultans of Turkey. When the last sultan, named Mohammed VI, was deposed from his throne and went into exile, his cousin became caliph (but not sultan) for a short time. This was in 1922. Two years later the caliphate was abolished, and since then there have been no more caliphs.

calisthenics

Calisthenics is a way of exercising your arms, legs, and body. It is mostly stretching, bending, and other movements of the body. Usually calisthenics is performed in a group, and a leader tells you what to do. For example, the director might say: "Hands on hips . . . PLACE!" and you and everyone else place your hands on your hips, exactly when the director says "place." Suppose the exercise is to be "deep knee-bends." You and the rest of the class would squat down, and rise up, down and up, down and up, beginning when the director said "Exercise!" and stopping when you got the signal to stop. Calisthenics makes the body strong and limber. In the United States Army and Navy and Marine Corps the men do calisthenics every morning. Some people do a few exercises by themselves in the morning, and we say that they are doing their "daily dozen," because there were twelve exercises in a course of calisthenics that was once very popular.

Calixtus

Calixtus was the name that three different Popes took when they were elected to the papacy. No one knows the real name of Calixtus I. He was a Roman who lived about 1,750 years ago. It is believed that he was born a slave about the year 160 and that he died as a martyr in 222.

Calixtus II was a Frenchman whose real name was Guy of Burgundy. He was a relative of the queen of France, the emperor of Germany, and the king of England. In France, he was the Archbishop of Vienne. He was very power-

THERE ARE 100 CALORIES IN

1 LARGE FRESH APPLE	1 SLICE BREAD and 1/8" pat butter	4 CARROTS (4 inches long)
1/2 BROILED CHICKEN	ONE FRANKFURTER	5/8 cup OF MILK
2 MEDIUM PEARS	2 tablespoons WHITE SUGAR	1 MEDIUM WHITE POTATO

ful and became Pope by a battle in which he captured and imprisoned the antipope (or false Pope) Gregory VIII. He died in Rome in 1124.

Calixtus III was a Spanish member of the famous Borgia family. His name was Alonso de Borja. When he became Pope in the year 1455, he was a very old man. He started a crusade against the Turks that was not very successful. The Borgia family in Italy became very powerful partly because of his help.

calla

The calla, which is also called the *lily of the Nile,* is a beautiful plant that is grown indoors, or outdoors in warm countries. It is a native of Africa. It has huge, glossy, dark green leaves, and white or golden heart-shaped "flowers." In the center of each "flower" is a fingerlike golden spike. On this spike are many little knobs, and these are the real flowers. The calla is very much like the jack-in-the-pulpit. They are closely related and belong to the same family of plants called *arums*. Another common arum is the wild calla that grows in ponds in northern America, Europe, and Asia. Its "flower" is very much like that of the cultivated calla, but smaller. The flowers on this spike produce pretty red berries. The leaves of the wild calla are about the size of an open hand, and heart-shaped.

calliope

A calliope is a musical instrument that is played in circus parades and outdoor shows. It is very loud and you can hear it a mile away. It has whistles of different sizes, tuned to notes of the scale like the pipes of an organ, and a keyboard like the one on a piano. When you press down a key, steam blows through a whistle and makes a loud tone. Modern calliopes use compressed air instead of steam. But lots of people think that the old-fashioned calliope, with its steam boiler with smoke and sparks coming out of it, and steam spouting from the whistles, was more exciting. Merry-go-rounds and other amusement park rides often use phonograph records of calliope music.

calorie

How many times have you heard some one say that he is overweight and must stop eating so many calories? Sometimes people also say that they must watch their calories. You are probably wondering what a calorie looks like. You will be surprised to learn that you cannot see a calorie nor can you chew one. A calorie is a unit of heat. It is the amount of heat that is needed to raise the temperature of one gram of water one degree. Since it takes almost thirty grams of water to make an ounce, you can see that one calorie is a very small amount of heat.

When people talk about how many calories they have eaten, they mean the amount of heat that will be created inside their bodies by the food they have eaten. The food we eat serves as fuel for our body which burns it just as a furnace burns coal. The heat that results serves as energy for our body when it does work. The less work we do the less energy we need and the less calories we should have.

These food calories are each equal to 1,000 small calories. They are called large calories, or *kilo-calories* (abbreviated K-cal). *Kilo* is from a Greek word meaning one thousand. When foods are said to contain calories, this means that when the food is burned inside our body it will give off a certain number of calories of heat to be used as energy. If we do not need the energy right away, the food will not be burned but stored in our body as fat. If we eat foods that contain more calories than we need, we will become overweight. That is why we should eat only enough to keep us healthy and give us energy to do our work.

Each particular food will supply a certain amount of calories. This amount can be found by burning a small bit of the food in a steel container with thick walls, called a *calorimeter*. After the food is burned, the temperature inside the calorimeter is measured and the amount of heat given off is determined. In this way it has been found that one slice of bread supplies 100 K-calories or 100,000 ordinary calories of heat, enough heat to boil a pound of water; an egg contains 80 K-calories; and a potato, 100 K-calories.

Boys and girls usually need about 2,400 calories a day to stay healthy. Of course, the amount of calories you should have depends upon how much exercise you do and also on how much you weigh. You should generally eat about 30 calories of food a day for each pound you weigh. Older people need fewer calories per pound. The amount of calories your body needs when it is completely at rest is called its BASAL METABOLISM. You can read about this in a separate article.

Calvary

Calvary is the name of the place outside the wall of Jerusalem where Jesus was crucified. It is from a Latin word that means *skull*. Calvary is mentioned in the Bible, but today no one knows where the exact place was. Some people believe that it is inside the Church of the Holy Sepulcher, because this church was built on the spot where St. Helena found a piece of wood that was supposed to have come from the cross on which Jesus was crucified. Another spot near the Damascus gate was said to be Calvary by an Englishman, Charles G. Gordon; it is called the *Garden Tomb* or *Gordon's Calvary*. The Hebrew name for Calvary is Golgotha.

Calvin, John

John Calvin was one of the great founders of the Protestant form of the Christian religion. He was born at Noyon, France, in the former province of Picardy, in the year 1509. At the age of 24 he had what he called a "sudden conversion" from the Roman Catholic Church to Protestantism. Because of this he had to move from one city to another. He finally settled in Geneva, Switzerland, where he changed the church and also the laws of that city. He believed in very strict church discipline. The Puritans who settled New

England were Calvinists. Calvin died in 1564.

The teachings of John Calvin influenced many people in western Europe, England, and even in America. There are several Protestant churches that believe in them. These churches are called the "Reformed churches" and the most important one is the Presbyterian Church. Calvinism was a part of the REFORMATION movement, which you can read about in a separate article.

calypso

The people of the islands of Trinidad, Tobago, and the British West Indies, in South America, sing a kind of song called *calypso*. The calypso singers usually make them up as they go along. Later they remember parts of what they sang, and little by little the songs are learned by other people. Usually they use a tune that they know, and make up new words to fit the tune. The words are about all kinds of things, and sometimes they do not fit the music too well. For example, in the song *Sly Woman* it is sung "She's a sly wo-MAN," because that fits the tune better. Calypso also refers to the people who live in the British West Indies, and they say "calypso man," or "calypso woman," as we would say "California man" or "New York man," if that is where they live. Calypso is also the name of a character in the *Odyssey*, the great poem by Homer.

Camacho, Manuel Avila

Manuel Avila Camacho was the president of the Republic of Mexico from 1940 to 1946. He was born in 1897, and when he was still a young man, he became interested in the problems of the Mexican people. At that time, Mexico was a republic, as it is today, but the people were not happy about conditions in the country. From 1911 until 1920, there were revolutions and fighting in Mexico. Camacho joined one of the revolutionary armies. He was an extraordinarily good soldier, and stayed in the army after the revolutions were over. Before he was elected president, he was a division general, the highest title in the Mexican Army. He died in 1955.

Cambodia

Cambodia is an independent nation in southeast Asia. It is one of the countries once called FRENCH INDO-CHINA. After being under Japanese control during World War II, Cambodia won its independence from France in 1955 and became a constitutional monarchy, which means that the king is head of the country but a parliament and prime minister actually control the government.

In area Cambodia is not much larger than Minnesota; in population, about six million, it is twice as large.

Most of Cambodia is level land, but there is a mountain range along the coast with peaks as high as 5,700 feet. There are large areas of jungle that are still wild, and full of tigers, leopards, buffaloes, and elephants. The climate is warm and damp, and there are only two seasons. The rainy season lasts from April to October. The rest of the year is dry.

Most Cambodians are descendants of the Khmer people who established themselves there thousands of years ago. They came from India. Their language, called Khmer, is like Chinese and their favored religion is Buddhism. Cambodians are mostly farmers; they grow cotton, rice (their main food), rubber, and spices, especially pepper. Cambodia has a seacoast on the South China Sea (Gulf of Siam) and fishing is an important industry. Exports include teak and ebony woods.

The children of Cambodia are still taught the arts of their ancestors. Girls of eight and nine learn to perform very complicated dances and boys are taught to carve designs in wood, stone, and bone.

About a thousand years ago the kingdom was called Khmer, and it was very powerful and very modern until it lost many wars. The ruins of the huge city of

CAMBODIA

French Embassy Press and Inform. Div.

1. The statue of this strange Cambodian god stands outside an ancient pagoda in Battambang. The club he is holding is to keep away evil spirits and enemies.
2. One of the most famous buildings in Cambodia is this temple, the Angkor Wat, built more than 700 years ago. Its lofty central tower rises more than 200 feet high. Inside the temple is the shrine of Vishnu, the Hindu god.
3. The king of Cambodia, Norodom Sihanouk, stands, during a ceremony, under the great sunshade that shows his high rank.
4. A Cambodian musician beats on a large drum that is like an African jungle tom-tom. The helmet he is wearing is the same kind worn by his ancestors.
5. The Cambodians are famous for their beautiful dances. These dancers are performing in richly embroidered costumes.

French Embassy Press and Inform. Div.

T.W.A.

Angkor, long covered up by the forest, have now been cleared and attract thousands of tourists every year.

When World War II ended the Cambodian people were given more freedom than they had enjoyed before, with a national assembly (parliament) formed in 1947. The king then was Norodom Suramarit, but power was given instead to his son, Prince Norodom Sihanouk, who insisted on free elections with himself a candidate for prime minister. Sihanouk won every election, and when his father died in 1960 he became head of the state but still refused the title of king.

CAMBODIA. Area, 88,780 square miles. Population (1964 estimate) 6,200,000. Government, constitutional monarchy. Capital, Pnom-Penh (population about 500,000). Monetary unit, riel, worth about 2 U.S. cents.

Cambridge

Cambridge is the name of two cities, each the home of a famous university.

Cambridge, England, is an ancient market town on the river Cam. It was originally a Roman fort and later a castle was built there by William the Conqueror. Both the fort and castle have long disappeared, but there are still many old inns, houses and churches in the town. Cambridge University is about 820 years old. It and Oxford University are the most famous universities in England.

CAMBRIDGE, ENGLAND. Population 91,800. On the Cam River.

Cambridge University, in England, is more than 800 years old.

Cambridge, Massachusetts, is the home of Harvard University, Radcliffe College, and the Massachusetts Institute of Technology. It is on the Charles River, across from the city of Boston. It was first settled by the Pilgrims in 1630, and was called Newtown. Harvard, founded in 1636, is the oldest college in the United States. The first printing press in the United States was set up in Cambridge and on it was printed a translation of the Bible for the Indians.

Cambridge is now a city of many industries; some of the products manufactured there are fine tools, machinery, rubber, chemicals, and candy.

CAMBRIDGE, MASSACHUSETTS. Population (1960 census) 107,716. County seat of Middlesex County.

Camden

Camden is a city in southwest New Jersey, across the Delaware River from Philadelphia. About 117,000 people live there. Camden has many large factories, shipyards, and oil refineries. The American poet Walt Whitman lived in Camden and his house there is now a museum. Camden was settled in 1681.

camel

The camel is a large beast of burden that has served men for the last five thousand years. It is able to carry heavy loads over long stretches of barren desert, and to go for several days without water. The shaggy brown animal is an invaluable friend to traders in Central Asia, North Africa, and Arabia. It is a familiar sight in the deserts and market towns to see the camel, with a heavy burden, plodding along under the hot sun.

Everyone can recognize a camel by the large hump on its back. The camel of North Africa and Arabia has just one hump, and is called a *dromedary*. But the camel in Central Asia has two humps, and is known as the *Bactrian camel*. During the rainy season, the camel enjoys its

CAMELLIA

1. The dromedary has only one hump. 2. The Bactrian camel has two humps. 3. The camel stores fat in its hump, and can go for long periods without eating. It also stores water in one of its stomachs, and can go for days without drinking.

richest diet, and its hump becomes large and well developed. But in the dry season the hump is shrunken and small. Usually, the camel eats grass and the branches and leaves of trees. But when this great beast is very hungry, it will eat the skin and bones of other animals, fish, and even a felt blanket.

The desert tribes keep camels in herds. The people drink the camel's nourishing milk, and eat the flesh. They clip the thick woolly hair that grows on the upper part of the camel's body during the winter months, and make it into soft camel's hair cloth. Clothing made of camel's hair is very popular in the United States and Europe. Though this animal is very useful, it is known for its stubbornness and nasty disposition. When it is angry, it kicks and bites, and is dangerous. Unlike other animals used by man, it shows little affection for its master.

camellia

One of the most beautiful shrubs is the camellia. It has dark green, glossy leaves, and large red or pink or white blossoms. Usually these are "double," that is, with more than one row of petals. In the southern United States, you will see camellias growing out-of-doors; but farther north they are grown only in greenhouses. Their native home is in Asia, where some of them grow into trees. They are closely related to the tea plant, and another name for camellias is *tea-flowers*. In fact, from one kind of camellia an oil is produced called tea-seed oil.

The double camellia is very beautiful and some varieties have a fine fragrance.

Camelot

Camelot was the town in England where King Arthur and his Knights of the Round Table are supposed to have lived more than one thousand years ago. No one knows exactly where this town was located, or if it really existed. But in the stories about King Arthur and his brave knights, Camelot is described as a very beautiful town, with great castles, and flags flying from its high turrets. There were fine roads over which the knights rode away to meet their adventures, and there was also a river that ran past the town. Many poems and stories filled with knights and fair ladies have been written about Camelot. It seems to have been an ideal town of long ago.

cameo

A cameo is a small stone which usually has a tiny face or a figure very delicately carved on it. These stones were first used over one thousand years ago in the Orient. They were attached to the backs of seals which people used to sign their letters. Sometimes the cameos were used, just as medals were, to show the high rank of the people who had them.

This beautiful ivory cameo was made by a skilled craftsman in ancient Greece.
N.Y. Public Library

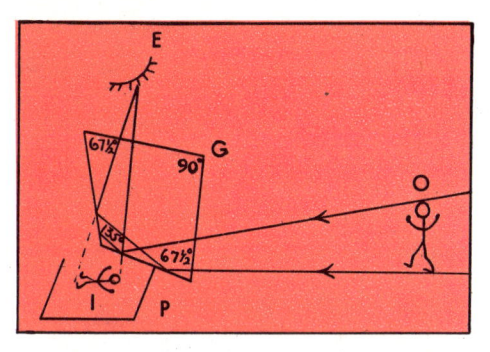

CAMERA LUCIDA. To see the little figure (O) in front of the piece of glass (G) called a prism, you must tilt the prism in a certain way. The prism is specially cut so that its corners are 90 degrees, 135 degrees, and 67½ degrees. This lets it catch rays of light from the figure and send them up to your eye (E) above the prism. If a piece of paper (P) is held underneath the prism, the figure can be copied in pencil.

Some of these cameos can be seen in museums today. The Greeks carved such fine designs on their cameos that people began to wear them on their clothes, and put them on their cups and drinking glasses. Some of the most beautiful cameos made today are carved in Rome, in Italy. They are used as ornaments on brooches, earrings, pins, bracelets and rings. Cameos are carved from semiprecious stones such as sardonyx and agate. These stones have veins in them and the carver has to know just how to use his tool so that he does not split the stone by carving against this grain.

camera, a device for taking pictures: see PHOTOGRAPHY

camera lucida

The camera lucida (pictured on this page, above) was invented more than 150 years ago by an English scientist named Dr. William H. Wollaston. Its name, *camera lucida,* means "light chamber." It is used to draw on paper the outline of objects of almost any size. It is made of a glass *prism* (which changes the direction in which light travels) and

CAMERA OBSCURA

a *lens,* or eyepiece, attached to a metal stand. The person using the camera lucida focuses it on the object that is to be drawn and then looks through the lens. Through this he sees not the actual object but an image of it shown on a piece of paper. This image can be adjusted to any size—larger, smaller, or the same size as the object. A perfect drawing can then be made with a pen or pencil.

The camera lucida is very useful to scientists, and to students of art and architecture. It can be used with a microscope to make drawings of very tiny objects, or with a telescope to draw objects that are very far away. Before the camera lucida was invented, another kind of instrument, called the CAMERA OBSCURA, was used to make drawings or tracings. You can read about it in the next article. Since the invention of photography, however, neither one is used as much as formerly.

camera obscura

The camera obscura is an optical instrument that was invented about four hundred years ago by an Italian named Baptista Porta. It was used as a toy, and also to draw outlines of all sorts of objects. Its name, *camera obscura,* means "dark chamber," or box. It has a glass lens at one end. Inside, at the other end of the box, a mirror is placed at an angle. The camera is focused on an object so that its image is shown on a ground-glass plate set into the top of the box. A sheet of paper is then placed on this plate, so that a drawing of the object can be traced with a pen or pencil.

The camera obscura was used a great deal until the invention of the CAMERA LUCIDA, about which you can read in the article just before this one. However, the most important use of the camera obscura was the part it played in the invention of photography. When a piece of photographic paper is used instead of a sheet of drawing paper, a photograph can be taken of the object.

Cameroon, Federal Republic of

The Federal Republic of Cameroon (formerly known by its French spelling, Cameroun) is a country on the west coast of Africa. In area it is 184,000 square miles, a little larger than California. More than five million people live in Cameroon. The country is composed of two states: the former territory of French Cameroons, which became independent in 1960; and the former territory of British Southern Cameroons, which voted to join the republic in 1961. The government is based on France's government, with a president, premier, and parliament.

The Cameroons area was discovered by the Portuguese toward the end of the 15th century, colonized by the Germans in 1884, and divided between the French and English by a League of Nations mandate after World War I, with four-fifths of the area going to France. Arabs live in the dry northern part of the Cameroons area. In the heavily wooded southern part along the coast, where the weather is always hot, the people are mostly Negroes, belonging to many different tribes. The area produces rubber, ivory (from elephant tusks), and cacao. Other products are peanuts, coffee, bananas, palm oil,

CAMERA OBSCURA. Rays of light from the little figure (O) go through a lens (L) and into a box called a camera obscura. The light then falls on a mirror (M). The mirror is set in back of the box at an angle. This sends the light to a screen (S), where an outline of the figure is seen as an image (I).

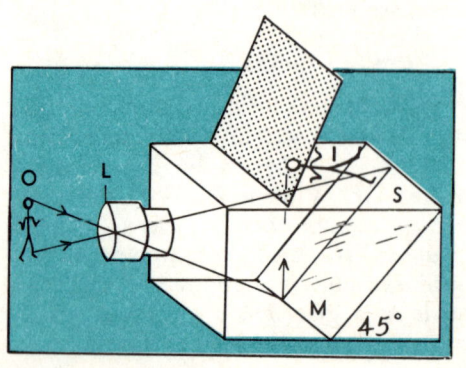

CAMOUFLAGE

A Cameroon tribesman is dressed up to entertain his friends at a celebration.

and hardwoods. Near the coast is Mt. Cameroon, an ancient volcano over 13,300 feet high.

CAMEROON, Federal Republic of. Area, 183,568 square miles. Population (1964 estimate) 5,150,000. Government, Federal republic. Capital, Yaounde (population 55,000). Largest city and chief port, Douala (population, 120,000). Languages, French, Foulbé Bamiléké, Bantu and many other dialects. Religion, native tribal religions, Christian, Moslem. Monetary unit, franc C.F.A. (African Financial Community), about 250 to the U.S. dollar.

camouflage

Many wild animals, such as the zebra and the tiger, have stripes or coats of other patterns that are very useful as disguises. When the animal wants to hide, in case of danger or in order to attack some other animal, it can stand in bushes or lie down in tall grass so that the pattern of its coat blends in perfectly with the shadows. When this kind of disguise is used by men in warfare, it is called *camouflage*.

Camouflaged soldiers wear coveralls with irregular colored patterns of brown, tan, green, and olive drab. This helps them to hide from the enemy. Sometimes they also paint their hands and faces with dark colors and put small leafy branches in their helmets so that, when lying down in the tall grass or standing in the forest, they look almost like bushes themselves. When they fight in the winter snow or on the sandy deserts, they wear white or other light colors to conceal themselves. Metal parts of weapons are blackened to prevent them from shining.

Camouflage is also used to disguise buildings, such as forts and factories, and military vehicles, such as automobiles, tanks, and even large guns. Buildings are painted to look like fields or forests. Large guns are covered with nets or wire screen strung with strips of dull-colored cloth that blends into the landscape. It would be almost impossible to hide ships completely. But they are painted in patches of gray or dull green to break up their outlines and to make them less easily seen against the sea and sky. Sometimes they even seem to be going in the opposite direction.

Scientific camouflage was developed during World War I by the French. During World War II camouflage was used by all the big countries, because there was so much bombing by airplanes that it was important to hide factories, airfields, and military bases. Sometimes real targets, like factories, were made to look from the air like fields, and sometimes open fields were made to look like factories. Complete make-believe towns and airfields were built as decoys, with dummy

CAMPANILE

During World War II, American soldiers often wore these camouflage suits.

This PT boat is camouflaged so that from a distance it seems to blend with the waves.

buildings, guns, and airplanes. The use of camouflage in Europe seems to have been very successful, though there is no way of telling exactly how many buildings were saved or how many bombs were wasted on false targets.

campanile

When a set of bells is hung in a separate building instead of in the steeple of a church, the building is called a campanile. The first campaniles were built in Italy hundreds of years ago. The famous "Leaning Tower of Pisa" is a campanile in Italy. The campanile of St. Mark's Church in Venice, and "Giotto's campanile" at Florence, designed by the great artist Giotto di Bondone, also are in Italy. The first campaniles were made round, but later builders made them square. They are generally made of brick and stone, with stairs going up to the belfry where the bells are hung. See the article on BELLS.

campanula

A campanula is a kind of plant with bell-shaped flowers which is often grown in rock gardens. It is also called *bellflower*. The flowers may be pink or white, but nearly always they are blue. One kind of campanula is called the "bluebell of Scotland," but its real name is the *harebell*. There are about three hundred kinds of campanula. The best known are the *Canterbury bell* and the *chimney bellflower*. The *rampion* is a kind of campanula whose roots and leaves are eaten in salads. Campanulas grow mostly in the northern parts of the world.

Campbell

Campbell is the name of one of the great clans (families) of Scotland. The heads of the family have been the earls and dukes of Argyll for hundreds of years. The traditional founder of the clan was named Colin. One of the famous

The campanile in Florence, Italy.

The photograph at the left shows Camp Fire Girls in Indian costumes performing a special ceremony with candles.

The photograph at the right shows a group of "Blue Birds" who are helping one another to bake a cake.

Camp Fire Girls, Inc.

Scottish folk songs is "The Campbells Are Coming." See the article on CLANS.

Campbell, Alexander

Alexander Campbell was the founder of one of the important Protestant Christian denominations, the Disciples of Christ (also called simply "the Christian Church" and sometimes "Campbellites"). Campbell was born in Ireland and settled in Washington, Pennsylvania, about 150 years ago. He had been a Presbyterian originally. There is a separate article on the DISCIPLES OF CHRIST. Campbell was born in 1788 and died in 1866.

Campbell, Malcolm

Sir Malcolm Campbell was a former English automobile and speedboat racer. He was born in 1885, and even as a boy he loved racing. He set many records in both automobile and speedboat racing, although these records have since been broken by men driving more modern cars and boats. During World War I, he was a captain in the British Royal Flying Corps. He was knighted by King George V after he had set an automobile speed record of 245 miles an hour in 1931. He set this record in his car, the *Bluebird*, along the beach at Daytona, Florida. Four years later, at Bonneville Flats, Utah, he was the first person to drive 300 miles an hour. Campbell died in 1949, at the age of 64.

Camp Fire Girls

The Camp Fire Girls are an organization of girls from 7 to 18 years old. The girls learn to play, camp, study, and work together in small groups. They follow their own law, "worship God, seek beauty, give service, pursue knowledge, be trustworthy, hold on to health, glorify work, be happy." Their emblem, or sign, of crossed logs and flame means both the hearth, or home fire, and the camp fire outdoors.

There are three groups in the organization. Girls between 7 and 8 years old may become "Blue Birds." "Camp Fire Girls" are between 9 and 11 years of age. High school seniors join the "Horizon Club," where the girls are between the ages of 15 and 18. Camp Fire Girls may be of any race or religion. Each group has from 6 to 20 members and an adult leader. Groups meet once a week, and also hold outdoor meets. At "cook-outs," the girls learn how to make fires and cook meals outdoors. They also go on nature-study hikes and camping trips.

The Camp Fire Girls follow many

customs of the American Indians. Each girl takes an Indian name that stands for what she would like to become. "Oka," for example, means to paint or sketch. The girl who chooses this name invents a design to go with it, and this design becomes her sign or monogram. She uses it on the special costume she wears at the council fire, which is a special meeting to welcome new members. The costumes are patterned after Indian ones, and so are many of the meetings.

Ceremonial costumes are decorated with colored beads that tell what each Camp Fire girl has learned to do. The girls have many different activities to choose from. These are divided into seven crafts: home, outdoors, creative arts, frontiers (in science), business, sports and games, and citizenship. For every skill or craft the Camp Fire girl learns, she is given a special wooden bead or "honor." A yellow bead means a business honor, green is for creative arts, blue for frontiers, and so on. The Camp Fire girl starts as a Wood Gatherer, and as she wins more honors she becomes Fire Maker, then Trail Seeker. The highest is Torch Bearer, which means a girl who has learned many skills that she is willing to share with others. The watchword of the Camp Fire Girls is *Wohelo*, a word made of the first two letters of the words *work, health,* and *love.*

The Camp Fire Girls organization was started in 1910 by Dr. and Mrs. Luther Gulick. Its program has been copied in 21 foreign countries, including Great Britain, El Salvador in Central America, and the Republic of the Philippines. More than three million girls have joined since the beginning. In 1961, there were about 600,000 members. The President of the United States is honorary president of the Camp Fire Girls.

The girls also join in community projects such as paper drives. During World War II, they helped sell war bonds, and worked in hospitals and nurseries. The headquarters of the organization is in New York City.

camphor

Camphor is a clear white substance that is made from the wood and bark of the camphor tree. It is useful to man in many ways. In the spring when housewives put away the family's winter clothes, they put camphor in with them to protect them against moths and other insects that like to eat cloth. If you have ever watched your mother do this, you probably remember the funny sharp smell that camphor has. Doctors use camphor as a sedative (to make a person relax), and in another form as a stimulant (to make a person feel more lively). Camphor is also used in making celluloid, perfume, and disinfectants. Scientists can make camphor artificially, from pine oil, and most camphor is now made this way. For many years, people in Japan, China, Formosa in the China Sea, and Borneo, have been boiling the bark and wood of the camphor tree and using the vapor to make camphor, which they send to many parts of the world. Camphor trees are now grown in the southern United States.

A flowering branch of the camphor tree.

Camping

camping

Camping means living outdoors instead of in a house. A camper sleeps in a tent or on the ground, and cooks and eats his food outdoors. There are some people who camp all the time. They are called *nomads.* They never stay in one place very long because they live by hunting or fishing and they follow the game or fish. Some nomads raise cattle or sheep, and they move their tents wherever their sheep and cattle find pasture and water. The Bedouins of Arabia are nomads who live in desert country, and the Jews in the Bible who lived in the days of Abraham were nomads. So were the American Indians of the Great Plains who lived in *tepees,* or tents made of the hides of animals.

Most of us like to go camping because we can learn interesting things about the woods, rivers, lakes, and seashore. It is a good way to spend a summer vacation. You can go camping with your family, or with a club; with the Boy Scouts or Girl Scouts or Camp Fire Girls; or with the YMCA.

WAYS OF CAMPING

When the early settlers had to go from one place to another, before there were any trains or buses or even any roads, they had to walk. Sometimes a trip might take days or even weeks, and every night they had to stop and sleep wherever they were. They took along only the things they really needed, because anything extra would just be more weight to carry. They took their guns or bows and arrows, a knife, a water bottle, blankets, and a flint-and-steel to make a fire. Sometimes they took some dried corn, called *pinole,* or a meat-paste called *pemmican* that the Indians made. Whenever they saw a squirrel or a rabbit or wild turkey, they shot it and roasted it over the fire. We can learn from them the first important rule of camping:

Take along only what you need.

Today there are many different ways you can go camping. You can go by automobile, by canoe on the lake or river, or by pack train (with your outfit packed on horses). Perhaps you may go on a real exploring trip into wild country. All these things have a lot to do with your "outfit," which means the things you need to take along in order to be dry and warm and comfortable and have plenty to eat.

WHAT YOU NEED IN YOUR OUTFIT

There are as many kinds of outfit as there are places to go. Before you can assemble your outfit you think of where you are going, and how long you are going to stay. Then you decide whether you will go by automobile, train, bus, or on foot. Next you find out if you will be near a store or a telephone. All these things have something to do with your outfit.

Good campers are careful about footwear. In rough and rocky country it is better to have boots or moccasins that come up over the ankles, and an extra pair of soft moccasins to wear at night around camp. Shoes or boots should be large enough so that you can wear wool socks without making them too tight. Nothing is more important than footwear, because if your feet get blistered or bruised by rocks, your trip will be spoiled. Put a little roll of adhesive tape in your kit, and if there is a place that rubs against your shoe, put a piece of tape over it. This is another important rule for campers: *Always wear shoes or boots that fit well.*

Socks should be made of wool, and have no holes or darned places in them. Cotton holds water, and holes and darned spots will make blisters on your feet. It is very important to take enough extra socks.

In the woods, even in a hot summer, nights are chilly. Be sure you have a sweater, extra underwear, and a warm jacket. All clothes should be strong and lightweight, and they should never be too tight. For winter camping and expeditions you need special clothes that are sold only at sporting goods stores.

Here is a list of things that should be in any outfit:

Knife: You will need a knife, either a belt or pocket knife. One blade, about 3½ inches long, is enough. In some places it is against the law to carry a knife that has a blade longer than 4½ inches.

Handkerchief: You need a big colored handkerchief. It has many uses: as a towel, to tie and carry things in, and to keep the sun and insects off the back of your neck. Never take a white handkerchief during hunting season, or some hunter might mistake you for a deer and shoot you.

Matches: You should carry matches in a waterproof case.

Compass: It is a very good idea to learn how to use a compass, because it can help you if you get lost. See the article on **COMPASS**.

Whistle: A whistle may help you signal your friends if you get lost.

Snake-bite kit: In any area where there are poisonous snakes you should have a snake-bite kit. You can buy one at sporting goods stores, or where Boy Scout supplies are sold.

Insect repellent: This comes either as a liquid or a paste. When you rub it on your face and legs it keeps insects from biting you for many hours.

First-aid kit: Some bandages, adhesive tape, salve, and iodine should be put in your kit for fixing cuts and scratches.

TENTS AND BEDDING

The kind of tent you need depends on the weather and the ground, and on how you are carrying your outfit. If you are going with your family in an automobile, the tent can be big and heavy. But if you are "back-packing," which means carrying your outfit in a knapsack, and are going by foot, your tent must be very light. The smallest tents, called "pup" tents, are just big enough to crawl into. "Wall tents," or "umbrella tents," are bigger and will hold several people, and there are many other kinds.

Most campers like "sleeping bags," but some like blankets. The best sleeping bags are filled with "down," the soft underfeathers of waterfowl, or a combination of down and feathers. They are really a sort of comforter or quilt folded in half, with a zipper or snap fasteners so that you can fasten yourself in.

Expert woodsmen know how to keep from freezing even without a tent or blankets. One way is to find a slope or big rock that will "break the wind," and then build a fire so that the heat will be reflected back toward your windbreak. Another kind of shelter is called a "lean-to." It is made by placing some poles against a low branch of a tree, and then piling leaves, brush, bark, or earth on the poles until it makes a windproof wall. Then you build a "reflector fire" against a flat rock or green log, in front of the lean-to. The back of the lean-to should be "into the wind," so that smoke will not blow in.

The ground is cold, even in the hottest summer; and nights are likely to be chilly, even in the jungle. In winter, you can freeze very quickly if you lie on the ground. This brings us to another rule:

Always have more bedding beneath than on top, and never let the body touch the ground—always have a waterproof ground cloth.

The problem of bedding also depends on what kind of camping you do. In an automobile camp, you can use folding cots and mattresses, but they are too heavy for hiking. Air mattresses are lightweight, but they are not warm enough for cold weather. The Indians made beds of willow sticks, laid close together across two logs. "Bough" beds are made of two logs laid about two feet apart and filled in with the tips of balsam or hemlock boughs. Some campers like a "bed-sack," which is a bag that you fill with dry grass and leaves at night. You carry it empty, or use it to carry other things in.

WOODCRAFT AND COOKERY

One of the first things a camper must learn is how to make a good fire, and how to keep it from spreading and causing a forest fire. The campfire should be small, so that it will not be too hot. The best woods are hardwoods, such as maple, birch, white ash, elm, oak, beech, and hickory. Softwoods such as pine, balsam, fir, spruce and cottonwood make good kindling or a quick fire for cooking lunch, but they will not burn down to a lasting bed of coals for cooking dinner and for a night fire.

Learning how to make a fire in the woods is not easy. You need a teacher and a lot of experience. A good camper gathers his wood first, and shaves up a little kindling. Then he clears a space on the ground so that nothing else will catch fire and lays his firebed. He seldom needs more than one match.

Fire regulations are laws that tell us when and where we may build a fire. The laws are not the same everywhere. Usually a permit is required. These laws are important because they are intended to prevent forest fires. Good campers love the woods and do everything possible to avoid setting them on fire. The principal rule about fires is this:

Before leaving a fire, be absolutely sure that it is really out. The best way to be sure the fire is out is to pour plenty of water on it, then rake it over with a stick, then drench it with water again. Unless you get it very wet it can start up again.

Cooking equipment can be any combination of pots and pans. There are special lightweight outfits that are very good, especially if you are back-packing. All the parts fit into each other, and they do not make much weight or bulk. You can do a lot of cooking with a kettle and frying pan and a little "know-how." Each person in a camping party should have a knife, fork and spoon, and an unbreakable cup and plate.

Before making up a "grub" or food list for camping, learn everything you can about which foods are light and nourishing, and will not spoil without refrigeration. All of these things are important.

WHEN YOU ARE LOST

A good camper never goes into the woods without telling his friends, or perhaps the Forest Rangers, where he is going and how long he expects to be gone. Then if he gets lost someone will miss him and start looking for him. One of the most important rules to observe when you are lost is this:

When you are lost stay where you are.

Every camper should have a compass and know how to use it, and should never be without matches in a waterproof match safe. But if you have neither, and if you have forgotten to tell anyone where you are going, try to find a shelter before it gets dark. Never try to find your way at

CAMPING 984

1. Taking a camping trip for the day can be a lot of fun. Early in the morning, you start out with your knapsacks, and hike through beautiful country. You can see many interesting things along the way.

2. If you have a pair of binoculars, you can watch the sky and see many different birds. You can also see animals in the fields and on the far hills and mountains.

3. A compass is very necessary on a camping trip. You need it to tell you what direction to take to reach your destination. Without a compass you can get lost.

4. If you know how to read a map, you will know where you are at all times.

Standard Oil Co.

CAMPING

1. If you have a trailer, you can take long summer trips. You can stay at trailer camps in many beautiful places.

2. Some of the best fun in camping is in cooking and eating out-of-doors. You can cook steaks and many other delicious things over an open fire.

3. On a camping trip, you may not have a refrigerator, but a cold stream makes an excellent icebox in which you can keep milk and other food.

4. After supper, everyone gathers around the campfire and sings songs. Someone may tell a story while you watch the logs in the fire burning brightly.

Standard Oil Co.

night, because you might fall and get hurt. If you have a whistle, blow three blasts from time to time. If you have a gun, fire three shots in the air. Three sounds of any kind mean "I am lost!" Above all, do not try to guess where camp is, and try not to be scared. If you know how to build a smoky fire, do that. Searchers will see the smoke and come to you.

WATER

Water is the most important thing in the world when you do not have it. Most of us are used to just turning a faucet when we want water. In the woods there is no running water except a spring or brook, but here is a very important rule:

Never drink water that you find in the woods unless you have boiled or purified it.

The best way to purify water is to boil it, but there are also tablets containing a chemical that purifies the water. You can use them when you have no way to boil the water.

Canaan

In the first book of the Bible, called Genesis, you can read the story of how the Lord promised Abraham a country for his people, who are the Jews. This country was called Canaan, and it lay about where the state of Israel is today. The Bible also tells the story of how Moses led the Jews out of slavery in Egypt, and how after much wandering and many difficulties they finally reached Canaan, the promised land.

Canaan was also the name of a grandson of Noah. He was disrespectful to Noah and was banished.

A shepherd takes his flock to market in that part of Palestine that was known as Canaan thousands of years ago, and was called "the Promised Land" by the Jews.

CANADA

An aerial view of Vancouver, British Columbia.

Late afternoon sunlight on the summit of Roger's Pass, British Columbia.

Photos by: NFB

A scene in British Columbia.

Simon Fraser University, Burnaby, British Columbia.

Two loggers felling a tree in British Columbia.

The Swiftsure Ocean Classic Fleet is docked at a harbor in Victoria, British Columbia.

Photos by: NFB

Halibut is being unloaded from the hold of a ship onto a wharf at Vancouver, British Columbia.

Salmon fishermen in British Columbia.

A night view of the Parliament buildings illuminated for Christmas in Victoria, British Columbia.

Hydro Quebec Power Dam near Portage du Fort, Quebec.

Photos by: NFB

An aerial view of Montreal, Quebec showing the University of Montreal.

Morning mists rising over a valley in autumn in Assomption Valley, Quebec.

A graceful modern church in Chibougameau, Quebec.

The city of Montreal, Quebec at night.

Photos by: NFB

The new Canadian flag on the Parliament building in Ottawa, Ontario.

The Parliament buildings illuminated at sunset in Ottawa, Ontario.

The City Hall of Toronto, Ontario.

Niagara Falls, located on the border between Niagara Falls, New York and Niagara Falls, Ontario.

A large factory in Hamilton, Ontario.

A view of Qu'Appelle Valley in Saskatchewan.

A fisherman tending his fish weir (a kind of trap) in St. John Harbour, New Brunswick.

The north Canadian Tundra in summer.

The community of Fogo in Notre Dame Bay, Newfoundland.

Photos by: NFB

Grain elevators and wheat fields at Indian Head in Saskatchewan.

Photos by: NFB

Peggy's Cove, Nova Scotia.

The North Star Oil Refinery
in Winnipeg, Manitoba.

Fort Prince of Wales at Port Churchill
in Northern Manitoba.

Citadel Hill in Halifax, Nova Scotia.

The Hudson Bay Mining and Smelting
Complex in Flin Flon, Manitoba.

An aerial view of Prince Edward Island.

Photos by: NFB

A radar station at Tukoyaktuk, Northwest Territories.

A scene in New Glasgow, Prince Edward Island.

Canon Fiord, Northwest Territories.

Eskimo hunters with their dog team in the Northwest Territories.

A cowboy on his bucking bronco at the annual "Calgary Stampede" in Calgary, Alberta.

A scene from Shakespeare's **Henry IV, Part 1** at the Stratford Festival in Stratford, Ontario.

A football game between the Ottawa Rough Riders and the Toronto Argonauts in Ottawa, Ontario.

A skier on the edge of a large drift in Banff, Alberta.

Photos by: NFB

A curling rink in Quebec City. (Curling is a game played by sliding a large, smooth stone along the ice at a mark 38 yards away.)

Canada

Canada

Canada is an enormous country that covers all of the North American continent north of the United States except Alaska. The border it shares with the United States is almost four thousand miles long. It has coasts on three oceans: the Atlantic on the east, the Pacific on the west, the Arctic on the north. It is bigger than the United States, and about the same size as China. But while China has a population of about 700,000,000, in all of Canada there are only about 20,000,000 people, or about as many as live in New York State or California. Most of northern Canada is too cold and barren for permanent settlement. In the frozen wastes of the far north, within the Arctic Circle, only the simplest kinds of plants will grow.

Yet in spite of all this, Canada is very rich. Its people live better than those of almost any other country. There is more than enough food to go around. Canada's farmlands are fertile; its forests are full of timber; its rivers, lakes and coastal waters abound with fish. Under the rich soil lie vast quantities of gold, silver, oil, uranium, iron, and many other kinds of natural wealth. Canada's industrial plants and factories are among the most modern in the world. So you can see that Canada could easily support twice as many people as it does now.

Canada is a member of the [British] Commonwealth. Like the other independent countries in the Commonwealth, such as Australia and South Africa, it has its own government. Like them, Canada was very important in World War II. The factories turned out war materials of all kinds and the farms produced food for the Allied Forces. The Canadian army, navy and air force fought with the Allies in Europe, North Africa, and the Far East. In the Korean War, Canadian soldiers battled alongside United States and British troops under the flag of the United Nations.

Canada is a member of the North Atlantic Treaty Organization (NATO) and is solidly joined with the other countries of the free world in the fight against communism. The United States and Canada are probably better friends than any other two countries.

THE PEOPLE OF CANADA

The people of Canada are almost all of European stock. The ancestors of almost half of them came from the British Isles—England, Scotland, Ireland, and Wales. Next in number are the descendants of French settlers; these number

CANADA

more than four million. The French language is spoken a great deal in Canada, especially in the big eastern province of Quebec. It is one of the two official languages; English is the other. Other Canadian people came originally from Germany, Russia, Scandinavia, Holland, Poland, and Italy.

Before the white men came, there were only scattered tribes of Indians in the vast land. The Indians were of many different types. In the north were the Eskimos. Seagoing tribes lived on the Pacific coast, and hunters and trappers lived in the east. However, there never were very many Indians. Little by little white settlers took their best lands, but they did not treat the Indians badly. Today there are about 165,000 Indians of all kinds in Canada, which is probably more than there were when the country was first seen by Europeans, five years after Columbus discovered the New World.

In religion, the citizens who speak French (called French Canadians) are almost all Roman Catholics. Most of those who speak English are Protestants. There are more than six million Catholics in Canada. The two principal Protestant groups are the United Church of Canada (which has almost three million members) and the Church of England, or Protestant Episcopal Church (which has more than two million).

HOW THE PEOPLE LIVE

Canada is such a rich country that its people do not have to depend on only one way of life, such as farming. They make their livings in a number of ways—farming, fishing, lumbering, mining, and manufacturing.

The first settlers who came to the rocky Atlantic coast of Canada almost four hundred years ago found the waters full of haddock, herring, cod, and lobster. Many people still live by catching these and other salt-water fish, particularly in Newfoundland, New Brunswick, Nova Scotia, and Prince Edward Island. These provinces are called the *Maritime Provinces* because they are by the sea. Although deep-sea fishing is a big industry in all of them, fresh-water fish like salmon, trout, pike and pickerel are also caught there in great numbers. Thousands of people work in the factories where fish are cleaned and packed in cans, or are frozen while fresh.

Along with the first fishermen, fur trappers came to Canada to hunt the foxes, muskrats, minks, beavers, raccoons, and other animals that brought high prices for their fur. Many Canadians still earn a living in the fur trade. But instead of hunting the animals in the forests, they raise them on big farms so as to have a steady supply of skins to be made into coats, jackets, and collars.

One of Canada's greatest natural treasures is its forests, which cover vast areas. Woodsmen living in lonely forest camps cut down the great trees and roll the logs to a river. The logs float down the river to a lumber mill. There they are sawed into planks for building, or crushed into the pulp from which paper and cardboard are made.

Farming has always been very important to Canada. Farmers use the most modern machines and methods to grow wheat, oats, barley, rye, potatoes, corn, tobacco, and a number of other crops. Dairy farms produce enormous quantities of milk and butter. After Canadians have used all the food they need themselves, there is always plenty left over for sale abroad.

On the western plains that stretch across the provinces of Manitoba, Saskatchewan, and Alberta, the people live much like their neighbors in North Dakota and Montana, just across the border. Big herds of cattle roam over the fine grazing lands. On higher ground shepherds watch over flocks of sheep. The sheep's soft white fleece, or coat, is made into wool. The meat of the cattle is sold for food. The hides become leath-

CANADA

Canadian Pac. Ry.

1. These great buildings are the Canadian Parliament, in Ottawa, Ontario, where the laws of Canada are made. You can visit Parliament to see the government at work.

2. This map of Canada shows its long and rugged coastlines and boundaries.

3. Canada is rich in many resources that have helped to make it a wealthy country. This map shows some of the most important products that come from Canada, and the sections they come from. The uranium deposits are the largest in North America.

4. If you were to visit Quebec, you might stay at the Chateau Frontenac Hotel.

Canadian Pac. Ry.

Standard Oil Co.
More and more oil has been found in Canada, and wells are built to pump it.

Canadian Pac. Ry.
This gigantic pile of pulpwood came from timber in the great Canadian forests.

er, to be used in shoes, belts, and other things.

Underneath the Plains region rich deposits of oil have recently been found. Oil refineries, where the crude oil is made into gasoline and oil for many uses, have been built near the oilfields. Thousands of Canadians work at bringing the oil up to the surface and refining it. In other parts of Canada miners dig for gold, silver, copper, lead, nickel, platinum, cobalt, iron ore, and coal. In northern Saskatchewan miners work the richest deposit of pitchblende in North America. Uranium, which is used in making atomic power, comes from pitchblende.

Across the Rockies from the Plains Provinces, in British Columbia, people work on farms, in factories, and in offices. They depend greatly on the shipping in and out of the Pacific port of Vancouver. In the northern part of British Columbia the Coast Indians still live as their forefathers did, fishing from boats made out of logs, and carving the giant statues of gods or special guardians called totem poles. In the Yukon Territory and the enormous Northwest Territories, which together take in the whole of Arctic Canada, the few white settlers are mostly miners and trappers. Some of the Eskimos have adopted the white man's ways, and live in the tiny settlements and trading posts. But most of them still live as Eskimos have lived for hundreds of years, hunting seals, snow foxes, and polar bears and living in ice huts called igloos.

The biggest Canadian provinces in size and population are Ontario and Quebec. More than half of all Canadians live in these two provinces. Quebec borders on the states of northern New England and New York State. More than three-quarters of its people speak French. Ontario, where most people speak English, borders on Minnesota and on all the Great Lakes except Lake Michigan. The people of both these provinces work at farming, manufacturing, lumbering, and mining. The Great Lakes region of Ontario is the industrial heart of Canada, where many thousands of people work in big, modern factories making machinery, automobiles, trucks, clothing, and leather goods.

CANADA

Canadian Pac. Ry. Photos

1. Many people riding in railroad cars pass through the magnificent Canadian Rockies with their towering peaks.
2. The royal Canadian coat of arms was a part of the flag of Canada. The crown at the top shows that the nation belongs to the British Commonwealth.
3. Niagara Falls are on the border between the United States and Canada. This picture of the falls is taken from the Canadian side.
4. Farmers in Canada raise great crops of wheat. The Manitoba wheat fields produce some of the finest grain.
5. One of the great industries of Canada is mining and smelting the rich metals found in the mountains. This is a smelting plant in British Columbia.

CANADA

992

1. These nuns in a convent in Quebec are making a beautifully embroidered garment that will be worn by a priest during a Catholic service.

2. People catch many kinds of fish in Canada's great rivers and lakes.

3. Hunters fly to the wilds of northern Canada to hunt moose and bring back the great antlered heads.

4. Boys and girls in many parts of Canada attend country schoolhouses. The ice on the windows shows how very cold it gets during the long winter.

5. A farmer and his oxen are on the way to market.

CANADA

The Nat'l Film Board of Canada Photo

1. People can enjoy many sports on their vacations in the Laurentian hills, in Quebec, Canada.

2. Southhead Cliffs is a magnificent sight on Grand Manan Island, New Brunswick. At the edge of the cliffs is the Southhead lighthouse.

3. People from all over the world come to see the great glaciers and snow-capped mountains at Jasper National Park, in Alberta, Canada.

4. Great flocks of wild birds gather on the cliffs of Quebec.

CANADA

Manitoba Gov't Bureau

Not all the deer in the Canadian woods are as tame as this fawn.

Canadian Nat'l Ry.

Most of the people in the Gaspé Peninsula live along the coast in little villages like this one.

Nova Scotia Bureau of Inform.

This Museum Chapel in Nova Scotia contains interesting relics.

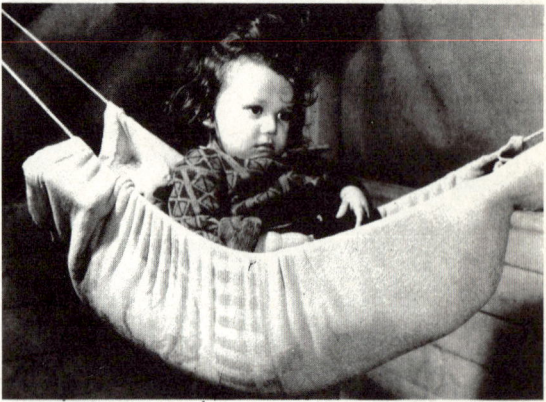

Standard Oil Co.

Many Indian families live in Canada. This little Indian girl is sitting in a homemade hammock.

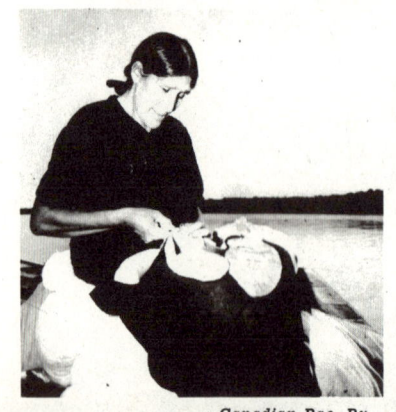

Canadian Pac. Ry.

An Indian woman making moccasins.

Canadian Pac. Ry.

Aerial view of the large city of Toronto, Ontario. It is the second-largest city in Canada.

CANADA

Canadian Pac. Ry.
Skiing on the mountain slopes in Canada is one of the biggest attractions for tourists.

The Nat'l Film Board of Canada
Children in Canada learn to ski at a very early age.

Canadian Pac. Ry.
Here you see the magnificent Parliament buildings in Ottawa, the capital of Canada.

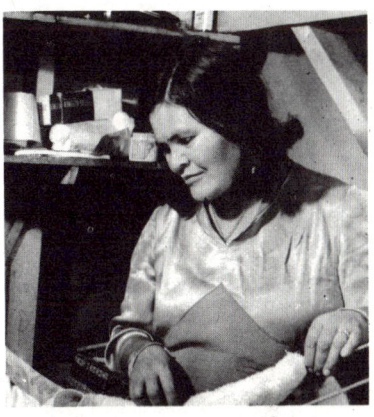

Standard Oil Co.
The Indian woman of northern Canada is rocking her baby to sleep.

Canadian Pac. Ry.
Ships from all over the world come to the port at Montreal, which is one of the largest in Canada.

Nova Scotia Bureau of Inform.
An Indian using a moose call. It sounds like a moose's cry.

WHAT THE LAND IS LIKE

Canada is an extremely varied land. In the east, the rugged, forest-covered Maritime Provinces lie around the Gulf of St. Lawrence, where the St. Lawrence River empties into the Atlantic. The Appalachian Mountains extend from the eastern United States into Quebec and New Brunswick. The many rivers and the beautiful scenery of this region make it a favorite with vacationers, particularly those who like to fish.

Farther west, the St. Lawrence valley opens out to the huge central plains around the Great Lakes. The St. Lawrence River connects the Great Lakes with the Atlantic. It contains thousands of islands, small and large. North of the Quebec farmlands rises the vast tableland called the Laurentian Plateau. This rocky plateau with its forests is sometimes called the "Canadian Shield," because it is really a huge barrier cutting off the northern region around Hudson Bay. It stretches from the Atlantic two-thirds of the way across Canada into Saskatchewan.

From the Great Lakes the central plain rises westward to the Rocky Mountains in Alberta. This region contains many lakes and rivers as well as flat prairie land. Banff and Jasper National Parks, in western Alberta, are world-famous vacation spots.

Along the Pacific Ocean, in British Columbia, are the steep Coast Mountains. Vancouver Island, which is large and covered with mountains, lies off the southwest corner of Canada. Further north a string of smaller islands runs up the coast to the border of Alaska.

Yukon, to the north, is generally mountainous and has an Arctic climate, with very long winters and very short summers. It is not a province, but a territory. It is drained by the Yukon River, which flows into Alaska and on into the Pacific. The important Alaska Highway, built during World War II, winds through the territory. Temperatures as low as 81 degrees below zero have been recorded in Yukon.

The immense Northwest Territories cover most of the northern edge of the North American continent, with vast empty islands out in the Arctic Ocean. There are huge areas of flat or rolling country called *tundras,* where no trees grow and the only plant life is a kind of lichen, or moss. Hudson Bay, a huge arm of the Atlantic Ocean, reaches south about five hundred miles into Canada to the northern edge of the Laurentian Plateau.

HOW THE PEOPLE ARE GOVERNED

Canada is a federation of provinces, as the United States is a federation of states. It is a member of the British Commonwealth of Nations. Elizabeth II is queen in Canada as she is in England. A governor general represents her at Ottawa, the Canadian capital. He is appointed on the advice of the Canadian government.

Laws are made by a parliament consisting of the queen, the Senate, and the House of Commons. Senators are appointed for life, rather than elected for a term. Members of the House of Commons are elected directly by the people. There are now 102 senators and 265 members of the House of Commons.

The prime minister is the leader of the party that has the most members in the House of Commons. He appoints a cabinet of ministers, each of whom usually assumes charge of one of the various government departments. By custom, only members of parliament can be cabinet members.

The provinces govern their own affairs, just as our states do. Each province has a lieutenant governor, appointed by the federal government, and a lawmaking assembly. The territories are governed by officials sent from Ottawa, who are advised by certain elected residents of the area.

Canada has a well-equipped army, navy, and air force. Law and order are enforced by the famous ROYAL CANADIAN MOUNTED POLICE, about whom you can read in the next article.

CANADA IN THE PAST

John Cabot, an Italian sailor in the service of England, reached the Atlantic shore of Canada in 1497. However, it was more than one hundred years later that the first settlement was established, by the French, at Port Royal in Nova Scotia. Later, English settlers came, and the two groups became rivals. The many wars between France and England in the next hundred years were matched in Canada by wars between the rival colonies. Finally, in 1763, New France was conquered by the British, and all of the settled eastern part of Canada came under British control.

During the Revolutionary War many Americans who still wanted British rule fled into Canada. These people helped to develop the land and to strengthen its ties with England.

Following many exploring trips, the Canadian colonists began to push westward into the wilderness during the nineteenth century. In 1867 four colonies banded together into a kind of union with a federal government. When a railroad was opened all the way to the Pacific coast, many more settlers moved to the west. New provinces were formed and admitted one by one into the Canadian federation. Since then, through two world wars and the Korean war, Canada has kept on growing richer and stronger.

The ten provinces of Canada are: Ontario, Quebec, British Columbia, Alberta, Saskatchewan, Manitoba, Nova Scotia, New Brunswick, Newfoundland, and Prince Edward Island. The territories are: Northwest Territories, and Yukon.

The chief cities of Canada are: Montreal, Quebec; Toronto, Ontario; Vancouver, British Columbia; Winnipeg, Manitoba. The capital of Canada is Ottawa, Ontario. There is a separate article on each of these provinces and cities.

CANADA. Area 3,851,809 square miles. Population (1967 estimate) 20,354,334 Government, self-governing federation within the (British) Commonwealth. Capital, Ottawa. Languages, English and French. Religion, Roman Catholic and Protestant. Monetary unit, the dollar, usually worth within 5% of the U.S. dollar. Flag, red maple leaf on white background, bordered on left and right by vertical red stripe.

Canadian Mounted Police

The Royal Canadian Mounted Police enforce the law throughout the entire Dominion of Canada. The men of the force are popularly known as the "Mounties," and many stories are told of their bravery.

This unusual police force was formed almost a hundred years ago. It was first called the Northwest Mounted Police, because its purpose was to keep order in the great unsettled region in northwest Canada. They protected the settlers from bands of robbers, and saw that there was peace between the Indians and the white men. They wore bright red coats and "campaign hats"—which looked like Boy Scout hats—and they became famous for their daring exploits. It was often said that the Mounties always got their man. Few smugglers or other criminals were able to escape from this police force.

Today, the Royal Canadian Mounted Police maintain federal law in all parts of Canada. They also enforce provincial and even city laws if the provinces or cities wish them to do so. The provinces of Ontario and Quebec have their own police forces, but all of the other provinces now engage the Royal Canadian Mounted Police to enforce their laws. Most large Canadian cities have their own police forces, but many small towns use the Royal Canadian Mounted Police for local enforcement.

Very few of these policemen ride horses any longer. Instead, they use modern equipment, such as small ships, automobiles, airplanes, and helicopters.

Above: The Royal Canadian Mounted Police are excellent horsemen. They also are trained to track criminals on skis, snowshoes, and dog sleds. *Right:* At the shows put on by the Mounted Police, the men go through troop drills to demonstrate their fine horsemanship. *Below:* Their horses are well trained and can do many tricks.

Nat'l Film Board of Canada

There is no police force in the United States exactly like the Mounties, for they not only fight against many kinds of crime, but they also enforce the laws that protect wild birds, they guard the rights of Indians, they prevent illegal trade in drugs, and they do secret work that in America is done by the Federal Bureau of Investigation.

canals

Canals are waterways made by man. They are among the oldest and most useful things man has ever built. When we speak of canals, we usually mean manmade channels like the Panama Canal or the Houston Ship Canal which ships and barges use. But there are many other kinds of canal. There is the kind that carries water into cities from out-of-town reservoirs. There is the irrigation canal that brings water to thirsty crops. Among the ship canals, there are those that connect one ocean with another to shorten the voyages of ships, those that connect large inland cities directly with the sea, and those that connect lakes and rivers and extend water travel throughout the interior of a country.

BUILDING CANALS

When engineers want to know how much a canal will cost, they examine the ground they have to cut through. Sand, clay, and soft stone are easy to cut through, but then there is the job of dredging. Children have the same problem when they build canals in the sand to bring sea water to where they sit on the beach. The sand falls in from the banks of their canals, and it must be dug out again so the water can flow. This is called dredging. The banks and bottoms of many canals are lined with concrete to avoid the need for dredging.

Much harder to build are the canals which are cut out of solid rock. The PANAMA CANAL took twice as long to build as the SUEZ CANAL although it is only half as long. There are separate articles on these two canals. The United States Army engineers who built the Panama Canal had to blast a path through mountains. They also had to build locks, so that the ships could go uphill.

LOCKS

Locks are like elevators for ships. They make it possible for a ship to go from a low body of water to a higher one. The ship sails or is pulled into a lock, which is a big tank open at the top. Watertight gates are closed behind the ship. More water is then let into the lock through pipes called *sluices*. As the water gets higher, the ship floats up to the level of the next lock. The gates open, and the ship moves into the next lock. The same things happen again. When the ship is in the last lock it is level with the body of water outside and it leaves the canal. When it comes back, it must go "downstairs" just as it went "upstairs." It enters a lock, the gates close behind it, and the water is let out through the sluice valves until the ship is floating at the level of the next lock. The gates open and the ship sails or is pulled out.

Ships can go through some canals under their own power but in others they are pulled through by engines that run on rails alongside the canal. Men, horses, and oxen used to pull ships and barges long ago, and on some canals in Europe they still do.

CANALS LONG AGO

One of the longest and oldest canals ever built was the Grand Canal in China. It was built almost 2,500 years ago. There was also an important canal between the Tigris and Euphrates Rivers in the land we now call Iraq. The French people built the famous Languedoc Canal several hundred years ago. It was almost 150 miles long, and connected the Mediterranean Sea with the Bay of Biscay. About the same time, the English were starting to build a system of canals which gave the country good waterways for its commerce. For hundreds of years the Belgians and the Dutch have used canals not only for transportation but to drain water off the land which in many places is below sea level. The people who live in the beautiful city of Venice, Italy, have canals instead of streets. They use gondolas and other boats as we use taxis and buses to go from place to place.

After the American Revolution, many people left the eastern cities and moved westward over the mountains. In their new homes, they needed supplies from the East, and they wanted to sell the food they grew and the fur of the animals they trapped. It was too expensive to send these things on slow wagons, so they built canals. The Erie Canal was the first. It stretched across New York State for 134 miles and connected Buffalo on the Great Lakes with Albany on the Hudson

CANALS

1. About 100 years ago, the Mormons built this canal in the rocky and hilly part of Utah.

2. This series of canals in Oregon carries water to farms where it will be used to irrigate the land. The water in the canals can be controlled by gates which are now open to let the water through.

3. This great canal in the state of Washington was built to turn dry and useless land into fine farming country.

Bureau of Reclamation

4. The Lachine Canal at Montreal Harbor is very important to Canadian transportation. It is connected to the St. Lawrence Canals so that large ships can travel more than 1,000 miles inland with their cargoes.

5. This barge is entering a lock in the Erie Canal, New York. The gates in front of the lock are already closed. When the barge is in the lock, the back gates will close and the water will rise.

Standard Oil Co.

Canadian Nat'l Ry.

CANALS

1. The famous Panama Canal was built to connect the Atlantic and Pacific Oceans. This shows the men at work in 1913, cutting through a mountain.
2. Today, great liners go through the Panama Canal by a series of locks, carrying passengers and products from all parts of the world.
3. When a lock is empty, it looks like a very deep and narrow swimming pool. You can tell how deep it is by comparing it to the height of the men standing at the bottom of the big lock.

Panama Canal Photo

4. The Panama Canal is more than 50 miles long and passes through both low and hilly country in the Panama Canal Zone.
5. The big ship at the bottom of the picture has just left one of the locks. Behind it, another ship is in the lock. When the water in the lock has risen fully, the gates will open and this ship will sail on to the next lock.
6. The many series of locks along the Panama Canal make navigation possible.

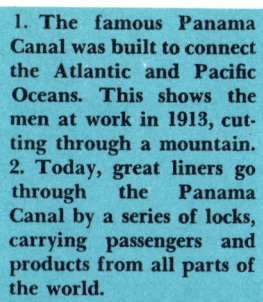

A man ties a barge in the Erie Canal to the wall of one of the locks before the water rises until it is equal to the level of water in the next lock.

River. The Erie made it easier to trade with the new West, and helped to make New York America's largest seaport. The Erie Canal is still in use as a part of the New York State Barge Canal. It is 150 feet wide and 12 feet deep.

During the 1850s, railroads began to take all the passenger and much of the freight business away from the canals. But today canals still carry many tons of freight like coal and oil because it is cheaper to ship it that way than by railroad.

Some inland cities build canals on which ships and barges can come right up to the city from the sea. Houston, Texas, is fifty miles inland from the Gulf of Mexico, but ocean-going freighters can reach it by using the Houston Ship Canal. The United States and Canada completed a canal system called the St. Lawrence Seaway in 1959 so that ships can sail from the Atlantic Ocean to Chicago, Cleveland and Canadian cities.

Canals make possible one of the most exciting trips you can make in the United States, a voyage through the Intercoastal Waterway. This route follows rivers, lakes, and canals for more than a thousand miles down the Atlantic coast line to Florida and then west to Texas.

Canal Zone, the region around the Panama Canal: see PANAMA CANAL.

ILLUSTRATED

WORLD

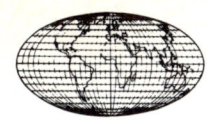

ENCYCLOPEDIA

LIBRARY
OF THE
LITERARY TREASURES

The novels, plays, poems, and other works of
the most celebrated and historic writers of
the English language in all lands and times

VOLUME
4

Bonds of Interest — Camille

Edited by ALBERT H. MOREHEAD
Designed by DONALD D. WOLF *and* MARGOT L. WOLF
With many new drawings by RAFAELLO BUSONI

ACKNOWLEDGEMENTS—Outlines in this volume were written by Elizabeth MacLean, Dina Dellalé, Nancy Starrels, Hanz Holzer, Martin Keen, Robert Condon, Christopher Lazare, Nicholas Bela, Susan Margulies, Phyllis Pollard, Gerard Meyer, Mary Louise Birmingham, Sue G. Walcutt, Ernst J. Schlochauer, James E. Tobin, Mildred Lee Marmur and the Editors.

Bobley Publishing a Division of
ILLUSTRATED WORLD ENCYCLOPEDIA, INC.

© **Bobley Publishing** a Division of
ILLUSTRATED WORLD ENCYCLOPEDIA, INC.

Illustrated World Encyclopedia, Inc.

Made in U.S.A.

Bonds of Interest

Play by Jacinto Benavente y Martinez, 1866–1954.

Produced 1907 (in U.S.A., in translation by John Garrett Underhill, 1917).

SPAIN'S NOBEL PRIZE dramatist (he won the prize in 1922) wrote this play as a farce along the traditional lines of the Italian comedy. The Spanish title was *Los intereses creados*. It was not produced in English until Benavente followed it with a second part in 1916—*La ciudad allegre y confiada,* The Gay and Confident City. *Bonds of Interest* is set in the 17th century and uses an old theme (its similarity to Farquhar's *The Beaux' Stratagem* is immediately apparent). It has survived as Benavente's most successful play.

Act. I. LEANDER and CRISPIN, two penniless young gentlemen, have just arrived in the city. Crispin explains that here there are really two different cities, one for the poor and one for the rich. To be able to live the life of the rich they can choose between robbing on the highway or using their intelligence to obtain the keys to the city. With Crispin posing as Leander's servant, they enter a fashionable inn. Crispin arrogantly demands the best service for his master and boasts that their baggage (they have nothing) is coming in 8 carts. Crispin tells the INNKEEPER that Leander is on a secret mission in the city. Leander strikes Crispin with his sword for disclosing this information and accidentally hits the innkeeper, who is so impressed by the manner of his guests that he asks for neither money nor identification. They go to their rooms.

HARLEQUIN, a poet, and the CAPTAIN enter. They, too, are without money for a meal. Harlequin cannot sell his poetry; the army is out of favor with the government, which sent the soldiers into an unjust war then made a disastrous peace to serve the commercial interests. They knock at the innkeeper's door. He refuses to let them in or extend them any further credit. The captain flies at the innkeeper with his sword and the poet threatens him with a deadly satire. The noise brings Leander and Crispin to the scene. Crispin takes the side of the poet and soldier, and speaking for the benevolence of his master assures Harlequin and the Captain that they will not want for anything. Crispin pretends to know the sonnets of the poet and the brave deeds of the captain. He insists that the innkeeper give the new guests 50 crowns on Leander's account. The party dines on good food and wine.

Act II. Doña SIRENA, a lady in reduced circumstances, and her young attendant COLUMBINE enter a garden before a fine house. Sirena is in distress; Columbine has just told her that none of the merchants will extend further credit. Sirena is to give a party that evening but the musicians and servants will not attend unless they are paid. Sirena wishes she were still young and could attract wealthy lovers. She reproaches Columbine for wasting time with the ragged Harlequin. Sirena is distressed because the rich merchant Signor POLICHINELLE is coming to her house to dine, with his wife and daughter SILVIA. Some impecunious nobles are also expected and if one can marry Silvia and secure the dowry, Sirena will be well rewarded. Columbine promises that Harlequin will provide the music and the service. Columbine goes to meet her lover in the corner of the garden but finds Crispin. Crispin assures Columbine that the evening party will be brilliantly taken care of if his master, the noble Leander, is invited. He offers a tremendous reward to Sirena if a match between his master and Silvia is arranged.

The party begins; the first guests, Laura and Risela, talk about the arrival in the city of a mysterious personage [Leander], who everyone thinks is an ambassador. Polichinelle comes, with his wife and daughter; he complains that his daughter is too interested in poetry and should think about making a practical marriage to a wealthy merchant. The mother and daughter will settle only for a nobleman. Crispin calls

L-191

Polichinelle aside and identifies himself as one who knows the merchant's criminal past and who was in the galleys with him. Crispin tells Polichinelle to separate his daughter from Leander, as Leander is as much a rogue as he, Crispin. Polichinelle storms into the house, pulling Silvia away from Leander. Later Leander confesses to Crispin his real love for Silvia. Crispin tells Leander that he has made the father oppose the match in order to intensify Silvia's love for Leander and win the mother's support. Silvia slips into the garden and meets Leander. They talk of love as Harlequin plays a song in the background.

Act III. Crispin has started a rumor that Leander was set upon by a dozen ruffians (hired, he implies, by Polichinelle). Silvia leaves her father's house and goes to Sirena's, where she insists she will stay until she has married Leander. Harlequin and the captain spread the false story of Polichinelle's assault. Crispin explains that intelligence, if used to its fullest extent, can win the world.

Sirena comes to the inn and asks Crispin for half of the money promised her. When he refuses, because he hasn't the money, she promises to see that the marriage will be performed before evening. Silvia believes Leander to be badly wounded and comes to the inn. Leander, who really loves Silvia, tells her that he and Crispin are penniless frauds. He wants to give her back to her father, feeling that he is unworthy. Polichinelle arrives with a doctor of law (LAWYER) and a crowd of angry people who have discovered that Leander and Crispin have no money. Leander hides Silvia in a back room, climbs out the window, and leaves Crispin to face the crowd. They are angry creditors roaring for justice. The lawyer insists on writing everything down and slows the proceedings with all the trivia of jurisprudence. Crispin explains that the creditors will be better off letting the marriage take place so that Leander can pay all his debts. If the creditors send Leander and Crispin to the galleys, they will get no money. The crowd agrees that Leander be allowed to marry Silvia. Crispin pulls away the tapestry on the back wall, revealing Silvia, Leander, Sirena, Columbine, and the wife of Polichinelle. Silvia and Leander say that they do not want the dowry money, but will live on pure love. The crowd insists that Polichinelle give them the dowry. Everything settled, Crispin leaves Leander, to go on to other adventures. He plans to become a success in politics. Silvia speaks to the audience, saying that love, among all the passions of man, has dignified the farce and makes us think something eternal remains when the farce of life is over.

Bonjour Tristesse

Novel by Françoise Sagan, 1938–
Published and © 1955 by E. P. Dutton & Co., New York. Translated from the French by Irene Ash.

THE TREMENDOUS INTEREST aroused by this very short novel, and its big sale, can perhaps be attributed chiefly to the interest in its youthful author, who was 16 when she wrote it. Mlle. Sagan is the contemporary and authentic voice of the "beat generation," in her native France affected by existentialism and living in shameless pursuit of thrills, speed in sport cars and rhythm in music. Nevertheless Mlle. Sagan has undoubted genius as a writer. She became the idol of teenage Paris and fulfilled her promise by almost killing herself in a motor accident. John Steinbeck satirized her in passing in his novel *The Short Reign of Pippin IV*.

Part 1. CECILE, spoiled and 17, vacations with her father, RAYMOND, and his mistress, ELSA MACKENBOURG, in a remote, white villa on the Mediterranean. Though cynical about love from the influence of this gay widowed father with his many

Cecile plans to destroy Ann, to restore the old days

affairs, Cecile starts a serious summer flirtation with CYRIL, a young college student. ANN LARSEN, a friend of Cecile's mother, arrives at the invitation of Raymond. She is 40, glamorous, serious, and intelligent, with high standards of good taste and fastidiousness. With good manners she hides her disapproval of the open situation of Elsa and Raymond, treating the mistress with gentleness. It soon becomes apparent that Elsa is no match for Ann's intelligence and refinement and after a drunken scene at the Casino she will not return to the villa, though she and Cecile were always friends in spite of the situation with Raymond. The next morning Ann tells Cecile that she is going to marry her father. An abrupt change comes over their pattern of life. Respectability is now their companion. Ann begins to organize Cecile's days, after catching her in a compromising position with Cyril. Sophisticated beyond her years, Cecile vows to destroy Ann in order to bring back the gaiety of the past two years with her father.

Part 2. Little by little the obsession to part Ann and her father develops in Cecile. She can think of nothing else. Elsa returns to the villa for her clothes and is encouraged by Cecile to think that Raymond is in love with her and is only trapped by Ann. Elsa agrees to Cecile's plan to stay at Cyril's and to pretend to be in love with him. Cyril and Elsa play their parts so well that even Cecile is slightly jealous. Raymond notices how Elsa is glowing and his possessive instinct is aroused. Cecile is so pleased that she is nicer to Cyril than ever before and they become lovers. Step by step the discord to be sown between the engaged couple is planned by the three plotters. A chance meeting is arranged at a bar in the village where Raymond and Ann are entertaining old friends. As Elsa passes, the old friends exclaim at her fresh beauty. Ann is hurt by Raymond's ready agreement to this remark, and Cecile with feelings of guilt praises Ann. As the elaborately planned chance meetings increase, Elsa blooms at the hope of recapturing her ex-lover. Cecile is torn between her desire to accomplish the break between her father and Ann, and a creeping sense of guilt at hurting the one woman she really respects and likes. She knows her father well, that he will be haunted until he gets the new desire for Elsa out of his blood even though he really loves Ann. Fate assumes a strange form. After what he considers successful maneuvering, Raymond finally is alone with

Elsa and embraces and kisses her. Ann accidentally sees them. Uncontrollably hurt, Ann runs for her car; but Cecile, running beside her, confesses her part in the whole mess and begs her not to leave. Ann does not believe Cecile and after a gesture of sincere affection drives off, with tears blinding her eyes. Raymond is frantic when he learns that Ann has left, and he and Cecile write her long, loving letters imploring forgiveness. Momentarily they are soothed, sure of Ann's final acceptance of their real feelings for her; but a telephone message informs them that Ann has met with a serious automobile accident on a treacherous stretch of road. She is dead. Dazed with shock, they return to Paris. Only Cecile realizes that it was no accident but was Ann's way of committing suicide. It does not take long for the fickle, pleasure-loving Raymond and his counterpart, Cecile, to return to their useless gaiety and they go back to their previous life, haunted only for brief moments.

The Book of Snobs

Humorous essays by William Makepeace Thackeray, 1811–1863.
Published serially 1846–47, in book form 1848.

THE BOOK OF SNOBS arose from a single sarcastic essay or sketch that Thackeray wrote for *Punch*. Popular (or at least editorial) demand caused him to expand it into a long series on "Snobs of England." The separate sketches were later called chapters when the whole was collected for publication in book form as *The Book of Snobs*. Thackeray enjoyed writing humor and fancied himself as a humorist but was not so good in the field as he supposed. *The Book of Snobs* is his best humorous writing but is not in a class with his novels.

Chaps. 1–8. History claims great men for great moments and I have been so chosen to write the History of Snobs. Chosen because I know snobs, have an Eye for them, in every class. I am one of them. First I turn my attention to the Manners Snob. Once I was revolted by my dear friend GEORGE MARROWFAT, who ate peas with a knife, a custom that should be reserved to foreign nobility. Then one day I saw him use his fork and I was happy once again to recognize him in polite society. The Snob Royal is a flunkey who admires snobs and has an impressive awe of titles. Snobs Royal are those who pretend to have contact with the nobility, and those who seek contact with the ranks above them. The lords and ladies who pride themselves on their titles and who carry themselves as if the universe were theirs for the mere beckoning are also snobs. They surround themselves with admirers and flatterers and forget that they might achieve something of worth if they tried. They do not feel called upon to show their hand. The ladies preen themselves like peacocks and the gentlemen, like prize stud horses, merely paw the ground. Many of them are feebleminded but hide their paltry wits behind the family crests. A lady of my acquaintance once fell in love with a young lord whom she knew only from hearsay. Being a merchant's daughter she could never meet the object of her affection, but this did not in the least prevent her from pining away in her chamber. She turned down several suitors who admired the affected airs she wore, and scared away several more young men who were unwilling to approach a woman with such advanced aspirations. She is now 45 and her beloved lord has been married twice. She has remained true to her first love, though I understand she is nasty to those who must live with her and she weeps in her room all the time. It is amazing how many people imagining themselves to be grand will stand in the rain to watch a duke's marriage and later his funeral. Merit, of course, has little to do with the matter. What a temptation to cringe we all have, and how we practice lordolatry. We are either arrogant or mean according to our fortune. A lord may be an ass and yet be respected. Excuses will be found for him. The piously respectable are also snobs. They think the church will fall if they fail to attend. These self-righteous snobs give to the poor and look down on those who don't. They talk about social matters as if without their attention the world would stop. They find all kinds of outrages everywhere but continue to live in comfort and style. They feel superior because of their goodness and use the word sin frequently when talking about others. They are close to the reverend and give, if not generously, conspicuously to his various projects.

Chaps. 9–17. We must not omit the Snob Clerical from our attention. Some members of this category are only as bad as everyone else. But others grow rich and fat on a sense of self-importance. One of the commonest clerical vices is leaving the service of ordinary folk at the bid of royalty. I know a parson once who left a wedding party and the young people standing hours by an altar waiting for him to complete the ceremony while he comforted a duke who had suffered a mild attack of gout. The clergy like to attend the mighty and often refer to their ministrations in the next week's sermon. I admit that I would jump out of my skin if two dukes would walk down Pall Mall with me. But nevertheless I think such temptations should be removed from the clergy. Among the Clerical Snobs the University Snob must be remembered. Universities are the last places to be reached by reform. Class distinctions according to wealth are as blatant as in feudal times. Students who are on scholarship are forced to wear garments of a certain color and eat together, apart from the more fortunate of their contemporaries. This makes matters more convenient for the student who wishes to make important contacts during his academic years. He can see at a glance whom to avoid. Among students there are Drinking Snobs, Dressing Snobs, Philosophical Snobs, and those who go to "rack and ruin aping their betters." University dons are a most remarkable type of snob. These gentlemen, who should be devoted to the various branches of learning, are in fact more involved in their petty powers. I have myself seen a don keep nine students standing in his elaborately comfortable study while he himself relaxed and smoked in a large chair. This he did not to teach the students manners, but to exercise the full power of his position. I have also known University Snobs who will curry favor with their noble pupils and be totally indifferent even to the most intelligent of the lowerborn. They will spend hours in the evening writing to the parents of their noble charges and attempt to gain their permission for an interview with these people, whom the dons respect despite the fact that their learning may be as negligible as their interest in their offspring.

Chaps. 18–26. As the Season draws to a close a great many Social Snobs have left London. The Party-giving Snobs are those who give parties in order to be invited in return. Dining-out Snobs are those who pretend to be richer and grander than they are. It is appalling how all the honesty of society is tainted by fashion-worship. Another form of snob is the Nationality Snob. Who has not sensed that calm British confidence that the British are the absolute center of the world? One of the dullest creatures under heaven, the Englishman, goes to every city of Europe being snobbish about what he sees. When he goes into churches in Italy he thinks about how superior his altar is to theirs. He looks down on the foreign religion without noticing its beautiful surroundings. He finds the food bad and the people dirty, though he cannot speak their language. He finds the trains and boats inferior and forgets the inconveniences of his native transportation. In the museums he says he prefers the painting over his own fireplace. His tastes for the new are dulled by his inordinate pride in his own.

Chaps. 27–35. In the country the situation is the same. I paid a visit to some country friends and found them eager for some news of the royalty. Guests would arrive in carriages, bearing their family colors. Everyone pretended connections in high places. Snobbishness is at war with love and human kindness and ruins many marriages. So many lives are spent in loneliness because of quarrels over a dowry. Bachelors rot in singleness and spinster women dry up like lemon peels, because the snob-walls prevent them from reaching each other.

Chaps. 36–43. In the final chapters we malign the Club Snobs. Clubs provide shelter for the moneyed, yet there are some clubs where no one speaks to anyone else. Club members are grave and concise in their speech. Their manner is weary. This is the Englishman relaxing. Actually the only men who belong in clubs are married men who have no profession or occupation. They are a nuisance to have around the house. The children want to practice their music. The chambermaid must clean and the wife wants to entertain. This sort of man belongs in the club, where he can waste his time at cards and conversation without really being in anyone's way. Other club members are all snobs of one sort or another. They will brag about their exploits with women, even repeating glorious details that never happened. They will boast of their boyhood pranks or military exploits, which also have a fictional basis. They will collect odd leather boxes or buttons from foreign lands and feel themselves distinguished because of their exclusive good taste. Without their clubs they would feel lost in the social structure, but with them they feel bloated with importance and immediately let strangers know how valuable they are by mentioning the names of their clubs. Wiggle and Waggle are two types of men found in the clubs. They like second-rate pleasures and fourth-rate women. They drop names of people and places. They are not precisely rogues, but see if they won't marry a fortune, ugly and old as she may be. Bacchus is the divinity whom they worship. Wine-amateurship is the distinctive mark of the Club Snob. It is next in boringness to food-amateurship. Captain Shindy has been known to destroy everyone's evening, creating a tremendous scene over a mutton chop. At the club he has ten servants to attend him while poor Mrs. Shindy and the six children are waiting in dingy lodgings for the wash to dry. Snobs despise their neighbors while they themselves lead small lives, following those that appear to have attained a higher degree. "Those who are proud of their pedigree and their wealth, they are the Snobs that Mr. Punch will laugh at. Hitting no foul blow, with his broadest grin, he will never forget that fun is good, truth is still better, and love best of all."

Boris Godunov

Play by Aleksandr Pushkin, 1799–1837. Published 1831 (written 1825). Various translations from the Russian; translation by Alfred Hayes © 1936 by Random House, New York.

WHEN PUSHKIN WROTE *Boris Godunov* in 1825 he was living under police surveillance, suspected of atheism. Pushkin is called the Russian Byron (because he was a contemporary of Byron's, was of similarly aristocratic birth, had similar poetic talent, and died similarly untimely) and he was influenced by Byron, but in this "dramatic poem" he was influenced chiefly by Shakespeare. *Boris* is based on events of the years 1598–1605 and is semi-historical. Its publication was delayed for six years after Pushkin wrote it and it was not performed on the stage until 35 years after his death in 1837. Then it was unsuccessful as a play. Nevertheless it proved to be the Pushkin work that brought him his most lasting international fame, because of the Moussorgsky opera based on it.

Palace of the Kremlin. Prince SHUISKY and Prince VOROTYNSKY discuss the treachery of privy councillor BORIS GODUNOV, who schemes to usurp the throne after having secretly contrived the assassination of Czarevitch DIMITRI, son and heir of Ivan the Terrible. Shuisky tells how the actual assassins were caught and killed by a mob,

BORIS GODUNOV

Waiting for news at the Kremlin

without any suspicion involving Boris. Laconically sly, Shuisky admits he parroted Boris Godunov's version of the murder, which he had been sent by Boris to investigate. Just between themselves, Shuisky and Vorotynsky contend that the succession to the throne should not go to Boris but to a member of their own family, the Ruriks.

The Red Square. SHCHELKALOV, secretary of the Council of Boyars, announces to the Moscow populace that the Patriarch of the Russian Orthodox Church will petition the widowed Czarina to have the crown rulership bestowed upon Boris Godunov.

The Maiden Field. Peasants and people of Moscow kneel in crowds as they wait anxiously for news that Boris has accepted the crown.

The Kremlin Palace. With a solemnly hypocritical display of humility and hesitation, Boris accepts the crown. The Boyar nobles pledge allegiance to him. Shuisky and Vorotynsky agree surreptitiously not to denounce Boris until a safer opportunity occurs.

Cell in the Chudov Monastery. An aged monk, Father PIMEN, is writing an historical account of Russia's contemporary troubles. GRIGORY OTREPYEV, a young monk who sleeps in the same cell with Pimen, is disturbed by dreams of grandeur. Grigory dreams he is looking down over the whole city of Moscow from the top of a great stairway. Old Pimen tells Grigory that worldly power is an illusion not worth considering. Grigory discounts this, saying Pimen is merely tired of life from having had his fill of it when he was young and a soldier.

Beside the Monastery Wall. A wicked monk intrigues Grigory with the idea that Grigory could pretend to be Dimitri, the murdered czarevitch, because Grigory and Dimitri were the same age. Grigory is tempted.

Palace of the Patriarch. The abbot of the Chudov Monastery informs the Patriarch of the Russian Church that Grigory has run away. At the Patriarch's demand, the abbot recites Grigory's family history and tells of Grigory's claim to the identity of the Czarevitch. The Patriarch calls Grigory a tool of the devil and will have his iniquity reported to the political police.

Palace of the Czar. Two courtiers are commenting on the curious extent to which Boris has fallen under the influence of magicians and fortune-tellers since he acquired the crown. Boris delivers a bitter soliloquy

BORIS GODUNOV

Maryna is ambitious

expressing the disappointments of his reign as czar, his fears, and his constant pangs of guilty conscience.

Tavern on the Lithuanian Frontier. Grigory is here on his way to seek Lithuanian support for his claim to the throne of Russia. He is traveling with two beggar monks, disguised as their companion. But Boris has discovered Grigory's rôle as an impostor and has sent agents to arrest him. At dagger's point Grigory escapes from the czar's officers, who try to seize him in the tavern.

Moscow—Shuisky's House. AFANASY PUSHKIN tells Shuisky there is news from Cracow that Czarevitch Dimitri, son of Ivan the Terrible, was not actually assassinated but is alive. Pushkin and Shuisky, both enemies of Boris, determine to support the new Dimitri, even if he is an impostor.

Palace of the Czar. Having been informed by his spies of the news given to Shuisky by Pushkin, Boris doubts Shuisky's loyalty and questions him as to the identity of the pretender. Boris reminds Shuisky that it was he whom Boris had sent to investigate the murder of the genuine Dimitri. Shuisky is under suspicion. Boris is gravely alarmed.

Cracow, House of Wisniowiecki. Grigory wins strong support from Polish nobles who hate the Muscovites, and from Russian foes of Boris. A Jesuit priest, Father CZERNIKOWSKI, also joins Grigory's conspiracy, offering to bring the influence of Rome to bear on behalf of the pretender. Grigory plans to march against Moscow at the head of a rebel army, menacing Boris with downfall and death.

Castle of Governor Mniszech in Sambor. MARYNA, daughter of Governor MNISZECH, is urged by her lady's maid to encourage the ardor of Grigory, who has fallen in love with Maryna. The possibility of becoming empress of Russia inflames Maryna's imagination.

Another Room in the Sambor Castle. The governor expresses gratification at seeing Grigory infatuated by his daughter.

Night. The Garden. The Fountain. In this romantic setting Maryna asks Grigory pointblank whether he really is Czarevitch Dimitri or merely an unfrocked monk pretending to be Dimitri, as she had heard rumored. The lovesick Grigory confesses his true origin to Maryna, whereupon she arrogantly refuses to consider his plebeian bid for her noble hand in marriage. She threatens to denounce him. He retaliates by insisting that he will be czar, then threatens to punish her for her disloyalty when he comes into power. His forcefulness impresses her. She promises to be his wife despite his lowly birth. She urges him not to delay his military campaign against Boris. Grigory declares he will march his men to war at daybreak.

The Lithuanian Frontier. Leading his rebel troops across the border into Russia, Grigory, the pretender, voices patriotic regret for the necessity of using foreigners to fight Russians.

The Council of the Czar. In Moscow, menaced by the rebellion, Boris asks the Patriarch what can be done. The Patriarch tells him that Dimitri's tomb has become a shrine of miracle-healing for the sick, the lame, and the blind, so the Patriarch advises Boris to have Dimitri's remains brought to the Kremlin for the performance of a public miracle. This would prove to the populace that Dimitri is dead and that Grigory is an impostor. Boris refuses to mix religion with politics; he declares he trusts the people to reject Grigory when they learn the truth directly from Boris himslf.

A Plain near Novgorod-Seversk. Foreign officers serving Boris discuss the trend of the fighting. They speak in French and German as well as in Russian. They praise the military talent of BASMANOV, one of Boris's generals.

Square in Front of the Moscow Cathedral. A street crowd waits to see Boris come from a requiem mass being offered in the cathedral in memory of the murdered Dimitri. When Boris appears, an idiot boy calls him "Herod," accusing him of having had Dimitri assassinated. Boris prevents his retinue of nobles from arresting the idiot.

Sevsk. Questioning a prisoner, Grigory learns that Basmanov has been made a member of the Czar's council and that Boris now has an army of 50,000 troops in the field against Grigory's 15,000.

A Forest. Grigory admits he is losing his last battle. He upbraids his Cossack followers for their inferior fighting and praises the German troops in the army of Boris. Afanasy Pushkin declares that Grigory's cause is not yet lost.

Moscow, Palace of the Czar. Boris gives supreme command of his army to Basmanov, remarking that brains are worth more than noble birth in a soldier, for Basmanov is of plebeian origin. Basmanov declares he has no sympathy for court intrigues, nor for the wavering sentiments of the populace. Boris goes to receive a delegation of foreign merchants. Soon after he leaves the room there is an outcry that he has been mortally stricken by a sudden illness and is bleeding to death from the mouth and ears. Boris, dying, is carried in on a chair. He names his son, FEODOR, to succeed him as czar, instructing Feodor to retain Basmanov as chief commander of the army and to observe all the traditional dignities of the court and the church. The Patriarch and prelates administer last rites to Boris Godunov as he dies.

Army Headquarters. Afanasy Pushkin, supporter of Grigory the pretender, makes a political bargain with Basmanov, persuading Basmanov to help put Grigory on the throne instead of Feodor. Basmanov hesitates, but finally agrees when convinced that Feodor's succession would be hopelessly defeated by popular acclaim for Grigory, because Grigory represents himself under the great, honored name of Dimitri. Basmanov proclaims his decision to lead the army in favor of Grigory.

Place of Execution, Red Square, Moscow. Afanasy Pushkin, in a public address to the townspeople of Moscow, denounces the harsh rule of Boris and makes an eloquent appeal for the acceptance of Grigory. The mob roars approval. Riotous peasants shout their determination to invade the Kremlin and kill Feodor. They yell, "Crush the race of Godunov!"

The Kremlin, House of Boris. Guards on the steps try to turn the mob back. Feodor is seen looking out through a window. From the crowd a few voices pity him but they are howled down. The Boyar nobles force their way past the guards. It is said they will make Feodor swear allegiance to Grigory, the false Dimitri. Screams are then heard from inside the house. A Boyar nobleman opens the door and announces that Feodor and the queen have committed suicide by taking poison. The Boyar says he has seen their dead bodies. He urges the mob to acclaim Dimitri, meaning Grigory. But the people stand silent, shocked speechless.

The Bostonians

Novel by Henry James, 1843–1916. Published 1886. (ML, 16)

THE BOSTONIANS is a novel of James's "middle period." He was in the realm of high society as usual, this time in the very starched Boston of the late 19th century. The novel was not successful when published and James was very unhappy. Among other things, it was considered wicked. Perhaps it was and still is, but it is among his most important works.

Chaps. 1–3. Miss OLIVE CHANCELLOR, an active feminist, dines in her fashionable Boston home with her cousin BASIL RANSOM. This is the first time they have met and mutual interest grows with mutual dislike. Olive, a tragic, morbid figure, broods on the sufferings of women; she longs to die for some ideal, so intensely does she find opposition to the world pleasurable. Basil, a handsome young man, has left the ruins of his Southern aristocratic family and settled in New York to make his fortune as a lawyer. Basil loves the Southern tradition and seeks everywhere a counterpart to the grace and order he knew as a child on his family's plantation. He also has the good sense to see that the South as he knew it is dead, and that he must go on to new challenges. Olive feels aggressive and angry in the presence of any man but finds Basil's indifference to the crimes against womanhood particularly unpleasant. Basil meets Olive's visiting sister, the flirtatious Mrs. LUNA, who is despised by the ascetic Olive. Mrs. Luna is struggling into a long pair of gloves and prepares to leave for a party. She loves the underprivileged position of women and thinks it is all very just. She criticizes Olive's hideous black bonnet and simple black dress. Olive decides to try to convince Basil of her side of the feminist issue and takes him to a suffragette meeting, especially to meet the famous feminist Miss BIRDSEYE and Mrs. FARRINDER. He goes out of curiosity and an amiable willingness to let life show him.

Chaps. 4–9. At the meeting Basil finds hundreds of black-bonneted women, most of them very unattractive, and their conversation seems humorless and silly, for to the end they take their agitations seriously. Basil does meet a wonderful woman doctor who is taciturn and cross because she believes women should do what they want, but not talk about it like hens in the coop. At the meeting, with her parents, is pretty, red-haired young VERENA TARRANT. Mrs. Farrinder, the expected speaker, refuses out of temperament to address the waiting audience. She says she has too much humility to speak before her sisters. After a disappointed silence, Verena is asked to speak. She claims to pronounce on vital issues only by means of another voice entering her body; everyone in the room must be very silent and she needs her father, a Mesmeric healer, to bring the spirits to her. After this mystic preamble she speaks on women's rights with purity and imagination. She still has a child's innocence when she reproves the terrible adult world. Ransom is enchanted by her manner and Olive is overwhelmed by the girl's eloquence and charm. Olive invites Verena to visit her and speaks to her parents, urging them to send Verena to her. The Tarrants have made money on all the mystic frauds, from séances to fortune-telling, but they are socially ambitious for their daughter and insist that she visit Olive on the very next day.

Chaps. 10–15. Olive, whose mind has become obsessed by Verena, greets the girl with open arms and insists that she devote her gift with words permanently to the feminist cause. She demands that Verena come to visit often and indicates that she wants to take the girl over and make her into a private possession. In the midst of this strange, subdued yet frightening conversation, Ransom enters. Again he is delighted with Verena, but Olive's cold reception and obvious dislike of his company forces him to leave. His business in Boston over, he returns to New York; but

L-200

he keeps Verena's image in his mind during the following months. Verena soon falls under the spell of the somber woman. She reads Olive's books, imbibes her ideas, and learns all of Olive's prejudices. Later, at the insistence of her parents, she invites Olive to take tea at her house. Verena seems to enjoy the company of some young men also at the tea, which produces a panic in Olive that blinds her to all else. As Olive leaves the tea she calls Verena out to the porch and standing in the snow tries to elicit a promise from Verena never to marry. The girl is very anxious to please her patroness but is frightened by the intensity of the request. She cannot really promise so great a thing. Olive rides home slumped in her carriage, for the first time afraid of some great grief that lies in her future. The next day Verena, seeing how tortured her friend is, gives the desired promise. As proof of her loyalty, Verena immediately turns down a journalist who wished to be her husband and to make money by taking her on lecture tours all through the country.

Chaps. 16–19. Verena and Olive continue to see each other constantly. Olive takes Verena to several feminist meetings and has her speak to the public. Verena gradually attains a reputation in Boston and a certain sort of fame follows. Verena develops a friendship with a Harvard student, **HENRY BURRAGE**. Henry is an amiable dilettante who simply wants to enjoy life in the manner of his New York social family. He has been captivated by a certain charm of Verena's and has proposed marriage. Verena takes Olive to tea with Henry at Harvard in hopes that Olive will approve of Henry and release her from her promise. Mrs. **BURRAGE**, Henry's mother, is also at the tea and she turns out to be very sympathetic to the feminist cause. Despite this, Olive suffers in the company and tells Verena that Henry is worth nothing and merely wants to exploit her, as do all men with their women. Verena acquiesces and breaks off her relationship with Henry, but she wishes that Olive did not always force her to think of the evilness in men. Out of affection for Olive she follows her completely in all her arguments and agrees to devote her own life to an oratorical career.

Chaps. 20–24. The winter season in New York goes badly for Basil. He has not succeeded as a lawyer and is living in rather extreme poverty. Besides that, he has grown to doubt his own ability to master the world. He has been plagued by Mrs. Luna, who first hired him as a tutor for her incorrigible son and then began to flirt with him in an embarrassing way. In Boston, Olive

Verena is frightened as Olive rides home alone

writes out a large check to Dr. Tarrant, who then permits Verena to live with Olive in her big house. The Tarrants are the kind of people who will let Verena go if they are paid. Henry Burrage refuses to take no for an answer; he comes to Olive's house one day and repeats his proposal. Verena again turns him down but Olive becomes frightened that his persistence will win Verena over. She decides to take Verena to Europe for several months. In Europe they visit feminist meetings and Verena gives speeches that are well attended and well received. At the end of this time Basil pays a long-overdue visit to Mrs. Luna and he learns that Olive and Verena have come back to Boston. His enthusiasm for life is rekindled as he thinks of Verena and he determines to go to see her. Mrs. Luna becomes jealous of his interest in Verena and warns him that Olive will never let him near her friend.

Chaps. 25–32. Basil goes to Boston on business and spends many hours searching for Verena. He finds her when he visits her parents and induces her to go walking with him. They argue; she tries to convince him of the justice of the feminist cause and he tries to explain to her his concept of the woman as a thing of grace and beauty that supports a man in all his efforts and bears him children to continue his love. These are all arguments Olive has taught Verena to despise and she tries to tell Basil that they have nothing to share and will never agree on the important things. But he feels differently. He is certain Verena really wants to believe in what he is saying and he tells her that he will stay near her for as long as she will allow him the honor. Verena becomes frightened of Basil as the conversation grows obliquely personal. She leaves him quickly, but unknown to Olive she sends him an invitation to a lecture to be given at Mrs. Burrage's party in New York some weeks later. At the party, despite Olive's entreaties, Basil seeks out Verena. However, the girl becomes really frightened by his threat to her way of life and promises Olive to remain with her forever.

Chaps. 33–40. But the next day Verena goes out with Basil. He tells her he wishes to save his own sex, to bring back order and grace into the world. Verena leaves New York and goes to the country. Basil follows her there and proposes marriage. He has just published an article and he feels encouraged. He believes his future will be brilliant if Verena will just aid him in his work. She has fallen in love with him and finds his plans of more interest than her feminist duties. But again she runs away from him because of Olive and the life to which she has already been committed.

Chaps. 41–42. Basil hears that Verena is again in Boston, where she is about to give an important lecture to a large audience. Basil comes to the stage door and Verena, sensing that he is there, refuses to begin her lecture. At last he convinces a policeman, posted by Olive, to let him through. Basil and Verena leave the hall together. Olive remains behind, suffering deeply as she faces the silent and disappointed crowd.

Basil finds a large crowd assembled for Verena's lecture

The Bourgeois Gentleman

Play by Molière, 1622–1673.
Produced 1670. (ML, 78)

THIS IS ONE OF Molière's two or three most popular plays with American readers. There are many translations and it is the title that has given the translators the most trouble. Among the efforts are "The Citizen-Gentleman," "The Middle-Class Gentleman," "The Citizen Who Would Be a Lord," and "The Citizen Who Apes the Nobleman." The last is perhaps most accurate, for Jourdain was not a gentleman, did not become one, and hardly aspired to become one; he merely wanted to associate with "the quality," act like them, and be thought one of them—not necessarily by them, but by others. His failures make a broad farce. In Molière's time was just beginning the 200-year process by which the rich middle classes pulled up to terms of equality with the gentry. In the first performances Molière himself played the part of M. Jourdain.

Act. I. 1. In the living room of Monsieur JOURDAIN, the MUSIC-MASTER and DANCING-MASTER discuss their services to Jourdain. The dancing-master is dissatisfied to work for a man who has no knowledge or appreciation of their arts, but the music-master finds that the large fees they collect are ample reward and the dancing-master agrees at least partly. 2. Jourdain enters, preening himself in a dressing-gown that his tailor has told him is a must for all men of quality. The two masters discuss with him the significance of music and dancing in life and current affairs and finally convince him that, to really be a man of the world, he must learn both. The act ends with a composition sung by a trio, followed by a ballet.
Act II. 1. Jourdain asks the two masters to prepare musical festivities for the afternoon, as he is entertaining a person of quality. Then he executes a few dance steps he has been learning and has the dancing master show him how to bow to a marquise because he expects one, DORIMÈNE, that afternoon. 2–3. The FENCING-MASTER arrives and Jourdain goes through some exercises after which the fencing-master gets into a dispute with the other two masters: He contends that fencing is far superior to dancing and music. The masters of fencing and dancing then insult each other violently. Jourdain tries to separate them. 4. A PHILOSOPHER whom Jourdain has hired to teach him logic enters and is asked by Jourdain to settle the dispute. The philosopher tries to reason but finds himself in the fight when the others all insist that their professions are more important than his. Despite Jourdain's pleas, they continue fighting and exit fighting. 5–6. The philosopher returns and prepares for the lesson. Jourdain wants none of logic, ethics, or physics, not understanding them; he wishes to be taught spelling. The philosopher tells him about the five vowels and demonstrates carefully how each is made, much to Jourdain's surprise and excitement. Then Jourdain asks to be taught how to compose a love letter. When told he must choose either prose or verse, he is amazed; he is then completely overcome when he learns that he has been speaking prose all his life. After a brief discussion of the love letter itself, the philosopher leaves. 7–9. Jourdain's MASTER TAILOR enters with a suit that has just been made for Jourdain. With orchestral accompaniment, which is how persons of quality do it, Jourdain is dressed in his new suit. To flatter Jourdain into tipping, the tailor and his men address him as Noble Sir, My Lord, and Your Grace, after each of which he is so overcome that he tips heavily, almost depleting his purse. The ballet at the end of this act consists of dancing while Jourdain is being dressed and then more dancing by way of rejoicing over his liberality.
Act III. 1–3. Jourdain, the maid, NICOLE, and Mme. JOURDAIN engage in a lengthy argument about his behavior in recent

M. Jourdain explains

weeks. He is outraged when both women ridicule his new suit and he explains that it is necessary to impress persons of quality. Mme. Jourdain states that he should be more concerned about getting his daughter LUCILE married but he insists that what he is doing is more important. He explains his discovery that he has been speaking prose all his life and with the fencing foils he tries to show Nicole that he is learning how not to be killed, but she bests him in a practice duel. Mme. Jourdain is mostly annoyed by his extravagant loans to Count DORANTE, who gives nothing in return. Jourdain explains that it is a very great honor to know the count and have him for a friend. 4–9. Dorante enters and, after flattering Jourdain, asks for more money. As Jourdain leaves to get it, Dorante tries without success to have a friendly conversation with Mme. Jourdain. Jourdain returns with the money and Dorante whispers to him that he has finally persuaded the Marquise Dorimène to accept Jourdain's gift and invitation to his house. Nicole overhears some of their conversation and reports to Mme. Jourdain, who lets it pass because she is more anxious about getting her daughter married. Mme. Jourdain dispatches Nicole to tell CLEONTE, who has been interested in Lucile, that she is ready to discuss marriage plans. Nicole gives Cleonte and his valet COVIELLE, who incidentally is interested in Nicole, her mistress's good news. But they are unfriendly toward Nicole and she leaves to tell Lucile. Their pride is hurt because they suspect that over the last few days both young women have been shunning them; Lucile snubbed Cleonte that morning. Cleonte suspects that Lucile is interested in Dorante, who has been visiting the Jourdains so often. 10–11. Lucile and Nicole come back together to try to discover what has so angered the two young men. The men still refuse to speak. In their turn, the women refuse to continue asking, at which the young men begin pleading with them to explain. Finally, Lucile explains that Cleonte was snubbed that morning because an old aunt was visiting who has very strict ideas about young ladies' speaking to men. Mme. Jourdain arrives to tell Cleonte that Jourdain is coming and he should ask for Lucile's hand. Jourdain enters and refuses to give his daughter to Cleonte because he must have a nobleman for a son-in-law. Mme. Jourdain is furious at his pose and, after he is gone, tells Cleonte not to be discouraged. Once alone, the two young men ponder Cleonte's problem and Coville gets an idea, which involves a masquerade (imposture) that might work. 15–21. Dorante arrives at Jourdain's, escorting Dorimène. Their conversation quickly reveals that Cleonte himself is courting Dorimène, giving her in his own name the gifts that Jourdain has been sending her. They greet Jourdain, who impresses Dorimène as a fool. Then they go in to dinner, which is introduced by an interlude ballet of the six cooks.

Act IV. 1–4. The dinner begins, with Dorante trying to hide from Jourdain the fact that Dorimène is not in the least interested in him (Jourdain). Three musicians with orchestra sing a drinking song, after which Dorante tries to quell Jourdain's ardor for the unsuspecting Dorimène. Mme. Jourdain arrives in a jealous rage and Jourdain is grateful to Dorante for explaining that the lady is not interested in Jourdain. But Mme. Jourdain insults Dorimène and the two guests leave. After a brief dispute Mme. Jourdain also leaves. 5–13. Coville, in disguise, comes in to tell Jourdain that he knew his father, who was a gentleman. Amazed and delighted, Jourdain is set up for further deception; namely, Covielle's report that the Grand Turk's son wants to marry Lucile and is arriving. Cleonte, disguised as a Turk, arrives, babbling incoherently in what Jourdain believes to be Turkish and which Covielle translates as the highest compliments. Dorante arrives and Covielle tells him privately about the masquerade. Jourdain undergoes a comic ceremony that makes him a "Mamamouchi," a fictitious Turkish title. This is part of the ballet, danced by Turks.

Act V. 1–7. Mme Jourdain enters and is stupified by the spectacle confronting her. Completely taken in by the rigamarole, Jourdain explains to her that he is a Mamamouchi and goes on babbling incoherently, which convinces her that he is mad. He leaves, followed shortly afterward by his distraught wife, discussing the absurdity of Jourdain's position. Dorimène decides to marry Dorante. Lucile arrives and, recognizing the "Grand Turk's son" as Cleonte, accepts her father's order to marry him. Mme. Jourdain refuses to allow her daughter to marry a Turk, but after Covielle explains the ruse, she consents. Jourdain, learning of Dorante's intent to marry Dorimène, is pleased because he believes it is being done to hide his own great love for the woman from his wife. Jourdain gives Nicole's hand to the "Dragoman" (Covielle). The final curtain falls with the company waiting for the notary who is to perform the double ceremony. An extravagant ballet ends the play.

Box and Cox

Play by John Maddison Morton, 1811–1891.
Produced 1847.

CHIEFLY, THIS FARCE deserves its immortality because it is a classic idea. It is not, however, merely a dramatic idea. Lodging houses in industrial cities—in the U.S., notably Pittsburgh—used to rent rooms in sleeping shifts, two or three each twenty-four hours, when the steel mills were busy. The idea made a musical show for Sir Arthur Sullivan in 1867; there the title was *Cox and Box*. The librettist was not Gilbert but Francis Burnand. It is very short and is usually produced in a double bill with a short Gilbert and Sullivan operetta.

Act. I. Cox, preparing to go to work one morning, is complaining aloud that his hair has been cut too short when Mrs. BOUNCER, the landlady, enters. Cox complains to her that his candles and coals are being pilfered and his room smells of tobacco. Mrs. Bouncer answers that the gentleman upstairs smokes a pipe and the smoke must come down the chimney to Cox's room. Cox is skeptical, but leaves for his job (he is a hatter). The landlady has actually rented the same room to a Mr. BOX, who has a night job on a newspaper. The landlady is thus receiving double rent. She is busy rearranging the room for her daytime guest when Box enters. He responds angrily to her suggestion that he should not smoke. He, too, finds his candles missing and complains. He puts some bacon on the fire. Then, still wondering about the mystery, he falls asleep. Cox returns because the owner of his shop has given him a holiday. He finds the fire going and the bacon cooking. Surprised, he puts his mutton chop on the grid and goes out for some rolls. Box wakes and throws Cox's chop out the window. Cox reënters and they confront each other with loud threats. Mrs. Bouncer comes in and explains the duplicity, promising another room for the following day. In the meantime Box and Cox begin a conversation. Cox admits that he has a fiancée who operates bathing machines at a resort. Box confesses that he was friendly with a young widow who wished to marry him and he, to avoid this drastic end, pretended to drown, leaving his clothes and a suicide note on the shore. It turns out that the same woman who chased Box is now pursuing Cox. Cox tries to make Box go back to the woman, PENELOPE ANN, so that he himself can slip out of their arrangement. They argue and call for pistols. Deciding that dueling is too dangerous they play at dice and then toss coins. The loser will have to take Penelope Ann. They both cheat and argue until Mrs. Bouncer brings in a letter saying that Penelope has drowned and wills her estate to her intended. Now Box and Cox, reversing themselves, argue over which of them is the heir. But another letter is delivered saying that Penelope is well and will arrive soon. Box and Cox now revert to their previous attitudes and both try to escape till they find out that Penelope has decided to marry a third party named Knox. This resolves the difference between Box and Cox and they decide they are long-lost brothers. They will continue to share the room.

Brave New World

Novel by Aldous Huxley, 1894–1963. Published 1932 by Harper & Bros., New York. © 1932 by Aldous Huxley. (ML, 48; Ban., AC1)

MIRANDA SAID IT, in *The Tempest:* "How beauteous mankind is! O brave new world, that has such people in it!" She was speaking ironically, so her words were an apt title for Huxley's satirical Utopia. In a 1946 Foreword to a new printing, Huxley apologizes for not foreseeing the atomic age (as he might have; Wells did, before the turn of the century). But no one ever said *Brave New World* is good science fiction. It is enough to be good satire.

Chaps. 1–2. In the year 632 A.F. (After Ford) the D.H.C., or Director of Hatcheries and Conditioning, shows a group of students through the small (34-story) building. All human beings are hatched in bottles. The lower orders (Gammas, Deltas, and Epsilons) are made as much alike as possible by the Bokanovsky process of splitting eggs to create as many as 96 identical-twin types. The Alphas and Betas are bred as individuals. The castes are carefully conditioned so that Alphas will have great intelligence, graded down to Epsilons of low intelligence to do the menial work. The highest are Alpha-Plus. Neo-Pavlovian conditioning trains the lower castes to dislike books, the beauty of nature, etc., but to consume manufactured goods and keep the economy going. While the children sleep they are conditioned by *hypnopaedia*, subliminal messages that among other effects make each caste contented with its station. "Mother" has become a very obscene word, "parent" and "father" only slightly less so. "Ford" is the god, used even in mild oaths such as "My Ford!"

Chap. 3. His fordship Mustapha Mond, Resident Controller for Western Europe, is in the garden where the children amuse themselves with sex play. He benignly talks to the students about ancient times when Ford and Shaw were on earth. In the Alpha Girls' Dressing Room LENINA CROWNE, a nurse, shocks her friend FANNY CROWNE (no relation, but there are only 600 surnames on earth) because she, Lenina, is going out again with HENRY FOSTER; she has seen almost no one else for months, which outrages the dogma that "Everyone belongs to everyone else" and that men and women both should be as promiscuous as possible. Lenina partly excuses herself by saying she is considering a trip with BERNARD MARX, who is Alpha but unseemingly short and also, more or less secretly, sensitive about the blatant promiscuity around him. The great entertainment medium of the age is the "feelies," which are like the movies or talkies except that the spectators grasp knobs and feel every sensation portrayed on the screen.

Chap. 4. Bernard visits his friend HELMHOLTZ, one of the few men with whom he feels comfortable because Helmholtz, a writer, also disapproves of some of the dogmatic rules of living.

Chap. 5. 1. Foster and Lenina fly (everyone flies everywhere) to the standardized fun of dining and dancing, then go to bed together. 2. Bernard attends a meeting of a singing group to which he belongs, and after the singing beds conventionally with one of the girls, but finds little enjoyment in it.

Chap. 6. 1. Bernard has a preliminary date with Lenina, who talks only in clichés reflecting her conditioning and is at ease only when he brings himself to become conventionally amorous. 2. The Director calls Bernard in; when he hears that Bernard is taking a girl to the New Mexican Reservation where the Indians still live as in prehistoric times, the Director reminisces a bit about a trip he took there once with a Beta-Minus girl, who got lost and whom he left there; then warns Bernard about the reports he has been hearing of Bernard's unconventional behavior. 3. Bernard and Lenina fly to Santa Fe (6½ hours from London). In the Reservation are about 60,000 savages and half-breeds, retaining all the old customs: marriage, families, Christianity, totemism, extinct languages, wild beasts, infectious diseases, priests, and no air-conditioning.

Chaps. 7–9. In the Reservation Bernard and Lenina see a [Hopi] Indian snake dance where a young man is whipped, and they meet JOHN, a young white man who to their amazement wishes he had been the young man in the ceremony and also knows much from the civilized world though he has been brought up as an Indian. Bernard learns that John's mother, LINDA, was lost in the Reservation long ago (and undoubtedly was the Director's girl, making the Director John's father). Linda taught him much, but also he learned much of the Indian and Christian philosophy. Lenina, on their return to Santa Fe, loses herself in the pleasant sleep induced by the drug *soma*. Bernard calls the Controller and is authorized to bring back John and Linda for scientific study. John, wandering into the room where Lenina is sleeping, falls in love with her.

Chaps. 10–13. When Bernard returns he is in disgrace with the Director and slated

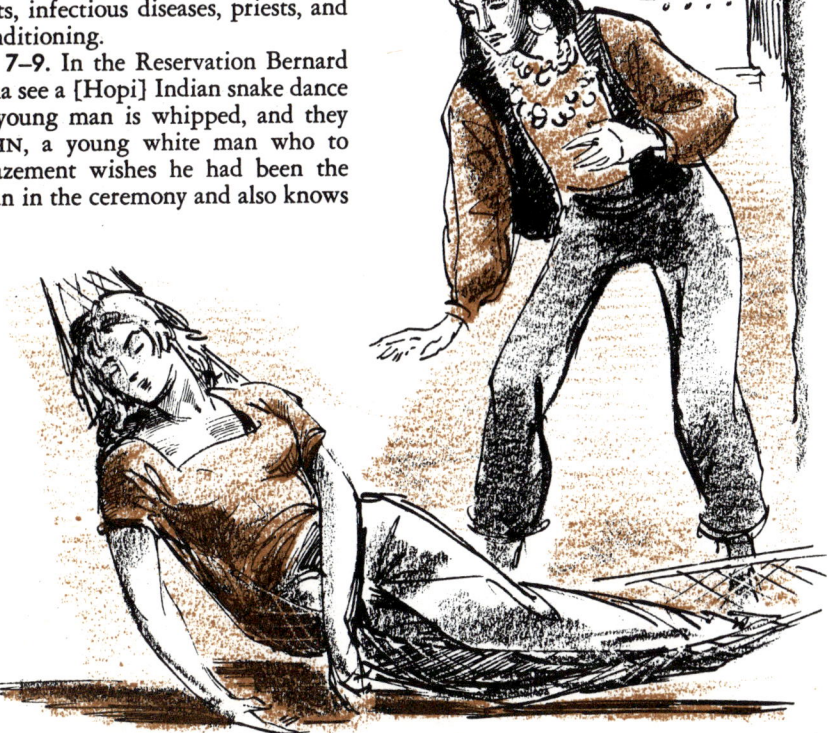

John sees Lenina asleep and falls in love with her

for a post on a remote island, but he turns the tables and makes the Director a laughingstock by bringing in John, who emotionally greets the Director as "Father." John then becomes the lionized curiosity of the entire civilized world and Bernard and Lenina (separately) are important personages by reason of the reflected glory. All the important people want to attend their parties and have sexual intercourse with them. John still nurses romantic love for Lenina, which she cannot understand. When once he begins to reveal it, she is reassured by the sign of normality and starts to go to bed with him, but he throws her out of his room. Then John ("the savage") disgraces Bernard by refusing to appear at a party attended by various important personages who have come only to see John; and once again Bernard is a nobody.

Chaps. 14–17. Linda dies in the hospital and John amazes everyone with his show of grief. He almost goes berserk afterwards and tries to start a rebellion of Deltas. Bernard and Helmholtz, from genuine friendship, take him away. The Controller and John have a talk in which the Controller tries to explain why the present system is best, as the least of evils, but John is not convinced.

Chap. 18. Bernard and Helmholtz are sent away to assignments in isolated places. John retreats to an old lighthouse and sets up an Indian-style home with various observances of worship. Some wayfarer observes him and then sightseers by the thousands come in helicopters to watch, especially after reporters write about his strange actions in the London papers. So John hangs himself.

Bread and Wine

Novel by Ignazio Silone (Secondo Tranquilli, 1900–   ).
Published and © 1937 by Harper & Bros., New York. Translated from the Italian by Gwenda David and Eric Mosbacher.

A NOVEL of almost straight antifascist propaganda, *Bread and Wine* was written while its author was living in exile from Fascist Italy. Silone's preoccupation with his message did not reduce the quality of the novel, which is generally considered a major work and his best. The English title is a literal rendering of the Italian, *Pano e vino*.

Chaps. 1–3. Old Don BENEDETTO, priest of the Italian village of Rocca, celebrates his 75th birthday with some of his former students. Only three have come, for many have died or been alienated by the priest's outspoken ways in the cause of liberty. One asks who was his favorite pupil and he replies PIETRO SPINA. There is a silence, for Spina has been expelled from Mussolini's Italy for championing the cause of the oppressed and now there is a rumor that he has returned surreptitiously.

One morning, Dr. NUNZIO SACCA, a classmate of Spina's, is called to the bedside of a sick man. He suspects it is the political agitator, Spina, and is fearful about attending him. When he finds Spina a prematurely old man (having disfigured his face with iodine), he is ashamed and not only heals him but obtains the clothes of a priest for his use in escaping and also chooses a name, Don PAOLO SPADA, for Spina to use in his disguise. Spina goes back to Fossa, the region of his birth, and stays at the Girasole Hotel. The next morning he is called to the bedside of a young girl, BIANCHINA GIRASOLE, who is thought to be dying as a result of a self abortion. He comforts her—uneasily—in his guise of a priest and prepares to leave the region to search for members of his party.

Chaps. 4–7. In Pietrasecca, Spina as Don Paolo rests and begins the recuperation necessary to go on his way to free the oppressed. He has great trouble avoiding priestly duties among the women of the valley. One morning Bianchina of Fossa appears to see him and tells him she is sure he is a saint for having saved her life. Her aunt has thrown her out, and having no place to go she puts her problems at his feet. A schoolfriend of hers, CRISTINA COLAMARTINI, who wishes to become a nun, lives nearby and gives her shelter. ALBERTO, Cristina's brother, falls in love with Bianchina and they go to live in an old deserted house of the Colamartinis without the benefit of marriage. Cristina comes often to see Don Paolo and they discuss liberty and God.

Don Paolo begins to go more among the peasants. There is a wild, destructive storm and he goes with the parish priest to see if Alberto and Bianchina are alive in their deserted house. They are alive but starving and with only a forlorn hope of marrying. Don Paolo speaks to Alberto's father, Don PASQUALE, in the hope of obtaining his consent. Before Pasquale can answer, Cristina, with her peasant pride, refuses the marriage because a Colamartini would lose caste by marrying a lowly Girasole. Don Paolo is appalled by Cristina's hardness and loses his respect for her. As Don Paolo's health improves, he goes more among the peasants and enters into their daily lives and conversations. It soon becomes apparent to him that he will not have success here in turning their minds toward his cause of liberty, for their intellects are too limited. He decides to leave the valley.

Don Paolo goes back to Fossa and begins his search for those interested in bringing about the revolution against Fascism. He feels that he is beginning to lay his cornerstone when he comes across Bianchina and Alberto again. They bring a young friend, POMPEO, to meet Don Paolo. Pompeo wholeheartedly joins in their ideas and plans and becomes one of them.

Chaps. 8–10. In Rome, where Don Paolo next goes, the clerical garb is cast aside and again Spina emerges. He meets ROMEO, his main contact with the anti-Fascists. Spina is distressed at the air of despair in the great city. He fights the futility of Romeo, who feels they are fighting a lost cause. Spina now believes that words alone are of no value, but that they must show others the way by living the deeds of which they speak. He is disillusioned when students demonstrate in favor of the Ethiopian war. He leaves Rome and returns to the Hotel Girasole again as the priest, Don Paolo. He can hardly believe the enthusiasm throughout the countryside for the victory over Ethiopia. His days are spent writing anti-war slogans on every available wall. His heart is broken when he discovers that Pompeo, his early convert, has been captivated by the war hysteria and has enlisted to fight. The people of the valley, steeped in victory, are furious with the writings on the walls but Don Paolo's identity as the instigator is kept secret by Bianchina's pleas to Pompeo, who knows of his activity.

Chaps. 10–12. Don Paolo as himself, Spina, goes to visit his old teacher, Don Benedetto. They find that their thoughts and ideals are similar and they determine not to compromise them in any way. Don Benedetto exhorts Cristina to be of aid to Don Paolo and to find a more tolerant attitude in her feelings toward him. The peasants are enraged at the candid statements of the old priest. They fear he will bring harm to their village. He is poisoned when, offering Mass, he drinks the sacramental wine.

Don Paolo has given Bianchina money to go to Rome and she sends word to him that Romeo has been placed under arrest. He goes to Rome and finds that Bianchina is now a prostitute but she protests her great and pure affection for the priest, Don Paolo, whom she considered a saint. Spina now takes over all Romeo's revolutionary activities in Rome and soon finds that the situation is hopeless, with exposure imminent. He rushes back to the valley to destroy all the evidence he hid there during his recuperation period. While he is doing this he receives a warning that his true identity has been discovered and he is about to be arrested. He flees to the snow-covered mountains, hoping to lose his pursuers in the coming blizzard. Hearing of his plight, Cristina, true to her promise to the dead Don Benedetto, hurries to gather food and warm clothes and starts to follow his tracks to help him escape. The snow mists become blinding and she loses her way. Realizing that she is hopelessly lost and that night has fallen, she knows that she will not survive and with religious fervor she sinks slowly to her knees and makes the sign of the cross as she waits for certain death from the wolves.

The Bride of Lammermoor

Novel by Sir Walter Scott, 1771–1832. Published 1819.

WHEN SCOTT WROTE THIS NOVEL he was still using the pseudonym Waverley; and his creation "Waverley" had become the world's most popular novelist. *The Bride of Lammermoor* is typical of the Waverley novels, neither better nor worse than the others. Its more lasting fame is due to the Donizetti opera *Lucia di Lammermoor*, based on it.

Chaps. 1–2. An impoverished artist who traveled in the Lammermoor section of Scotland came upon a strange legend, notes of which he has given to the writer of this tale. Out of these notes comes the story of the bride of Lammermoor.

The impoverished noble family of Ravenswood is deposed from its ancestral castle by a man appointed "King's Keeper" at the time when James VI of Scotland left to become James I of England. The new Keeper is Sir WILLIAM ASHTON. He is the father of LUCY ASHTON, a beautiful and sensitive young woman of 19. His wife, Lady Ashton, is a domineering, determined matron who brooks no insubordination from anyone, including her husband. The Ashtons are Presbyterians and are rigidly opposed to the Church of England. When Lord Ravenswood (who has been a bitter enemy toward Ashton) dies, his Church of England burial service is interrupted by an official sent by Ashton's authority to stop it. EDGAR RAVENSWOOD, now Master of Ravenswood, holds the officer off with a sword so that his father's remains may be properly interred.

Chaps. 3–5. Lucy Ashton takes her father for a walk to see old BLIND ALICE, a former servitor of the Ravenswoods. Blind Alice is possessed of acute perceptions. She warns Sir William that a Ravenswood means great danger to him, and Sir William is impressed by the warning, having heard of the legend concerning Ravenswood vengeance in the past. He is preoccupied on the homeward walk and is quite unprepared when one of the wild cattle that roam the vicinity charges him and Lucy. A shot from an unknown source saves them, and Lucy faints. The young man who fired the shot remains with Lucy as her father goes to seek help. It is Edgar, as Sir William learns on his return. Sir William then alters his report of Edgar's offense at his father's funeral.

Chaps. 6–11. In a tavern not far from the dreary tower where Edgar Ravenswood now lives, two men are awaiting him. They are Captain CRAIGENGELT, a soldier of fortune, and Mr. HAYSON OF BUCKLAW, an impoverished young man whose only hope of wealth is through an inheritance from his aunt, Lady GIRNINGTON. With Ravenswood, they had expected to leave for France and commissions in the French army. Ravenswood appears and tell them he has decided not to go. Craigengelt is angry and Bucklaw offended. In the resulting conversation Bucklaw considers himself insulted.

Consulting Blind Alice

He follows Ravenswood and they have a brief duel. Ravenswood wins easily and spares Bucklaw's life. This cements their friendship and Bucklaw goes to Wolf's Head, Ravenswood's castle, for refuge; for Craigengelt has been arrested for his political activity and it is probable that Bucklaw is in danger. While he is at the tower there is a festive hunt. Ravenswood attends, as do a young lady and her father, both masked, as is the custom. When a violent thunderstorm breaks out, the elderly man asks for shelter and Ravenswood takes them to the tower. He learns that his guests are Lucy Ashton and her father, Sir William, the sworn enemies of the House of Ravenswood. The tense situation is relieved by the ridiculous pretenses of CALEB BALDERSTONE, the old butler of the Ravenswoods, who wails that the storm has destroyed the sumptuous repast they might have had. He will never admit to anyone that a Ravenswood is suffering from poverty.

Chaps. 12–18. Caleb goes to the hamlet of Wolf's Hope to obtain food and there meets LOCKHARD, Sir William's servant. At length—through some considerable chicanery—he has supplies for a meal and returns to the tower. The news that Sir William is at Wolf's Crag astounds the people, and Caleb has implied a possible romance between Ravenswood and Miss Ashton. Back at the tower, a fine meal is enjoyed, and all retire for the night, but not until Sir William has made some overtures of friendship toward Ravenswood. Edgar is puzzled, but is attracted to Lucy. Sir William is aware that there may be some political changes soon that would make it advantageous to him to have Ravenswood's friendship. The time soon comes when the Ashtons must return to Ravenswood and Edgar decides to go with them to return their visit. Caleb is horrified and reminds Edgar of the prophecy concerning the last Laird of Ravenswood. The old verse says that the last Laird will win a dead maiden to be his bride, and will disappear then in the quicksand that is named after the water sprite, Kelpie. Edgar scoffs, and makes the journey. Lucy's younger brother HENRY interjects an ominous note when he refuses fearfully to approach Edgar when introduced. He declares to his sister that Edgar is the same man who is pictured in an old portrait of Sir Malise of Ravenswood—famous for dealing murderous vengeance upon his enemies.

Chaps. 19–26. The visit of Edgar is pleasant and free of contention. Lucy takes him to visit old Blind Alice, who warns him, privately, that only ill can come of his staying at Ravenswood. She tells him that without question Lucy loves him, but that this can never be good for either of them. Edgar is to meet Lucy at the Mermaiden's Well, which according to legend has always been a fatal spot for Ravenswoods. At the well Edgar finds Lucy alone, Henry having gone off to wander through the woodlands. Soon his love and hers are openly avowed, and they pledge their troth in a sacred oath, commemorated by breaking a thin gold coin in two pieces, one of which each would keep until their marriage. Lucy ties hers on a ribbon about her neck. When Sir William tells Edgar that the Marquis of A——, Edgar's kinsman and politically differing from Sir William, is about to pay a visit to Ravenswood, Edgar accepts his host's invitation to remain longer. Bucklaw, who by now has inherited both his aunt's fortune and the title of Laird, disapproves of the friendly connection between Ashton and Ravenswood. He has reason to suppose that his own suit for Lucy Ashton's hand is welcome, and Ravenswood's, if it exists, is not. Lady Ashton is the reason for this supposition, and Lady Ashton will as ever make all important family decisions. Craigengelt calls on Lady Ashton, who is in Edinburgh, and insidiously lets it be known that Edgar has been visiting a considerable time at Ravenswood and that a marriage is rumored. Lady Ashton seethes in fury and hastens to get home. The result is a near-race between her coach and the coach of the Marquis, which she concedes at the last moment, so that the noble guest enters the gate first. Inside, there is confusion and trepidation. Lady Ashton demands that her husband evict Ravenswood, which he refuses to do. She herself then writes him a note, and he leaves immediately. He rides toward the house of old Blind Alice, and as he approaches the Mermaiden's Fountain along the way, he sees Blind Alice—or her apparition—standing before him, silently mouthing words he cannot make out. Proceeding to the hut, he finds that Blind Alice has died. Shortly thereafter Edgar meets the Marquis and learns that there is a mission for him in a foreign land. They plan to go to Wolf's Crag, and a message is sent ahead to Caleb. As they approach the tower, a tremendous glow fills the sky. The tower is afire. Caleb meets them and conducts them to the inn at Wolf's Hope, where he has contrived to establish the notion that the Marquis is about to select those who will receive lucrative and dignified offices when the political picture clarifies. The Marquis and Edgar are received and treated royally. Ravenswood elicits from Caleb the information that he set the fire to prevent the arrival of the Marquis in a castle lacking in food, furnishings, and comfort. The tower itself did not burn, only some tinder.

Chaps. 27–32. Edgar and the Marquis reach Edinburgh without incident and go to the nobleman's house. Political events put the Marquis in power and Sir William out of favor. A letter from Edgar to Lady Ashton elicits a scathing reply, one to Sir William is answered in most ambiguous legal terms, and one to Lucy is answered merely by a note that affirms her fidelity but pleads the danger of further communication for the present. Bucklaw still believes that his suit is favored by Lady Ashton and attributes Lucy's lack of eagerness to her vow to Edgar, which she cannot in good conscience break. Her letters to Edgar, and Edgar's to her, are intercepted by her mother and burned. Lucy thinks Edgar has not tried to communicate with her but refuses to violate her oath until he releases her. Even the intervention of the local minister finds her obdurate, but he persuades her that a reasonable length of time without a reply would constitute a release by implication and he promises that nothing will interfere with the delivery of at least one letter. The date approaches when the official agreements for Lucy's marriage to the Laird of Bucklaw are to be signed. Lady Ashton has hired the services of one known locally as a witch, to influence the mind of her daughter. Lucy suffers, and gradually her mental condition becomes intolerable. Still no answer comes to her last letter to Edgar. Finally she can wait no longer; the day arrives and Lucy signs. No sooner have the contracts been completed than there is a sound of hoofbeats, and Lucy cries aloud that Edgar has come.

Chaps. 33–35. Edgar asks Lucy to tell him if the handwriting in a letter he carries is hers. The letter was dictated by Lady Ashton and expresses nothing of Lucy's feelings, but she must admit that it is her hand. Edgar gives her his half of the coin and releases her from her oath. He departs. Four days later, the wedding takes place. While the guests are celebrating, horrible screams come from the bridal apartment. Bucklaw is found unconscious and bleeding from a dozen wounds; Lucy is covered with blood, and in her hand is a dagger. She is completely mad and dies without recovering her sanity. On the challenge of Colonel DOUGLAS ASHTON, Lucy's elder brother, Edgar agrees to meet him in a duel. At dawn on the day set, Edgar rides toward the point of rendezvous. The Colonel sees him approach and Caleb, watching from Wolf's Crag, sees him go forth. He disappears from the sight of both watchers, and when they seek him there is no trace. The prophecy of long ago has been fulfilled. Edgar, the last Laird of Ravenswood, has "stabled his horse in the Kelpie's flow." He has sunk in the quicksand.

Lucy is seen holding a dagger

Brideshead Revisited

Novel by Evelyn Waugh, 1903–1966. Published 1945 by Little, Brown & Co., Boston. © 1944, 1945 by Evelyn Waugh. (Dell, D163)

ANYONE WHO HAS KNOWN the younger upper classes of London after either World War can testify that Evelyn Waugh did not overpaint their wildness, their excesses, for they could hardly be overpainted. In fact, in *Brideshead Revisited* Waugh was quite moderate. As a novel it is great. When all the arguments about Waugh's other works are ended, *Brideshead Revisited* will remain to testify that the man could write. The ambivalence produced by Catholicism in Englishmen, a favorite theme of Waugh's, is accented in this novel.

Prologue. The entire story is told in the first person by Captain CHARLES RYDER. During World War II Ryder, a captain in the (British) Reserves, at 39 old for a captain, moves his company with the rest of the regiment to a new billet in England. He is preoccupied with military matters—the unreasonable new colonel; the untrained young lieutenant, HOOPER. Then the regiment arrives and he finds that their new place is the estate Brideshead; and his whole life is recalled to his memory.

Book I. Chap. 1. Charles went to Oxford in 1923, when he was not quite 19. His father, who had not noticed the world very much since Charles' mother died, and who lived alone with Charles in a large house in London and confined his attention to scholarly pursuits, gave Charles £550 and little advice. Charles got good advice from his Oxonian cousin JASPER but nevertheless found himself drawn into a group of aesthetes, dissolute and in some cases degenerate, of whom Jasper and the solid Oxford community disapproved. One was ANTHONY BLANCHE, world-traveled scion of a rich South American family, a brilliant (though often outrageous) conversationalist despite his slight stutter. The principal one was Lord SEBASTIAN FLYTE, younger son of the Marquis of MARCHMAIN, whose houses were Marchmain House ("Marchers") in London and Brideshead (a former tremendous castle that had been moved physically more than 100 years before to a new location nearby). The Marchmains were very rich. Sebastian affected to make his best friend and confidant a Teddy-bear that he called ALOYSIUS. Sebastian took Charles one day to Brideshead to see his old nurse, NANNY HAWKINS. Charles discovered that Sebastian did not like his family, and though his sister JULIA—about a year older—was there, Charles did not meet her.

Chaps. 2–4. Despite Jasper's disapproval, Charles and Sebastian became inseparable friends. Like the rest of their group they drank too much—Charles from youthful unrest but Sebastian because he was an incipient alcoholic. Charles discovered that Lord and Lady Marchmain were separated, Marchmain living in Italy with his mistress. They were Catholics, Marchmain having become one to marry Lady Marchmain, who was very devout and was considered saintly. Lord BRIDESHEAD (by his familiars called BRIDEY), the elder son, was unlike Sebastian, very conservative and very Catholic. When Charles returned home for the summer his father, disliking having his solitude disturbed, made his life unpleasant and Charles was glad when Sebastian sent a telegram saying he had been seriously injured and asking Charles to come at once. Charles found that the injury was minor and Sebastian just wanted company, but he spent the rest of the summer with Sebastian. He briefly met the beautiful Julia and saw much of the younger sister, 12-year-old CORDELIA, who like Bridey was very devout. Charles became almost a member of the family to the servants, headed by WILCOX, the butler. Then Sebastian and Charles visited Lord Marchmain in Venice. Marchmain's mistress,

CARA, a middle-aged woman who was accepted in good society, was very outspoken and told Charles that Marchmain did not really love her, his principal emotion being his hatred of his wife.

Chap. 5. In the new term at Oxford, Anthony Blanche did not return, the former group of aesthetes was broken up, and usually Charles and Sebastian had only each other's company. Charles met Lady Marchmain when she visited Oxford briefly, trying to arrange for Sebastian to live with Monsignor BELL and redeem himself for the escapades that had got him in trouble at Oxford. Charles was struck by Lady Marchmain's beauty and charm, which however did not captivate him as much as most. Julia also visited Oxford, bringing REX MOTTRAM, a rich Canadian and now an M.P. Charles, Sebastian, and an Oxford friend, Viscount "Boy" MULCASTER, went to a party given by Rex in London and later were arrested for drunkenness. The result was small fines but unpleasant publicity and a black mark at Oxford. At Brideshead, Sebastian's drinking disturbed his family. Sebastian was unwilling to move in with Monsignor Bell and Oxford would not have him otherwise, so he was sent abroad with his Oxford tutor, a don, Mr. SAMGRASS.

Chap. 6. Charles went to Brideshead for Christmas. Sebastian and Samgrass were back from their tour. Sebastian persisted in drinking, and when Lady Marchmain learned that Charles had lent him money she was vigorous in her condemnation and Charles left. Cordelia wrote him a loving letter saying that she too was in disgrace for stealing Wilcox's keys and giving Sebastian whiskey. Charles saw Rex in London and learned that Rex and Julia would probably marry and that the Marchmains were living far beyond their means.

Chap. 7. A digression on information about Julia that Charles learned from Julia much later: Rex's political career had been furthered by his being a favorite lover of the influential Mrs. BRENDA CHAMPION, but he knew the proper kind of wife was necessary and was determined to marry Julia. In the meantime Julia fell in love with him. Rex was totally pliable about family conditions—becoming a Catholic, marriage settlement, etc.—treating it all as unimportant. Just before the wedding, Bridey discovered that Rex had been married and divorced. Rex could not understand how this made the marriage seem impossible to the Catholic family; but when they persisted, he appealed to Lord Marchmain, who authorized a Protestant wedding, being sure this would displease his wife. They were married without the family present. Then Julia discovered that Rex was not quite a complete human being—unaware of everything except power, money and politics (and also he continued his affair with Brenda Champion).

Chap. 8. Instead of continuing at Oxford, Charles studied art in Paris. He returned to London for the general strike of 1926, falsely thinking it an emergency in which his help would be needed. Julia told him Lady Marchmain was dying and wanted to see Sebastian, who was living in degradation in Morocco. Charles volunteered to get him and went to Fez, where he found Sebastian in the hospital, temporarily, as a result of his alcoholism, but regularly living with a German émigré, KURT. Sebastian found some solace in waiting on Kurt and being mistreated by him. Charles returned to London, where Bridey asked him to make some paintings of Marchers (which was to be torn down); these paintings were the start of Charles' reputation as an artist. While painting he saw Cordelia, now 15, and they talked about why Lady Marchmain, who had died, had been so loved by all others but had failed to be loved by her husband and children.

Book II. Chaps. 1–2. Ten years later, Charles was an established artist. Finishing a painting trip of about two years in Central America, he was joined in New York by his wife, Lady CELIA, sister of Mulcaster. They had been married almost ten years and had two children, the second of whom Charles had never seen. He had not been happy in marriage, though his wife was always very dutiful (except for her infidelities). On the ship taking them to Europe Julia was also a passenger. She was still married to Rex but her trip to America was to chase another man she believed she loved but found out she did not. On the ship a storm made most of the passengers seasick but not Charles and Julia, who became intimate for the first time and discovered they were in love. In London Celia continued to

Julia was a passenger on the ship

be a helpful wife, working to make Charles' exhibition a success (as it was). Anthony showed up at it and he and Charles briefly renewed their acquaintanceship. Charles refused to go home with Celia, even to see the daughter he had never seen. Instead he "visited" Julia and Rex at Brideshead, and stayed there.

Chaps. 3–4. Bridey came to Brideshead and told Julia and Charles that he was going to marry a widow, Mrs. BERYL MUSPRATT, whom he met because her husband, like Bridey, collected match boxes. Beryl, a Catholic of course and very proper, would not visit Brideshead while Charles and Julia were there in their sinful relationship; Julia was not only offended but disturbed. Charles and Julia both decided to get divorces so they could marry. Rex was puzzled at the necessity; he did not object to their present relationship. Cordelia, now 26, had been nursing in Spain (where the Civil War was on). She came back for the wedding and told what had happened to Sebastian: Kurt went back to Germany and pretended to be an enthusiastic Nazi. Sebastian followed him and finally convinced him that he did not like it and should escape; but Kurt was caught. Sebastian then retired to a monastery in Tunis, back to the faith.

Chap. 5. Lord Marchmain came back to Brideshead to die. He had a bad heart. Cara was with him. A compromise had to be worked out between Wilcox and Marchmain's chief servant, PLENDER; both were made *grooms of the household,* with equal rank. Bridey, Beryl and Cordelia all wanted Marchmain to have final rites, when the time came, from Father MACKAY; Marchmain at first objected and Charles and Julia fought about it, Charles thinking the priest should not be forced on Marchmain. Marchmain decided not to leave Brideshead to Bridey, largely because he disliked Beryl so much. Marchmain's impending death made Julia feel more and more guilty about her own departure from the faith, of which she was reminded by her father's case. Marchmain finally died, and almost as he died, though he was unable to speak or nod, he managed to make the sign of the cross. After his death, Julia told Charles she could never marry him; it was an act of penance on her part. It was no surprise to him, for he had seen it coming during the preceding weeks. He told her he hoped her heart would break, but that he understood.

Epilogue. So the reminiscence ends. Charles, the reserve captain, is with his troops at Brideshead. Lady Julia, the owner, is abroad, and so is her sister Cordelia, but Charles sees Nanny Hawkins. She is impressed by the fact that Rex Mottram is now a cabinet minister and many of the friends he used to bring up are similarly important in the government. Charles goes about his duties.

The Bridge of San Luis Rey

Novel by **Thornton Wilder**, 1897–
Published 1927. © 1928 by A. & C. Boni, Inc. (PB, PL 36)

Thornton Wilder made his first great success with *The Bridge of San Luis Rey*. It is very short, not 35,000 words—hardly a novel at all by most standards—but it ranks with such magnificent miniatures as *A Christmas Carol* and *Of Mice and Men*. It won a Pulitzer Prize.

Part I. On July 20, 1714, the Bridge of San Luis Rey in Peru suddenly collapsed and five persons dropped to their deaths in the deep gorge below. The bridge was old and famous, and to those who used it it was unthinkable that the bridge could ever collapse. The people of Peru considered the disaster an act of God. One person, Brother **Juniper**, determined to find out if possible why those particular five people were selected by God for death at that particular moment. He investigated the life of each of the five.

Part II. The Marquesa de Montemayor was one of those thrown to their deaths. Today the letters of Doña **Maria**, Marquesa **de Montemayor**, are classics of Spanish literature, but at that time Brother Juniper had a difficult research. He learned that she had been an ugly, unprepossessing child, the despair of her mother. To compensate for her homeliness and her habit of stuttering, her mother decked her in costly jewels. Doña Maria was very unhappy. She resolved never to marry but was eventually forced into marriage with an impoverished nobleman and bore him an exquisite daughter, Doña **Clara**. The girl was like her father, cold and selfish, and from an early age was contemptuous of her mother. The Marquesa, however, formed an almost worshipful love for her daughter. Their relationship was never pleasant. At last Doña Clara accepted a proposal of marriage that took her to Spain. The Marquesa started her immortal letter-writing at this time. She combed the city for anecdotes and sketches. Doña Clara scarcely glanced at the painstakingly penned epistles, but her husband delighted in them.

In her loneliness, the Marquesa took to drink and remained in a semi-conscious state for the greater part of each month, sobering herself only to produce one of her elaborate letters. As a companion she had taken in an orphan girl named **Pepita**, whose life she made miserable with her selfishness and bitterness.

When news came that Doña Clara was to have a child, the old Marquesa began using all manner of magic charms to help her daughter and to protect the unborn child. One of these observances was a visit to a shrine across the famous Bridge of San Luis Rey from Lima. On this journey she read a letter that little Pepita had written to the Abbess of the convent where she had been reared. The girl's misery and bravery touched the Marquesa as nothing else ever had. The masterpiece of all of her letters was written then. In this letter, she poured out her heart with love—but a truly selfless love in this case. Two days later, she and Pepita died in the collapse of the bridge.

Part III. Twin baby boys were left in the foundling basket at the convent at Santa Maria Rosa de las Rosas. The nuns named them Manuel and Esteban and brought them up. No one ever devised a method of telling one brother from the other. They lived apart from the world, close to each other but to no one else. They even devised a secret language in which they spoke when alone. At one time a professor and priest determined to probe into their language and discover its source; he failed.

The boys worked at many different jobs. The education the nuns had given them made it possible for them to become scribes and write letters for the more ignorant people. They also wrote theater programs. One day Manuel was asked to write a letter for a beautiful and popular actress in town, **La Perichole**. He fell in love with her, creating for the first time a barrier between himself and his brother. Esteban assured Manuel that he need not be troubled about having another love; Manuel tried to pretend that he cared nothing for La Perichole. He wrote letters for her to her various lovers, which made him violently angry. When he cut his leg and developed blood poisoning, his delirium revealed that he did love her. Manuel died. Esteban pretended that it was he and not his brother who died. He took Manuel's name and lived an aimless, deranged life. He accepted a job aboard a ship setting forth on a world trip; on the way he had to cross the Bridge of San Luis Rey and went down with it.

Part IV. Uncle Pio had encountered a young girl singing in a tavern, long ago when he first came to Peru, and had groomed and coached her until she became one of the most famous names in the country—La Perichole, the great actress. She was beautiful and gay and the toast of Peruvian gallants. She had many love affairs, as Manuel well knew—and resented—but the one that most influenced her was with the viceroy, during which time she decided loftily that the stage was unfit for one of her station and withdrew from such a life. All was well until she contracted smallpox and lost her beauty. She withdrew to a small farm and refused even to see Uncle Pio, but at length he tricked her into opening the door by engaging the services of a young girl for whom he felt sure the door would be opened. He begged her to let him take Jaime, her illegitimate son, away so that he might be educated as a gentleman, and at length she agreed. Like the others, Pio and Jaime set out to cross the Bridge of San Luis Rey, and like the others they fell to their deaths.

Part V. Long after the mass funeral for the victims, events were still evolving out of the accident. Brother Juniper was accused of heresy in attempting to interpret the will of God, and after a trial with the usual amount of bigotry and superstition he was sentenced to be burned at the stake. He tried to interpret the will of God in this, still convinced that everything happens when it does as an act of God. La Perichole abandoned her resentment over her lost beauty and became a friend of the Abbess of the Convent. Doña Clara, remorseful, also became the Abbess's friend.

Uncle Pio encountered the girl when she was singing in a tavern

The Brothers Karamazov

Novel by Fedor Mikhailovich Dostoevski, 1821–1881.
Published 1880. Translated from the Russian by Constance Garnett. (ML, G36 & T12; NAL, T1488)

SEVERAL OF Dostoevski's novels have been nominated as his greatest, but despite its defects in novel-construction and literary finesse *The Brothers Karamazov,* his last work, should have unchallenged position also as his best. Neither Dostoevski nor any other novelist ever explored the souls of his characters so completely as Dostoevski did in this novel, traveling the full range from the depths of depravity to the heights of exaltation, from the meanness to the nobility of which the ambivalent human spirit is capable. The characters are Russian and their emotions may seem unreal or exaggerated to English-language readers, but these readers would be better advised to accept the characters as the novelist portrays them. *The Brothers* is a long novel, overlong in fact; it is one of those Somerset Maugham named as the world's greatest but said were candidates for "artful skipping." Also enjoyment of *The Brothers* in English is lessened by the fact that there is only one translation and it is a very poorly written one, though it may be quite faithful in sense. There is an excellent revision of the Garnett translation by Princess Alexandra Kropotkin, but it is published only in a "cut" version.

Part I. Book I. 1–4. FYODOR PAVLOVITCH KARAMAZOV is a well-to-do landowner but known as a dissolute man, a toady in his youth, a man who will clown to make an impression. Somehow he managed to marry a beautiful heiress but she ran away, leaving her 3-year-old son DMITRI (MITYA), who is now 27. By his second wife, whom he abused, and who became insane and died, Fyodor has two other sons, IVAN, who is 23, and ALEXEY (ALYOSHA), who is 20 and has recently entered the monastery to study and perhaps become a monk. Mitya has been a cavalry officer. Ivan is studious, intellectual. Alyosha loves everyone and everyone loves him. Mitya and Ivan hate their father—Ivan for mistreating his mother, and Mitya for all but abandoning him and for having stolen the fortune his mother left him. Mitya is living in lodgings, not at home, and is all but penniless. **5.** It is arranged for all four Karamazovs, along with a friend, PETER MIÜSOV, to visit the elder of the monastery, the saintly Father ZOSSIMA, to seek reconciliation.

Book II. 1–2. They assemble at Father Zossima's cell. Fyodor, acting the buffoon, exaggerates his piety. **3–4.** They wait while Father Zossima goes to see other visitors who have come for his blessing. Among these are the young, wealthy widow Mme. HOHLAKOV and her crippled 14-year-old daughter LISE. (Both are just a bit unbalanced mentally.) Mme. Hohlakov gives Alyosha a message that KATERINA IVANOVNA (a rich, beautiful young woman who is ostensibly engaged to Mitya), wants Alyosha to come to see her. Lise has a crush on Alyosha. **5–8.** The Karamazovs' interview with Father Zossima fails, ending in a loud quarrel between Mitya and his father. The principal issue between them is a woman, an "enchantress" (named AGRAFENA ALEXANDROVNA and nicknamed GRUSHENKA), whom apparently both want. RAKITIN, a fellow-student of Alyosha's who is poor and jealous of the Karamazovs' wealth, chides Alyosha on the sensuality of the Karamazovs—for example Mitya, who could marry Katerina and be rich, but instead pursues Grushenka.

Book III. 1–2. The Karamazovs' big house is served by three servants: GRIGORY, old, faithful, honest; his wife MARFA; and a young man, SMERDYAKOV ("the stinking one"), who is generally supposed to be the illegitimate son of Fyodor and a half-witted girl of the town. **3–4.** Alyosha starts out to call on Katerina. He encounters Mitya. In a long conversation, Mitya tells him the history of his relationship with Katerina. Mitya was a young officer; Katerina, the colonel's daughter, was aloof to him. The colonel became 4,500 rubles short in his accounts and was threatened with disgrace. Mitya told Katerina's sister he would supply the money if Katerina came to him. Katerina came, ready to sacrifice herself; but Mitya, after humiliating her with words only, gave her the money and would not touch her. Soon afterward they became betrothed. Now she wants to marry him—in gratitude, Mitya believes; Mitya says she is an angel, he is unworthy of her, and he thinks she should marry Ivan, who loves her. **5.** Mitya also reveals that he owes Katerina 3,000 rubles that he virtually stole from her, and he is desperate to repay it and save his honor. Yet his father, who stole most of his fortune, will not give him even that. Instead, Fyodor keeps 3,000 rubles in an envelope for Grushenka if she will come to him. Mitya sends Alyosha on to Katerina to "give her his compliments"—in effect, break his engagement to her. **6–8.** Alyosha first goes home to dinner, at which Fyodor carouses and makes outrageous and irreverent assertions. **9.** Suddenly Mitya rushes in wildly; he has a false notion that Grushenka has come to see Fyodor. Fyodor is afraid for his life, but Mitya leaves. **10.** Alyosha calls on Katerina. She says Mitya owes her nothing; also, that Grushenka (whom she calls an "angel") has promised to give Mitya up. Katerina brings into the room Grushenka herself, who was calling on her when Alyosha arrived. Grushenka changes completely, mocks Katerina, says she was only fooling and will take Mitya again if she wishes. She reveals also that Mitya has told her about Katerina's first visit to him. Katerina becomes like a tigress and throws Grushenka out. **11.** Mitya confesses to Alyosha that he did dishonorably tell Grushenka that secret; he calls himself a scoundrel. Alyosha receives a love letter from Lise insisting that he come to see her.

Part II. Book IV. 1–2. Alyosha returns to the monastery, then goes to his father's house, where he asks his father to give Mitya the 3,000 rubles. Fyodor refuses, fearing that Mitya will use the money to buy Grushenka. **3.** On the street Alyosha sees a group of schoolboys, about 10 or 11, defied by a lone schoolboy of 9; they are throwing stones at one another. He stops them but the lone boy is unfriendly to him too and bites him. **4–5.** At Mme. Hohlakov's Alyosha finds both Katerina and Ivan. He can tell they are in love with each other, but Katerina will not relinquish her self-imposed obligation to Mitya. Katerina asks Alyosha to take 200 rubles from her to an improvised captain whom Mitya insulted. **6–7.** Now Alyosha understands why the boy bit him—the boy is the son of this Captain NICOLAY SNEGIRYOV—and the boy fights the other boys because they tease him about the captain's beard, which Mitya pulled. Alyosha offers the captain the money; he first takes it, then is revolted by shame and gives it back.

Book V. 1. Alyosha goes to see Lise. Mme. Hohlakov tells him Katerina had hysterics after they left and is still delirious. **2–5.** Going home, Alyosha enters through the back alley and the summer house, where Smerdyakov is playing his guitar to a neighboring girl. Inside, Alyosha has a long talk with Ivan, who expounds on the conflict of faith (Christian) and natural skepticism. **6–7.** Smerdyakov speaks very cryptically to Ivan, advising him to be out of town for a while and adding that "a word to the wise is sufficient." Ivan does not understand, but the implication is that this will give him an alibi while Mitya kills his father.

Book VI. 1–3. Father Zossima is dying. Alyosha has written down notes on his life, constituting a fairly long autobiography: Zossima was born of a good family. His father died and his mother put him in a cadet corps. He lived the usual wild life and became involved in a duel. His adversary fired first and wounded him slightly; then Zossima, over whom a complete change of heart had come, threw his pistol away. A man confessed to him an old murder for which he could never be caught but which he was impelled by conscience to confess publicly; however, all thought him merely mad. Father Zossima then expresses his faith and exhorts others to faith, good works, and prayer.

Part III. Book VII. 1–3. After Father Zossima's funeral, Rakitin asks Alyosha to go to Grushenka's with him and Alyosha goes. He discovers that Grushenka has promised to pay Rakitin if he would bring Alyosha

BROTHERS KARAMAZOV

to her. Grushenka expresses love (the pure kind) for Alyosha. Grushenka was deserted by her first love (a Polish officer) and was befriended by a very rich old merchant, KUZMA SAMSONOV, who has guided her investments so well that she is now financially secure. Grushenka tells Alyosha that she has seen Mitya lately only because she is afraid of his violence if she does not. Her officer, after several years, has reappeared and summoned her and she is joyously going to him.

Book VIII. 1–3. Mitya, desperate for the 3,000 rubles, has been to Samsonov to try to borrow against the inheritance he expects he will legally recover from his father. Samsonov, who actually is unfriendly, sends Mitya on a trip to see a peasant who has a woodland to sell, on which a large profit can be made. Mitya finds it is a wild goose chase. He returns and tries to borrow from Mme. Hohlakov, who leads him on with apparent promises but in the end merely advises him to go off gold-prospecting. Half-mad by this time, Mitya goes by Grushenka's, makes threatening remarks when he finds she is not at home, and dashes off to his father's house. **4–5.** Grigory tries to stop Mitya, who seizes a brass pestle and knocks the old man out, then rushes inside. Later Mitya returns to Grushenka's. His hands are bloody. Grushenka's terrified maid, FENYA, tells him Grushenka has gone to Mokroe to meet "her officer." With a bundle of 100-ruble notes in his hands, Mitya goes to PETER PERHOTIN, a young official, to redeem a pair of dueling pistols on which Perhotin lent him money. Then Mitya buys a load of champagne and fine foods, hires an expensive carriage, and sets off for Mokroe. **6–8.** After a wild ride, Mitya arrives at the inn at Mokroe and finds Grushenka with the Polish officer, Pan (Mr., or Sir) MUSSYALOVITCH, and Pan VRUBLEVSKY, his Polish friend. Also there are Mitya's friend KALGANOV and an older man, MAXIMOV. Mitya soon discovers that the Poles are deadbeats, seeking merely to win some money with marked cards and get money from Grushenka. Mitya privately offers them 3,000 rubles to leave Grushenka to him and they accept, but then they refuse when they find that Mitya can pay no more than 700 in cash and the rest is a promise. Mitya then spends his money recklessly on a party, including gypsy girls for singing and dancing. But Grushenka does admit she loves him, and lets him kiss her, but pleads with him to do no more till they are married. She will repay Katerina, of whom her jealousy is extreme. Their love scene is interrupted by the arrival of officers who have come to arrest Mitya for murder. Fyodor has been murdered that night.

Book IX. 1–6. Perhotin, suspicious when Mitya showed up with so much money, promptly investigated, which led to Mitya's arrest. The prosecutor, IPPOLIT KIRILLOVITCH, and the investigating attorney, NIKOLAY PARFENOVITCH, have excellent circumstantial evidence against Mitya, though there is no evidence from Smerdyakov, who has had an epileptic fit (to which he is subject) and is unconscious. Mitya indignantly denies being a parricide but refuses to explain how he so suddenly became possessed of so much money. Grushenka clings to Mitya and says "Punish us together!" Mitya is overemotional and distraught when examined and he can not or will not give lucid or convincing answers. **7–9.** Finally Mitya admits that he had kept 1,500 of the 3,000 rubles of Katerina's, in a bag around his neck, and this was the money he spent. But he had spent so wildly that he cannot prove he did not spend 3,000 rubles—the amount Fyodor had in the envelope for Grushenka, which has disappeared. Protesting his innocence, Mitya is put in jail.

Part IV. Book X. 1–4. Alyosha becomes friendly with the schoolboys—KOLYA KRASSOTKIN, one of the group of boys who were throwing stones; ILUSHA, Snegiryov's son, whom the other boys were persecuting; and the others. **5–7.** Ilusha is very ill, probably dying. Alyosha comforts him and inspires Kolya to do the same.

Book XI. 1. Ivan goes to see Grushenka. She has taken in the old man, Maximov, because he is destitute, and she has received regular begging letters from the two Poles, to whom she has given a few rubles—largely because of her happiness at the end of her dream that she still loved the Polish officer. She loves Mitya and Ivan assures her that Mitya loves her. **2–3.** Lise gives Alyosha a private letter for Ivan. **4.** Alyosha goes to the prison to visit Mitya. Both Grushenka and Katerina visit him, and

BROTHERS KARAMAZOV

Dmitri in jail

Katerina is active in his defense, which makes Grushenka jealous. Mitya wants to marry Grushenka in prison if the authorities will permit it. Grushenka wants to follow Mitya to Siberia. Katerina is trying to have Mitya declared insane and Ivan is working on escape plans. Ivan thinks Mitya is guilty. **5.** Alyosha next drops by Katerina's. Ivan is there. He seems to think Smerdyakov was the murderer; yet Alyosha has heard Ivan say, in delirium, that he—Ivan—actually killed their father. **6.** Ivan goes to see Smerdyakov, in the hospital, and grills him, but Smerdyakov admits nothing—not even that his fit was a sham. **7–10.** When Smerdyakov is released, Ivan goes to see him at home. This time Smerdyakov says he knows Ivan wanted Fyodor dead but wanted Mitya to kill him, to increase his own inheritance. Ivan is aghast at this thought. Meanwhile Ivan reads the letter—a letter Mitya wrote to Katerina, the day of the murder, promising to have the money "tomorrow"; and at last Ivan thinks Mitya guilty. But then Ivan has a third interview with Smerdyakov, and this time Smerdyakov confesses that he faked the fit and murdered Fyodor, expecting to be rewarded by Ivan; and Smerdyakov proves it by showing Ivan the 3,000 rubles he took from Fyodor. Ivan goes home, knowing that the next day he can prove Mitya's innocence. But when he wakes the next morning he learns that Smerdyakov hanged himself during the night. Now Ivan has only his own testimony as to Mitya's innocence, and it will not be believed.

Book XII. 1–3. The trial of Mitya begins. The first evidence builds a case against Mitya. **4–5.** Katerina's testimony creates sympathy for Mitya. Ivan, ill and distraught, gives his true testimony and produces the money Smerdyakov stole, but of course it is unconvincing; and Katerina is so distressed by what she considers Ivan's sacrifice for his brother that she has herself recalled to the stand and this time she shows the damning letter. **6–9.** Ippolit Kirillovitch delivers an eloquent summation, skillfully directed at the prejudice of the peasants on the jury against the excesses of the nobility. **10–14.** Mitya's lawyer, the great orator FETYUKOVITCH, delivers an eloquent and persuasive summation, but the peasants cannot be swayed. They find Mitya guilty and he is in for at least a sentence of 20 years in the mines.

Epilogue. 1–2. Katerina has collapsed after the trial, from remorse at her vengeful act that led to Mitya's conviction. Ivan also is unconscious, in a high fever. When she is able, Katerina goes to the prison hospital—for Mitya also has collapsed. Mitya now considers escaping, with Grushenka, though America seems to him as bad an exile as Siberia. When Katerina comes, he and she ask each other's forgiveness. Then Grushenka comes, and she is venomous toward Katerina. Katerina flees and Mitya, still forgiving, sends Alyosha to comfort her. **3.** Ilusha has died. At his funeral Alyosha tells the boys to be good and have faith, as he will, despite his grief.

Buddenbrooks

Novel by Thomas Mann, 1875–1955. Published 1901. English translation by H. T. Lowe-Porter published and © 1924 by Alfred A. Knopf, New York. (PB, C 60; GC 3)

MANN'S FIRST NOVEL is still ranked among his best. It pictures the high-bourgeois business family of which Germany's commercial cities have had a superabundance for at least a century and it portrays the problems of the monster or mutant of artistic soul born into such a family. The novel is wholly authentic because Thomas Mann was such a person born into such a family.

Part I. The Buddenbrook family in 1835 is solidly prosperous and solidly united—with the exception of JOHANN BUDDENBROOK'S eldest son, GOTTHOLD, offspring of his first marriage. JOHANN Junior, upon reading a letter from his half-brother, in which Gotthold demands a third interest in his father's estate, advises old Johann to give nothing. Gotthold married against his father's wishes, voluntarily cutting himself off. Old Johann agrees, and the subject of Gotthold and his demands is dismissed.

Part II. The Buddenbrook business continues to thrive. Old Frau Buddenbrook, Johann's second wife, dies about two years after the day when Gotthold's demands were denied, and shortly thereafter Johann signs over the business to his son Johann, whom most people call JEAN. The old man dies and Jean's children start to mature. TOM, Jean's eldest son, leaves school at 16 and enters the business with his father. The younger boy, CHRISTIAN, is quite unbusinesslike and most unlike the stolidly practical family. The youngest child, ANTONIE—nicknamed TONY—shows signs of growing up, and when she goes so far as to take afternoon strolls with a boy, she is packed off to boarding school. She is 15.

Part III. Tony is 20. She has a suitor that her family approves but she finds detestable. Herr GRUNLICH, the suitor, is an eminently respectable business man. Tony avoids him as much as possible. She goes to the seashore to avoid him, and there she becomes attached to a young medical student. MORTEN SCHWARTZKOPF. She writes her family that she has fallen in love. Grunlich goes to Morten's father, declaring that the boy has infringed on his prior claim. The elder Schwartzkopf sends his son away to punish him for this violation of convention, and Tony's family takes her home. She submits at last to the betrothal, and Herr Grunlich acquires a dowry from her father of 80,000 marks.

Part IV. Tony is married to Grunlich. Her letters to her family complain that he is very trying and unreasonable, miserly and asserting his will upon her in everything. She soon bears him a child, a daughter. She wants to name her daughter Meta but Grunlich insists on ERICA.

Things go from bad to worse with Grunlich, and his creditors finally force him to ask his father-in-law for additional funds, to spare Johann's daughter and grandchild the humiliation of bankruptcy. In the course of his pleas to Johann, Grunlich is uncovered as an unscrupulous cheat by the drunken boasts of a friend who happens to be present. Grunlich had sought Tony's hand solely for the dowry. Johann takes Tony and Erica back home and arranges for a divorce.

The Buddenbrook business is enriched further with the death of Johann's mother-in-law, who left a substantial sum. Tony lives a useful domestic life and feels that there is nothing amiss that a good second marriage would not cure. Johann Buddenbrook dies suddenly and the business falls into the capable hands of his elder son, Tom.

Part V. Tony, still of the opinion that she should remarry, speaks to Tom. The proper social and financial level is a most important point with the Buddenbrook family. The result is that each marries someone almost exactly like himself, insuring the standardization of offspring. Tom marries the statuesque GERDA, whom Tom had known in boarding school. Christian is still unconventional, by Buddenbrook standards, and is sickly.

Part VI. Tony sets out to travel and broaden her interests. There is little chance that she will meet an eligible male in her mother's house.

She meets a hop-dealer from Munich—Herr PERMANEDER—who calls when she returns home. Permaneder proves to be a substantial, reliable, well-to-do businessman—all the Buddenbrook qualifications. Tony marries him, which seems to settle her domestic situation. This does not endure for long. Permaneder, after an exceedingly profitable investment of Tony's dowry, is most willing to relax and live on income. He has enough money and is not a mercenary man. Tony, conditioned to a completely mercenary way of life, is bewildered by Permaneder's attitude.

The knowledge that she is going to have a baby gives Tony cause for rejoicing, but the baby, a little girl, lives only a few minutes. Her relationship with Permaneder becomes worse. After a brief period of mourning, Permaneder returns to his tavern friends each evening. One night Tony finds her husband and the maid, BABETTE, in an amorous embrace. She goes home again, taking Erica, and demands a second divorce. The reaction of Herr Permaneder astounds everyone. He does not contest either the divorce or the restitution of the dowry.

Part VII. Gerda and Tom have a son to carry on the name of Buddenbrook. JUSTUS JOHANN KARPAR BUDDENBROOK is christened at a gala celebration. Christian returns from his latest business venture, at which he has failed again, and this time he is sent to London. A senator dies and Tom is elected to fill his place. Tom works harder than ever, in spite of the doctor's warning. Old Frau Buddenbrook does something unthinkable: At the request of her youngest daughter, CLARA, who is dying of tuberculosis, she signs over Clara's dowry and inheritance to Clara's minister husband.

The fortunes of war in 1865 cause the total bankruptcy of a wholesale firm in Frankfort, and the firm of Johann Buddenbrook is involved and loses at one stroke 20,000 thaler.

Little Johann Buddenbrook, called Hanno, is a quiet, shy child of about 4½ years.

Part VIII. Erica is now 20 years old. She becomes engaged to HUGO WEINSCHENK, a director of an insurance company. Though not outstandingly rich in the merchant world of the Buddenbrooks, he holds a respected position and is found suitable for Erica. They are married and Tony goes to live with them and manage their house. Erica has a daughter, a frail and delicate child. Tom's son, Hanno, is also frail. He

Tony sets out to travel and broaden her interests

shows great talent as a pianist, but Tom is bewildered by the shy, imaginative child. Weinschenk is involved with shady manipulations of insurance and is sent to jail for 3½ years. The Buddenbrooks are deflated only temporarily; the man was an outsider away.

Part IX. Old Frau Buddenbrook dies of pneumonia. A violent argument occurs between the three heirs. Tom and Christian quarrel bitterly and Tom refuses to agree to Christian's marrying—not so much because Christian wants to marry his mistress, ALINE, as because Christian's inheritance would eventually pass to Aline's children, out of the reach of all true Buddenbrooks.

The dissolution of the family is emphasized when the old home is sold. Tony sees the new name over the door and weeps unashamedly in the street.

Part X. Tom watches little Johann (Hanno) hopefully for signs that the boy is developing interest in the Buddenbrook firm. Tom fears he is heading swiftly toward his end. Christian has a similar premonition. An excruciating toothache takes Tom to the dentist. The attempted extraction fails. On his way home Tom falls in the snow, after a sudden and violent seizure of dizziness, and dies later.

Part XI. With Tom's death, and the permanent disappearance of Erica's husband, there seems little to cause concern in the family when Christian marries Aline and is later committed by her to a mental institution. Hanno dies of typhoid, and Gerda departs for America. Tony reviews her life and finds that everything is gone. The family of Buddenbrook has descended the implacable slope to oblivion.

Bulfinch's Mythology

Stories (retold) by Thomas Bulfinch, 1796–1867.
Published 1855; republished with additions by Edward Everett Hale, 1894.

THIS IS ONLY ONE of many retellings of the classical myths and legends for young readers, but it has been the most successful book of its kind (except for Hawthorne's *Wonder Book* and *Tanglewood Tales* in their day) and it has survived as the standard book on the subject. ⁋ Bulfinch devotes most of the book to the Greek mythology, which however he takes chiefly from the Roman poets Virgil and Ovid and in which he uses the Roman rather than the Greek names of the gods and goddesses. Then come chapters on Eastern (Persian and Hindu) myths; and Norse mythology; the Druids of the ancient Celtic nations; and Greek sculpture. There are many quotations from English poets such as Milton and Shakespeare, giving their allusions to the mythological stories and characters.

The Greeks, Romans and Germans all belonged to the Aryan race or stock and their stories often bore much resemblance though found in different forms.

The (ancient) Greeks believed the world to be flat and circular, with Greece (especially Mount Olympus) in the center and the "River Ocean" flowing all around. The Dawn, Sun and Moon were supposed to rise out of the Ocean. The gods lived on Mt. Olympus, and when summoned they assembled in the palace of Jupiter, where they ate ambrosia and drank nectar. The Roman names of the Greek gods were not mere translations; in many cases there were equivalent gods among the two peoples. JUPITER (in Greek, ZEUS), the chief god, was the father of many gods and goddesses; he himself was the son of SATURN (or, in Greek, KRONOS, or Time) and OPS (in Greek, RHEA), who were Titans, the original race that came before the gods. Jupiter and his brothers and sisters rebelled against the Titans and conquered them. They imprisoned some and punished others; for example ATLAS, a Titan, was condemned to bear the heavens on his shoulders. Then Jupiter and two of his brothers divided the universe: Jupiter got the heavens, NEPTUNE the seas, and PLUTO the underworld. Jupiter was the king of gods and men. His wife Juno was queen of the gods.

The chief gods and goddeses who were children of Jupiter were: VULCAN, artist of the heavens; MARS, god of war; PHOEBUS APOLLO (a Greek name), god of the sun, and his sister DIANA, goddess of the moon; VENUS, goddess of love and beauty, mother of CUPID, the god of love; MINERVA (in Greek, PALLAS ATHENE), goddess of wisdom; MERCURY, Jupiter's messenger; the nine Muses; and BACCHUS, the god of wine. Others, not children of Jupiter, were: CERES, Jupiter's sister, goddess of agriculture; JUNO, wife of Jupiter; the three Graces, the three Fates, and the three Furies, all goddesses; NEMESIS, the avenging goddess; PAN, the god of shepherds; MOMUS, the god of laughter, and PLUTUS, the god of wealth. There were many others. All the foregoing were recognized by both Greeks and Romans. In addition the Romans had gods unknown to the Greeks: SATURN; JANUS, the two-headed porter of heaven; and the household gods, Penates who guarded the family and Lares who were the spirits of dead ancestors.

The creation. Ovid tells the story of creation: First there was CHAOS, all the elements of nature in a disordered jumble. God and Nature separated earth and sea, and the fiery part, being lightest, sprang up and formed the skies. The Titan EPIMETHEUS made men and animals, and his brother PROMETHEUS went up to the sun, stole fire, and brought it down to man. Woman was not yet made; Jupiter made her and sent her to Prometheus to punish him for stealing fire. The first woman was named PANDORA. Curiosity caused her to open a jar in which Epimetheus had confined all unpleasant things such as disease and envy; they escaped to plague men forever, but Pandora managed to put back the top of the lid in time to save Hope, which accordingly never leaves man.

Stories of gods and goddesses. Apollo slew with his arrows a terrible serpent, PYTHON, which appeared at the time of the creation. At Delphi, Apollo founded the Delphic oracle, which all nations came to consult.

Apollo offended Cupid, who thereupon shot Apollo with an arrow that made him love the nymph DAPHNE and shot Daphne with an arrow that made her abhor Apollo. When Apollo pursued her, she ran; and when she was almost caught, she cried for help to her father Peneus, the river god, and he changed her to a laurel tree. Apollo adopted the laurel as his tree and victors at the Pythian games, founded by Apollo, were crowned with laurel wreaths.

PYRAMUS, a handsome youth, loved THISBE, a beautiful maiden, but their parents would not let them marry. They arranged to meet secretly. Thisbe arrived first but was frightened away by a lioness, dropping her veil as she ran. The lioness rent the veil with her jaws, bloody from a previous kill. When Pyramus arrived he saw the lion's footprints and the bloody veil; and thinking Thisbe was dead, he plunged his sword into his heart. Thisbe found him dying and killed herself with his sword. Their parents acceded to Thisbe's dying wish and buried them together.

CEPHALUS, a youth fond of hunting, was loved by the goddess AURORA, the Dawn; but he loved his wife PROCRIS, who had been given a never-failing javelin by Diana, who also was goddess of hunting. Cephalus had the habit of speaking to "the sweet breeze" when he was alone. Someone heard him and told Procris he was wooing another woman. She hid to hear for herself, and Cephalus heard the rustling in the bushes, thought it was game, and threw his magic javelin, which killed Procris.

Io was a maiden loved by Jupiter; when JUNO spied on him, he changed Io to a heifer to deceive her. Juno took the heifer and assigned ARGUS, who had a hundred eyes, to guard it. Jupiter sent Mercury to kill Arbus and liberate Io. Mercury had trouble doing this, for he could not get Argus to sleep so soundly that all his hundred eyes were closed; but finally he put Argus wholly to sleep by telling him a long story. Then he cut Argus's head off. Juno took Argus's hundred eyes and put them in the tail of her peacock. Juno then sent a gadfly to torment Io, who swan all over the world to get away; finally Jupiter promised he would not see Io again and Juno changed her back to a woman.

CALLISTO was another maiden of whom Juno was jealous. Juno changed her to a bear. Callisto's son, when hunting, encountered this bear and was about to kill it, but Jupiter stopped him by changing them both to stars, the Great and Little Bear.

ACTAEON, a son of King Cadmus, was resting in the course of a hunting expedition when he happened to see the goddess Diana being dressed by her nymphs. Diana changed him to a stag so that he could tell no one; and his own dogs pursued and killed him.

PHAETON, son of Phoebus Apollo (the sun), was boasting to Epaphus, son of Jupiter and Io. Epaphus would not believe him. So Phaeton went to his father and asked to be allowed, for one day, to drive the chariot of the sun through the heavens. Apollo urged him not to attempt this, and offered him anything else, but Phaeton persisted and Apollo gave in. Phaeton set off but could not control the fiery horses; the chariot of the sun through the heavens. Jupiter finally averted total disaster by killing Phaeton with lightning.

MIDAS, a king, befriended Silenus, the foster-father of Bacchus. As a reward Bacchus offered Midas whatever he might wish and Midas asked that everything he touched might turn to gold. Bacchus granted the wish, but now even Midas's food and drink turned to gold. He prayed for relief to Bacchus, who allowed him to rid himself of the unwanted gift by plunging into the River Pactolus.

BAUCIS, a pious old dame, and her husband PHILEMON had grown old together. They lived in a hut in Phrygia. Jupiter and Mercury, journeying in that land and seeking shelter for the night, were turned away at one house after another; but Baucis and Philemon received them hospitably, and placed all they had to eat before them. As a reward, the gods built a fine temple in which Baucis and Philemon lived the rest of their lives, and in accordance with their wish Baucis and Philemon died together, being changed to a linden and an oak tree; but the rest of the village, for its inhospitality, was sunk beneath a lake.

PROSERPINE, daughter of Ceres, was loved by Pluto, who carried her off to the underworld. Ceres searched for her daughter all over the world; embittered when she could not find her, Ceres withheld agriculture from the earth and all plants died. The fountain Arethusa, at the entrance to the underworld, then told Ceres that Proserpine was the bride of Pluto and was queen of Erebus (the underworld). Ceres appealed to Jupiter, who agreed to have Proserpine released—on one condition, that Proserpine should not have eaten any food while she was in the underworld. But Proserpine had sucked a few seeds of a pomegranate that Pluto had given her. So a compromise was made, by which Proserpine would spend half of each year with her mother and half with her husband. This story is an allegory of the planting of seed underground and the emergence of the plant in the spring.

GLAUCUS, a fisherman, ate some grass that affected him strangely, drawing him irresistibly into the water. There he was welcomed by the sea-gods, changed in form, and became one of them. From the water he saw and loved the maiden SCYLLA, but she would not have him. He appealed for advice to the enchantress Circe, who advised him to abandon Scylla; but he refused to do this. Circe found this an occasion to persecute Scylla, rooting her in the water with serpents and monsters attached to her. Scylla's temper grew as ugly as her form and she devoured all mariners who came within her grasp. Later she was changed to a rock.

PYGMALION saw so much to blame in women that he came to hate them. He was a sculptor and made an ivory statue of a woman, so beautiful that he fell in love with it. (He named it Galatea.) He prayed to Venus for a wife just like the statue; but Venus knew that he really wanted the statue itself, and she caused the statue to come to life.

Venus, playing one day with her boy Cupid, wounded her bosom with one of his arrows. Before the wound healed she saw and fell in love with ADONIS. She loved to hunt with Adonis, but warned him to be careful. He was too noble to heed her counsel, and soon after this he was slain by a boar. Venus changed his blood to a flower, the anemone, which blooms briefly each

Jupiter, disguised as a bull, carries away Europa (see next page)

year. Another flower story is: Apollo was passionately fond of a youth named HYACINTHUS. One day when they were playing quoits the god threw one with too much strength and it bounced back from earth and killed Hyacinthus. Apollo in his grief changed the youth's blood to a flower.

PSYCHE, the youngest of a king's three daughters, was so beautiful that Venus became jealous. Venus commanded her son Cupid to make Psyche fall in love with some mean, unworthy being. Cupid obediently touched Psyche with one of his arrows; but accidentally he also touched himself with the arrow. An oracle told Psyche's parents that she must marry a god—but a monster—who lived on a mountaintop. Obediently they took her to the mountain and left her. She fell asleep and awoke to find herself in the garden of a beautiful palace. A voice told her that she had a host of invisible servants and might have anything she desired. So she lived in luxury but never saw her husband, who came to her only in the darkness and fled before dawn. Her husband allowed her to visit her sisters, who reminded her that her husband was supposed to be a hideous monster. Filled with suspicion, she armed herself with a knife. The next time her husband visited her, when he fell asleep, she uncovered her lamp and looked at him. She saw not a monster but a beautiful god, Cupid. But Cupid, waking, reproached her for her suspicion. He said she could go back to her sisters; then he left her, and the next morning the palace had vanished.

Psyche wandered day and night trying to find her husband again. She prayed at the temple of Ceres, who sent her to Venus, so she prayed at the temple of Venus. Venus gave her a series of impossible tasks, but (unknowingly helped by Cupid) Psyche was able to accomplish them all. Then Cupid asked Jupiter to help him and Jupiter persuaded Venus to relent. Psyche was made a goddess and married Cupid, and they had a daughter, Pleasure.

CADMUS was a son of Agenor, King of Phoenicia. Jupiter, disguised as a bull, had carried away Cadmus's sister, EUROPA, to Crete; and Cadmus went there in search of her. Failing to find her, he consulted the oracle of Apollo and it told him to follow a cow he would see; and when it stopped, he should build a city and call it Thebes. The cow stopped and Cadmus sent his men to find water. They encountered a horrid serpent (or dragon), which killed them. Cadmus, discovering this, managed to kill the serpent. Then Cadmus heard a voice commanding him to sow the dragon's teeth in the earth. He did so and armed warriors grew from them. The great crop of warriors fought one another until only five were left; these were peaceful and joined Cadmus, helping him to build Thebes.

ECHO, a beautiful nymph but too fond of talking, offended Juno. As punishment, Juno took away Echo's power ever to speak first, leaving her only the power to reply, as she had always liked to have the last word. Echo saw and loved the beautiful youth NARCISSUS, and had a conversation with him, repeating his words; but he spurned her and she grieved until she lost her beauty and faded away. Her bones were changed to rocks. But she is still ready to reply to anyone. Narcissus fell in love with his own image in a fountain and he too lost his beauty and died of unrequited love.

LEANDER was a youth of Abydos, a town on the Asian side of the strait between Asia and Europe, and on the opposite shore, in the town of Sestos, lived the maiden HERO. Leander loved her and used to swim the strait nightly to see her. One night, in a tempest, he was drowned; and Hero in her despair cast herself from a tower into the sea and perished.

Minerva, who is said to have sprung forth from Jupiter's brain fully grown and clad in complete armor, was a warlike goddess. Athens was her own city, awarded to her for winning a contest with Neptune. Once a mortal maiden, ARACHNE, dared to challenge Minerva to a contest at needlework, of which Minerva was the goddess. Both wove magnificent work; Minerva had to admire Arachne's, but still punished Arachne for her presumption and impiety. She transformed Arachne into a spider.

Niobe, queen of Thebes, also presumed to challenge a goddess, Latona, mother of Apollo and Diana; Niobe thought she had a right to be prouder of her own fourteen children. Latona complained to her children, who slew Niobe's children one by one. Niobe at the end cried, "Spare me one!" but that last one was killed too.

The king of Argos, Acrisius, was told by an oracle that he would be slain by the child of his daughter DANAE. He shut Danaë up in a tower but Jupiter went to her there and they had a son, PERSEUS. Unwilling to kill his daughter and grandchild, Acrisius placed them in a chest and sent them floating out to sea. They reached an island, Seriphus, when Perseus was brought up by a fisherman. When Perseus was grown, the king of Seriphus sent him to bring back the head of MEDUSA, one of the three GORGONS, whose hair was coiled serpents that would turn to stone anyone who looked at it. (Minerva had turned the hair to serpents, to punish Medusa for vying with her beauty.) Minerva and Mercury helped Perseus: Minerva lent him her shield and Mercury lent him his winged shoes and sword. Perseus saw Medusa's reflection in the shield and killed her by cutting off her head, which he put in a bag.

On his way home, Perseus arrived in Ethiopia, of which CEPHEUS was king and CASSIOPEIA queen. Cassiopeia's vanity had offended the sea nymphs, who sent a prodigious sea-monster to ravage the coast. An oracle told Cepheus he must sacrifice his daughter, ANDROMEDA, to this serpent; so Cepheus chained her to a rock by the sea. Perseus, flying over, saw the monster approach. He killed the monster and so was awarded the hand of Andromeda. But PHINEAS, her betrothed, objected and attacked. Outnumbered, Perseus told his friends to turn their faces away and then took from his bag the head of Medusa, turning all his enemies to stone.

OEDIPUS was the son of LAIUS, king of Thebes. An oracle warned Laius that his newborn son was dangerous to him and Laius gave the infant to a herdsman to destroy; but the herdsman pitied the child and simply abandoned him, and he was found and raised to manhood by another herdsman. When Oedipus was a young man, the Delphic oracle prophesied that he would kill his father and marry his mother.

Oedipus resolved to leave the country. On his way, he encountered Laius driving to Oedipus; there was not room for two chariots to pass and in a quarrel that ensued Oedipus killed Laius, his own father. Oedipus journeyed on toward Thebes, which was afflicted by a monster, the SPHINX, which had the body of a lion but the head and torso of a woman. The Sphinx blocked the road and killed all travelers who not could answer "the Riddle of the Sphinx": What animal is that which in the morning goes on four feet, at noon on two, and in the evening on three? Oedipus gave the correct answer: Man, who creeps as a child, walks in manhood, and uses a staff in old age. The Sphinx, mortified, killed herself. The people of Thebes were so grateful to Oedipus that they gave him their widowed queen, JOCASTA, as his wife; and so he married his mother. When later this was discovered, Jocasta killed herself and Oedipus tore out his eyes and wandered till he died, accompanied however by his faithful daughters.

PEGASUS was a winged horse that grew from the blood of Medusa, when Perseus cut off her head. The CHIMAERA was a fearful monster, breathing fire; its fore part was lion and goat and its rear part was dragon. BELLEROPHON, a gallant young warrior, was charged with the task of killing the Chimaera. With the aid of Minerva, who gave him a magic bridle, Bellerophon found Pegasus drinking at the well of Pirene, tamed him, and by riding him was able to kill the Chimaera. Bellerophon and Pegasus together performed many other feats until Bellerophon became so proud that Jupiter sent a gadfly to sting Pegasus and make him throw Bellerophon. Bellerophon became lame and blind and wandered miserably until his death.

NEPHELE, a queen in Thessaly who had been put away by her husband, feared for the lives of her two children. Mercury gave her a ram that had golden fleece and could fly, and she set her children on it. The girl, HELLE, fell off; but the boy, PHRYXUS, safely reached the kingdom of Colchis and was welcomed by its king, AETES. The ram was sacrificed to Jupiter and the golden fleece was hung in a consecrated grove guarded by a dragon. JASON, the prince of another kingdom, was sent in quest of the golden fleece by his uncle PELIAS, who actually wanted to get rid of him. Jason employed Argus (not the monster) to build a ship that would carry fifty men (at that time considered a gigantic undertaking). The ship was called the *Argo* and Jason and his men, including such heroes as Hercules, Theseus, Orpheus and Nestor, were called Argonauts. The Argonauts had various adventures in sailing to Colchis, which was on the Black Sea.

The king of Colchis, AETES, consented to give up the golden fleece if Jason would yoke to the plow two fire-breathing bulls and also would sow the dragon's teeth as Cadmus had done. Jason had already become engaged to marry MEDEA, the king's daughter, who was a potent sorceress. With the help of her magic he yoked the fire-breathing bulls; then he sowed the dragon's teeth and when the warriors sprang up and rushed to attack him he threw a stone in their midst, which set them fighting among themselves until all were killed. Aetes promised the golden fleece the next day, but that night Medea told Jason that actually her father planned to attack him. They went to the grove, where Medea put the dragon to sleep with a magic potion. Then with the golden fleece they sailed back to Thessaly. Medea had other adventures: With her magic she restored Jason's aged father, Aeson, to youth; then, under pretext

The riddle of the Sphinx

of doing the same for Pelias, she killed Pelias and fled to Athens, where she married the king, Aegeus.

HERCULES (in Greek, HERACLES) was the son Jupiter and ALCMENA. Juno, jealous as always, sent two serpents to destroy him in his cradle but he strangled them with his hands. However, under Juno's curse Hercules had to undertake the twelve "Labors of Hercules," set for him by his cousin Eurystheus. The chief ones were: 1, to kill the terrible Nemean lion; Hercules strangled it. 2, to kill the Hydra, a nine-headed monster. Each time Hercules cut off a head, two others grew. Eventually Hercules burned away all heads but one, which was immortal, and this one he buried. 3, to clean the Augean stables, which housed three thousand oxen and had not been cleaned for thirty years. Hercules turned two rivers through them and cleansed them in one day. 4, to procure the girdle of HIPPOLYTA, queen of the Amazons, a nation of warlike women. Hippolyta was willing to give Hercules the girdle; but Juno spread the rumor that Hercules was carrying off the queen and the Amazons attacked Hercules. Thinking Hippolyta treacherous, Hercules slew her and sailed off with the girdle. 5, to bring home the oxen belonging to Geryon, a three-headed monster; to do this Hercules had to kill a giant, Eurytion, and a two-headed dog, who guarded the oxen. 6, to to get the golden apples of the Hesperides, which had been Juno's wedding present. Hercules did not know where they were, but he persuaded the giant Atlas to get them for him while he held up the heavens in Atlas's place.

Other exploits of Hercules included killing the giant ANTAEUS, son of Terra (the Earth), who forced all strangers to wrestle with him. Hercules found it was of no avail to throw Antaeus, who rose with renewed strength from every fall; so Hercules lifted him from the earth and strangled him in the air.

THESEUS, son of AEGEUS, king of Athens, after various exploits, went to Crete to save Athens from paying a terrible annual tribute: Seven youths and seven maidens had to be sent each year to feed the MINOTAUR, a monster with a bull's body and human head, which belonged to MINOS, king of Crete. The Minotaur was kept in a labyrinth built by Daedalus, so artfully that no one in it could find his way out. Theseus won the heart of ARIADNE, daughter of Minos, and she gave him a thread of which she held one end, to guide him out. Theseus entered the labyrinth, slew the Minotaur, escaped from the labyrinth, and sailed back home, taking Ariadne with him. Then he treacherously abandoned her on the island of Naxos. But he had promised his father to fly white sails instead of black if he succeeded, and he forgot; so when the old king, watching from the coast, saw the ship approach with black sails he thought his son had perished and he killed himself.

PROCRUSTES was one of the evil-doers that Theseus overcame in his journeyings. Procrustes had an iron bedstead on which he tied all travelers who fell into his hands. If they were shorter than the bed, he stretched them; if they were longer, he lopped them off. Theseus served him as he had served others.

DAEDALUS, a most skillful artificer, made wings for himself and his young son ICARUS; the wings were made of feathers held together by wax. Daedalus warned Icarus not to fly too high, but Icarus disregarded this and flew too near to the sun. The wax melted, the wings fell apart, and Icarus fell into the sea and died.

ORPHEUS was the son of Apollo and Calliope, the Muse of music. He was the greatest musician. He married EURYDICE, but soon afterward she killed by a snake bite. Orpheus followed her to the underworld, where his music so charmed the gods that Pluto consented to let him take Eurydice back to earth—with one condition, that Orpheus should not look back at her until they reached the upper air. But Orpheus forgot and looked back and lost her forever.

The Valkyrie ride

THE NORTHERN MYTHOLOGY

The mythological records of the Scandinavians are contained in two collections called the *Eddas*, of which the oldest, in poetry, dates back to 1065, and the more modern or prose Edda is dated 1640.

Once there was no earth or heaven but only a mist, in which flowed a fountain. From the fountain twelve rivers issued and froze. The vapors in the air formed clouds, from which sprang the giant YMIR, the Frost, and his progeny; and the cow AUDHUMBLA, whose milk nourished the giant. The cow licked the hoar frost and salt off the ice, revealing a god, whose children were three brothers, ODIN, VILI, and VE. They slew Ymir and made the earth from his body and the seas from his blood. They made a man, Aske, from an ash tree and a woman, Embla, from an alder.

A mighty ash tree, Ygddrasil, was supposed to support the whole universe. It had three immense roots, one extending into Asgard, the abode of the gods; another into Jotunheim, the abode of the giants; and the third into Niffleheim, the regions of darkness and cold.

The root that extends into Asgard is guarded by the NORNS, three goddesses who dispense fate; they are URDUR, the past, VERDANI, the present, and SKULD, the future. Access to Asgard is only by crossing the bridge Bifrost, the rainbow. Asgard consists of golden and silver palaces, the most beautiful being Valhalla, the residence of Odin. Here he feasts with his chosen heroes, those who have fallen bravely in battle. The Valkyrior [Valkyries] are warlike virgins, mounted on horses and armed, whom Odin sends to every battlefield to choose those to be slain; the Aurora Borealis is the reflection from their armor as they ride.

THOR, the thunderer, Odin's eldest son, is the strongest of gods. He has three precious possessions: his hammer, Miölnir; his belt of strength, which when worn doubles his strength; and his iron gloves. The god FREY presides over rain, sunshine, and the fruits of the earth; his sister FREYA is the goddess of love, music, spring, and flowers. BRAGI is the god of poetry and HEIMDALL is the watchman of the gods and guards the bridge Bifrost. LOKI is the god of fraud and mischief.

THOR, with his servant THIALFI and with Loki, set out on a journey to Jotunheim, the abode of the giants. At nightfall they were in an immense forest with no shelter until they found a large hall, where they slept. At dawn they discovered that the supposed building was the glove of a giant, who said his name was Skrymir and proposed that they travel together. That night, while Skrymir slept under a tree, Thor tried three times to kill him with mighty blows of his mallet; but each time the giant seemed to think merely that a leaf, or some moss, or an acorn had fallen on his head. They journeyed on and came to the city of King UTGARD-LOKI. The city was peopled by giants. Loki, Trialfi and Thor tried feats of strength and of eating and drinking with the giants but were easily beaten. Thor lost a wrestling match to an old crone, could not lift the king's cat, and failed to drain a horn of liquor in three tries. When they left the city, Utgard-Loki confessed to Thor that all their defeats were illusions and in reality Thor was the strongest god he could imagine: The old crone was Old Age; the cat was the earth; and the horn was connected with the oceans. Thor angrily tried to kill Utgard-Loki, but he vanished.

BALDUR THE GOOD dreamed that his life was in peril and told the other gods. Then Frigga, wife of Odin, made fire, water, metals, disease, all animals, and poisons promise not to harm Baldur. But she forgot to exact the promise from mistletoe. Loki, learning this, took a twig of mistletoe. The gods were amusing themselves by casting things at Baldur, to prove his immortality. Loki suggested that Hodur, a blind god, cast the twig at Baldur; Hodur did so, and Bladur fell lifeless.

Frigga offered a reward to anyone who would go to Hel, in Niffleheim, the abode of HELA, daughter of Loki, and ransom Baldur. HERMOD undertook the journey. He reached Hel, but Hela refused to release Baldur unless all things on earth, alive and lifeless, wept for him. Hermod returned with the message and all things did weep for Baldur except one old hag, Thaukt, who refused. So Baldur had to remain dead.

Loki fled the vengeance of the other gods and turned himself into a salmon. As he was trying to escape, Thor caught him by the tail; so salmon have very thin tails.

The ELVES were lesser gods. The white elves lived in Alfheim. They loved the light and were kindly disposed toward men. The black or night elves were ugly, long-nosed dwarfs. They were the most skillful artificers of things in metal and wood, making among other things Thor's hammer and the ship Skidbladnir, large enough to hold all the gods and their possessions but so skillfully wrought that it could be folded and put into a side pocket.

Ragnarok, or the Twilight of the Gods, was a prophesied time when all the gods and the universe would burn up, the earth would sink into the ocean, and time would be no more. Then ALFADUR, the Almighty, would create a new world in which there would be no wickedness and misery.

THE DRUIDS

The Druids were the priests of the ancient Celtic nations in Gaul, Britain, and Germany. They taught the existence of one god, named Be' al, identified with the sun. Fire was a symbol of the divinity. They had no temples, their sacred place being a circle of great stones 20 to 30 yards in diameter; the most celebrated of those remaining is Stonehenge, in England. They also worshiped at piles of stone, called cairns, on the summits of hills.

The Druids offered sacrifices to their deity, and according to Roman writers these were sometimes human sacrifices.

There were two festivals each year. The first, at the beginning of May, was called Beltane or "fire of God." The other was called Samh' in, or "fire of peace," and was held the first of November. At this time the Druids acted as judges, settling all questions and crimes.

The Bards were part of the Druidical hierarchy. They preserved the history and genealogy of the people in songs and stories. They were thought to be inspired.

The Cabala

Novel by Thornton Wilder, 1897–
Published 1926 by A. & C. Boni, New York. © 1926, 1954 by Thornton Wilder.

THIS IS Thornton Wilder's first published novel. It did not create much of a stir at the time, but after he made his great success less than two years later with *The Bridge of San Luis Rey* readers went back to *The Cabala* and found it good. ¶ The original cabala was an occult religious system, but also any principal group or council of scholars considered authoritative on the system was known collectively as "the Cabala."

Book 1. The narrator of the story, a young American writer (SAMUELE), arrives in Rome a couple of years after the end of World War I. He is accompanied by his friend JAMES BLAIR, a classical scholar, and through Blair meets a group of rich and talented people. This group, known as the Cabala, are absorbed in antiquarian lore and they attempt to create the present in terms of the long-dead past. Blair takes the narrator to the home of Miss ELIZABETH GRIER, an American member of the Cabala, who entertains lavishly. She has her own private orchestra and stays awake all night. She is constantly inviting favored guests to tea, dinner, and late supper. The members of the Cabala accept the narrator and call him SAMUELE. He meets other members of the group at Miss Grier's and finds them a fascinating group. There is Cardinal VAINI, who has been a missionary in China. The Cardinal is concerned with the inner affairs of the Church, but also, as the friend and counselor of the Duchessa D'AGUILANERA, he is worried about her 16-year-old son MARCANTONIO, who is living a wild and dissolute life. Samuele also meets ASTRÉE-LUCE DE MONFONTAINE, a religious fanatic who as a French royalist believes in the divine right of kings; Mme. BERNSTEIN, the daughter of a German banker, and the Princess ALIX D'ESPOLI, who has beauty and charm but not enough intelligence to hold the man she is attracted to.

Book 2. Samuele has tea and dinner at Elizabeth Grier's, leaves, and returns later in the evening for a late supper. The Duchessa d'Aguilanera begs him to come to her home and talk to Marcantonio. She thinks Samuele can influence the boy to change his wayward life. Samuele agrees and goes to the duchessa's Renaissance villa for study and rest. There he spends much time listening to Mme. Bernstein play the piano. The Cardinal has told Samuele that Marcantonio is completely dissolute, immoral in character, and habituated to his evil life with older companions. This shocks but does not deter Samuele from undertaking the reformation of Marcantonio. The boy tells him that he likes to drive fast cars, but that also he has an ambition to run in the Olympic games. Samuele agrees to coach him, but soon becomes disgusted by the boy's way of life and castigates him with a torrent of Puritan invective. Marcantonio is deeply affected and in a state of religious frenzy jumps from a balcony and kills himself.

Book 3. Samuele becomes the intimate friend of the Princess Alix d'Espoli and he introduces her to James Blair. The princess falls madly in love with Blair, but as is usual with her the love is not reciprocated. She mistakes Blair's friendly attitude and begins to visit him uninvited. Blair is annoyed and leaves Rome to escape her insistent demands on him. The princess pours out her grief to Samuele and plunges into the weird life of the artistic colony of Rome. Blair returns a month later and he and Samuele visit a Rosicrucian seer. At a public séance they encounter Alix. They try to avoid her but she sees them, and evidently realizing that Blair is through with her she leaves the place in a fit of anger. Samuele later hears that she has left Rome for Greece, but has returned and is once more the subject of gossip for her attempts to snare a man.

Book 4. Samuele next becomes involved

with Astrée-Luce de Monfontaine and finds that the deeply religious woman is shy and full of goodness. She wants Samuele to intercede with Cardinal Vaini and persuade him to use his influence to establish the Divine Right of Kings as a dogma of the Church. She wants the Bourbons restored to the throne of France to help save Europe from destruction. Samuele visits her at her villa and at Anzio and he agrees to approach the Cardinal with her plan. The Cardinal, instead of agreeing to Astrée-Luce's royalist schemes and joining forces with her in this impossible venture, rebukes her for her exaggerated faith in prayer. Astrée-Luce is disturbed and when the Cardinal visits her at her villa she cries out to her other guests that "the devil is here" and takes a shot with a pistol at the Cardinal. He is not hurt, but he cannot be reconciled to her. He decides to return to missionary work in China, but en route he falls ill and dies and is buried at sea.

Book 5. As Samuele prepares to leave Rome he visits places where strange events with members of the Cabala occurred. He makes a last call on Elizabeth Grier, who tells him that the members of the Cabala are in reality the reincarnation of the pagan gods of antiquity. Despite this ancient knowledge they are lost in the complexities of the modern world. She shows Samuele a document written by a Hollander who insisted his body had been entered by the god Mercury. Samuele leaves Rome to return to America. On board ship he invokes the shade of the poet Virgil and it appears to him in mid-air, telling him, "hurry and die."

Cabbages and Kings

Novel by O. Henry (William Sidney Porter, 1867–1910)
Published 1899.

THIS IS ABOUT AS CLOSE to a novel as O. Henry ever wrote. It is a series of short stories, but they are tied together by the same characters and they reach a conclusion as though they had been written as a novel. The quality of O. Henry's work was so uniform that it is hard to pick his best, but he was at his best in *Cabbages and Kings*. The title is from the poem "The Walrus and the Carpenter," in *Through the Looking-Glass:* "The time has come, the walrus said,/To talk of many things—/Of shoes—and ships—and sealing-wax—/Of cabbages, and kings . . ."

The Proem. A little love, plus plotting and counterplotting with warm U.S. dollars, begins the tale of Doña ISABEL GUILBERT, young American opera singer, who only once gave the key to her heart and then to President MIRAFLORES, the brilliant but now dead President of the volatile Latin republic of Anchuria. It is said there that he died by his own hand while fleeing with Doña Isabel and a valise filled with a hundred thousand dollars. The valise disappeared but Isabel quickly married FRANK GOODWIN, an American resident of the coast town of Coralio.

Fox-in-the-Morning and **The Lotus and the Bottle.** A telegram to Goodwin, who is secretly allied to the Out Party, revolutionary in its attempt to overthrow the In Party, is a delight; for it brings the news of the flight of President Miraflores. It advises Goodwin to be sure to retrieve the valise; the money will be needed when the new party takes over. His reward for these endeavors is many thousands of coffee-bearing acres. To pass the days that must elapse before the departing Miraflores reaches Coralio, Goodwin calls frequently on WILLARD GEDDIE, the consul for the United States. Geddie is a young man escaping from a lover's quarrel with the beautiful Miss IDA PAYNE of New York.

His year in Coralio has greatly eased his heart's pain and he has definitely decided to marry PAULA BRANNIGAN, a most delectable native girl with a tinge of Indian blood and a very rich Irish father. Though his attentions have not been voiced, he is confident of his decision until he reads in a newspaper that Ida is cruising on a yacht in his vicinity. Trying to analyze his feelings, he walks along the beach, where absentmindedly he picks up a bottle washed ashore. There is a note inside and he perceives that it is from Ida. Resisting the temptation to remove and read it, he goes immediately to Paula and proposes. He is accepted and returns to the sea to throw the bottle as far as he can—only to half-drown while swimming to recover it again!

Meanwhile Frank Goodwin quietly prepares to take all the precautions necessary to keep the fleeing president from making good his escape. By chance, the barber ESTEBÁN DELGADO tells Goodwin he has just shaved off the president's whiskers. He takes Goodwin to where Miraflores is staying for the night. First Goodwin enters Doña Isabel's room and she, in anger at allegation of money stolen from the treasury, brings the valise and opens it. Her astonishment when she sees the money is vocal and brings Miraflores into the room. He immediately grasps the situation and with a farewell kiss to Isabel goes into his room and shoots himself. It is said in Coralio that they still search for that valise with its dollars. No one has ever seen it, but Mr. and Mrs. Frank Goodwin have a paradise of a home and Doña Isabel has forgotten her waywardness and Miraflores to become a happy and perfect wife.

Cupid's Exile Number Two. The Phonograph and The Graft. Mr. JOHN DE GRAFFENREID ATWOOD is the successor to the consulship when Geddie resigns to go into his future father-in-law's business. Atwood, too, is a fugitive from a shattered romance. He proceeds to do absolutely nothing as consul, but he does it very charmingly. BILLY KEOGH becomes his boon companion and one still, alcoholic evening tells him how he introduced the first phonograph to South America. Keogh and a partner had set up their one machine in the small town of Solitas, where they were immediately wined and dined by the American secretary to the President, HOMER P. MELLINGER, a man proud of his honesty in a country of graft. Mellinger invited Keogh and his Indian partner, HENRY HORSECOLLAR, to demonstrate the novelty at his reception. A district governor was coming and Mellinger knew the governor was about to offer him a bribe to betray the President. When the bribe came it was so enormous that Mellinger faltered; but just at that moment Keogh played a record of "Home Sweet Home" and Mellinger resisted the temptation and stayed honest. The next day Mellinger insisted on buying the phonograph for many times what it was worth. He put the cost on his expense account because it was worth that much to the government to keep him honest.

Money Maze and **The Admiral.** The new administration that takes over now in Anchuria has one major concern, to recover the Miraflores valise with its monetary content. The secretary to the new President, Colonel EMILIO FALCON, comes to Coralio to investigate, and all clues lead to Frank Goodwin. It is surprising that privately Goodwin and his wife, Doña Isabel, admit taking the money but both being of such honest mien, the reason is a mystery, the more so since Goodwin denies it to the Colonel. In jest, the new government appoints that fine sailor but half a man, FELIPE CARRERA, Admiral of the Navy of the Republic. It seems fitting, since Carrera is half-witted, for him to have this appointment, for there is no navy. Carrera proceeds to do the best he can with one small freighter, and waits and waits for government orders.

The Flag Paramount. One morning orders finally come for the faithful "loco" admiral and he rushes his small boat to the River Ruiz, where instead of beef and provisions he finds three men who board his ship. He recognizes the leader, Don SABAS PLACIDO; who, being exceedingly talented, plays with revolutions and collects naval flags. The admiral knows Don Sabas for a traitor to the In government and reveals that he will have him shot. Don Sabas regretfully kills the admiral and turns the small craft towards the ship that is waiting to take him into exile and safety. He does not forget, however, to take the admiral's flag to complete his collection.

CABBAGES AND KINGS

Clancy works with pick and shovel

The Shamrock and the Palm. In the heat of a relaxed evening CLANCY tells Johnny Atwood the story of his fight for liberty in Guatemala. He is shanghaied under false pretenses by General DE VEGA to build a railroad that is politically needed, and he spends months hard at work with a pick and shovel instead of fighting in the glorious cause. He finally escapes, and he discovers that the general has just staged an unsuccessful *coup d'état* and has stowed away penniless on the same freighter to New Orleans. In New Orleans Clancy gets his revenge by turning the general in as a vagrant and watching him serve his sentence with a rake and shovel in front of the Irishman's favorite saloon.

The Remnants of the Code. BEELZEBUB BLYTHE, Coralio's town drunk and former U.S. gentleman, awakes one morning with all his credit exhausted and not one cent to his name. When he is refused his reviving morning drink everywhere, he is faced with his last resource, to blackmail Frank Goodwin about the lost valise with the hundred thousand dollars. Because he likes Goodwin, it is with great regret that he tells him he was the only witness to Goodwin's stealing the valuable valise and asks for a thousand dollars. Goodwin agrees, with no explanation, and says he will deliver the money when Blythe boards the afternoon ship to leave for the States. Blythe refuses brandy, though he desires it desperately; for one does not drink with the man one blackmails.

Shoes and Ships. The same evening the heartsick American consul and Billy Keogh are leisurely passing the time by ignoring all the consulate's mail. Keogh spies a letter from Atwood's home town. The letter seriously asks if a first-rate shoe store would be profitable in Coralio. Hysterical with laughter at the thought of a shoe store in this village of barefoot natives, they draft a jesting reply praising such a venture to the hilt. Never dreaming anyone would take them seriously, they are surprised weeks later when the would-be storekeeper arrives accompanied by packing cases of shoes and his beautiful daughter. In horror Atwood discovers that the daughter is his lost love ROSINE HEMSTETTER. He discovers also that she loves him and not his hated former rival, PINK DAWSON. Atwood is frantic. He solves his problem by cabling his rival, Dawson, to send thorny cockleburrs. These he and Keogh, secretly at night, spread on all the roads and streets. The natives are forced to buy shoes and Atwood confesses his love to Rosine. He resigns and returns to the U.S. to live in marital bliss.

Masters of Arts. Keogh decides to strike it rich with the aid and concert of the new dictator of Anchuria, President LOSADA. He goes to New York and enlists the aid of an old friend, CAROLUS WHITE, a down-and-out portrait painter. They return to Coralio during the only weeks of the year when it is a popular resort, and Losada is relaxing there. In no time, White is demeaning his art by painting the dictator to look like Washington and Napoleon combined. When he is finished and is paid $10,000 for his efforts he cannot bear what he has done and tears the check to pieces. Keogh is furious. He goes about taking pictures with his camera. There is a brief flurry of revolution over an English money deal. Losada quashes it quickly, but not before Keogh has taken an incriminating picture of him negotiating with the Britisher. Losada pays him $20,000 without a murmur and Keogh, impressed by his good sportsmanship, is as big a fool as White and rejects the money.

Dicky. DICKY MALONEY drops from the clouds into Coralio to add to its odd fish. He is gay and compatible with a free-and-easy style. Soon he opens a small tobacco and sweet shop and meets, woos and marries PASA, the beautiful daughter of Madame ORTIZ. The Commandante flirts with Pasa and Dicky teaches him a painful lesson with his fists. Dicky is put into jail and being temporarily without funds he languishes for three days. Pasa's fidelity weakens slowly with the absence of his love. But an American ship arrives in the harbor and its captain hurries to supply Maloney with all the funds he needs, so he and Pasa are reunited.

Rouge et Noir. Two Recalls. Dictator Losada antagonizes the Vesuvius Fruit Company, mighty in American dollars, by trying to shake them down for additional graft. The company gets busy at replacing this annoying President, who placed an extra cent on the price of bananas. A startling thing happens when the people are whipped into a frenzy of remembering their poor honest Président, OLIVARRA. Dick Maloney jumps to the high steps, tears off his red wig, and reveals himself as the son of the dead Olivarra. He is proclaimed President and he lovingly draws Pasa with him to his future and Anchuria's future.

Caesar and Cleopatra

Play by George Bernard Shaw, 1856–1950.
Produced 1900. (ML, 19)

TO SHAW THERE WAS nothing temerarious about approaching one of Shakespeare's major characters. In a preface to the play, Shaw deprecates Shakespeare as well as Bardolatry and explains why his Julius Caesar is far superior to Shakespeare's. Many readers have agreed with him. *Caesar and Cleopatra* is masterful historical drama as well as magnificent comedy. Caesar is wholly believable as he transforms Cleopatra from a convincing juvenile into a convincing woman prepared to conquer Antony. The characters speak in modern language and the frequent anachronisms Shaw treats with the disdain they deserve. A sly touch is Britannus, Caesar's Briton henchman, Shaw's portrayal of the timeless Englishman in his conservatism and doggedness.

Prologue. The first act is preceded by a prologue and an alternative to the prologue. In the first, the Egyptian god Ra, arrogant and cynical, gives a brief history of Caesar's conquest over Pompey and Pompey's flight to Egypt and death. Caesar, following Pompey, enters Egypt to set up a Roman governor of his own and settle the dispute between young Queen Cleopatra and her younger brother Ptolemy. The *alternative to the prologue* is a brief dramatic section introducing the audience to Cleopatra's chief nurse FTATATEETA, an imperious battle-axe; the captain of the palace guards, BELZANOR, a gruff warrior; a sly Persian recruit; and the proud Egyptian soldier, BEL AFFRIS. They discuss the imminent arrival of the Romans and plan to sell Cleopatra to her brother so that when Caesar comes they can join him in her rescue and remain as palace guards to the joint rule of the Roman and Cleopatra. Cleopatra and a sacred white cat have disappeared, however, and the prologue ends with panic.

Act I. In the desert, by a sphinx, CLEOPATRA is found by an old stranger and they

CAESAR AND CLEOPATRA

Caesar and Cleopatra

talk about the approaching Romans. The old man, in reality CAESAR himself, tells her she must be brave to meet the Roman conqueror. Together, they go to her palace just before the Roman soldiers arrive and hail their leader. Cleopatra is stunned but relieved to find that her friend turns out to be the man she had feared so.

Act II. At Alexandria, PTOLEMY is in the palace attended by his tutor, THEODOTUS; the chief of his army, ACHILLAS; and his guardian, POTHINUS. The boy is being encouraged to fight his sister and the Romans. At that instant, Caesar enters accompanied by his officer, RUFIO, and his secretary, BRITANNUS. Caesar decides to settle the dispute over Egypt's throne by calling out Cleopatra and declaring that the two young people will rule jointly, which dismays the court. When Caesar learns of Pompey's brutal assassination he is horrorstricken. He sends Ptolemy and his entourage away and makes plans to set up Cleopatra's court. He tells her about Mark Antony, whom she met when she was younger, and with whom she is deeply infatuated, and promises her that he will bring Antony back to her. Learning that Achillas has brought the Egyptian army into the city and incited riots against his men, Caesar prepares to withdraw his troops to a lighthouse and the quay by the palace. Pothinus returns to offer Caesar an ultimatum and is warned by Caesar to stop the rioting. Theodotus enters, hysterical because the library is burning from the fire spreading from Caesar's burning ships. Caesar remains unruffled and gets dressed for battle, with the help of Cleopatra. Then he leaves for the refuge of the lighthouse.

Act III. APOLLODORUS the Sicilian, a dapper young nobleman, confronts a Roman sentinel on the shore by Caesar's island lighthouse. He has some carpets for Cleopatra's palace but the sentinel refuses to let him pass. Ftatateeta arrives to ask that Apollodorus may pass and after some angry debate the Roman allows the merchant and the nurse to go to the palace. Cleopatra runs out, asking for a boat to go to the lighthouse, and, once again a fight ensues. She is not permitted to go and decides to send Caesar a present of a carpet. She retires in the palace to make her choice, asking Apollodorus to take the gift to Caesar for her. The carpet is then brought out, with Ftatateeta's warning to Apollodorus that it is very fragile and must be handled with care, and he sails off with it toward the lighthouse. Meanwhile, at the lighthouse, Rufio and Caesar discuss the progress of the battle. Britannus brings Caesar a bagful of letters which could reveal the names of all Roman traitors and Caesar throws the sack into the sea, not wishing to waste time suspecting and condemning people. Apollodorus arrives, angry because his boat was destroyed by the falling bag of letters, but his carpet is safe and Caesar has it brought up to him by a crane. The present is opened, revealing Cleopatra. During this action the Egyptian army has cut them off from the Roman troops and they must escape. Following Apollodorus's lead, Caesar, Rufio and a reluctant Cleopatra dive into the water to swim to the safety of their incoming ships, leaving Britannus to be rescued later.

Act IV. Six months later, Cleopatra is with the women of the palace. She has grown older and wiser under Caesar's guidance. Pothinus arrives, angry because she has apparently sold her country to the Romans—who, though outnumbered, still hold the

Egyptian troops at bay. A sumptuous dinner is set for Caesar, who arrives with Rufio. Pothinus, now a prisoner, comes to warn Caesar against the treachery of Cleopatra. He is interrupted by her arrival. Caesar makes him speak in her presence and is not at all surprised at his news; Caesar shrugs it off as a natural and inevitable course of affairs, and one he expected. Cleopatra denies everything hotly but Caesar, amused, tells her that it is true. Left alone to compose herself, Cleopatra sends for Ftatateeta to kill Pothinus. The nurse leaves and the men return to eat and chat. They hear the dying scream of Pothinus; and Caesar, suspecting the truth, questions Cleopatra. The people in the streets, enraged by the assassination, rise up against the palace. Caesar, disgusted, prepares to leave Cleopatra. Just as the situation grows desperate outside, a Roman relief army approaches, to Caesar's great joy. Caesar leaves to join the incoming army. Rufio, staying behind, warns Cleopatra against further murder. Suspecting Ftatateeta of having committed the crime, he slits her throat and departs.

Act V. The conflict over, Caesar prepares to embark for Rome. He sets up Rufio as governor and promises once again to Cleopatra that he will send Mark Antony to her. Amid great pomp and celebration, Caesar departs; Cleopatra cries at the loss of her great old friend but awaits the arrival of the young Antony.

Caesar's Commentaries

History by Julius Caesar, 100–44 B.C. Written: *The Gallic Wars*, about 50 B.C.; *The Civil War*, about 47 B.C. (ML, 295)

CAESAR WAS ONE of history's remarkably versatile men and among other gifts he was a great stylist in classical Latin. This gift is perhaps inadequately appreciated by the generations of schoolboys who have had to learn the first line of *The Gallic Wars:* "*Gallia est omnis divisa in partes tres, quarum unum incolunt Acquitaniae . . .*" It is unfortunate that an outline necessarily cannot include any of the details of strategy, tactics and military engineering so painstakingly described by Caesar. There are many good translations and it would amaze many ten-o'clock Latin scholars to read one and find themselves enjoying it.

The Gallic Wars

Book I. 58 B.C. Gaul was divided into three major tribes, the Belgians, the Aquitanians, and the Gauls (Celts). The Helvetians were the bravest of the Gauls. They were constantly at war with the Germans and attempted to gain supremacy over the rest of Gaul. The leader of the Helvetians died and the tribe, wishing independence from Rome, attempted a march through the Province. The Helvetians tried to force their way across the Rhone. CAESAR built a barricade and pushed the Helvetians back. The Romans with their organized phalanx and superior discipline destroyed the enemy's army. The barbarians could not withstand the pikes and artillery of the Roman legions. The Helvetians fled and attempted to find safety in neighboring villages, but the vastly depleted army was captured and returned to their territory. Chiefs of the other tribes came to Caesar and thanked him for vanquishing the Helvetians. They asked the Roman general's protection against the German Sequanians, who, under the leadership of the tyrannical ARIOVISTUS, had moved into Gaul. Caesar sent overtures of friendship to the Sequanians but was curtly rebuffed. At a battlefield near Mulhausen, Caesar's army thoroughly defeated the German force.

Book II. 57 B.C. Caesar brought his army to Cisalpine Gaul to spend the winter. After they were installed in camp he learned that the Belgians had attacked the Roman garrison at Bibrax. The barbarians, with a multitude of soldiers, had surrounded the fortification and cast stones to knock down the Romans from the top wall. Holding their shields over their heads, they advanced on the garrison. The line of Belgians with shields raised looked like a giant tortoise to the men in the garrison. Caesar came to Bibrax and attacked the Belgians. They were forced to retreat from the garrison but later that day stormed Caesar's camp across the Sambre river. The Roman soldiers fought the Belgians in the river and the blood of both armies ran in the water. In the evening the Belgians decided to retreat and fight Caesar in their own territory, but he surprised them on their midnight march, killing and capturing many. The battle ended with the rout of the tribes and their survivors surrendered to Caesar. Caesar settled his legions in winter quarters and sent word of his victory to Rome and the Senate declared 15 days of thanksgiving.

Book III. 57–56 B.C. Caesar sent SERVIUS GALBA, with the 12th Legion, to open a pass through the Alps, which the Nantuates, Veragrians and Sedunians were holding. Caesar wanted this pass to be opened for Roman merchants. Galba, despite one defeat, fought a successful campaign and established a garrison. Caesar at last believed Gaul to be under Roman control, but a coastal tribe, the Venetians, protested a grain tax and gathered the other seacoast tribes together in a new rebellion. Caesar depended, in this battle, upon his well-equipped and skillful navy. The Roman fleet was victorious and the defeat of the Venetians was accomplished. Caesar decided to punish the tribe and killed or sold as slaves the members of its Senate. Caesar then campaigned against the mutinous tribes of Morini and Menappi. He chased them from their homes into the hills and ravaged the countryside.

Book IV. 55 B.C. The German tribes, hungry for land and war, moved across the Rhine. Their strength was extraordinary but their discipline weak, and the individual fighters were pushed back by the Roman line. Caesar decided to chase the Germans across the Rhine, but feeling that boats were an undignified means of transportation for the Roman army, he built a bridge to carry his men and supplies into German territory.

Caesar made an expedition to Britain. There he made a landing and despite the loss of ships and supplies brought some of the Britons under his control. Since Caesar's horses had been lost at sea he was unable to pursue the Britons after the battle. He wished to stop them from sending aid to Gaul. Back in Gaul, Caesar again vanquished the erring Morinians and Menapians, and when he sent word of his triumphs to the capital, the Senate decreed 20 days of thanksgiving.

Book V. 54 B.C. Caesar planned the preparation of his fleet for a second expedition to Britain, and left with hopes of a brilliant success. The landing was unopposed and the following day the Britons were again defeated. Caesar had to return to Gaul because of several new rebellions. He demanded hostages from the Britons and fixed a tribute that they were forced to pay to Rome each year. Britain was milder in climate than Gaul. Its people were settled in small agricultural communities and had the strange custom of painting themselves blue, which made them frightening in battle. In Gaul, Cicero had been attacked and surrounded by the Nervians. Caesar, back in Gaul, rescued the Romans and his soldiers brought in the head of the Gallic leader, INDUTIOMARUS.

Book VI. 53 B.C. There was a new revolt in Gaul. Caesar moved his legions against the Nervians, Senones, Carnates, and Menapians. He crossed the Rhine to prevent the warring tribes from obtaining asylum in Germany. The Gauls were very religious. They were Druids and led an elaborate ritual life. The Druid priests were the leaders of the society, along with some powerful nobles. Most of the people were slaves. The Germans were not as religious as the Druids. They recognized only the useful gods, such as Sun and Water. The Germans were better fighters and stronger people.

Book VII. 52 B.C. Another conspiracy of the Gauls was formed under the able leadership of VERCINGETORIX. His personal power and ability with words brought many tribes into the rebellion. Vercingetorix spoke of freedom and liberty and the rights of the people who tilled the land. After several minor battles Caesar managed to end the rebellion at the town of Alesia. The town was besieged and women and children ran terrified in the streets. The men were

Caesar's strength was in his Roman legions

cornered and killed and their houses burned. Vercingetorix, a brave and intelligent leader, was captured and the tribes who had followed him were punished and forced into submission. Caesar went on to subdue the Aeduians and the Avernians, and 20 days of thanksgiving were decreed in Rome.

Book VIII. 51–50 B.C. The final book of the Gallic war was written not by Caesar but by GALUS HIRTIUS, who was one of Caesar's officers. A successful campaign against the Bellouacians was described, and Caesar's glorious welcome on his return to Italy.

The Civil War

Book I. 50–49 B.C. Caesar has crossed the Rubicon into Italy, which precipitates the Civil War.

Chaps. 1–13. Caesar sent a letter offering to resign if POMPEY also would resign. Consuls refused to have the letter read in the Senate. SCIPIO, who spoke for Pompey, said that he would stand by the Senate if they were firm, but if they were irresolute he would not support them in a future crisis. Pompey's army was near Rome and his spokesmen in the Senate were loud and aggressive. It was decided to demand that Caesar disband his army by a specific date or be considered a traitor. In the evening the session was adjourned and Pompey's friends rallied to him and new soldiers came to his side. Caesar's enemies CATO and Scipio bore him ancient grudges and desired more power for themselves. They turned Pompey against Caesar even though he had once been Caesar's son-in-law. After an election in which Caesar's enemies were placed in control, Caesar's friends and members of the tribune came to Caesar at Ravenna. In Rome, Pompey and his friends divided the control of the Roman Empire. All rights of the people, sacred and secular, were taken away. On hearing of this, Caesar addressed his troops and told them of the wrongs done him. They promised to defend him and the liberty of the Roman citizens. ROSCIUS and LUCIUS CAESAR came to Caesar at Rimini, where he had advanced with his soldiers, and entreated him to disband his army for the sake of unity within the state. Caesar asked the messengers to request a conference for Caesar with Pompey. They did, but Pompey refused to see Caesar until he disbanded his army. Caesar

CAESAR—THE CIVIL WAR

took several towns around Rimini. He heard that one of Pompey's generals had taken Gubbio but that the townspeople were for Caesar, so he sent several cohorts there under the charge of CURIO. Pompey's men withdrew and the townspeople cheered Caesar's troops.

Chaps. 13–25. Caesar marched to Osimo. The people let him into the town and Pompey's forces fled. News of this created panic in Rome, where Pompey's government was sitting. From Osimo Caesar moved swiftly through the entire region of Picenum. He was provided with supplies and welcomed by all the towns. Caesar surrounded the town of Sulmo and then the town of Corfinium. He forced these towns to surrender and absorbed Pompey's cohorts into his own army. He did not punish in any way those in the town who had conspired against him.

Chaps. 26–50. Caesar again demanded an interview with Pompey and designated Brindisi for the meeting. Caesar put floats into the harbors to prevent Pompey from attacking. As a countermeasure Pompey fitted large freighters with armed three-story towers. He drove the freighters against Caesar's works. Caesar decided to abandon all attempts at negotiation and concentrate on war. Pompey and his troops left the harbor and escaped to Asia. Caesar proceeded to Spain.

Chaps. 50–86. AFRANIUS, an officer of Pompey's, almost conquered Caesar in a battle at Lerida, because Caesar had lost important bridges in a rainstorm and could not attack or retreat. But he was ultimately able to cross the river and attack. There was a naval battle at Marseilles, in which Caesar's fleet vanquished the enemy. Caesar forced Afranius's army up a hill and cut off their food supply. Some of the enemy soldiers deserted to Caesar's camp but there was a fierce battle, which Caesar won, taking Afranius's army and releasing the soldiers to return to their own homes.

Book II. 49 B.C. BRUTUS led Caesar's fleet against a second unsuccessful attack by the Massilians, and Marseilles capitulated to Brutus. Curio, one of Caesar's generals, went to Africa to fight Pompey's forces under the leadership of VARUS. Curio underestimated his opponent and took too small an army. Caesar's legions were badly defeated. Many of the men were killed and others taken prisoners. Curio declared that he would never face Caesar after losing so many of his men and he was killed on the battlefield. Caesar maintained control of Italy and Europe while Pompey's forces gathered strength in Africa.

Book III. 49–48 B.C. Pompey had assembled a large fleet from Asia and borrowed large sums from the various potentates of Asia and Syria. But Caesar transported his men and supplies from Brindisi and landed in Asia. He sent a message to Pompey, asking again for a peace conference. Pompey refused to accept and his army panicked, many of the men deserting to their homes. Pompey's fleet was unable to reach the mainland and in many areas his men were starving. He asked for a truce only in order to force Caesar to release his blockade, and Caesar, perceiving this, went on with his plans for war. Caesar was waiting for ships from Rome, bringing more men and supplies. MARK ANTONY came from Rome to aid Caesar. Pompey planned to ambush Antony's forces as they marched to join Caesar, but Antony was informed of the plan and kept his men in camp until Caesar had joined him. Scipio was notified of Antony's arrival by Pompey and brought his forces out of Syria to join Pompey. Pompey's army was down in the swamplands and Caesar in the mountains. Caesar built dams to prevent the clear mountain water from reaching Pompey. Pompey's army was forced to charge uphill because the men were starving. Due to a sudden panic among Caesar's soldiers, they were successful in splitting the army in two and killing many men. Caesar withdrew and spoke to his soldiers to uplift their morale.

At the decisive battle some weeks later the Pompeians were overconfident and fanciful in their battle plans. Caesar's army broke into Pompey's camp and Pompey fled. Caesar chased his opponent to prevent him from securing new soldiers and arms. Pompey was assassinated by the generals of PTOLEMY's army. Caesar followed to Alexandria, where he tried to settle an inheritance quarrel between CLEOPATRA and her brother Ptolemy. Ptolemy's forces, under the rule of a regent, marched on Caesar in Alexandria, and this was the beginning of the Alexandrine War and the end of the Civil War between Pompey and Caesar.

The Caine Mutiny

> *Novel by* Herman Wouk, 1915–
> Published 1951 by Doubleday & Co., New York. © 1951 by Herman Wouk.
>
> IN THIS, HIS SECOND NOVEL, Wouk fulfilled the promise of his earlier work and was rewarded by one of history's biggest best-sellers, plus a successful Broadway play and Hollywood movie (*The Caine-Mutiny Trial*). *The Caine Mutiny* is perhaps not a "war novel," for its principal characters see no battle action, but it is an excellent novel about men in the war. It won the Pulitzer Prize for 1952.

Chaps. 1–5. WILLIE SEWARD KEITH, a young man of wealthy family whose mother tries to spoil him, is admitted to midshipman school during World War II, mainly to escape the Army for the Navy. He is billeted with a young Southerner named KEEFER and a pessimistic young man named KEGGS. Willie has been in love with MAE WYNN, a nightclub singer whose real name is Marie Minotti, and he plans that their romance will come to a natural end when he is shipped out to sea after his four months in midshipman school. The experience he receives in training has a profound effect upon him and he finds that he wants genuinely to succeed in the naval service. After many vicissitudes, and near expulsion for excessive demerits, he is at length graduated and assigned to Destroyer Minesweeper 22, U.S.S. *Caine*. He is now Ensign Keith.

Chaps. 6–8. While Willie is in San Francisco awaiting orders to board the *Caine*, he learns of his father's death. He fails to make connections in Hawaii with the ship, because of an error in his orders, and at a party attracts the attention of an admiral, through his piano playing. He is given a part in the officers' pool that will keep him ashore for some time, but he seeks a means of reaching the *Caine*, with no success. After several months, Willie is awakened early one morning by Ensign PAYNTER, a member of the *Caine's* complement, and learns that Keefer's brother TOM is on the same ship. On boarding the ship, Willie receives an impression that is to remain with him indefinitely: The *Caine* is a "pile of junk in the last hours of decay." Life aboard the *Caine* is uncomfortable and dull. Willie thinks that Captain DE VRIESS is responsible for the slovenly condition of the ship and is delighted when an order arrives to transfer him elsewhere and put in command instead one Lieutenant Commander PHILIP F. QUEEG.

Chaps. 9–14. At first Captain Queeg is pleasant and agreeable. He holds a meeting of his officers and tells them that everything aboard the *Caine* is henceforth to be done with rigid obedience and conformity to regulations, and with no deviations permitted. Soon the meaning of "conformity" becomes painfully clear. The free-and-easy days under Captain de Vriess are over. Every smallest detail is checked and enforced by Captain Queeg, and soon an atmosphere of tension develops aboard the *Caine*. The first evidence of Queeg's incompetence in handling a ship comes when orders arrive to send the *Caine* to tow targets for ship's gunnery practice drills. Queeg botches his orders for getting the ship clear of the dock, and in his report of the resultant grounding of the propeller in the harbor mud, he blames failure on the part of the engine tenders to respond to his commands. The entire ship knows that the fault was solely Queeg's. Next, the captain appoints Willie Keith as morale officer, with instruction that all officers and crew keep their shirts tucked in the trouser bands at all times. Queeg's habit of constantly rolling steel balls between his fingers has been noted by all his staff. An incident concerning the manner of giving orders to the helmsman causes Queeg to run down the wrong side of a channel. Although they barely miss a battleship, Queeg refuses to admit that they are on the wrong side of the channel. The next unpleasant incident occurs when Queeg spends so long berat-

L-243

CAINE MUTINY

ing a sailor for having a shirttail out that he forgets to give the orders to straighten out after a turn. Before he corrects this the ship has made two complete circles and has severed the tow-rope attached to the target. Queeg refuses to send out a boat to retrieve the valuable target, and heads for home, blaming a defective tow-rope for his own stupidity. Returning to the *Caine*, he finds young STILWELL, the helmsman of the day before, reading while on watch, which has been permitted in the past, but which Queeg sternly forbids. Stilwell is given six months' restriction to the ship for it. Word comes that the *Caine* is to go to the States for general overhaul, and everyone is pleased.

Chaps. 15-18. Queeg buys all the unused liquor rations of the officers, having in mind the far higher cost of liquor in the States. It is against regulations, but he orders a crate to be made to hold his loot. He takes the ship out of its way to debark the liquor, and the extremely heavy weight causes the crate to slip from the handlers into the harbor. Queeg blames Willie, and withholds shore leave until Willie gives him the cost of the lost liquor. When the ship finally docks, both Mrs. Keith and Mae are waiting for Willie. The *Caine* stays in port a shorter time than was expected, but Willie and Mae go skiing at Yosemite and see a great deal of each other. Mrs. Keith hopes they will not marry.

Chaps. 19-23. Orders come, sending *Caine* in advance of an attack force on Kwajalein. The DMS is supposed to steam ahead on the proper course, so that the attack force will know exactly where to go. Queeg hurries toward the point too fast for the attack boats to keep up, and drops a yellow dye marker by the spot, turning and getting away as quickly as possible. This earns him the nickname of "Old Yellowstain," which sticks. A day later orders come to detach Lieutenant RABBIT, and Queeg attempts to procrastinate. He is foiled when the captain of the ship to which Rabbit is transferred comes aboard the *Caine*. Queeg's frustration puts him in a vile temper, and he cuts off all water for bathing and drinking, as he learns that on the day of the Kwajalein operation water consumption increased ten percent. Forty-eight hours of sweltering tropic heat without water has a powerful effect on officers and crew. Queeg extends the officers' water ban for an extra 48 hours when he catches an ensign taking a shower with the water left standing in the pipes. Shortly after the water famine, a court-martial is scheduled for Stilwell, accusing him of falsifying a report of his mother's illness in order to see his wife. The officers who judge are forced to find him guilty, but they deliberately insult Queeg by ordering as punishment the loss of a few days' leave.

Chaps. 24-27. STEVE MARYK, executive officer, has listed the strange and eccentric behavior of Captain Queeg in a "medical log," on the basis of Tom Keefer's earlier and emphatic declaration that Queeg is on the verge of a psychological disorder. Keefer is prevented from seeing his brother, Roland, on a carrier moored nearby. Queeg refuses to let him leave because of some unimportant filing that is incomplete. Next day Roland is killed as the result of a Japanese suicide plane that crashes the carrier. One of the other ships in the group is a tender, and Ensign JORGENSEN acquires a gallon of frozen strawberries from a friend aboard. There is a feast of strawberries and ice cream, but late that night the Captain sends for more, only to be told that the strawberries are gone. In a rage, he summons a meeting and goes through a wild and furious investigation to account for the missing strawberries—which he calculates must be about a quart. No one admits eating them, and Queeg becomes violent. The scene verges on farcical madness as he demands an inspection of every key in the possession of every man aboard, determined to uncover the extra—but nonexistent—key to the supply room. The frantic and senseless search leads Tom Keefer to remark to Maryk that this seems like the behavior of a raving lunatic. Subtly, he asks Maryk if he has read Article 184 of *Navy Regulations*, which states that the commanding officer of a ship may be "relieved" if he is completely unable, because of illness, to continue in his command. Queeg seems at least mentally "unfit" as he insists on continuing a fruitless search for a key that does not exist, even after two witnesses have declared they saw the mess boys scraping out the strawberry can.

Chaps. 28-30. During a typhoon, Queeg indicates general incompetence, and in the opinion of the ship's personnel he does not know what to do. The danger seems imminent when Maryk assumes command and brings the *Caine* through safely. After the storm, the *Caine* picks up three survivors of a ship they see floating bottom-up. Queeg would not have troubled to look for survivors, he says.

Chaps. 31–33. Maryk is to be court-martialed, but not on a charge of actual mutiny. The charge is "Conduct to the Prejudice of Good Order and Discipline." Before the trial, Willie has time to go East for a brief visit with his mother, and an even briefer visit with Mae, at which time he tells her that their romance is finished. Meanwhile, the defense for Maryk encounters some difficulty in finding a lawyer to represent him. At length BARNEY GRUENWALD, a young Jewish lawyer from Albuquerque, agrees to take on the task, after he learns from Maryk that Tom Keefer was the source of all the rumors of Queeg's mental unbalance. Maryk was Keefer's victim, and Gruenwald declares that he can unquestionably get an acquittal.

Chaps. 34–37. The trial produces the recounting of all the events that have taken place on the *Caine* since Queeg took command. Queeg often tells direct untruths, but it is his word against that of one officer or sailor in each case, and only his contradictory statements can be challenged. At length he becomes so excited and so angry that he speaks incoherently and shrilly, for far too long. He is not insane, but merely stupid, disagreeable, and inept. However, Barney Gruenwald wins his case by emphazing that at the times noted, Queeg *was* mentally ill, for it is quite inconceivable for an officer in the United States Navy to be either incompetent or a coward. Maryk is acquitted. Tom Keefer comes rushing up to him with the news that he has sold his novel, which he worked on aboard the *Caine,* and that he is giving a grand dinner party that night. Maryk and Gruenwald must attend, as guests of honor. Gruenwald arrives late, already half intoxicated. He makes a speech, when asked to propose a toast, in which he excoriates the "sensitive civilians" who scoff at regular Navy procedure and personnel, when it is the regulars who give the civilians freedom in which to scoff if they wish.

Chaps. 38–40. Tom Keefer is captain of the *Caine,* and when a Kamikaze plane strikes the ship, setting fire to one engine room, Keefer jumps overboard, leaving Willie, his executive officer, to save the ship and take charge of extinguishing the fire. Soon the war is over, and Keefer is in line for a fast discharge on the point system. Willie becomes the last captain of the *Caine* and takes the ship from Okinawa to Bayonne, New Jersey, for de-commissioning. He then goes to find Mae, knowing that she is the woman he will always want to have beside him. After some difficulty he locates her and convinces her of his sincerity. Both Mae and Mrs. Keith realize that he is not the same boy who joined the Navy so long ago. Willie Seward Keith has become a man.

A kamikaze strikes the ship

Cakes and Ale

Novel by W. Somerset Maugham, 1874–1966.
Published 1930 by Doubleday & Co., New York. © 1930 by W. Somerset Maugham. (ML, 270)
ASHENDEN THE WRITER has been used by Maugham as narrator in many stories, notably his excellent stories of spying and intrigue during World War I. *Cakes and Ale* is considered one of Maugham's major novels.

Chaps. 1–3. My name is WILLIAM ASHENDEN and I am a writer by profession. When I learn that ALROY KEAR wishes to see me, I assume that he has in mind some purpose advantageous to himself, for he does almost nothing without such a motive. His talent for advancing himself has won him great fame as a novelist, and great personal popularity as well. He likes people in general, and in general they like him. I lunch with Roy at his club. I do not learn the reason for his seeking me out, but our conversation is guided skillfully by him to the subject of the late EDWARD DRIFFIELD, who at this time is acknowledged to have been one of the best of Victorian novelists. I knew Driffield and his wife when I was a boy living with my aunt and uncle in Blackstable, a Kentish town near the sea. My opinion of Driffield's work is not very high, and Kear seems somewhat irritated by that. He leaves without asking the favor —whatever it may be—that I am certain he has in mind. His mention of Driffield recalls to my mind the first time I had heard of him. He was considered rather common in Blackstable, and socially unacceptable. Worse, his then wife, ROSIE, was a former barmaid!

Chaps. 4–10. I receive a note from AMY DRIFFIELD, the writer's second wife, now his widow. It invites me to call. I remember the only time I met the second Mrs. Driffield. She had been the nurse who attended Driffield during a long and serious illness some time before. At the time when I met her, Driffield was an acknowledged personage in the literary world, and something of a celebrity. He mentioned that he had taught me to ride a bicycle, and the associations with that incident recalled events of earlier times. My aunt and uncle were most scornful of Driffield and his wife and disapproved heartily of my seeing them. I thought also of Rosie, who had been a most disarmingly likable person. My aunt's maid, Mary Ann, had known Rosie from childhood, and mentioned to me that Rosie had "carried on" with many different men while employed as a barmaid. One of these was GEORGE KEMP, our local coal merchant and occasional dealer in real estate. I myself observed positive evidence that Rosie and George had not ceased their friendship with her marriage. I saw them slip away into the fields for a romantic tryst, which shocked me deeply. My acquaintance with Rosie and Edward Driffield continued through my holidays from school. It was at Easter holiday that I learned suddenly of their departure, leaving behind them many debts. All the shock of this discovery sweeps over me again as I am reminded by Amy Driffield's note of those times so long before.

Chaps. 11–16. In a conversation with Roy, I learn that he is to write Edward Driffield's biography. He seems to think that there are many things about Driffield's life that should be touched upon only lightly and subtly, if at all. Rosie, for example— who Roy says has been dead for years—is one of the "unfortunate" parts of the great man's life. So also are his dislike of bathing, and his regrettable habit of conversing with all manner of common persons at the local pub, a place that he visited far too regularly. In short, the biography of Edward Driffield is to paint an artist, a genius, and a solemnly important literary figure, with little trace of the man himself. I do not contemplate with relish a visit with the second Mrs. Driffield and I agree to go to Blackstable only if I may stay at the inn and enjoy complete privacy whenever I wish it. Some whim to recall the past sends me to my former lodging house in town, where Mrs. HUDSON, my former landlady, is still the humorous, likable, warm-hearted woman I remember. So much has happened since I lived in her house! It was after two years there that I met the Driffields in London. Quite accidentally I encountered Mrs. (Rosie) Driffield and realized for the first time that she was very pretty. I went to their flat, and found Driffield as hospitable as ever. Soon I developed the habit of dropping in every Saturday, when various and assorted groups of people congregated there. Eventually Mrs. BARTON TRAFFORD, a socially prominent and influential woman, took Driffield under her competent wing and set out to make him famous in what she termed "the right circles." That she succeeded most admirably is a matter of history. Mrs. Trafford was, incidentally, the only person I ever knew Rosie to dislike—heartily and uncompromisingly. The indescribable charm and very real beauty of Rosie impressed itself more deeply on me each time I saw her, and before long I was occasionally escorting her to the theater or to the interesting occasions of the day. Driffield worked at night, and there was no reason for Rosie to sit alone in their flat while he worked. One night after attending a popular play we sat down for a moment in the park. It was a beautiful night. Suddenly we were hungry and stopped for fish and chips at a small place I knew. Heading back toward her flat, we passed my lodgings and I invited Rosie in to see them. She spent the night with me.

Chaps. 17–18. I suspected that she might be sleeping with some of the other men who took her out, but chose to deny the suspicion to myself. I was able to continue my self-deception until the episode of a rich Dutch Jew named JACK KUYPER. He squired Rosie for some time, and just before returning to Amsterdam gave her a sable cape and muff that cost more than I earned in two years. Then I knew. Still, Rosie was warmly sweet and human, and she somehow made it seem utterly unimportant. It was at about this time that Driffield in *Cup of Life* caused a major sensation. Critics said that it was shocking, dreadful, and wicked—should be banned. Not a word in it would even ruffle the modern reader, but this was the Victorian era. Driffield simply shrugged and continued to write.

Chaps. 19–21. (Still reminiscing.) A telegram from Mrs. Trafford asked me to call and I obeyed the summons. I learned that Rosie had left Driffield and had run away with George Kemp. At the exhortation of the Traffords, I went to Blackstable and found ample confirmation of the report. Kemp had left his wife and two sons, and a mountain of debt. The scandal rocked the town, but I personally was merely hurt and angry that Rosie should prefer George Kemp, as a lover, to me. Back in London, Driffield was staying with the Traffords and was not well. Time passed, and I lost touch with him. Money from America was forthcoming to Rosie's mother, but never with a message or a return address. When her mother died, no more was heard of Rosie.

Chaps. 22–25. This was all in my recollection. On Friday, Alroy Kear and I meet as scheduled in Victoria Station, en route to Blackstable. From him I learn that Isabel Trafford tended Driffield for some time and as a reward was honored by a dedication in his novel *By Their Fruits*. He became very ill with pneumonia shortly thereafter, and since he was away from London Mrs. Trafford hired a nurse for him. Three weeks later she learned that he had married his nurse by special license. This was Amy. We reach Blackstable and I find things much changed. A former schoolmate of mine is a grandfather three times over, which is somehow a shock. The second Mrs. Driffield is more than a shock. She obviously ruled the home life of Edward Driffield with a velvet-clad iron hand. She made over his appearance, his house and his manner of living into what she considered proper for one of his eminence. At that meeting with Roy and Amy, I feel constrained to dispute their coarse conclusions with regard to Rosie. I know better. Amy never told Driffield when she heard from one of Kemp's sons that Rosie was dead. She did not want to disturb the great man with a sordid note out of the past!

Chap. 26. Alroy wants material for his biography of Edward Driffield, but he wants only the sugar-coatings. I could give him far more than he suspects to exist—for Rosie Driffield Iggulden is very much alive. I know, for I saw her not long ago in New York, where I received considerable publicity in connection with the opening of one of my plays. She and George Kemp had changed their name to Iggulden, and George was dead. Rosie was then about 70, but still vital and appealing, and still filled with love of life. I learned from her that Driffield had completely understood her infidelities and had accepted them. Her attraction to George Kemp she summed up most succinctly: "He was always such a perfect gentleman."

The Call of the Wild

Novel by Jack London, 1876–1916. Published 1903. Copyright 1903, 1931 by The Macmillan Co., New York. Published by Grosset & Dunlap, New York. (PB, 593)

PERHAPS TO PROVE the doctrine that dog books are the surest successes and the longest-lived in the world of books, *The Call of the Wild* has long been the most popular of Jack London's books. It is one of the best-written of the dog stories and has several emotional high points. It is written from the dog's point of view.

Chap. 1. From a house in the Santa Clara valley the dog BUCK is stolen, to be sold for use as a sled dog in the Alaska gold rush of 1897. Buck is a magnificent large dog with luxuriant fur. His father was a St. Bernard and his mother a shepherd. Buck is treated cruelly by the man who is taking him to his new owner. He fights angrily against each new outrage, from the strangling rope about his neck to the cramped cage in which he eventually rides. He learns that a man with a club is not to be disputed. Soon he is resold —this time to a French Canadian named PERREAULT, who with another man, FRANÇOIS, is commissioned to purchase sled dogs for carrying government dispatches. CURLY, a Newfoundland; a large white dog from Spitzbergen called SPITZ; a sullen, unfriendly dog called DAVE, and Buck are all taken aboard ship and transported to the coast of Alaska, where Buck sees his first snow.

Chap. 2. Buck learns quickly that he is in a land where the only law is the law of club and fang. Curly is killed swiftly in a brief fight with a husky and his body is torn to pieces by the circle of dogs that witness the battle. Buck learns that once a fighter goes down, the pack closes in to finish him off. Spitz has a way of rolling out his tongue and laughing, and he laughs as he sees the end of Curly. Buck suddenly hates the big white dog with an undying hatred. Almost immediately he is introduced to the sled harness. Dave is impatient with mistakes, nipping him sharply to correct him. Spitz is the lead dog. Buck learns fast, and François is delighted with him. Sleeping in the bitter cold poses a problem until Buck sees one of his teammates curled in a hollow dug in a snowdrift. He proceeds to dig one for himself. The warmth of his body quickly heats the tiny area and he sleeps comfortably. Instincts long buried under domestication come to life again and Buck swiftly hardens into a cunning, powerful, resourceful dog of the north.

Chap. 3. Buck's hatred for Spitz continues. One night they begin a fight but a pack of starving huskies raid the camp and precipitate a free-for-all. Buck's feet are not as hard as those of the other dogs and a set of boots is made for him by François. Shortly afterward, one of the dogs bitten in the fight with the huskies goes mad, and it is Buck that she chases. He is saved when François' club hits his pursuer, and he sinks exhausted to the ground. Spitz, seeing Buck's weakness, attacks viciously but is beaten by François, who says that some day Buck will kill Spitz. Buck is now an accomplished sled dog and resents the fact that Spitz is the leader. One day the dogs are chasing a snowshoe rabbit, filled with the thrill of the chase. Spitz cuts across a curve and seizes the rabbit, which Buck felt to be his legitimate prey. He flies at Spitz and the long-awaited battle is on. Spitz has killed many another rival but goes down at last to be torn to pieces by the circle of huskies, while Buck looks on—triumphantly victorious.

Chap. 4. Buck steps into the lead dog's place next day, but the dog drivers put him out and place another in the traces. Buck drives the interloper away three times, until he is threatened with a club. He keeps his distance, but refuses to go into the old place. The drivers at length acknowledge defeat and put him in the lead dog's place. François and Perreault receive orders to go elsewhere and the team is turned over to a mail train group. This is hard, gruelling work and soon the dogs are in poor condition—badly in need of a rest period. Dave is obviously in pain but refuses to be taken out of harness, as is the way with true sled dogs. It is more merciful to let him die in the traces; he would die anyway, of a broken heart, if he were not allowed to work. Finally Dave is shot.

Chap. 5. When the team reaches Skaguay, both drivers and dogs are in a state of utter exhaustion. The team is sold to two greenhorns named HAL and CHARLIE. With them is MERCEDES, Charlie's wife and Hal's sister. They overload the sled, they pack it improperly, they carry dozens of unnecessary things. The two men think to lighten the load with a team of fourteen dogs. Fourteen is too many, because a single sled cannot carry enough food for fourteen dogs. Hal and

The dogs are turned over to a mail train group

Charlie mismanage what food they have. One by one, dogs begin to starve to death. The five left reach the camp of JOHN THORNTON with the beginning of the spring thaw. Thornton warns them against the rotting ice ahead. Hal sneers at him, determined to continue despite the warning. Buck refuses to move and Hal takes the club to him. Buck is beaten unmercifully, until he is only a quarter conscious. Thornton warns grimly that if another blow falls on the dog, he will kill Hal. He takes Buck out of the traces, and the remaining dogs drag the sled away. Dogs, sled and the three humans disappear in an ice hole. John Thornton is Buck's new master.

Chap. 6. Buck learns for the first time the meaning of true love for a man. He adores John Thornton. HANS and PETE, Thornton's associates, remark that they would not like to be the man who attempted to lay hands on John Thornton. In Circle City Thornton good-naturedly steps between two quarreling men and BLACK BURTON, an ill-tempered man, strikes out with his fist. Buck goes for him but is driven off by the crowd. The opinion of the miners is that Buck was within his rights. Later Buck saves Thornton from certain death in the rapids of the river —breaking three of his own ribs in the act. Still later, he enables Thornton to win a substantial bet by the unheard-of feat of pulling by himself a load of one thousand pounds on a sled frozen in the snow—breaking it out unaided. This achievement earns $1,600 for John Thornton. A famous passage in the book occurs when Thornton refuses to sell Buck.

Chap. 7. The money won by Thornton makes it possible for him to seek a certain lost mine, and with Pete and Hans he sets out. For months they travel, and after many hundreds of miles, they come upon a shallow basin in which the gold is so plentiful that it can be seen gleaming through the water. Day after day, they fill sacks with gold dust and nuggets. There is nothing for the dogs to do. Buck becomes aware of a call that seems to come from the depths of the forest. It is the call of the primitive—and of the wild. One night he awakens with a start at the sound of a certain call in the forest. He approaches the source of the sound and at length sees the lean form of a timber wolf, muzzle pointed skyward, and howling. The wolf dashes away and Buck follows. At length the wolf is cornered and turns to snarl and snap at him. Buck circles about, making friendly advances, but the wolf is fearful. At length they sniff noses, then they run together through the night. But Buck remembers John Thornton and returns to Thornton's camp. On another of Buck's lonely prowls he encounters a herd of buffalo—with one old bull that has an arrow protruding from his shoulder. Buck stalks the beast for four days until at last he closes in for the kill. Four days more of eating and sleeping beside his prey, and Buck is ready to go back to the camp. Doom seems to hang over him as he lopes along. At the approach to the camp it is suddenly clarified. The body of Hans is lying with many arrows protruding from it. Strange men are moving about rhythmically, chanting strange sing-song chants. An over-powering fury possesses Buck, and with no warning he leaps into the circle of men, slashing and killing with lightning speed. So vicious and so fast are his movements that the Indians—Yeehats—flee in panic. Buck follows the trail of John Thornton to the edge of the pool—and there the trail stops. Buck raises his nose and howls. Pete he has already found dead in his blanket roll. Buck remains near the camp and hears timber wolves approaching. He stands and awaits them, motionless. When the boldest attacks, Buck breaks its neck. Three others try, but withdraw slashed and bleeding. Now Buck must fight the whole pack. He fights so powerfully that at length the wolves stand back, uncertain. One of their number moves forward slowly, the wild brother with whom Buck ran in the woods, and they touch noses. An older wolf moves up next, and after a warning snarl, Buck sniffs noses with him also. The old wolf sits down and howls, and the rest of the pack follows his example. Buck then does the same thing—and when the pack yelps and courses away, Buck runs with them.

As the years go on, the Yeehats notice a change in the breed of timber wolves—and they tell tales of a Ghost Dog that runs with the pack. The Yeehats do not visit the valley where John Thornton's camp was once located, but each summer a great wolf visits the valley, sits quietly there for a while, then lifts his muzzle to the sky and howls just once.

Camille

(The Lady of the Camellias)

Novel by Alexandre Dumas *fils*, 1824–1895.
Published 1848. (ML, 69)

IN THIS CASE the fame of the novel is as nothing compared to the fame of the play that Dumas *fils* made of it. The play appeared in 1852 with Eleonora Duse in the title rôle. The part is one of the best ever made available for an actress. The title of both novel and play (*La Dame aux Camélias,* The Lady of the Camellias) and the name of the heroine have been all but forgotten in the survival of her sobriquet, Camille. The novel is short and the play introduces new scenes and characters.

Chaps. 1–2. I learn that at an apartment at 9, Rue Lantin, the furniture is to be sold at public auction some days hence. The owner, a woman of ill repute, died in debt. I follow the curious crowds of sightseers and learn that this was the apartment of a MARGUERITE GAUTIER (Margherita Gauthier), whom I knew by name and sight only. I knew also the story of Marguerite's daughterly relationship with a wealthy and elderly duke, who had been entranced by her resemblance to his dead daughter and asked her to allow him a father's interest in her, not knowing of her profession. Even when he became aware of her past, and she herself resumed her gay life between his visits, he refused to reject the girl so like his daughter. Marguerite was seen and known everywhere. She always wore camellias.

Chaps. 3–4. At the sale of Marguerite's effects, I buy a copy of *Manon Lescaut*, inscribed in front "Armand Duval." Some days later, Armand Duval himself appears at my house to ask if I will sell him the book. I give it to him willingly. From him I begin to learn what a wonderful woman Marguerite Gautier really was.

Chaps. 5–7. I seek the grave of Marguerite, for a reason I cannot explain even to myself, and find that it is kept covered perpetually with fresh camellias, at the order of Armand Duval. I learn also that Armand has gone to obtain permission from Marguerite's sister to have the body removed and placed in another grave. This entails an identification of the uncovered corpse, and Armand provides it, nearly fainting in horror at the sight. He becomes ill and is confined to his bed for several weeks. I remain with him, and he tells me the story of the love between him and Marguerite Gautier.

Chaps. 7–13. Armand tells me of the first time he saw Marguerite and of the tremendous attraction she exerted toward him. He did not see her often, and always at a distance. Suddenly he failed to see her at all, and learned that she was ill. She was consumptive and had gone to Bagneres for her health. There she met an elderly duke, rich and kind, whose daughter died of tuberculosis a few days after Marguerite's arrival. In his grief, the startling resemblance between Marguerite and his daughter caused him to ask her if she would take his daughter's place in his life, and she agreed. He visited her regularly, and it was during this period that Armand met and fell in love with her. He called at her apartment in the company of her next-door neighbor, PRUDENCE DUVERNOY, and another young man, GASTON. He learned that she was very ill with tuberculosis and could not expect to live very long. They became lovers, and the next day Marguerite told him of her plan for them to spend the summer in the country, far from Paris and the life she lived there.

Chaps. 14–15. A jealous quarrel separated Armand from his love, but reconciliation was swift, for both were truly in love. NANINE, Marguerite's maid, prepared them a supper and they were happy together again.

Chaps. 16–18. Armand and Marguerite spent the day in the country at Bongival and saw a cottage that delighted them. Marguerite determined to ask the old duke to rent it for her, and he did so. Armand moved to a suite in an inn nearby. The old duke, who had been so generous, suddenly stopped supplying Marguerite with money, and Armand's income was inadequate. Marguerite sold and pawned her possessions, to pay some debts, and Armand determined to help somehow.

Chaps. 19–22. Armand's father came to Paris, arriving just after Marguerite and Armand had taken a small house in town. Armand had started making arrangements for an income left him to be turned over to Marguerite. Monsieur Duval was angry and distressed over his son's relationship with Marguerite, whose past he knew. He could not convince Armand, however, and instead approached Marguerite with a plea that she give up Armand so that his sister's engagement would not be endangered by a scandal. Her fiancé was of a stern and unbending family. Marguerite's sympathy for another woman's love caused her to tell Armand that all was over between them. He did not know of his father's responsibility.

Chaps. 23–24. Armand, in his hurt, was intentionally cruel and appeared with a new mistress in all the places where he was sure to see Marguerite. At length she could stand no more and went to England. Armand also was miserable and went to Alexandria, where he learned that Marguerite was dying.

Chaps. 25–26. Armand did not reach her in time to see her before she died, but her letters told him the entire story of her great sacrifice and told him also how great was her love. His father confessed that Marguerite was indeed a great and noble woman.